Tolkien and Shakespeare

CRITICAL EXPLORATIONS IN SCIENCE FICTION AND FANTASY
(a series edited by Donald E. Palumbo and C.W. Sullivan III)

1. *Worlds Apart? Dualism and Transgression in Contemporary Female Dystopias* (Dunja M. Mohr, 2005)

2. *Tolkien and Shakespeare: Essays on Shared Themes and Language* (edited by Janet Brennan Croft, 2007)

3. *Culture, Identities and Technology in the* Star Wars *Films: Essays on the Two Trilogies* (edited by Carl Silvio and Tony M. Vinci, 2007)

4. *The Influence of* Star Trek *on Television, Film and Culture* (edited by Lincoln Geraghty, forthcoming 2007)

5. *Hugo Gernsback and the Century of Science Fiction* (Gary Westfahl, forthcoming 2007)

Tolkien and Shakespeare

Essays on Shared Themes and Language

EDITED BY JANET BRENNAN CROFT

CRITICAL EXPLORATIONS IN
SCIENCE FICTION AND FANTASY, 2
Donald E. Palumbo *and* C.W. Sullivan III, *series editors*

McFarland & Company, Inc., Publishers
Jefferson, North Carolina, and London

COPYRIGHT ACKNOWLEDGMENTS: Excerpts from *The Lord of the Rings*. Reprinted by permission of HarperCollins Publishers Ltd. © J.R.R. Tolkien, 1965. Excerpts from *The Lord of the Rings* by J.R.R Tolkien, edited by Christopher Tolkien. Copyright © 1954, 1955, 1966 by J.R.R. Tolkien. Copyright © Renewed 1982, 1983 by Christopher R. Tolkien, Michael H.R. Tolkien, John F.R. Tolkien, and Priscilla M.A.R. Tolkien. Copyright © Renewed 1993, 1994 by Christopher R. Tolkien, John F.R. Tolkien, and Priscilla M.A.R. Tolkien. Reprinted by permission of Houghton Mifflin Company. All rights reserved. Excerpts from *The Letters of J.R.R. Tolkien*. Reprinted by permission of HarperCollins Publishers Ltd. © Humphrey Carpenter, 1981. Excerpts from *The Letters of J.R.R. Tolkien*, edited by Humphrey Carpenter with the assistance of Christopher Tolkien. Copyright © 1981 by George Allen & Unwin (Publishers) Ltd. Reprinted by permission of Houghton Mifflin Company. All rights reserved. Excerpts from "On Fairy-Stories." Reprinted by permission of HarperCollins Publishers Ltd. © J.R.R. Tolkien, 1966. Excerpts from "On Fairy-Stories," from *Tree and Leaf* by J.R.R. Tolkien. Copyright © 1964 by George Allen & Unwin Ltd. Copyright © Renewed 1992 by John F.R. Tolkien, Christopher R. Tolkien, and Priscilla M.A.R. Tolkien. Copyright © 1988 by The Tolkien Trust. Reprinted by permission of Houghton Mifflin Company. All rights reserved. Excerpts from "Sitting Down to the Sacramental Feast: Food and Cultural Diversity in The Lord of the Rings" by Jonathan Langford, from *Food of the Gods: Eating and the Eaten in Fantasy and Science Fiction*, edited by Gary Westfahl, George Slusser, and Eric S. Rabkin. Reprinted by permission of The University of Georgia Press. Portions of the Introduction and "'Bid the Tree Unfix His Earthbound Root': Themes from *Macbeth* in The Lord of the Rings" were originally published in the article "'Bid the Tree Unfix His Earth-bound Root': Themes from *Macbeth* in The Lord of the Rings." *Seven: An Anglo-American Literary Review* 21 (2004): 47–60.

LIBRARY OF CONGRESS CATALOGUING-IN-PUBLICATION DATA

Tolkien and Shakespeare : essays on shared themes and language / edited by Janet Brennan Croft.
    p.   cm. — (Critical explorations in science fiction and fantasy ; 2)
    Includes bibliographical references and index.

    ISBN-13: 978-0-7864-2827-4 (softcover : 50# alkaline paper)

    1. Tolkien, J.R.R. (John Ronald Reuel), 1892–1973—Criticism and interpretation.   2. Tolkien, J.R.R. (John Ronald Reuel), 1892–1973—Knowledge—Literature.
3. Shakespeare, William, 1564–1616—Influence.
4. Shakespeare, William, 1564–1616—Knowledge—Literature.
5. Mythology in literature.   6. Myth in literature.
I. Croft, Janet Brennan.
PR6039.O32Z8395   2007
823'.912—dc22   2007001370

British Library cataloguing data are available

Cover art ©2006 Photodisc

Manufactured in the United States of America

McFarland & Company, Inc., Publishers
Box 611, Jefferson, North Carolina 28640
www.mcfarlandpub.com

IN MEMORIAM

Daniel Timmons
1961–2005

Contents

MAGIC

THE OTHER

Introduction

Tolkien and Shakespeare: Influences, Echoes, Revisions

JANET BRENNAN CROFT

Why bring together Tolkien and Shakespeare? At first glance they would seem to have little in common—one a prolific popular dramatist and poet of the Elizabethan era, the other a twentieth-century scholar of Old English and the "great but dilatory and unmethodical" author of a much smaller body of finished narrative and poetic work (C.S. Lewis, qtd. in Carpenter, *Tolkien* 199–200). Both have been condemned as superficial or hack writers with a shaky or undeserved spot in the canon, and both have also been nearly deified as among the greatest who ever wrote. Both also appeal equally strongly to a general audience and to amateur and professional scholars, and inspire creative works in many other fields.

But more intriguing are the parallels to be found in their bodies of work. What particularly interests us in this collection of essays is uncovering Shakespeare's influence on Tolkien through echoes of the playwright's themes, motifs, and even word choices, and discovering how Tolkien used, revised, updated, "corrected," and otherwise held an ongoing dialogue with Shakespeare's works.

Tolkien's Encounters with Shakespeare

Because of the evidence in his letters and biography, J.R.R. Tolkien is often thought of as being "unswervingly hostile" to William Shakespeare and his works (Shippey 310). As a schoolboy at King Edward's he had already formed his opinion of the playwright, and did not enjoy

1

studying Shakespeare, whom he "disliked cordially" (*Letters* 213). The Carpenter biography records that in a debating society speech at age sixteen Tolkien "poured a sudden flood of unqualified abuse upon Shakespeare, upon his filthy birthplace, his squalid surroundings, and his sordid character" (40). As an adult, Tolkien blamed Shakespeare for playing an "unforgivable" part in the "debasement" of the English concept of the Elves (*Letters* 185) and wished "a murrain on Will Shakespeare and his damned cobwebs" (143n). His plans for curriculum reform at the Oxford English School, based on the program he had developed at Leeds University, reduced the emphasis on Shakespeare and Milton that he felt privileged modern literature studies at the expense of historical linguistics (Shippey 137). He thought that the Honour School of English Language and Literature course should have a rigorous language component "based on ancient and medieval texts and their language, with at most only a brief excursion into 'modern' literature"—"modern" being anything after Geoffrey Chaucer (Carpenter, *Inklings* 24).

But how much did Tolkien really dislike Shakespeare? In *The Inklings*, Carpenter speculates that Tolkien "took an impish delight in challenging established values" and in "declaring that Shakespeare had been unjustifiably deified" (25). In Carpenter's "imaginary meeting" of the Inklings, in which he reconstructs a typical meeting from the published and unpublished writings of the participants, Carpenter has Tolkien saying "*Hamlet* is a fine enough play ... providing you take it just so, and don't start *thinking* about it. In fact I'm of the opinion that Old Bill's plays in general are all the same—they just haven't got any coherent ideas behind them" (135).

But while Tolkien may have disliked Shakespeare, he was not so hostile as to totally avoid reading, thinking about, and teaching his works. He spoke on *Hamlet* as part of a sequence of lectures with Coghill, Dyson, Lewis, Wrenn, and others during his early career at Oxford (Ryan 50), and his essay on *Beowulf*, particularly the longer versions recently edited by Michael Drout, is full of references to *King Lear* and other plays (*Beowulf and the Critics* 7, 97, 140, 159, passim). However, the opinions he expressed in writing were not always consistent, particularly when it came to his thoughts on reading Shakespeare versus seeing the plays in performance. In "On Fairy-Stories" (OFS) he says that the witches in *Macbeth* are intolerable on stage but significant in reading, and Shakespeare ought to have written *Macbeth* as a story instead of a play (OFS 50). Tolkien thought it was impossible to translate fantasy to the stage without violating the "Secondary Belief" of the audience. In this essay Tolkien illustrates his point about the inability of Drama to represent Faërie by describing how depicting the witches through stage trickery detracts from the power of their portrayal in the reader's imagination. Being brought into the Primary World, they cannot help but be exposed as shams. In his opinion, Drama cannot truly depict Fantasy because it prevents total suspension of disbelief by its very nature (OFS 49–51). He feels fiction does the job better.

On the other hand, in a 1944 letter to his son Christopher, Tolkien writes about attending a performance of *Hamlet* featuring a "young rather fierce" Prince of Denmark, in which Ophelia's mad scene, which he found boring in reading, became "almost intolerably" moving. Here he says Shakespeare should not be read in the study but seen live in performance: "Could one only have seen it without ever having read it or knowing the plot, it would have been terrific" (*Letters* 88). He says nothing of the fantastic elements in *Hamlet* and whether they worked on stage or not, although the Ghost of Hamlet's father is fully as fantastical as the witches in *Macbeth* and as difficult to present convincingly in performance.

Whatever his attitude toward a writer who was, after all, a fellow coiner of rich and strange new words, possessed of an astoundingly fertile imagination like his own, and raised in Warwickshire as he himself was, Tolkien was not ignorant of Shakespeare's writings. It does take a certain familiarity with the sources to be able to casually write in a letter that Sam "treats Gollum rather like Ariel to Caliban" (*Letters* 77), or disparage a critic's "Shylockian" turn of phrase in a scholarly essay (*Beowulf: The Monsters and the Critics* 10). As the essays in this collection will show, Tolkien's knowledge of Shakespeare appeared in some surprising forms in his writings.

The Essays

The essays in this book are grouped according to the broad themes and motifs which concerned both authors: Faërie, Power, Magic, and The Other (there is, of course, a great deal of overlap between these categories; they are all interrelated).

The depiction of Elves and the world of Faërie, and how humans interact with them, are some of the most obvious points of comparison and difference for the two writers. Allegra Johnston leads off with a survey of the historical roots of Shakespeare's and Tolkien's Elves in Celtic and Germanic fairy lore. Jessica Burke examines Victorian depictions of Shakespeare's fairies and how they may have influenced Tolkien's radically re-visioned Elves. Rebecca-Anne C. Do Rozario describes the significance of the encounters between each writer's most mundane beings—the Hobbits and the Athenian workmen—and Faërie. Romuald

I. Lakowski's paper focuses on the specific image of the Fairy Queen in Tolkien and Shakespeare, and their Renaissance and medieval sources.

Both Tolkien and Shakespeare were deeply concerned with the uses and abuses of power: with princes, politics, war, and the lessons of history. Daniel Timmons provides a fascinating look at the depiction of war, and critical reactions to these depictions, in *Henry V* and *The Lord of the Rings*. Kayla McKinney Wiggins is concerned with the parallels and contrasts between Aragorn and Hamlet, their differing types of heroism, and the influence of Machiavelli's *The Prince* on portrayals of political leadership. Judith J. Kollmann's paper looks at Aragorn from another angle, this time comparing his development with Shakespeare's description of Henry V's growth throughout the *Henriad*. Annalisa Castaldo discusses all of Shakespeare's history plays in her broader view of Tolkien's uses and interpretation of the cycles of history. Leigh Smith's paper delves into the deep thematic parallels between *King Lear* and *The Lord of the Rings*, looking closely at motifs, plot devices, and character groupings. Anne C. Petty concludes this section with a discussion of dramatic catharsis in the fall of the great and powerful, finding particularly strong examples in Tolkien's Thorin Oakenshield, Denethor, and Fëanor.

Magic and prophecy were also concerns of both authors. How did magic work in their worlds, and how did it function as a metaphor for power? What differing philosophies are revealed in the way users of magic are portrayed? Nicholas Ozment approaches the topic by examining the ethics of magic as revealed in the actions and personalities of Prospero and Gandalf. Frank P. Riga broadens this discussion by going back to the historical roots of both characters in Merlin, and showing how Tolkien used aspects of Merlin and Prospero in both Gandalf and Saruman. Last in this section I look at the sources for several incidents in *The Lord of the Rings* in *Macbeth*, and discuss the use and function of prophecy for both writers.

The works of both Tolkien and Shakespeare are full of encounters with the Other: with masks and disguises, mirrors that hide and reveal, clear glasses full of light or seeing stones that show only part of the truth. Maureen Thum's paper challenges us to look behind the masks of the women in *The Lord of the Rings* and *Twelfth Night*, to find that some of the most powerful women are hiding in plain sight. Race is another representation of the Other, and Robert Gehl looks at fears of racial otherness as revealed in the characters of Othello and Gollum. Anna Fåhraeus demonstrates how Tolkien turns the table in *The Silmarillion* and shows Man to be the Other from the point of view of the Elves. Is the past populated by the Other? Lisa Hopkins examines the power of the idea of evolutionary change in critical interpretations of Caliban and in the Victorian and Edwardian adventure literature which influenced Tolkien. Finally, Charles Keim looks at the Other within in a study of the fatefully divided minds of Othello and Gollum.

Shakespeare's precise influence on Tolkien may be debatable—absent any clear statement from Tolkien about the sources and influences he found in Shakespeare, we are reduced to speculation—but it is abundantly clear that these widely different authors can usefully illuminate each others' works across the centuries.

Note on Editions Used

Since there are many different editions of J.R.R. Tolkien's *The Lord of the Rings*, references in all of the essays have been standardized to the 1994 paperback edition published by Houghton Mifflin, with a note on the text by Douglas A. Anderson. The page number is preceded by the book and chapter number (for example, "You cannot pass!" [*LotR* 2.5.322]) for the convenience of those using another edition. Likewise, citations to *The Hobbit* are given by chapter and page number to the 1966 Houghton Mifflin hardback edition.

References to Shakespeare's plays have been standardized to the 5th edition of the *Complete Works*, edited by David Bevington and published by Pearson. References are given to act, scene, and line numbers. Title abbreviations confirm to MLA style.

Works Cited

Carpenter, Humphrey. *The Inklings: C.S. Lewis, J.R.R. Tolkien, Charles Williams, and Their Friends*. Boston: Houghton, 1979.

_____. *Tolkien: A Biography*. Boston: Houghton, 1977.

Ryan, John S. "J.R.R. Tolkien's Formal Lecturing and Teaching at the University of Oxford, 1929–1959." *Seven* 19 (2002): 45–62.

Shippey, Thomas A. *J.R.R. Tolkien: Author of the Century*. Boston: Houghton, 2001.

Tolkien, J. R. R. "Beowulf and the Critics." Ed. Michael D.C. Drout. *Medieval and Renaissance Texts and Studies*. Vol. 248. Tempe: Arizona Center for Medieval and Renaissance Studies, 2002.

_____. *Beowulf: The Monsters and the Critics*. Oxford: Oxford University Press, 1936.

_____. *The Letters of J.R.R. Tolkien: A Selection*. Ed. Christopher Tolkien. Boston: Houghton, 2000.

_____. "On Fairy-Stories." *The Tolkien Reader*. New York: Ballantine, 1966. 3–84.

FAËRIE

Clashing Mythologies
The Elves of Shakespeare and Tolkien

ALLEGRA JOHNSTON

... I now deeply regret having used Elves, though this is a word in ancestry and original meaning suitable enough. But the disastrous debasement of this word, in which Shakespeare played an unforgivable part, has really overloaded it with regrettable tones, which are too much to overcome [*Letters* 185].[1]

The overwhelming success of J.R.R. Tolkien's fiction suggests that the "debased" perception of Elves, which he lamented in the letter quoted above, was *not* too much to overcome, though it may have seemed so when he wrote those words. Part of Tolkien's goal in writing *The Lord of the Rings* (*LotR*) was to endow England with a more weighty mythology than that previously attributed to it. He believed English lore was lacking, and objected to the way an author like Shakespeare, despite his greatness as a writer, downplayed and debased creatures and elements of mythology—specifically Elves. He deliberately moved away from Shakespearean traditions in his effort to create a new and comprehensive body of myth suitable for England. Whether or not his creation was specifically adopted by England, Tolkien's Elves did set a new standard for numerous other fantasy writers, Hollywood producers, and board gamers.

The full complexity of Tolkien's Elves was something that developed over time. The Elves in Tolkien's early work, such as *The Hobbit*, share considerable similarities with their Shakespearean counterparts, but those found in *LotR*, Tolkien's later work and masterpiece, are quite distinct from the small, fairy-like creatures of Shakespeare's work. A close comparison of key Elven characters in the two authors' works, as

well as an examination of the traditions each author drew on in creating those characters, demonstrates that by the time he finished *LotR*,
Tolkien's Elven race was a unique creation that, for the most part, went
directly against Shakespearean tradition.

The differences, while apparent to any reader, are made understandable when one considers the mythologies each author relied on
in his own work. Regarding fairy-stories, Tolkien warned that the very
"richness and strangeness" of Faërie make it both difficult and dangerous to report its wonders accurately ("On Fairy-Stories" [OFS] 3). Yet
Tolkien did try to answer the question of how fairy stories originated,
and it is that question that concerns me now in comparing his idea of
Elves to that of Shakespeare.

Shakespeare drew on an English country tradition with Celtic roots
when writing about these mythical characters. In Shakespearean works,
the term *Elf* or *fairy* usually represents a mischievous character, and the
word "Elf" in particular is used in several plays to insult another person's physical form. Overall, Shakespeare treats Elves with a light hand,
while Tolkien, drawing primarily on Norse mythology and early Anglo-
Saxon traditions, prefers to see them as more serious, spiritual beings.
Though Tolkien's Elves are not perfect (they commit atrocious acts in
The Silmarillion), they represent a set of aesthetic ideals, particularly
those involving beauty, music, and appreciation for knowledge and lore.

Elves Within the Works

Perhaps the simplest way to show the distinction in the two authors'
treatment is to show some examples from their works. The most famous
Shakespearean play featuring Elves is *A Midsummer Night's Dream* (*MND*).
To be sure, it is not entirely fair to compare the Elves in *MND* with those
in *LotR*; Shakespeare's play is a comedy, which necessitates a different
tone than that found in an epic struggle between good and evil (such
as Tolkien's work). However, Shakespeare did not feature Elves in his
more "serious" plays, and that choice alone demonstrates the two
authors' different approaches. Shakespeare's comedic works embody
much of his genius, and given that comedy is where his Elves are found,
we must compare two different genres in assessing the Elves of each
author.

In *MND*, Shakespeare uses the terms "fairy" and "elf" more or less
interchangeably. The fairy folk have a substantial role in the plot and
lead a parallel existence with the human characters, occasionally min-
gling with them to suit their whims. They play tricks on one another
and on humans, and are subject to very human emotions like jealousy.

They do have some supernatural powers, such as the ability to traverse the globe in mere minutes, become invisible or change their appearances, and cast spells and enchantments, but their motivations for using these powers are primarily personal.

One of the primary characters, Puck, or Robin Goodfellow, is a mischievous fairy who acts as an instigator for much of the plot. He is King Oberon's jester and takes pleasure in interfering and complicating the lives of others in ridiculous ways: he turns the head of a human character, lowly theater-player Nick Bottom, into that of an ass for his own enjoyment. He is lively and more-or-less good-natured, though he does make mistakes (he smears love potion on the wrong human) and is not averse to playing cruel tricks. Oberon refers to him as a "mad spirit" (3.2.4), suggesting that his nature is inherently unpredictable.

While the character of Puck could be described as earthy, the other fairies of *MND* are more airy in nature. In the beginning of Act II, Puck is on stage speaking with a fairy, who says

> I must go seek some dewdrops here,
> And hang a pearl in every cowslip's ear.
> Farewell, thou lob of spirits; I'll be gone.
> Our Queen and all her elves come here anon [2.1.14–17].

Several things can be seen in this passage: first that the fairy's "tasks" are seemingly inconsequential, and second, that the elves belong, as subjects, to Queen Titania. Also, the fairy refers to Puck as a "lob," or bumpkin, of spirits, adding to his earthy reputation. Later in the scene the fairy says that Puck is also called a "hobgoblin," which is also a non-human creature of the fairy sort, but with more negative connotations.

Puck continues in this scene by warning the fairy to make sure Titania and Oberon do not meet up with one another, because they are fighting over a changeling:

> And now they never meet in grove or green,
> By fountain clear, or spangled starlight sheen,
> But they do square, that all their elves for fear
> Creep into acorn cups and hide them there [2.1.28–31].

One common British folkloric belief in the Middle Ages and Renaissance was that fairies would steal unattended children and raise them in the fairy world. This was sometimes used to explain lost or runaway children. Here we see Shakespeare playing on this idea, using the stolen child as a source of conflict between the King and Queen of Fairies. Another notable part of Puck's speech is his reference to the size of the elves. When they are afraid they "creep into acorn-cups," suggesting they are minuscule in stature.

Later, in Act III, when Queen Titania wishes to lead a mortal man into the fairy realm, she tells the elves:

> And pluck the wings from painted butterflies
> To fan the moonbeams from his sleeping eyes.
> Nod to him, elves, and do him courtesies [3.1.167–69].

In this scene Titania is directing the elves, as her minions, to "tend to" a mortal man by playing tricks of enchantment on him so that he will do the Queen's will. The tasks she assigns are whimsical, gossamer matters. And although she is royalty, Titania is not immune to foolish tricks. She succumbs to the love potion Puck procured for Oberon and dotes on the character of Bottom. Only when Oberon is satisfied that he has had his revenge is she released from the spell.

These examples from *MND* show Elves as mischievous and fanciful creatures. They are small and elusive, and though they use magical qualities to lead humans (and each other) astray, their power to affect the greater course of humanity (such as the fate of battles or nations) is quite limited and not their primary concern.

Fairies appear in *The Tempest*, a romance, as well, though they do not have such a large part. Instead, they are controlled by the magician Prospero, a man who is not above using magic to cause destruction or manipulate events to suit his will. Prospero's chief magical servant is a spirit named Ariel, though it is unclear exactly what kind of spirit he is. He is not a fairy like those of *MND* (though he shares Puck's ability to traverse the globe at amazing speeds), and much about him as a being remains ambiguous. His primary role is that of servant, for he must do Prospero's will until the magician releases him. This demonstrates that despite his status as a non-human, he can be controlled by a human (though one with magic).

Finally, there are a few other examples in which Shakespeare used the term "elf" (or some variation thereof) as a description or insult, rather than to refer to an actual being. In *King Lear*, the word "elf" is used with a negative connotation in describing appearance. Edgar, son to the Earl of Gloucester, says in Act 2, scene 3:

> My face I'll grime with filth,
> Blanket my loins, elf all my hairs in knots,
> And with presented nakedness outface
> The winds and persecutions of the sky [2.3.9–12].

Edgar is attempting to disguise himself as a madman in order to avoid persecution. The phrase "elf all my hairs in knots" refers to elf-locks: hair full of tangles and snarls because Elves had been messing with it.

In *Richard III*, there is a more dramatic use of "elvish" as an insult. Queen Margaret, the widow queen, in an argument with the Duke of Gloucester (who is to become Richard III) cries "Thou elvish-marked, abortive, rooting hog!" (1.3.228). Queen Margaret curses a number of characters in this scene, but her use of the term "elvish-marked" refers to the Duke's hunchback, a historically inaccurate physical defect which Shakespeare gave to his revisionist version of Richard III. This insult plays, once again, on the folkloric belief that fairies might steal a child and replace it with one of their own. The belief sometimes served as an excuse for the deformed or mentally unstable, for the changeling child would exhibit physical or mental traits that differed from the rest of the human population. Though Queen Margaret is not actually suggesting the Duke is a changeling, she is insulting him by saying he has been touched by the unnatural.

While these examples do provide insight into Shakespeare's perception of Elves, it is important to end this section by reiterating that on the whole, Elves do not feature prominently in the vast majority of Shakespeare's work.

This is not the case for J.R.R. Tolkien, whose masterpiece work *LotR* features Elves in key roles, as do *The Hobbit* and *The Silmarillion*. The Elves in Tolkien's first novel, *The Hobbit*, which was aimed at a youthful readership, come closest to resembling those found in Shakespearean works, though they are human-sized or taller. The Elves found in Tolkien's later works grow increasingly distinctive, ending with *The Silmarillion*, which contains the weighty history of his Elven race and was published after Tolkien's death.

The first elves we come across in *The Hobbit* are those of Rivendell, residing with Elrond in the Last Homely House before the Misty Mountains. Bilbo, Gandalf, and a party of dwarves pass through on their way to the Lonely Mountain. The first thing they hear when arriving in Rivendell is the song of the elves:

> *O! What are you doing,*
> *And where are you going?*
> *Your ponies need shoeing!*
> *The river is flowing!*
> *O! tra-la-la-lally*
> *here down in the valley!* [3.58].

This is only one verse of the song, but as Tolkien writes at the end of the verses, "So they laughed and sang in the trees; and pretty fair nonsense I daresay you think it" (3.59). He notes that the Dwarves consider Elves foolish folks, and although he says that is "a very foolish thing to think" (3.59), the reader does not get much evidence in this chapter to suggest otherwise, other than the fact that Elven song is won-drous and the Elven people always seem to be abreast of news from afar. The elves also tease Bilbo and the dwarves, much as their Shake-spearean counterparts tease humans. The only exception is Elrond, who is described as an elf-friend because he has both Elvish and human ancestry. He is described as "noble," "wise," and "venerable"—not terms to be taken lightly (3.61). Elrond aids them in interpreting moon-runes on their treasure map and is able to give them the background on the swords they found in a trolls' lair. Still, he is only part–Elf, and the full–Elves of Rivendell appear far less serious creatures.

The other notable set of Elves in *The Hobbit* are the Wood-Elves inhabiting Mirkwood, a dense forest described as "dark, dangerous, and difficult" (7.143), and filled with savage creatures and strange enchant-ments. The Dwarves and Hobbit leave the only safe forest path when they see twinkling lights and Elves feasting merrily—just when their own party is nearing starvation. Yet when they get close to the feasting Elves, the lights go out and the Dwarves become lost, following the magical feasters further and further from the path. Whether or not the Elves deliberately lured the party into the dangerous forest is debatable; the Dwarves certainly felt tricked and ill-used, though the Elves claimed innocence. However, the narrator says of these Elves:

> These are not wicked folk. If they have a fault it is distrust of strangers.... They differed from the High Elves of the West, and were more dangerous and less wise. For most of them ... were descended from the ancient tribes that never went to Faerie in the West. There the Light-elves and the Deep-elves and the Sea-elves went and lived for ages, and grew fairer and wiser and more learned [8.178].

The distinctions between the different types of Elves become much clearer in *The Silmarillion* and *LotR*, but here it is enough to know that the Elves of Mirkwood, while tricky and distrustful, are still "Good Peo-ple" (5.179). They do make prisoners of the Dwarves, but since Tolkien's Elves and Dwarves have a long history of mistrust and even war, this is not unexpected. Late in the novel they join forces with the Dwarves, Eagles, and Men in the Battle of Five Armies, demonstrating their skill as fighters and their hatred for evil.

Already there are some differences between the Elves of Tolkien and their Shakespearean counterparts: their size is that of humans, and they participate in the greater events of the world around them. They are not servants who can be controlled by their human counterparts like the fairies in *The Tempest*. Still, like Shakespeare's fairies, they are often seen singing foolish songs and using magic deep in the woods.

The Elves of Mirkwood, with their dangerous tricks, could possibly be described as somewhat "Puckish."

Such similarities disappear in Tolkien's later works. *The Lord of the Rings* is imbued with a far greater sense of the history of Middle-earth, with a particular emphasis on the allure of decayed grandeur found in lost or ruined civilizations (both Human and Elvish). The previously light-hearted Elves of Rivendell are portrayed in a more serious and ethereal manner, while the tricksy Elves of Mirkwood are represented only by the character of Legolas, who joins the Fellowship of the Ring with a noble purpose. The Elves of *LotR* and *The Silmarillion* are also great warriors, with a long history of battling evil (and, occasionally, fighting among themselves). This is a definite break from Shakespearean fairies, who may influence human events through magic, such as by changing the weather, and who may have conflicts between themselves, like Oberon and Titania's disagreement over the changeling child, but are never portrayed as a warrior people.

One character that serves particularly well to demonstrate the differences between the Elves of Shakespeare and Tolkien is Galadriel. Like Titania of *MND*, she is a queen (though the Elves refer to her as the "Lady of Lothlórien," her function and bearing are quite queenly). Galadriel is serious and considerate, as well as powerful; it is difficult to imagine her ever falling for the same trick that had Titania doting on an ass-headed commoner, nor do she and her elves romp freely through the woods like Shakespeare's Elves.

Galadriel is first seen toward the end of *The Fellowship of the Ring*, as the fellowship passes through Lothlórien. There is a great deal of mystery surrounding the land in which she dwells, and Gimli the Dwarf relates tales suggesting she is a witch to be feared. Aragorn assures him she is not evil, yet the mystery remains and there is much ceremony to their approach to Galadriel's city. Galadriel herself, with her consort, Lord Celeborn, lives high above the ground in a tree, adding to the ethereality of her person. She is not of this earth, and yet she is. While Shakespeare's Elves can also be found in the woods, they generally remain on the ground and have a far less ethereal quality. Shakespearean Elves are light-hearted and airy, but their mystical qualities are not beyond human understanding, as they are in Tolkien's story.

The first description we have of Galadriel's physical person is very ceremonial. She and Celeborn stand to greet their guests, in what is described as an Elvish custom followed even by rulers. Their appearance and bearing are stately, dignified, and the epitome of otherworldly beauty, "but no sign of age was upon them, unless it were in the depths of their eyes; for these were keen as lances in the starlight, and yet profound, the wells of deep memory" (2.7.345).

Here we see elves that are not only tall, they are "grave," "beautiful," and ageless, possessed of keen and far-reaching memories. Galadriel has power to see what is going on outside her domain and, to some extent, to view what may happen in the future. She is wise enough to know the limitations of her own powers, using her brand of magic to gain knowledge but not for trickery or deceit. She also has keen insight into other characters, sensing that the members of the Fellowship can only succeed if they are wholly dedicated to their quest, and not to any other desires or loyalties they may have.

She tests them, both by looking into their minds and seemingly tempting them with those other desires, and, for Frodo and Sam, by offering them a glimpse into the Mirror of Galadriel, where they see the frightening things that may lie ahead on their path. While Frodo and Sam, and indeed most of the Fellowship, are able to pass Galadriel's test, not all are so strong. Not long after Galadriel's warning about remaining true, Boromir succumbs to his own desire for the power of the One Ring, thereby tearing apart the fellowship (but confirming Galadriel's abilities).

Those who have read more of Tolkien's works will know that Galadriel has a long history before she appears in *LotR.* In *The Silmarillion,* which concerns the history of Elves, we find out that she is a member of a group of Elves called the Noldor, who rebel against the Valar (holy and powerful beings who reside in the undying West). Though she decides to return to Middle-earth, the fact that she has been to Valinor, land of the Valar, places her in the category of "Light-Elves" (those who have seen the light of that great land, as opposed to the Dark-Elves, who were too fearful to make that first journey to the West when it was offered them). The Light-Elves have, in general, a greater understanding of their world and the powers that lie within it, for they have spent time in the presence of the Valar. Those that rebelled, however, including Galadriel, angered the Valar and were banished from returning. Galadriel is able to gain great power in Middle-earth, particularly as she is the bearer of one of the Three Rings, but her banishment is the reason that, as she says in *LotR,* she must "diminish" if she is to return to the West. Her sins of pride and ambition can be forgiven, but she will no longer have the power she once desired, and she must come to terms with this. She does so, for when Frodo offers her the One Ring, the power to control all, she turns it down, demonstrating her wisdom and humility.

Another elf who plays a major role in *LotR* is Legolas. We first meet him at the Council of Elrond, though he plays only a small part there. He is chosen as one of the Fellowship to accompany Frodo on the quest to destroy the One Ring, and his presence proves quite valuable. Legolas has physical abilities beyond those of Men or even Hobbits, such as the ability to see further, to move in silence, or to endure wearying journeys without sleep. He functions as an ambassador when the Fellowship enters Lothlórien, and his skill with bow and arrow protects his companions more than once. When necessary he can fight with deadly accuracy, and the dangers of the wild hold little fear for him. He is not immune to grief, for even as the other elves sing songs of Gandalf after his fall in Moria, Legolas refrains from translating for his companions, "saying only that he had not the skill, and that for him the grief was still too near, a matter for tears and not yet for song" (2.7.350). Although the loss of Gandalf affects him, Legolas has something of the otherworldly about him, for the hardships and worries of the journey seem to touch him less than his mortal companions, allowing him, for the most part, to remain light of heart when others are downtrodden. He has an appreciation for mischief and competition (for example, competing with the Dwarf Gimli to see who can kill the greater number of enemies), but he can hardly be compared to Shakespeare's earthy Puck. Like Galadriel, he bears little resemblance at all to the Shakespearean fairies, sharing only physical beauty and a connection to nature.

A final mark of greatness for Tolkien's Elves bears mentioning. Of the rings of power originally intended by Sauron to control their bearers (though the Elven-smiths who created them did not share those intentions), only those belonging to the Elves did not fall back into his hands. The Dwarves and Men did not fare so well, for they were more easily controlled by Sauron's evil. The Elves, however, were able to withstand the pressure to cave in to Sauron and used the rings to protect their own domains. This ability to withstand being externally controlled stands in direct contrast to the fairies in Shakespeare's *The Tempest*, who are under the direct control of a magician. (One might argue that the fairies of *MND* did have some level of control over humans, but never did they keep them as servants.) Tolkien's Elves have a direct impact on all of Middle-earth, while Shakespeare's fairies concern themselves primarily with the people and events of their immediate surroundings.

Folklore and Literary Traditions Concerning Elves

A primary reason for the conceptual differences of Elves lies in the cultural sources the two authors used, with each adapting specific traditions to suit their own purposes. Shakespeare favored English traditions with Celtic roots while Tolkien drew on Germanic myths—though the two are not entirely unrelated. As the various peoples of Europe had contact with one another over the centuries, so elements of their cultures intermingled. As Tolkien said, "the history of fairy-stories is probably more complex than the physical history of the human race, and as complex as the history of human language" (OFS 20).

It is particularly difficult to trace the exact traditions that Shakespeare drew on in his conceptualization of Elves, because England's history is one that is, until the later Middle Ages, marked by invasions and struggles for power. Because of this, the mythology of England was influenced by the mythologies of its invaders, including the Vikings and Anglo-Saxons. However, it was the indigenous population of the British Isles that had a lasting impact on the folklore of that country, despite being conquered and assimilated under the laws of various rulers. Celtic and pagan folklore lived on in the countryside of the British Isles, sometimes mixing with Christian beliefs as the society's power structure changed and developed.

The changing nature of myth itself causes problems when trying to attribute an author's ideas to a particular body of myth. For example, the very early Celtic beliefs did feature gods and spiritual beings like fairies that were both divine and impressive in nature. They were immortal and powerful, but, as Celtic scholar Charles Squire has noted, "they had taken on the semblance of mortality by the time their histories were fixed in the form in which we have them now. Their earliest records, if those could be restored to us, would doubtless show them eternal and undying, changing their shapes at will, but not passing away. But the post–Christian copyists, whether Irish or Welsh, would not countenance this" (17). The Christian church frowned on fairy beliefs, particularly belief in immortal, god-like fairies that required respect and even worship. Belief in lesser fairies, while not officially approved, was less threatening to the Church.

By Shakespeare's time, secular and fantastic topics, including fairy lore, were becoming more acceptable in literature and the arts. Few people by then would have told stories about the ancient, powerful Celtic gods, but many would have known to bar their doors at night to prevent mischievous fairies from stealing away family members. So when I suggest that Shakespeare drew on Celtic traditions for his conceptualization of Elves, I mean the popular rural folklore of his day, which was Celtic in origin but certainly not unaffected by the course of time.[2] Katharine Briggs, author of *The Anatomy of Puck* and *The Fairies in English Tradition and Literature*, attributes this new acceptance of fairy lore (with smaller, more lighthearted fairies) in literature to the rise of the yeoman writer in England. Writers with a country background, like Shakespeare, could draw on the fireside tales of their youth in a way that delighted audiences without forcing anyone to take the idea of fairies too seriously (which would still be frowned upon in a time of scientific advancement and strong Christian influence in government) (Briggs 6).

Regarding fairies, Shakespeare's portrayal of these non-humans as very small and mischievous can be linked to lore from throughout the British Isles, though not all fairies were of that nature. In fact, the fairies of Celtic tradition came in a number of various guises, some more powerful than others. Celtic scholar Bob Curran, in *The Creatures of Celtic Myth*, describes the fairy folk as "the representation of the elemental forces of nature who, at best, were capricious in their attitude towards mankind and, at worst, were fully prepared to do humans some fatal mischief" (52). Briggs acknowledges the connection to nature, but also divides the fairy peoples into four types: the ordinary or domestic fairies, like brownies; the hobgoblins, who are rougher and more earthy (like Shakespeare's Puck); mermaids and water or nature spirits; and monsters (like giants and hags) (14–16). Of these, Shakespeare primarily makes use of the first two (though hags appear in *Macbeth* and the exact nature of the spirit Ariel is uncertain). Shakespeare also combines elements of the domestic and nature spirits in the fairies of *MND*.

Domestic fairies were known by many names throughout the British Isles: fairies, Good People or Fair Folk,[3] sprites, goblins, Elves, brownies—the list goes on. Often the names varied according to the natural setting the particular fairy was thought to inhabit. Along with the variation in names came variation of the "seriousness" of fairies. The brownies of the Scottish and English countryside, for example, were mere household sprites, while the more dangerous Pookas (or pwccas, or pixies, depending on regional differences) were known for leading travelers astray. The name "Puck" is an adaptation of the term "Pooka," with origins in the Celtic character Pouk. Shakespeare's Puck, like a pooka, is a fairy who leads humans astray.

There is a spiritual dimension to Celtic fairies, perhaps, as Curran suggests, because the fairies were a folkloric reinterpretation of the ancient Celtic gods after those gods were stamped out by Christianity (52). It is notable that although Celtic fairies often had spiritual power, they were not necessarily credited with great wisdom or skill. Instead, the close association of fairies with nature, and the respect that most people had for the power of nature, were what gave them weight.

Shakespeare downplayed the spiritual element: his fairies do reside in natural settings and hold some supernatural powers (for example, being able to travel the globe at amazing speeds), but they do not garner a great deal of respect or fear from human characters. Shakespeare also seems to have toned down the hostility of his fairies, for although they do perform some mischief (like stealing away a human child, a very popular theme in Celtic folktales), they do not kill humans. In fact,

Briggs points out that the benevolence of Shakespeare's fairies, especially in *MND*, is particularly striking, and that even Queen Titania's theft of a human child is motivated by her love for its dead mother (46). English lore was not devoid of kindly fairies, but Shakespeare's choice to emphasize that aspect of their nature was unusual.

Although Tolkien did not appreciate the way Shakespeare portrayed fairies, he did acknowledge that it was not without cause: "It is perhaps not unnatural that in England, the land where the love of the delicate and fine has often reappeared in art, fancy should in this matter turn towards the dainty and diminutive" (OFS 6). He also stated that one of the reasons the elements of fantasy in Shakespeare's plays bothered him is because of the difficulty in staging anything that is supposed to be fantastic. He said that on the stage, men were likely to achieve "buffoonery or mimicry," but not Fantasy, and that it only worked when portrayed as a farce (thereby relieving the audience of the requirement to actually believe in the story) (OFS 49). Tolkien's stories are meant to be read rather than performed, which he found far more conducive to creating stories of real, if fantastic, power.

By the time Tolkien began his work in the early twentieth century, the Shakespearean conceptualization of Elves was the standard that permeated most British literature. Tolkien, however, was a scholar of Anglo-Saxon and Old English, which brought him into contact with texts unfamiliar to the general public. Here he discovered the traditions and myths of Germanic cultures, which differed considerably from those of his own time. He was not necessarily opposed to the Celtic traditions that informed Shakespeare's writing; indeed, he stated in a letter to Milton Waldman that he had been affected by Celtic stories, among others, and that one of his goals in creating his own body of legend for England was "possessing (if I could achieve it) the fair elusive beauty that some call Celtic (though it is rarely found in genuine ancient Celtic things)" (*Letters* 144). Here he seems to suggest that while actual Celtic history is not something he chooses to emulate, there is a secondary meaning to the term "Celtic" which relates to beauty and mystery—qualities very important to his Elves.

However, in creating this beauty and mystery, Tolkien actually drew on traditions from Anglo-Saxon, Norse, and ancient Germanic cultures—the material he was so familiar with from his scholarly work. Though he professed to be creating mythology and lore for England, he found these other mythologies to be more compelling when compared to his "impoverished" home country, which he said "had no stories of its own" (*Letters* 144). A few of his ideas are similar to Celtic beliefs, such as the concept of Valinor as the undying lands across the ocean, which is like the Celtic belief in an otherworld (often an island) where everything was better. But when it came to Elves specifically, the modern British traditions, influenced by Shakespearean fairies, offered little that appealed to him.

In comparison, the Norse and Anglo-Saxon cultures featured Elves that were human-sized and powerful. Jacob Grimm's *Teutonic Mythology* is a worthy, though dense, resource on such matters; in a chapter on wights and Elves he states

> the Elder Edda several times couples *æsir* and *âlfar* [elves] together, as though they were a compendium of all higher beings ... *this apparently concedes more of divinity to elves than to men.* Sometimes there come in, as a third member, the *vanir*, a race distinct from the *æsir*, but admitted to certain relationships with them by marriage and by covenants.... *âlfar* have skill (understanding), and *vanir* knowledge [443, emphasis added].

This description sounds strikingly similar to the Elves of Tolkien, who, like the Old Norse *âlfar*, have a more direct connection with the spiritual world than does the race of Men. Tolkien's Elves also interact (primarily in *The Silmarillion*) with the Valar (a name notably close to *vanir*), a race similar to gods that resides in the undying lands. The Valar have a great deal of knowledge and understanding but are quite separate from the human world.

Norse mythology also distinguished between "Light-elves," "Dark-elves," and "Swart-elves" (or "black-elves")—distinctions that Tolkien appropriated for his own fiction. Tolkien scholar Tom Shippey notes in *J.R.R. Tolkien: Author of the Century* that most of what we know of the ancient mythology comes from the Icelander Snorri Sturluson (who composed *The Prose Edda*, somewhat later than the Elder Edda, containing a manual of poetics and many mythological tales). It unfortunately leaves many questions unanswered, such as the nature of the difference between the types of Elves (228–29). Shippey suggests in a recent essay that Tolkien, as a philologist, was frustrated by the lack of clarity in the many terms used to describe Elves—the Anglo-Saxon, Scandinavian, and Germanic myths had points of commonality but many inconsistencies in terminology. Tolkien saw an opportunity in his own fiction to provide a more satisfying, if fictional, answer as to the varying natures and types of Elves ("Light-elves" 2, 5).

While earlier scholars guessed that the distinction between Light and Dark Elves had to do with actual color or size, or possibly the relationship between Elves and Dwarves, Tolkien addressed the question by separating his Elves based on their history. Thus the Light Elves of Tolkien's work are those who went to Valinor, where the Valar reside, and saw the Light of the Two Trees, while the Dark Elves, unsure of the journey, remained behind in Middle-earth. Later, many of the Light

Elves are exiled from Valinor and return to Middle-earth, which explains why both types of Elves are present during the stories set at the end of the Third Age. All of this is explained in *The Silmarillion*, though Tolkien hints at the Elvish history in *The Hobbit* and *The Lord of the Rings*. As for the swart-elves of Icelandic mythology, Tolkien rejects the idea they could be Dwarves and eliminates this group completely—though, as Shippey points out, the account of Eöl, a black-clad Elf who associates with Dwarves, allows Tolkien's mythology to remain compatible with that which he was drawing from ("Light-Elves" 11).

Not only the character of the Elves, but the complexity of their history and their language, Quenya, are also influenced by these traditions. Modern readers are sometimes frustrated with *The Silmarillion* because, in order to follow the storylines, it is vital to be able to remember complex family history and genealogy for the Elves. As Shippey points out, this is another element of Norse influence showing in Tolkien's work, because such complex relationships were common in the Norse and Icelandic sagas (*Author* 244). Their audiences would have been accustomed to seeing the subtleties and importance of such relationships, while contemporary readers do not catch these same distinctions.

Contemporary readers have, however, accepted the presence of the Elvish language, Quenya, in *LotR* and *The Silmarillion*, in part perhaps because Tolkien wove it into the narrative so well. Quenya is a language of Tolkien's invention, but Shippey suggests it has links to the Finnish language—a language Tolkien particularly appreciated as a philologist (244). Certain story elements of *The Silmarillion* parallel the Finnish *Kalevala* (an epic compiled of traditional Finnish songs and lays, reconnected in the 19th century in a poem), strengthening the link between that culture and Tolkien's Elves (*Author* xv, 244, 250, 255).

Finally, even the *attitude* of the Elves (and of the Men, Dwarves, and Hobbits) toward the battle against Sauron is one that stems from Norse mythology. The Norse tales told of a Day of Doom (Ragnarok) in which, unlike in the Christian stories that promise an eternal life, the gods and men battle the giants and monsters until all are destroyed. Great warriors were expected to have courage in spite of certain doom. As Shippey describes it, "Northern mythology asks more of people than Christianity does, for it offers them no heaven, no salvation, no reward for virtue except the sombre satisfaction of having done right" (*Author* 150). In *LotR*, the Elves show this same fortitude. Though Sauron does not actually win, the odds for the Fellowship do seem nearly insurmountable. Still, Elrond, Legolas, and Galadriel all press on, aiding the cause in whatever ways they can, in spite of the fact that the Elves are, as a whole, leaving Middle-earth for the undying lands in the west. They are not hopeful so much as resolute, in line with the attitudes found in Norse mythology. Thus, while Tolkien's Elves may have a "Celtic" sort of beauty, their origins are far closer to the Elves of Teutonic or Old Norse mythology.

It is evident, then, that the differences between Shakespeare's fairies and Tolkien's Elves stem from the authors' primary sources: the Celtic folklore of the English countryside versus ancient Norse mythology. Despite such differences, one point of commonality in the two authors' attitudes toward the Elves and fairies is a sense of nostalgia in the works that contain them. *A Midsummer Night's Dream* can easily be read as a paean for a passing time. In the sixteenth century there were many opponents of festivals that had pagan roots, such as the rites of midsummer. The Catholic Church had allowed and absorbed some of these rites, but the new Church of England proclaimed them immoral and many pastors wrote condemnations of such celebrations. It later became illegal (shortly after Shakespeare's time) to celebrate midsummer's night and the traditional rites that went with it. The power of the church spread even to small towns like Stratford-upon-Avon, and anything that smacked of paganism was stamped out with a vengeance. Yet Shakespearean scholar Stephen Greenblatt suggests that Shakespeare would have grown up with knowledge of the folk traditions, even if he himself was Christian, because many were celebrated during his boyhood, and even Queen Elizabeth held some fondness for them (38–53). There is a sad or nostalgic undertone to *MND*, perhaps because the author realizes his society is losing a part of its history.

Similarly, many scholars have commented on the constant awareness of an ending era in *LotR*, which goes beyond nostalgia to an almost elegiac tone. Regardless of the outcome of the battle with Sauron, the Elves are leaving Middle-earth forever, and the age of Men is beginning. This sense of ending is comparable to the sentiment of Anglo-Saxon elegiac poems like *The Wanderer* or *Beowulf*, which celebrate a warrior culture while simultaneously acknowledging that the Christian era is taking over. Given Tolkien's scholarly work in Anglo-Saxon studies, it is likely that those works influenced his thinking more heavily than the nostalgia found in Shakespeare's plays. Still, this is one area in which the two authors are not at odds with one another.

In conclusion, then, Shakespeare and Tolkien may share a deep interest in folklore and the creatures of myth, but the works they produced are quite different, in part because of the sources they used. The English folklore Shakespeare drew on had Celtic roots (however watered down) that contrast significantly with the Old Norse sources Tolkien found most compelling. Shakespeare's lighthearted, tiny Elves enchanted Elizabethan society, while Tolkien's Elves captivate readers with their ethereal beauty, knowledge, and power. Both authors continue to be popular and influence new writers, but the Elves Tolkien created have set the standard for modern fantasy.

Notes

1. J.R.R. Tolkien wrote these words in a letter to Hugh Brogan, in which he attempted to explain his choice of names for the non-human races in his fiction.

2. We do have evidence of Celtic tradition in other areas of Shakespeare's work as well. For example, the play *King Lear* is, according to Charles Squire, loosely based on Celtic legends about the sea-god Llyr. The figure of Cordelia in that same play is related to the Celtic maiden Creudylad, daughter of Lludd (whom Squire describes as "the British Zeus" or sky-god) (Squire 258, 270). Of course these legends also had changed considerably from their original forms by the time Shakespeare was using them, but the groundwork for his ideas was essentially Celtic.

3. These names, according to Curran, were used not out of respect, but to appease the fairies, for many humans feared what they might do (52–53).

Works Cited

Briggs, K.M. *The Anatomy of Puck.* London: Routledge, 1959.

Curran, Bob. *The Creatures of Celtic Myth.* London: Cassell, 2001.

Greenblatt, Stephen. *Will in the World: How Shakespeare Became Shakespeare.* New York: Norton, 2004.

Grimm, Jacob. *Teutonic Mythology.* Trans. James Steven Stallybrass. Vol. 2. New York: Dover, 1966.

Shakespeare, William. *The Complete Works of Shakespeare.* Ed. David Bevington. 5th ed. New York: Pearson, 2004.

Shippey, Thomas A. *J.R.R. Tolkien: Author of the Century.* Boston: Houghton, 2000.

_____. "Light-elves, Dark-elves, and Others: Tolkien's Elvish Problem." *Tolkien Studies* 1 (2004): 1–15.

Squire, Charles. *Celtic Myth and Legends.* New York: Portland, 1997. Revised edition of *Mythology of the British Islands.* 1905.

Tolkien, J.R.R. *The Hobbit.* 2nd ed. Boston: Houghton, 1966.

_____. *The Letters of J.R.R. Tolkien.* Ed. Humphrey Carpenter. Boston: Houghton, 2000.

_____. *The Lord of the Rings.* 2nd ed. Boston: Houghton, 1994.

_____. "On Fairy-Stories." *The Tolkien Reader.* New York: Ballantine, 1966. 3–84.

"How Now, Spirit! Whither Wander You?"

Diminution: The Shakespearean Misconception and the Tolkienian Ideal of Faërie

JESSICA BURKE

Be thou spirit of health or goblin damn'd,
Bring with thee airs from heaven or blasts from hell,
Be thy intents wicked or charitable,
Thou com'st in such a questionable shape
That I will speak to thee [*Hamlet* 1.4.40–44].

In some form or other, fairies have been around since the beginning of time. Every culture around this planet has its own brand of fairy, but there is one unfortunate English version of the fairy that twitters about within our collective imaginations and threatens to overwhelm all others. These fairies are the essence of cuteness, trivialized and made small: romantic renditions of an idealized humanity. Such was not always the case—as reflected in the quote above. Here we hit upon the historical unblemished ferocity and raw enchantment of the fairy. But how do we get from the roots of an ancient past ripe with goblins and imps, with untamed fairies that kidnap and cajole, lure and punish, to effervescent tree sprites all bedecked in cobwebs, dewdrops, insect wings, tulle, and sequins? How do we get from Yallery Brown[1] to Disney's Tinker Bell? Tolkien attributed this link to no other source than Will Shakespeare, and no other play more than *A Midsummer Night's Dream* (*MND*). It was undeniable that Tolkien felt Shakespeare, and Shakespeare's fairies in particular, lacked enchantment, the essence of Faërie. Yet I find it somewhat dubious that Shakespeare really was the sole culprit. Despite Shakespeare's first steps toward what would become a machine-driven theatrically influenced fairy of minuscule proportions, it was the Victorians who truly capitalized on this trend and made the fairy into an industry of its own. Did Tolkien detest Shakespeare not for planting this seed, but because Tolkien harbored some embarrassment for his own early diminutive creations, as gossamer as any produced by the Victorian fairy machine? Eventually, he corrected the Victorian mistake: he gave the fairy back her majesty.

But what is a fairy? Can we honestly say that Shakespeare got it wrong and Tolkien got it right? Is there a right and wrong when it comes to Faërie, or are we all just groping blindly? Let us first define the differences between "fairy" and "Faërie." The term "fairy" refers to the creatures often portrayed as diminutives, with supposed magical abilities, popularized by Shakespeare, the Victorian stage's pantomime and transformation scenes, and the likes of Andrew Lang, Richard Dadd, and Walt Disney. Faërie can be deemed a polar opposite, a Tolkienian ideal, an entity, a state-of-being, a creation beyond mortal thought, both "The Perilous Realm" and its denizens, beyond describing, but not beyond perceiving (*Essays Presented to Charles Williams* [*EPCW*] 42–3).[2] Tolkien's Elves are creatures wholly of the enchanted lands, set apart from the concerns of mortal men.

An extensive taxonomy of the multifarious fairy denizens of our space-time continuum can be found in the many works of the folklorist Katherine Briggs. However, Diane Purkiss' enlightening and pragmatic *At the Bottom of the Garden* brings out a point perhaps unheeded by the eminent Briggs—while there are hundreds of fairy names, there are only a few categorical fairy "types" (Purkiss 8–9). For our purposes, with specific regard to Shakespeare's fairies and those presented in *MND*, we can turn to Peter Holland, who discusses the various trouping fairies that influenced Shakespeare and shared interests with their Celtic ancestors—hunting, riding, and feasting (Holland 23). These are interests of a leisure class, specifically of the aristocracy or of an aristocratic household, and imply a rigid class structure within the fairy realm. Shakespeare additionally draws on other fairy traditions, such as shape-shifting, variant but generally diminutive size, and a tendency to punish mortals (with chastisements ranging from a mere pinch to kidnapping), all of which reinforce the notions of fairies as frivolous, unimportant, minuscule, lacking both power and a voice of their own.

Faërie, however, is a notion of pure, unadulterated enchantment that draws us from our everyday mundane world: this is the very quality Tolkien finds missing in *MND* (Carpenter 35, 48; *Letters* 185). In "On Fairy-Stories" (OFS) Tolkien discusses this notion of Faërie in terms of joy as "poignant as grief" (*EPCW* 81). And, for the most part, this anguished joy is lacking in many of Shakespeare's fairies, from Mercutio's Queen Mab (*Rom.* 4.53–94) to the ever-trivial fairies in *MND.* This lack of joy, this absence of epiphany, glory, revelation—fairies devoid of Faërie—is where the diminution begins.

In childhood, I was indoctrinated into the world of the fairies through the body of literature erroneously called fairy-tales. As Tolkien points out, among the collected fantastical tales of the Brothers Grimm, Charles Perrault, Andrew Lang, and Hans Christian Andersen, even the pop-cultural notion of the fairy is lacking. There are, however, talking beasts, magical flowers, enchanted rings, bewitched castles, and many an inanimate object with the brusque personality of an in-law, but no creatures genuinely of the realm of Faërie. This is not to say that there isn't some merit or cultural value in reading this legendarium—but it is a falsehood to call them "fairy tales."

Despite being surrounded by Disneyfied fairies and fairy tales without fairies in them, in childhood I clung to the grace of Faërie, the beauty of enchantment that I discovered in the works of Tolkien, in *The Hobbit* and in *The Lord of the Rings* (*LotR*). In these works Tolkien harkens back to an earlier concept of Faërie and endows his Elves with "perilous joy" when he makes them the Firstborn, higher and fairer than Man. In *The Silmarillion,* Ilúvatar granted that the Elves would be the bearers of grace in all its forms; they would create more beauty than any race save the Valar themselves; and the joy of the Elves would be the greater, but so would their sorrow. *The Lord of the Rings* is a record of their passing out of Middle-earth, and the coming of the Age of Man, our current Age. Tolkien's Elves are thus neither trivial nor diminutive. They are shapers of the very foundations of the earth, their language is song, and they are anything but peaceful. The "Valaquenta" and "Quenta Silmarillion" have enough bloodshed, treachery, war, vice, lust, and bad-temper to make the mighty gods of even Mount Olympus blush. Written at the time of World War I, *The Silmarillion* reflects the same end of innocence that Tolkien's own world was experiencing.

Tolkien's Eldar are physically distinctive as well. Glorfindel and Elrond are tall, fierce, beautiful, kings among their people. Arwen is seen as the female form of Elrond in a sense, and all three are both timeless and ageless, though the weight of many years shows in the depths of their eyes. More impressive still are the Elves who overrun Smith as he wanders through the lands of Faërie:

> The elven mariners were tall and terrible; their swords shone and their spears glinted and a piercing light was in their eyes. Suddenly they lifted up their voices in a song of triumph, and his heart was shaken with fear, and he fell upon his face, and they passed over

him and went away into the echoing hills [*Smith of Wootton Major* 28].

This is rather a contrast to Shakespeare's sprites as we first meet them in *MND*.

Shakespearean and Other Elizabethan Fairies

Shakespeare's descriptions of the physical appearance of his sprites must be deduced from dialogue, since there are no descriptions of the fairies' appearance in the stage directions, while Tolkien, in his element as a narrative writer, could provide the reader with very distinct imagery. It is also useful to keep in mind that aside from the fact that the authors worked in different media—fiction and drama—Shakespeare literally churned out his work, writing over thirty plays in less than thirty years, in addition to the sonnets and narrative poems. Tolkien, on the other hand, took the better part of half a century to write his literary legacy, the majority of which was neither published nor finished in his lifetime. This is not to say Tolkien was an idle scholar, or a lazy author. He wrote thousands of pages of text, scores of versions of any particular scene, hundreds of lines of verse: he was a perfectionist, and, if it wasn't "right" then it wasn't finished and therefore not suitable to print.

Shakespeare was ambiguous in various places, distinct in others. Take, for example, the first Fairy's response to Puck's infamous question: "How now, spirit, whither wander you?" (*MND* 2.1.1–13). The reader is led to assume from this passage that the fairies are as tall as a "cowslip." This is by no means a blanket description of all fairies, nor does Shakespeare intend it to be. When the fairy bids Puck "Farewell, thou lob of spirits," this may imply that Puck is larger than the other fairies whose diminutive proportions are reflected in their names Mote, Mustardseed, Peaseblossom—Puck could even have been played by an adult actor (Holland 153). "Lob" does refer in a general sense to larger, lumbering fairy types—the brownie, the house-spirit, the shape-shifting mischief maker—but there is no real evidence to suggest that Robin Goodfellow was not a contemporary of Shakespeare's century rather than a throwback to any hardy Anglo-Celtic past. Purkiss discusses fairies as having much to do with a rural tradition from both the ancient cultures of the world, and the not so ancient. Fairies involved the so-called unexplainable things in life, the darknesses from before and after, the blank outer spaces on the map: birth, death, sex, and beyond. Fairies dealt with the uncertainties of life—love, the acquisition of wealth, the loss of favor, fortune, health. They ranged in purpose from helpful spirits who tinkered about the house or farm, to kidnapping specters reminiscent of the revenant—a wraithlike ancestral phantom that was the predecessor to the vampire legend. Purkiss notes that the crossing of the threshold—from the fairy as a thing to be feared, to a thing to be coddled and cooed over—came primarily from Shakespeare and the time of the Protestant Reformation (Purkiss 11–30, 158). Fairy lore was demoted from dire warnings about the outer limits of humanity and the unknowable reaches of life, to a handbook of dos and don'ts for the working class. Fairies after Shakespeare became creatures that would punish a servant for not cleaning the grates properly, and became a means for the upper classes to keep the rural folk in order. Fairies were also used—most particularly—as a means for the making of rules for women (Purkiss 164–65). In the 1628 *Mad Pranks and Merry Jests of Robin Goodfellow*, we have fairies who were exceptionally brutal and troublesome to idle serving-women not performing their duties to the express satisfaction of their betters. While Shakespeare briefly touches on this aspect of fairy-lore in the trick played on Falstaff in *Merry Wives of Windsor* (5.5.41–53), it can be seen more readily in the poetry of Robert Herrick, specifically his poem "The Fairies":

> If ye will with Mab find grace,
> Set each platter in his place;
> Rake the fire up, and get
> Water in, ere sun be set.
> Wash your pails and cleanse your dairies,
> Sluts are loathsome to the fairies;
> Sweep your house; Who doth not so,
> Mab will pinch her by the toe [Herrick 15–16].

Published in 1648, Herrick's main body of work, *Hesperides*, includes hundreds of poems—and quite a few references to fairies. Herrick's stance on the fairies is an odd one. His fairies are diminutives, quite akin to the likes of Queen Mab from Shakespearean perspective—and they do reflect a need for the upper classes to impose a means of social control on their servants. At the same time, Herrick's fairies are also expressions of a vehement anti–Papist sentiment rampant in England at the time, and he takes the anti–Papist imagery in Spenser's *The Faerie Queene* one step further. In Spenser's work, the Papists are strong and not to be underestimated or trivialized, but they are not associated with Faërie. For Spenser, the knights of the realm—the Redcrosse Knight for example—and Queen Elizabeth herself are the only ones pure enough to be coupled with fairyland. However, Herrick does just this in "The Fairy Temple" and "Oberon's Feast," at the same time trivializing both fairies and Catholicism:

the Fairies would have known,
Theirs is a mixt religión:
And some have heard the elves it call
Part Pagan, part Papistical.
If unto me all tongues were granted,
I could not speak the saints here painted.
Saint Tit, Saint Nit, Saint Is, Saint Itis,
...
Saint Frip, Saint Trip, Saint Fill, Saint Filly;
Neither those other saint-ships will I
Here go about for to recite
Their number, almost infinite;
Which, one by one, here set down are
In this most curious calendar [Herrick, lines 22–37].

He goes further, describing the ceremony—the Holy water is placed in
the "shell of half a nut" (line 44), and:

They have their cups and chalices,
Their pardons and indulgences,
Their beads of nits, bells, books, and wax-
Candles, forsooth, and other knacks;
Their holy oil, their fasting-spittle,
Their sacred salt here, not a little [Herrick, lines 113–22].

Marjorie's Swann's "The Politics of Fairylore in Early Modern
English Literature" explores the notion that the expression of the fairies
in Shakespeare, Herrick, and Michael Drayton weren't to be taken as
literal flights of fancy. Rather, these diminutive fairies were conscious
attempts at the authors to articulate political views and a deep mistrust,
ambivalence, and contempt for the cultural and economic elite of Elizabethan and Jacobean society. Swann states that the authors writing of
fairies in the 17th century took their fairy imagery from Shakespeare—
primarily the images he conjured of Queen Mab. And, aside from
succeeding in planting a political awareness into the collective subconscious of Jacobean England, poets such as Herrick and Drayton also succeeded in extinguishing the fairy that truly arose from the folklore of
the people. The fairy of Purkiss' ancient past verily was dead, and with
her death arose the frustration of Tolkien.

Victorian Fairies

The fairy was further humiliated in the decades before Tolkien's
birth and during the age of his upbringing in the arena of Victorian
pop culture. As a polar opposite to the fairies of folklore and even the

fairies of later poets from Milton to Keats—poets who depicted the fairy with the cutting edge of fear or the scintillating thrill of the grotesque—fairy painting and stage productions of the 19th century served to strip every shred of mystery from the fairy's corpse.

Fairy painting reached its quintessence between 1840 and 1870 with such Romantic artists as Richard Dadd, John Anster Fitzgerald, and Joseph Noël Paton. The majority of fairy painters were indistinguishable from the Pre-Raphaelites, and in today's art markets many of the classics of fairy painting—*Midsummer Eve* by E.R. Hughes or John Simmons' *Titania*—are lumped together with the Pre-Raphaelites (Maas 11–12). Many other talented artists—from Richard Dadd to Richard Doyle—were dismissed for the lightness of their composition or the supposed frivolity of their subjects. The majority of fairy paintings adhered to the dominant notion of the diminutive fairy, which suffered from a trivialization which reflected the common Victorian's lack of personal power, just as the sheer numbers of fairies displayed both on canvas and on the stage represented the population explosion that plagued a newly industrialized nation.

Fairy painting as a genre arose from the renderings of specific scenes from Shakespeare's *MND* onto canvas. We literally have dozens of versions of Titania, and of the quarrel between Titania and Oberon. All too often, these painted renditions of Shakespeare disregard Shakespeare's own words to further diminish the fairy. John Anster Fitzgerald's depiction of Ariel in his watercolor *Ariel* is one such example. It shows the powerful spirit as a bewinged and pompadoured fairy languidly reclining upon a hawthorn bough, though Shakespeare never described Ariel this way. While he is called a fairy, he is also a "brave spirit" (*Tempest* 1.2.206). When Ariel first appears, he commands fire and a kind of madness. Later in the play, Ariel is a harpy, a harbinger of fate and time—reminding us that such creatures weren't entirely tamable. Prospero also reveals Ariel's lack of substance when he tells the creature to take the form of a sea nymph (1.2.300–305). The spirit is a shapeshifter, an ethereal spirit of unruly the elements air, fire, and water. This is a far cry from Fitzgerald's depiction.

The only specific reference to Ariel as a fairy comes from Stephano, who, when addressing Caliban, calls Ariel "your fairy" (5.1.195). Prospero also calls his spirits "goblins" (4.1.260), and later he addresses them as "Ye elves of hills, brooks, standing lakes, and groves" (5.1.33). The only reflection of the diminutive fairies of *MND* found in *The Tempest* can be seen in Ariel's song:

> Where the bee sucks, there suck I.
> In a cowslip's bell I lie;
> There I couch when owls do cry.

On the bat's back I do fly
After summer merrily.
Merrily, merrily shall I live now
Under the blossom that hangs on the bough [5.1.88–94].

I do have to wonder if Fitzgerald even bothered to read the play beyond this little ditty. Richard Doyle likewise put his own stamp on *The Tempest* with his *More Nonsense by Dick* and *The Enchanted Fairy Tree* (Maas 126–128). Doyle was often dismissed for his supposed lack of formal training, and for his caricature-like images. Yet Doyle is almost a standard—and he epitomizes the Victorian fairy painting.

As Maas points out, the genre was an essential part of the Victorian subconscious. Fairies were the outlets through which many divergent facets of the Victorian psyche were brought together. From exploration into spiritualism and the occult, to an expression of undaunted sexuality, fairy paintings made it possible to experience the culturally provocative and even explore the taboo in a repressive social order. While it can be argued that artists such as Doyle, Paton, and Fitzgerald portrayed a trivialized fairy world—fairies donning insect wings and flower stamens, fairies rowing down a rivulet of rainwater in a water-lily, fairies sleeping in birds' nests—others from Dadd to John Atkinson Grimshaw to Edmund Dulac and Estella Canziani gave Faërie back to the fairies. Dulac depicts a fairy world that is magical and frightening—as in *The Entomologist's Dream*, which depicts a terrified collector of butterflies awakening from a nightmare to find that his worst fears have been realized: the butterflies have broken their bonds to possibly take revenge. Not a fairy subject, per se, it is a fantastical piece, harkening both to Fitzgerald's wretched butterfly-winged fairies and the fairies of the ancient past, which were part of the nightmare world. Fitzgerald also forayed briefly into this weird realm of the frightening fairyland with *The Artist's Dream* and his different versions of *The Nightmare* and *The Stuff That Dreams Are Made Of*—all of which feature a sleeper beset by wicked goblins and fearsome fairy creatures.

Contemporary with fairy paintings were stage productions presenting a similar interpretation of the fairy. Purkiss notes the change in the fairies of this age as representative of the changing fashions of the day. The fairy could no longer represent the uncertain monstrosity that is at the heart of Mab—the strange little insect-like creature that feeds off men's dreams, crawling through ears and eyes, provoking desires—instead, the Victorians elaborated on the Romantic fascination with innocence and created a wholly unique creature. The Victorians linked the unadulterated innocence of childhood with the fairies (Purkiss 120), bringing forth another monstrosity: the fairies of the Victorian theater.

A Midsummer Night's Dream was one of the most frequently produced of Shakespeare's plays (for full accounts of the various productions see Gary Jay Williams' *Our Moonlight Revels: A Midsummer Night's Dream in the Theatre*). The stage production of *MND* by Lucia Elizabeth Vestris in London in 1840 in particular would influence all productions of Shakespeare—especially *MND* and *The Tempest*—for nearly a century afterward. Vestris herself portrayed Oberon in her 1840 production, and the fairy king would be performed by a woman for the next 74 years. Vestris' production also served to further sexualize the fairies, providing both Oberon and Titania with trains comprised of adult women attired in alluring and flimsy gauze dresses akin to those worn in the ballet (Williams 96). This was diametrically opposed to the depictions of fairies on the stage in ages prior. In early productions of *MND*, those of Shakespeare's day and in the century following the death of the Bard, the fairies were more analogous to the Muses, classical sylphs, or the Vestal Virgins of the goddess Diana. Shakespeare himself alludes to such imagery when Titania speaks of the mother of the changeling child as having been a "vot'ress" of her order (*MND* 2.1.123). While Vestris kept the color of the gowns classically white, her fairies were no longer stately Muses, or sylphs: instead, they donned insect-like wings and crowns of flowers and were remade in the Victorian image. They were sexually accessible—eye-candy for the scores of proper Victorian gentlemen who did not have such a luxury from the women in their own lives. Williams even likens Vestris' performance—the sensuality she brought to Shakespeare's masterful comedy, her cross-gendered role, the personal power she exhibited as being the owner the theaters performing her own productions of Shakespeare, the physicality of her being thronged by fluttering women in revealing attire—to the allure of the dominatrix (Williams 97–101). There was one positive aspect of Vestris' production of *MND*: her interpretation, despite all its musical numbers, had more of Shakespeare's own words than any other performance of the play had in over a century.

One interpretation of *MND*, however, that attempted to instill a little morsel of Faërie back to the fairy was the 1853 production by Samuel Phelps. While Phelps did follow Vestris' general outline of the play, he deleted the superfluous songs, and added two novelties to his production: the magic of illusion and good acting. Phelps attempted to make the fairies believable, and chose to use subdued effects of sheer fabrics and gauze as opposed to the brilliant harshness of the Vestris productions. He also employed actors—himself included—who did more than prance about the stage in artful costumes (Williams 111–112). The fairies portrayed in Vestris—and later productions of Charles Kean, Charles Calvert, William Burton, and Sir Henry Beerbohm Tree—were the antithesis of any "real" fairy. They were apart from nature in their sequins and white tulle, designed for an audience that wanted to be "spoon-fed with fairies" (Purkiss 237).

Is it possible that Tolkien's frustration with and essential rejection of Shakespeare comes not from his dislike of the Bard's works per se, but from his exposure to Victorian fairy painting and the pantomimes masquerading as Shakespearean productions? This style in the visual and performing arts, which began as a need to counteract the "growing alienation in the public sphere due to industrialization" (Zipes 114)—a genuine move toward enchantment of a kind—turned into just another facet of the machine. Fairies of the Victorian age weren't true fairies: they had no lives of their own, no voices of their own: they were merely pantomimes, mere shadows of Faërie.

"On Fairy-Stories" and Diminution

"On Fairy-Stories" was an Andrew Lang lecture given by Tolkien at the University of St. Andrews in 1939. In Carpenter's *Biography*, he places the lecture as contemporary with Tolkien's first explorations into a sequel for his "children's" tale, *The Hobbit*. These explorations took Tolkien beyond the parameters of Lang's own construct of the fairy tale as suitable for children, and Tolkien began toying with the idea of the fairy tale for adults. This of course became *LotR*, and his explorations were set down in the lecture. In the beginning of the essay, Tolkien ponders the origins of the diminution of the fairy, and harkens to the French romance *Huon of Bordeaux* when he notes that the ranks of ancient fairies may have counted pint-sized fairies among their numbers, though they were by no means the norm. *Huon*, as noted by Purkiss, is a romance widely read by the likes of Spenser, but now fallen into obscurity. *Huon's* Oberon, unlike Shakespeare's, is about three feet high and crook-backed—yet his face is angelic. The romance Oberon has been cursed into the body of a child, but he gains magics and possesses a legendary ancestry: he is the offspring of Julius Caesar and the grandmother of Alexander the Great.

Tolkien continues to note how the diminutive fairy is a product of literature and particularly of Shakespeare (*EPCW* 39–40); however, alongside Shakespeare in culpability, Tolkien cites the poet Michael Drayton and his uber-fairy epic *Nymphidia*. I find it interesting to note that while Tolkien discusses his dislike for Drayton's fairies and the wretchedness of Drayton's verse at length (*EPCW* 40–42), he does not even mention any of Shakespeare's plays by name. Yet most critics and scholars of Tolkien skim over this difference. Even the estimable Humphrey Carpenter—most notably in his *Biography*—harps on Tolkien's dislike of Shakespeare, making much of a 1909 debate Tolkien took part in at the tender age of seventeen. Tolkien put forth his vehement dislike of Shakespeare in this discussion, which was perhaps a forerunner to the staunch ideas Tolkien would have concerning curriculum reform.[3] Yet, as Garth points out, Carpenter perhaps overestimated Tolkien's dislike of Shakespeare primarily because of this overbearing debate—in which Tolkien may have taken this stand for simple shock value (81). Shakespeare was deemed an "untouchable" in most literary circles in the 19th century. Take Alfred Darbyshire's worshipful tone in his introduction to a lecture given in 1893:

> We are here to-night ... to thank Providence for that twenty-third day of April, 1564, which ushered into the world that spirit 'whose great name we revere.' ... [O]ur Poet's name is ... enshrined with Homer and Dante, and ... the purity and beauty of our language are due to his magic pen.... [T]o attempt a panegyric on his genius would only be
>
> > To gild refined gold, to paint the lily;
> > To throw a perfume on the violet
> > Or with a taper light
> > To seek the beauteous eye of heaven
> >   to varnish... [Fishwick 77–78].

This is the environment—combined with the pantomime and fairy paintings—that Tolkien was rebelling against. Garth points out—as does Tom Shippey—that if Tolkien so detested Shakespeare, why then did he take up so many threads from Shakespeare in his own works? As evidenced by Tolkien's own commentary in OFS, Drayton should be the poet most known as the object of Tolkien's distaste—not Shakespeare, or at least not Shakespeare alone.

Drayton's *Nymphidia* is written in the form of a mock-heroic tale which, according to Swann, reflected the socioeconomic structure of post–Elizabethan England circa 1627. The tale is purely a flight of fancy, clothing Arthur's failing Camelot and Guinevere's dalliances in the guise of fairy wings and emmets' eyes, and to believe that Tolkien took it for a serious work is a touch troublesome. The only "serious" fairy within the piece is Puck, here also known by one of his original names "Hob"—as in Hobgoblin.[4]

Given the attitude expressed towards the diminished fairy in OFS, we are left with a central question about Tolkien's earliest works. Tolkien does not explain why—if he did indeed detest Shakespeare's moonbeams and cobwebs from youth (*Letters* 143)—he himself composed poems that fell into the very trap sprung by Shakespeare. The fact of the matter, as pointed out by Garth (75), is that Tolkien's first encounter

with fairies and the realm of Faërie—as both an author and a poet—
came when he crossed paths with the sprites of Victorian England.
"Wood-sunshine," written when Tolkien was barely eighteen, has not
been published in its entirety, but a fragment can be found in the *Biography* (Carpenter 55). A delicate poem, "Wood-sunshine" bears a resemblance to both Shakespeare's *MND* and Ariel's song (*Tempest* 5.1.88–94),
as well as Milton's "Comus," and perhaps shows the influence of a typically "Victorian" Birmingham production of *Peter Pan* which Tolkien
saw not long before he wrote it (Carpenter 55). Tolkien's poem could
also serve as a companion piece to Hughes' *Midsummer Eve* or some of
the images of fairyland preserved by Richard Doyle—in particular *Wood
Elves Hiding and Watching a Lady* and *Under the Dock Leaves: An Autum-
nal Evening's Dream* (Maas 126, 134, 145). "Wood-sunshine" seems a bit
squeamishly effervescent, although there is the element of "joy." Yet,
this poem seems so very young when compared with the beauty of the
verses of the Elves in *LotR* or the resplendent prose of *The Silmarillion*.
Consider the poem which Frodo hears upon leaving the Hall of Fire
(2.1.231–32). Written in Tolkien's invented language of Quenya, the
poem exemplifies Faërie and harkens to the epiphany found in pure
language, the glory of the voice. Every writer needs the chance to grow,
and admittedly there is a space of twenty or more years between the
two poems, but there is a marked difference between their essences.
The first, while potentially dealing with the treacherous realm of Faërie,
depicts a fairy creature very much akin to Tinker Bell or Peaseblossom,
even to Drayton's pitifully short diminutions Pip, Trip, and Skip. The
second, written in one of Tolkien's invented languages, a dialect of the
High-Elves, portrays the beauty and the sadness cast upon the Elves by
their deity Ilùvatar.

Another poem, "Goblin Feet," written in 1914, shows more maturity. Tolkien hasn't fully grown beyond the tripping creatures of "Wood-
sunshine," and there is still a marked difference between these fairies
and Tolkien's later Elves. These fairies are very much like Shakespeare's
and Drayton's, but in both early poems there is some discernable essence
of enchantment. "Wood-sunshine" and "Goblin Feet" were not the only
poems Tolkien wrote about diminutive fairies, but it was not long after
this that his work began to shift from "fairy" to "Faërie," most likely influenced by his discovery of Cynewulf's *Christ*. As both Carpenter and Garth
show, this stanza changed Tolkien's thinking about fairies and Faërie:

> Eala earendel engla beorhtast,
> Ofer middan-geard monnum sended
> And soð-fæsta sunnan leoma
> Torht ofer tunglas. Þu tida gehwane
> Of sylfum þe symble inlihtes [Cynewulf 10].

Gollancz translates it thus:

> Hail, heavenly beam, brightest of angels thou,
> sent unto men upon this middle-earth!
> Thou art the true refulgence of the sun!
> radiant above the stars, and from thyself
> illuminest for ever all the tides of time [Cynewulf 11].

Tolkien wrote his own version of the verse entitled "The Voyage of Eär-endel the Evening Star" (Carpenter, *Biography* 79), and discovered the ability to fuse language with myth with what would become part of "The Lay of Eärendel"—"The Shores of Faëry" (Garth 84–85; Carpenter, *Biography* 84–85). With this poem came another pivotal moment in the germination of Tolkien's Faërie: the outbreak of World War I and Tolkien's wartime marriage to Edith Bratt. Tolkien briefly returned to the idea of diminutive fairies in a prose piece and poems about a place called the "Cottage of Lost Play." The first poem, in which two sleeping children visit the land of Faërie in their dreams, is entitled "You & Me and the Cottage of Lost Play" and alludes to fairy-rings and gardens being the tiny villages of the fairies (*Book of Lost Tales* [*BoLT*] *1*:20–24). The final version, "The Little House of Lost Play," has grown beyond the delicate tripping verse of "Wood-sunshine," yet the children witness inhabitants of the realm of Faërie watering the flowers in their garden town. The language is very diminutive, and the fairies even have a tiny king. Yet it is worth noting that while the small fairies in "The Little House of Lost Play" seem like a regression back into the machine of Victoriana, Tolkien's wife, Edith, dearly loved the little fairies of popular fancy. The poems may represent a (later abandoned) effort to bring together Tolkien's nascent mythology and his young wife's preferences, as witnessed by the character Littleheart, who ties "The Cottage of Lost Play" to "The Fall of Gondolin" and the story of Eärendel.

Littleheart appears in the second volume of *BoLT*, where we encounter another interesting version of Tolkien's fairies—what would later become the Elves of Middle-earth. Written around the same time as "The Cottage of Lost Play" are Tolkien's variations on "The Fall of Gondolin" (*BoLT* 2:148–49). In an early version of "Gondolin," the Gnome Ilfiniol, or Littleheart, is the Gong-warden of Mar Vanwa Tyaliéva (The Little House of Lost Play), and provides a link between all the tales of Middle-earth of the period of 1916–1917. Littleheart sailed with Eärendel to Valinor, appears throughout *BoLT*, and is the teller of the tale of Gondolin (*BoLT* 2:147). Littleheart is not a diminutive fairy; neither is he one of the tall sons of the Eldar or a Man. He is of Gnomish descent, and Tolkien's Gnomes later become the Noldor. Littleheart's eyes are blue, merry, and ageless, though he is weather-worn and older

than first assumed. This agelessness—or agefullness—found in the
depths of his eyes is more than a little reminiscent of Tom Bombadil.
Tom is another anomaly of Faërie—bigger than a hobbit, yet smaller
than either Elf or Man, Tom is a veritable lord in the realm of Faërie.
Could Littleheart and Tom be a bridge connecting Tolkien to the fairy
world that spawned Puck and Oberon just as assuredly as it did "Goblin Feet"?

Another way in which Tolkien rejects the idea of Faërie presented
by Shakespeare, Drayton, and the Victorians lies in the element of
dream. In OFS Tolkien emphatically separates Faërie from the realm
of dream and the mechanics of the dreamer. Dream imposes a sense of
unreality on a realm that he considers very much real (*EPCW* 45). The
Mab of Shakespeare's Mercutio is a grotesque creature, a parasitic insect
that delights in attacking mortals in the realm of dreams, very much
the opposite of Tolkien's later Elves. Puck chalks up the entirety of *MND*
to a dream:

> If we shadows have offended,
> Think but this, and all is mended,
> That you have but slumbered here
> While these visions did appear.
> And this weak and idle theme,
> No more yielding but a dream... [5.1.418–423].

The Tolkien of OFS would have been infuriated by this dismissal of
Faerie as a "but a dream." But the poems and prose of the Cottage of
Lost Play, composed long before OFS, are deeply concerned with
dreams. The children of Man visit Valinor in their dreams—the place
Vairë tells Eriol of is called the "Path of Dreams" (*BoLT 1*:7–8). How-
ever, the later versions of the tales as set forth in *Lost Tales*—what becomes
The Silmarillion—has had all vestiges of the dream removed.

As Carpenter notes, the Elves in *The Silmarillion* bear little resemblance to the tiny fairy folk much admired by Edith (*Biography* 100). Yet
a similar shift from dream-like fairy-folk to angelic forces like the Valar,
Maiar, and the Eldar may be found in the poems of Francis Thompson—particularly "Sister Songs," with which Tolkien was intimately familiar. "Sister Songs" weaves elements paralleled in "Goblin Feet" and "The
Cottage of Lost Play" alongside a recurring image of fairies as creatures on the verge of human thought enveloped in light. Almost too
small to see, Thompson's creatures appear as crystalline motes of light
and song. Both the Music of the Ainur and Tolkien's vision of angels
held in the light of St. Gregory's Church as recounted to Christopher (*Letters* 99) are paralleled in Thompson's piece. Carpenter emphasizes this more-human-than-Man motif as he notes that the Elves of *The*

Silmarillion—like the motes of light Tolkien sees in the church—are images of man before the Fall: they are a dream that has been shattered by the folly of man (*Biography* 101).

In OFS Tolkien makes it clear that the road to Fairyland is neither the narrow path to Heaven nor the broad highway to Hell; fair Elfland has its own "bonny road," and its denizens are natural, not supernatural—more "of nature" than man, in fact (*EPCW* 39). The fairy tradition leading through Shakespeare and Drayton to Milton, however, had a whiff of brimstone about it. Shakespeare's Mab, the foundation for Drayton's own Queen Mab (Drayton, lines 130–52), is a fairy by Shakespearean standards, but she can likewise be termed a demon—the very opposite of Tolkien's angelic mote of light. This demonic likeness is echoed in the antics of Puck, a spirit plainly out to wreak havoc upon mankind and delighting in his own mischief. W.B. Yeats echoes this demonic fairy notion in his *Irish Folk Stories and Fairy Tales* as he calls the *sidheòg* or *daoine sidhe*, "Fallen angels who were not good enough to be saved, nor bad enough to be lost" (Yeats 1). We see this again at the end of the first book of Milton's *Paradise Lost*:

> Behold a wonder! They but now who seemed
> In bigness to surpass Earth's giant sons,
> Now less than smallest dwarfs, in narrow room
> Throng numberless—like that pygmean race
> Beyond the Indian mount; or faery elves,
> ...
> Thus incorporeal Spirits to smallest forms
> Reduced their shapes immense, and were at large,
> Though without number still, amidst the hall
> Of that infernal court.... [Milton, lines 757–792].

As we saw above, some of the Victorian fairy painters shared this demonic vision as well. But by hearkening to the romance of *Huon* and Milton's mixed court of "great seraphic lords and cherubim" (Milton, line 794), Tolkien redeems the winged creatures of Victorian imagination, particularly in the tale of Elwing. One of the Teleri, Elwing was mother to Elrond and wife of Eärendil. During the attack of Sirion by the brothers of Maedhros—the remaining sons of Fëanor—Elwing dove into the sea bearing the Silmaril upon her breast. Pitying her plight, Ulmo rescued Elwing from the deeps and gave her the form of a great white bird. She flew to the arms of her husband, whose ship had been placed among the stars by the Valar. Ever after she spoke the language of birds, and learned flight from them (*Silmarillion* 250). This image is markedly different from the petty winged fairies of Doyle and Fitzgerald, Vestris and Kean. Here Tolkien links the Elves to the very angels.

In bridging the gap between the fairy and Faërie, Tolkien successfully communicates the essence of enchantment, the epiphany of joy, and the wondrous peril he describes in "On Fairy-Stories." Despite his early forays into the realm of the delicate, frivolous, and commercial Victorian version of the fairy realm, with his mature work Tolkien reclaimed honor for Faerie.

Notes

1. Yallery Brown is a squalid creature described in Purkiss. Yallery Brown wreaked havoc on a kindly farmer, who wished nothing more than to help the fairy spirit. In return, Yallery Brown drove the man to destitution and death (Purkiss 1–2; Briggs 71–72).

2. The version of "On Fairy-Stories" in *Essays Presented to Charles Williams* was chosen as the reference for this essay because it is the most contemporary with the composition of *The Hobbit* and *The Lord of the Rings*, and is free of some of the editorial changes and revisions later made to the lecture.

3. Tolkien championed the desire that no student of language need be burdened with the need of reading Post-Chaucerian literature (Carpenter, *Inklings* 25).

4. This Puck is quite clearly a darker creature, assassin-like, sent out to find Oberon's Queen and her lover, the knight Pigwiggen:

> "Dear Puck," quoth he, "my wife is gone:
> As e'er thou lov'st King Oberon,
> Let everything but this alone,
> With vengeance and pursue her;
> Bring her to me alive or dead,
> Or that vile thief Pigwiggen's head;
> That villain hath defiled my bed,
> He to this folly drew her" [Drayton, lines 297–304].

Rather than the fickle fairy of *MND*, he is a throwback to the Puck of supposed tradition—or the concocted tradition of Jacobean England. Drayton's Hob can be argued to be more sinister than the Robin Goodfellow of Scot's 1584 tract "The Discoverie of Witchcraft" or *Robin Goodfellow, His Mad Prankes, and Merry Jests* (1625). Shakespeare was familiar with Scot's work.

Web Resources

Dadd, Richard: http://en.wikipedia.org/wiki/Richard_Dadd; "The Richard Dadd Page": http://www.noumenal.com/marc/dadd/
Fitzgerald, John Anster: http://www.illusionsgallery.com/Fitzgerald.html; http://www.victorianweb.org/painting/fitzgerald/

Works Cited

Briggs, Katherine. *The Fairies in Tradition and Literature*. London: Routledge, 2002.
Bullough, Geoffrey, ed. *Narrative and Dramatic Sources of Shakespeare*. London: Routledge, 1961.
Carpenter, Humphrey. *Tolkien: A Biography*. Boston: Houghton, 1977.
_____. *The Inklings: C.S. Lewis, J.R.R. Tolkien, Charles Williams, and Their Friends*. Boston: Houghton, 1979.

Cynewulf. *Cynewulf's Christ: An Eighth Century English Epic.* Ed. and trans. Israel Gollancz. London: Nutt, 1892.

Drayton, Michael. *The Baron's Wars: Nymphidia and Other Poems.* London: Routledge, 1887.

Fishwick, Henry. *Shakespearean Addresses.* London: Sherratt, 1912.

Garth, John. *Tolkien and the Great War.* Boston: Houghton, 2003.

Herrick, Robert. *Chrysomela: A Selection from the Lyrical Poems of Robert Herrick.* Ed. Francis Palgrave Turner. London: Macmillan, 1892.

Holland, Peter, ed. *The Oxford Shakespeare: A Midsummer Night's Dream.* Oxford: Clarendon, 1994.

Maas, Jeremy. "Victorian Fairy Painting." In *Victorian Fairy Painting.* Ed. Jane Martineau. London: Merrell, 1997. 11N21.

Milton, John. *Paradise Lost.* London: Routledge, 1905.

Purkiss, Diane. *At the Bottom of the Garden: A Dark History of Fairies, Hobgoblins, and Other Troublesome Things.* New York: New York University Press, 2003.

Shakespeare, William. *The Complete Works of Shakespeare.* Ed. David Bevington. 5th ed. New York: Pearson, 2004.

Spenser, Edmund. *The Faerie Queene.* London: Penguin, 1987.

Swann, Marjorie. "The Politics of Fairylore in Early Modern English Literature." *Renaissance Quarterly* 53.2 (2000): 449–73.

Tolkien, J.R.R. *The Book of Lost Tales 1.* New York: Ballantine, 1992.

_____. *The Book of Lost Tales 2.* New York: Ballantine, 1992.

_____. "Goblin Feet." *The Annotated Hobbit.* 2nd ed. Boston: Houghton, 2002. 113.

_____. *The Letters of JRR Tolkien.* Ed. Humphrey Carpenter. Boston: Houghton, 2000.

_____. *The Lord of the Rings.* Boston: Houghton, 1994.

_____. "On Fairy-Stories." *Essays Presented to Charles Williams (EPCW).* Ed. C.S. Lewis. Michigan: Eerdmans, 1978.

_____. *The Silmarillion.* 2nd ed. Boston: Houghton, 2001.

_____. *Sir Gawain and the Green Knight; Pearl; Sir Orfeo.* Boston: Houghton, 1978.

_____. *Smith of Wootton Major.* Boston: Houghton, 1978.

Williams, Gary Jay. *Our Moonlight Revels: A Midsummer Night's Dream in the Theatre.* Iowa City: University of Iowa Press, 1997.

Yeats, William Butler, ed. *Fairy and Folk Tales of the Irish Peasantry.* London: Scott, 1888.

Zipes, Jack. *When Dreams Came True: Classical Fairy Tales and Their Tradition.* New York: Routledge, 1999.

Just a Little Bit Fey

What's at the Bottom of The Lord of the Rings *and* A Midsummer Night's Dream?

REBECCA-ANNE C. DO ROZARIO

"You take after Bilbo," said Gandalf. "There is more about you than meets the eye, as I said of him long ago" [*The Lord of the Rings* 2.5.319].

"Bless thee, Bottom! bless thee! thou are translated!" [*A Midsummer Night's Dream* 3.1.113–4].

Could "a crew of patches, rude mechanicals" (*A Midsummer Night's Dream* [*MND*] 3.1.9) and "small rag-tag" (*The Lord of the Rings* [*LotR*] 3.10.569) be stitched together from the same geography and source of inspiration? Both J.R.R. Tolkien and William Shakespeare drew on the local inhabitants of Warwickshire for the Hobbits of *LotR* and the mechanicals of *MND*. These native English creations, ostensibly rustic, serve both fictional realms as mediators between the fey and mortal mythological. They are walking, laughing, drinking and singing anachronisms who, while seemingly very much like us, are really far more uncanny than many have supposed. There is more to the patches and rag-tags than ever a mischievous sprite or wizard could tell.

A Midsummer Night's Dream is recognized as one of Shakespeare's original works, but, drawing on diverse mythological and fairy tale sources, is itself to a degree a patched drama. Set in Athens and the woods outside Athens, the play switches between the city-dwelling lovers—the mythological couple, Theseus and Hippolyta, and a quartet of lovestruck youths—and the squabbling fairy King and Queen,

Oberon and Titania, with their diminutive attendants including Robin Goodfellow or Puck. Existing side by side with fairies influenced by British folklore and mortals based in Greek mythology are the mechanicals, local artisans who, as Puck declares, "work for bread upon Athenian stalls" (3.2.10), and gather to put on a play for Theseus and his bride. The mechanicals, however, do not sound at all Greek or fey. They include Nick "Bully" Bottom, the weaver, Peter Quince, the carpenter, Francis Flute, the bellows-mender, Robin Starveling, the tailor, and Tom Snout, the tinker. These craftsmen sound English; in fact, they sound rather like Shakespeare's own father, John Shakespeare, the glover, of the Warwickshire village, Stratford-upon-Avon.[1] The woods outside Athens, in which they rehearse by moonlight, can likewise be related back to the Forest of Arden in Warwickshire, which would have been as ready a retreat for Shakespeare, who grew up on its fringes, as the palace wood is for the mechanicals.[2]

In the context of the play, set in myth-bound Athens, these English artisans are ultimately anachronisms, more likely to be working for their bread on stalls in Elizabethan Stratford-upon-Avon. Yet they and, in particular, Bottom, have ready congress with the other inhabitants of the ancient, classical world. Bottom seems no more surprised to be amorously accosted by the Queen of the Fairies (he may later remark upon the strangeness, but at the time accepts her love with aplomb: "reason and love keep little company together now-a-days" [3.1.138–39]), than he is to perform before the legendary Theseus and his bride, being more concerned about the beard he should wear for the occasion and that no one gets bad breath from eating onions. T. A. Shippey notes Bottom's "Tolkienish bravura" (*Road* 64), one that resonates most particularly with Tolkien's Hobbits.

The Shire Hobbits are a little more surprised and amazed by their fellow inhabitants of Middle-earth, though undaunted and just as English as the mechanicals. Tolkien, in a letter to Rayner Unwin, confirms: "The toponymy of *The Shire* ... is a 'parody' of that of rural England, in much the same sense as are its inhabitants: they go together and are meant to" (*Letters* 250). More specifically, Tolkien indicates in a letter to Allen and Unwin that the Shire's heart, Hobbiton, is virtually "a Warwickshire village" (230), placing the Hobbits in precisely the same geographic area as the mechanicals. Tolkien's *The Hobbit* introduces the region with Bilbo Baggins, a waistcoated, comfortable Hobbit who greets wizards with a typically English good morning. Bilbo lives comfortably before Gandalf the Wizard and a group of dwarves take him away from the Shire to burglarize a dragon. His journey takes him, incidentally, by the Last Homely House in the woody valley of Rivendell, home to the Elves, and he takes his first leave of Rivendell the morning after

Midsummer Eve, coinciding with Bottom's exit from the woods, though
Bilbo's departure marks the beginning of his adventures rather than
the culmination. The woods indicate a crossroads between the ordinary
and supernatural for both Bilbo and Bottom, epitomized by inflected
solstice symbolism, and watched over by fey creatures who offer respite
from care and woe. Bilbo and his later Hobbit compatriots find refuges
in the woody homes of Elrond, Tom Bombadil, Galadriel, and Treebeard. With excellent meals and splendid songs, these woodland havens
cater generously to the hobbits' comfort. Bottom likewise experiences
the delights of an attentive host when Titania orders her fairy attendants to "be kind and courteous to this gentleman" (3.1.159), supplying him every desire, even the honey-bags from the bees.

The feasting and celebration is a "holiday-time," or May-time, in
the narratives, whose curious echo of pagan and medieval ritual and
tradition recalls the magical conjunction of everyday life with supernatural forces and the attempts to engage and honor the green men and
sprites and spirits of the natural landscape on days set specifically aside
for such humors.[3] In taking his second leave of Rivendell, Bilbo reflects:
"Merry is May-time! ... But our back is to legends and we are coming
home" (*Hobbit* 19.311). Like Bottom leaving behind woodland May
games of love and illusion, Bilbo forsakes festivities at the Last Homely
House.[4] For, as the narratives suggest, neither Bilbo nor Bottom fully
belongs in May-time; it is only an interval in their life's journey. Their
own home lies beyond May-time and legend: geographically and temporally in the post–Medieval villages and towns of Warwickshire where
such adventures and supernatural merrymaking are fading from local
memory.

It is Bilbo's nephew and heir, Frodo Baggins, who embarks upon
the consequent quest to destroy the One Ring, joined by Samwise "Sam"
Gamgee, Meriadoc "Merry" Brandybuck and Peregrin "Pippin" Took.
The Hobbits, who live in cozy holes in the ground, smoke tobacco and
eat tomatoes, are, despite the antiquity of the Middle-earth in which
they live, quite modern.[5] Shippey confirms the point that they "are, and
always remain, highly *anachronistic* in the ancient world of Middle-earth"
(*Author* 6). Just like the mechanicals, the Hobbits are roughly contemporary with, or just a little prior to their author, even as the author
looks back to a mythological past. They remain forever out of synch with
their fictional surroundings, although they easily hobnob with Elves,
Dwarves, Wizards and even Orcs and likewise confidently address great
kings; witness Pippin remarking that Théoden, King of Rohan, is "a
fine old fellow" (3.8.545), and later delivering a lively, familiar greet-
ing to Aragorn as King of Gondor, startling Prince Imrahil (5.8.845).
The Hobbits stand in no awe of greatness as informs legend. Just like

Bottom, who graciously addresses "masters" and "mistresses" with equality, they retain a curiously modern sense of self, conducting themselves democratically and courteously, affording a useful liaison between the author and the mythical past he seeks to recount.

Their down-to-earth, modern viewpoint is likewise a tempting "ingress" for the audience, as these characters respond to fantastical and mythological elements as if to explain and clarify. For instance, Tolkien notes that some time after the actual narrative events of the novel, Pippin sought to explain the impact of the Ent Treebeard's eyes, then quotes Pippin's retrospective description (3.4.452). It is not unusual for Tolkien to give such space to the observations of the Hobbits on the various wonders and predicaments they encounter. In fact, Tolkien tells that the entirety of *LotR* is somewhat based upon a Hobbit history, the Red Book, allowing the story itself to ostensibly originate from their perspective and rumination. Likewise, on being introduced to Titania's retinue of fairies, Bottom's response is virtually exposition: "Good Master Mustard-seed, I know your patience well: that same cowardly, giant like ox-beef hath devoured many a gentleman of your house" (3.1.186–89). Bottom's ready analogy of the fairy's name to the condiment is more than a play on words: it renders the wondrous knowable, even mundane.[6] Through their recorded or spoken reflections, the mechanicals and Hobbits make over the remarkable through their very ordinariness; as Shippey suggests, creating a link between the mythological time and the reader's time (*Author* 6). Yet the Hobbits and mechanicals are not quite in themselves as modern, as similar to the reader's sensibilities as it would seem. This is simply the impression they give by seeming so ordinary, their Warwickshire roots linking them to the known world. Bottom and Bilbo still resonate with audiences in the twenty-first century, a time well removed from their original anachronistic appearances. There is more to them than first appears.

The Hobbits and mechanicals have also troubled modern criticism because their humor seems at odds with serious import. As Laura Mooneyham has argued: "Comic narratives, unfortunately, rarely find acceptance with modern audiences except when they occur in popular culture" (115). Mooneyham locates this rejection of comedy in modernism itself, and this abhorrence or condescension is arguably most evident in responses to Bottom's buffoonery and the comically inept performance of the legend of Pyramus and Thisbe, and the hobbits' high jinks.[7] Tolkien mused in a letter to Charles Furth of Allen and Unwin: "I am personally immensely amused by hobbits as such, and can contemplate them ... making their rather fatuous jokes indefinitely," unlike C.S. Lewis and Rayner Unwin, who had read early drafts (*Letters* 38). The hobbits are regarded as childish, at best childlike.[8] In part this is because of their comedy, in part their diminutive size. On occasion, the hobbits are even kitted out in the costumes of children, and although they join in battle and undertake perilous adventures, their value in such grave enterprises is all too frequently underestimated by those who do not know them very well; consider Théoden questioning Merry's martial potential in the fighting at Gondor: a "swordthain," but "greater of heart than of stature" (5.3.786). The hobbits preoccupy both Sauron and Saruman, and the Ring-bearer is himself a Hobbit, but even after their resounding success, when Aragorn calls for the gathered armies of Men and Elves to honor Frodo and Sam (6.6.933), Aragorn as King ultimately remains the "protector" of the Shire and its small inhabitants.

A paternal relationship exists between Men of greater stature and the Hobbits, likewise the mechanicals. Louis A. Montrose notes: "Like their companion Bottom in his liaison with Titania, the mechanicals are collectively presented in a childlike relationship to their social superiors" (218). Snug, as Montrose indicates, reflects that in performing for Theseus they would be "made men" (4.2.18), as Merry and Pippin both are "made men" of the Mark and of Gondor. The achievement of some status among Men *seems* to be equated with maturity. In fact, the Hobbits' role as "men" of these kingdoms is to entertain. Théoden makes the request of Merry, who joins the Riders, to "lighten my heart with tales" at the dining table (5.3.779). Likewise, when Pippin offers his service to Denethor, Steward of Gondor, he learns that part of his role will be to talk and sing to Denethor whenever he has a moment free from political and military duties (5.4.788). Pippin feels that no Hobbit song of his is appropriate to Denethor's hall since they mainly describe humorous subjects or meals, and although Denethor insists they should not be disdained in such grave times, Pippin still does not "relish" performing them for his intimidating lord (5.4.789). The role of the hobbits in the halls of great lords as comic relief, rustics of great heart whose tales relieve the serious cares of their lords, is like that of the mechanicals in performing their play for Theseus. This noble and heroic duke has wondered "how shall we beguile / The lazy time, if not with some delight?" (5.1.40–41). Of course, the concerns of Theseus on his wedding eve are not so grave as those of Théoden and Denethor, even though his bride be an Amazon, but the motivation is similar, identifying in their rustic origins a source of peaceful merriment. Indeed, the Hobbits and mechanicals are enshrined twofold in these works as comic relief: internally helping to cheer great lords, but also acting as narrative and dramatic tools by which to lighten the mood for the audience or reader.

The Hobbits nonetheless willfully retain an identity separate from

Men, in part by self-deprecation, distinguishing themselves from the loftiness of more renowned counterparts. Pippin, for example, notes that he is neither a Man nor "valiant," unless he has to be (as when he battled Orcs, escaped his armed captors and helped to bring down Saruman) (5.1.733). Bottom also, as David Mikics says, "remains, always, just what he is" (118) and is wont to disclaim any virtues of his own, besides those of the actor, remarking in response to Titania's claim of love inspired by his "fair virtue's force": "Methinks, mistress, you should have little reason for that" (3.1.137–38). The humble habit again makes them appear deferential to their supposed superiors, effectively reinforcing a paternal relationship.[9] As Puck and Saruman suggest in slighting them by calling them patches and rag-tags, they are made of sturdy, though inelegant, stuff and paternalism readily turns to patronization in the less astute mind. Philostrate, for example, announces that the mechanicals are "hard handed men," who "never laboured in their minds till now" (5.1.73–74), a sketch that is sometimes applied to Hobbits. Patrick Curry indicates that Tolkien's particular brand of Englishness as represented in the latter is not relentlessly nor unduly positive: "it includes greed, small-minded parochialism and philistinism" (27). Yet, both works also reveal in these characters a distinctive, if tattered, genuineness. Theseus himself, though ready to take sport in the stumblings of the mechanicals, notes: "Love, therefore, and tongue-tied simplicity / In least speak most, to my capacity" (5.1.104–5). Theseus recognizes that though their eloquence is garbled, it is more often sincere and respectful. Aragorn likewise recognizes the sincerity in wrong words, or, as Merry describes such tongue-tied fits: "We fear to say too much. It robs us of the right words when a jest is out of place" (5.8.852).

"I See a Voice": Embodiment in Verbosity

Both *MND* and *LotR* present the particular verbosity of the mechanicals and Hobbits in dialogue with other forms of speech and discourse. Within the fictional worlds generated as ancient Athens and Middle-earth, the mechanicals and Hobbits do not make great claims for their eloquence or aptitude in art, though it be honest, frequently shrugging it off, as Bottom does in response to Titania's fulsome praise of his singing: "Nay, I can gleek upon occasion" (3.1.141).[10] Yet their observations and tales are more unaffected than the philosophical, often long-winded speeches of Wizards and Fairies, cutting through to simplify and move along both events and the story itself. Gandalf, for example, acknowledges when Merry repeats a practical question to him after a fulsome discourse on the political situation, that every Wizard should be accompanied by a persistent, indeed hard-headed, Hobbit who can put them right when they get preoccupied with their own deliberations (3.11.574).

Nonetheless, Hobbits and mechanicals themselves are given to talk, particularly where the subject closely concerns them: just try to keep Bottom or a Hobbit quiet for any length of time. As Gandalf warns when Théoden begins to converse with Merry and Pippin, they "will sit on the edge of ruin and discuss the pleasures of the table" and their family and ancestors' "small doings" with little persuasion (3.8.545). Bilbo himself confirms: "There are no folk like hobbits after all for a real good talk" (2.1.232). Peter Quince, Titania and Theseus likewise have a most difficult time putting an end to Bottom's inexhaustible conversation. Even during the play's performance, he will stop to tell the Duke a cue (5.1.183), while earlier Titania orders her attendants to "tie up my lover's tongue" (3.1.196) after his extensive greetings to each. However, in their verbal responses to others, they wholeheartedly declare their being.[11]

Their verbosity articulates their virtue and amiability. Treebeard says Merry and Pippin's "nice little voices" prevented him from squashing them (3.4.453). The meeting of the two hobbits with the Ents is timely, the hobbits' talkativeness contrasting significantly with the slowness of Entish speech in which a long time is taken to say anything. The alacrity with which the hobbits speak their mind allows them to act spontaneously when required, free of the overt deliberation and formality that impedes Entish action. The mechanicals, who attempt more courtly prose, nonetheless appear to hopelessly garble the language in their haste to put across their meaning, the Prologue announcing: "If we offend, it is with our good will. / That you should think, we come not to offend, / But with good will" (5.1.108–10). Their good will and desire to be as open and honest as possible, even at the cost of maintaining dramatic illusion, may spoil formal speech and dramatic art, but lets them cut to the chase. Ultimately, as they rightly assert, Pyramus *is* Bottom the weaver, the lion *is* Snug the joiner. Their verbosity thus defines their candid existence among fantastical and mythological characters. In *LotR*, Treebeard has never met a Hobbit, and so Merry and Pippin themselves helpfully suggest a line for Hobbits in the lists of living creatures, confirming that Hobbits gave themselves their name (3.4.454). The Hobbits speak for themselves, and they speak with their own words. Tolkien's interest was, of course, itself linguistic, so this makes perfect sense. It is through language that the Hobbits declare their uniqueness; in this case, a blend of invented, ancient and modern language. Shakespeare in a similar vein used words as a dramatic tool to create character, his mechanicals coming to be through their rustic, "pidgin-courtly" turns of phrase. To such creatures, language is a fundamental animation of genuine self.

The way they utilize language in their cultural pursuits further asserts their identity. Although Bottom and his fellow craftsmen work with their hands for a living, they also engage in writing and producing plays. Bottom's enthusiastic will to undertake additional roles, even the damsel and the lion, shows his eagerness to reveal the full potential of himself, whether with "a monstrous little voice" (1.2.46) or a roar to "do any man's heart good to hear" (1.2.65). The mechanicals' plain speech and frequent misuse of words likewise exerts their individual elocution even over the script—Bottom blithely pronouncing "odious" for "odorous" for example (3.1.77)—but while the imperfect erudition ostensibly exposes a lack of sophistication, it has its own comic logic unique to the mechanicals. Hobbits, likewise, are literate, and though they tend to prefer books about genealogy, they also collect and translate songs and tales. While Bottom is anxious for Peter Quince to turn his romance with Titania into a song, Bilbo requests Frodo bring back songs and stories from his adventures for inclusion in a book (2.3.271). The interest in song and story from other sources reveals the mechanicals and Hobbits engaging in adaptation, even of ostensibly high or superior works of art and literature. Inevitably, they bring their frankness to these works, mediating their value and meaning for contemporary audiences.

Bottom and his fellow players are undaunted to appear before Theseus and his bride with a play inspired by the classic legend of Pyramus and Thisbe, but largely written and directed by themselves. The performance is usually viewed as one of humorous ineptness, but its apparent clumsiness reveals an underlying comprehension of dramatic principles. William Hazlitt, remarking upon Bottom's suggestion for a prologue to clarify that he is not Pyramus dying, but Bottom playing Pyramus dying, writes: "Bottom seems to have understood the subject of dramatic illusion at least as well as any modern essayist" (472). Bottom may not accurately apply his understanding (indeed, his hazy comprehension leads him to destroy the illusion at least as well as Bertolt Brecht would do in the twentieth century for wholly artistic reasons), but his comments show an awareness of the mechanics if not the art of drama. Yet Hazlitt goes so far as to say that "Bottom the Weaver is a character that has not had justice done him. He is the most romantic of mechanics" (471). In fact, Quince indicates that he is "a very paramour for a sweet voice" and although Flute insists he means "paragon," for a paramour is "a thing of naught" (4.2.11–14), there is something of the lover in Bottom's approach to performance. His romantic ideals are not matched by his truthful, mechanical grasp of the art; as he himself says,

"I am to discourse wonders: but ask me not what; for if I tell you, I am no true Athenian" (4.2.28–29).[12] It is not in his nature as a craftsman to be equipped to deliver such a discourse, but he himself is such a discourse as a romantic mechanical.[13]

Bilbo Baggins also tackles high art, rendering it into a more common tongue. He writes a song based on the tale of Eärendil that he gamely performs before the great Elven lord, Elrond, Eärendil's son. He admits to Frodo that Aragorn told him it was impertinent, which he placidly concedes to be true (2.1.231). Yet, Bilbo's verses meet with some approbation from the Elves, who request a repeat performance, just as, despite the often mocking interjections of the noble audience, Theseus calls for a final dance from the mechanicals, proclaiming that "this palpable-gross play hath well beguiled / The heavy gait of night" (5.1. 362–63). Entertainment is afforded by the imperfect effort to engage in these artistic dialogues. It is the simpler, native art of the mechanicals and hobbits, however, that properly reflects their particular brand of romanticism.

Sam, for instance, in a childlike posture reciting his own composition on trolls, qualifies that his efforts are "just a bit of nonsense," not a "proper" poem (1.12.201). Yet, his tale is articulate with no doubting its significance or value, particularly as recited at the location of Bilbo's Troll encounter, where the stone Trolls still sit.[14] When Frodo is later inspired by the singing of the Elves of Lothlórien, mourning Mithrandir (Gandalf), he creates a song of his own, one that reflects his higher education in the lyricism of the Elves, to which Sam suggests another stanza with basic rhymes describing Gandalf's fireworks. Sam remarks that his stanza falls short, yet the rustic sentiments perhaps do Gandalf, who delights in Hobbits, greatest honor, for they capture the genuine affection and wonder in which he is held by Sam. It is, in the end, a fitting tribute. Hobbit song and verse, after all, most often express love for everyday occurrences. Hence they have a song for taking a bath, raucously performed by Pippin on the relevant occasion (1.5.99). Although a song about merrily splashing in a hot tub does not seem particularly insightful, the verses articulate the Hobbits' earthy romanticism, as mispronunciations and muddled phrases embody the true nature of the mechanicals.

Ragged Wit for Patched Fools

Francis Flute describes Bottom to Quince thus: "he hath simply the best wit of any handicraft man in Athens" (4.2.9–10). The wit of Bottom is a peculiar one, related in his translation into an ass. Marina

Warner raises an Elizabethan proverb concluding "'more hair than wit,' which associated abundant locks with the primitive and the inferior, hence the sexual, the beastly" (360). Shakespeare's Speed in *The Two Gentleman of Verona*, in fact, quotes, "she hath more hair than wit" (3.1. 346). Bottom's translation renders him hairy, bestial and with the added effect of the flower juice, sexier to Titania, but Tolkien's Hobbits have always been hairy without necessarily being sexy. They have abundant curly hair upon their heads and their feet. In fact, the vigor of the hair on their feet is such that it is rare for a Hobbit to wear shoes, Tolkien noting that only shoemakers were rare among their tradespeople (Prologue.2). The most common kind of Hobbit, furthermore, is the Harfoot, proclaiming this striking physical appendage, while some families, such as the Proudfoots, obviously rejoice in their attributes. Warner suggests that like hair, feet could have a sexual connotation, but the hobbits plainly have no reputation that indicates it. Instead, the distinctiveness of their hairy feet highlights their earthbound nature, somewhat recalling the Elizabethan analogy to the natural or primitive. Yet any inferiority attached is also problematized by the traditional association of peculiar feet with witchcraft and wisdom.[15] The hairy feet of the Hobbits remind the reader that they are not human and although they appear to have long ago lost the fey qualities or esoteric wisdom associated with their non-human pedate status, vestiges of it remain to distinguish them from Big People.[16]

Unlike the Hobbits, the mechanicals are themselves of quite ordinary hairiness and, to quote Titania, "mortal grossness" (3.1.154). In fact, Bottom contemplates an addition to play Pyramus: "I will discharge it in either your straw-colour beard, your orange-tawny beard, your purple-in-grain beard, or your French-crown-color beard, your perfect yellow" (1.2.84–87). Bottom's desire for such wondrously colored facial hair is translated into the ass's head with which he is endowed by Puck in a fit of mischief. Thus Bottom is cursed with *un*natural hairiness.[17] As a man with an ass's head, he becomes supernatural; as Quince screams, "O monstrous! O strange!" (3.1.99). Bottom appears oblivious, though he begins to suspect his paranormal condition in requesting Cobweb to scratch him: "I must to the barber's, monsieur, for methinks I am marvellous hairy about the face; and I am such a tender ass, if my hair do but tickle me I must scratch" (4.1.23–26). As is the case with most "asses," there is more truth to his remark than he is aware.

As with feet and hair, the ass is linked to sexuality. In Warner's words, it "transgresses human society's norms by aggressive wantonness" (145). Warner notes Bottom's appeal to Titania (145), but there is more to Bottom as the ass than wantonness, for Bottom's translation divides him from the ordinary human, making him a little bit fey. Warner observes: "Talking animals in general could be considered a more reliable denominator of folklore than fairies themselves, especially the donkey" (142). Bottom, just as voluble as an ass, is thus a consistent, fey incarnation. The point of his translation is often mistaken, though, in the wordplay of "ass," for, as Warner argues: "The animal most closely associated with merriment and folly is the ass; but, paradoxically, donkeys are also the beasts most endowed with powers of divination and wisdom in fairy and folklore" (136). Lucius Apuleius' *The Golden Ass*, for example, with which Shakespeare was most likely familiar, concerns a man translated, whole, into an ass. *The Golden Ass* also includes the story of Cupid and Psyche, as *MND* includes Pyramus and Thisbe, underscoring the plights of their translated heroes through tales of star-crossed lovers.[18] Both asses are foolish, but they find wisdom through their adventures and encounters.

This paradox of wisdom and foolishness is thoroughly explored in Bottom. He understands his experiences as remarkable—"I have had a most rare vision. I have had a dream, past the wit of man to say what dream it was. Man is but an ass, if he go about to expound this dream" (4.1.203–5), which he nevertheless attempts—and he recognizes the inability of grasping the wisdom in his dream. Yet for all Bottom's buffoonery, like the hobbits, he may act the fool, but he does realize some wisdom. Pippin, for example, is the youngest hobbit of the fellowship and the most foolish. In the Mines of Moria, when his curiosity imperils them all, Gandalf turns on him with "Fool of a Took," reminding him that they aren't a walking-party (2.4.305). Yet *LotR* is at heart a Hobbit walking-party. The hobbits travel vast distances and for all the seriousness of their endeavors, they still retain their essential foolishness while gaining wisdom and the ability, at the end, to deal with the Shire's troubles.

Getting to the Bottom of the Road

Hobbits in general are not known for going far from home, but the particular hobbits of Tolkien's work are not typical in this respect, and one of the recurring motifs of both *The Hobbit* and *LotR* is a walking-song first sung by Bilbo in *The Hobbit*. It is an evolving song, added to and adapted by the hobbits as they journey through Middle-earth on their quest, finally wrapped up, at least within the confines of *LotR*, by Frodo when walking with Sam to the Grey Havens, his verse inferring "hidden paths" yet to be discovered beyond the earthbound branches of the road (6.9.1005).

Either Frodo or Bilbo sing the walking-song; its significance to these two intrepid hobbits is hinted at in Frodo's memory of his uncle's warning about the dangers of leaving your cozy hole to be carried away along the road (1.2.72–73). The road itself is a physical metaphor for destiny and experience. For Frodo and Bilbo, it originates at the bottom, at the door of Bag End. Shippey points out that "bag end" is a literal translation of the French "*cul-de-sac*," indicating a road with no outlet or a "dead end" (*Author* 10), which is appropriate as the hobbits start from the very bottom of a road that takes them through the many realms and landscapes of Middle-earth and back again. Not only do they have to at last face Saruman, who as Sharkey takes Bag End as his headquarters in "The Scouring of the Shire," but Bag End is itself finally bequeathed to Sam, who returns to this comfortable hole from the Grey Havens with the novel's final words, "Well, I'm back" (6.9.1008). As Don E. Elgin notes, it is "a song about the roads that go ever on until they return at last to the familiar things they have always known" (1). The road serves as an end that, paradoxically, has no end, since it is likewise the beginning—it is the bottom of a journey that effectively has no bottom.

Bottom also undertakes a journey from his home through perilous woods, but his is a much more romantic, brief sojourn. He reflects upon it in a famous soliloquy, known as "Bottom's Dream," though it refers to Bottom's inclination to have his experiences recorded in a song of that title: "The eye of man hath not heard, the ear of man hath not seen, man's hand is not able to taste, his tongue to conceive, nor his heart to report, what my dream was" (4.1.209–12). Bottom's garbled analogies indicate the hidden meaning of the dream, akin to the unknowable reaches of the road the hobbits sing about, "the hidden paths" that Frodo seeks. The soliloquy appears inspired, as has been often argued, by Pauline philosophies, Isaiah quoted in Corinthians: "eye hath not seen, nor ear heard" (1 Cor. 2:9). Bottom's Dream, therefore, may be directly interpreted as a spiritual journey, a mystery that Mikics remarks demands "further pondering" (117), as Shippey suggests the walking song includes ideas to "be brooded upon" (*Road* 188). Understanding and wisdom are not simply achieved, they are always just a bit "beyond," and only foolishness would have either a hobbit or mechanical claim to have understood completely. As Corinthians continues: "natural man does not receive the things of the Spirit of God, for they are foolishness to him" (1 Cor. 2:14). The *un*natural man, however, may receive this wisdom, though he be unable to comprehend and articulate it and consequently appear a fool.

Bottom's desire to have his experience put into song, despite his assertion that "man is but an ass" should he speak about it, is never realized. Bottom is, in fact, quite understandably unable to describe the ineffable beyond the essential paradox of the situation: "it shall be called

'Bottom's Dream,' because it hath no bottom" (4.1.213–14). The hobbits are happily more able to sing about the ineffable through the analogy of the road, which "goes ever on and on" (1.3.72). Although the road returns to the doorstep of Bag End, ultimately the road has no end, no bottom, and even Sam will one day leave Middle-earth, the road and the Far Shores calling him. Indeed, the journey of these creatures is itself wholly ineffable: their future, elucidated within the narratives, is unknowable; for though they appear anachronistic and therefore futuristic within their ancient settings, even as they were written, they had not been. There were no hobbits in Victorian Warwickshire and there was no mechanical magically metamorphosed into an ass in the Elizabethan Forest of Arden. They are anachronisms that never were on a road without end in a dream without bottom.

With the Fairies: A Eucatastrophe

Bottom's Dream more directly describes the enchantment of Titania and the translation of Bottom. Bottom quite readily suits himself to being adored and embraced by the fairy queen, who declares lovingly, "the female ivy so / Enrings the barky fingers of the elm" (4.1.42–43). Bottom's affair in the wood is a prelude to his portrayal of the doomed Pyramus. The tale of Pyramus and Thisbe of Babylon is ancient and recorded in Ovid's *Metamorphoses*. Pyramus and Thisbe are lovers kept apart by a wall, through the gap in which they may communicate. After fixing the place at which to meet to run away together, Thisbe, the first to arrive, is forced to flee a lion. Pyramus, then arriving, mistakes her torn veil as a sign of her death and kills himself. Thisbe returns to find Pyramus dead and so kills herself. The tragedy is thus concluded.

The mechanicals' performance is rife with error. Bottom, for example, mispronounces the name of the tomb by which they should meet as "Ninny's," a playful pun on his own intellect. Bottom's performance is fulsome and he dies verbosely:

> Thus die I, thus, thus, thus.
>   Now am I dead,
>   Now am I fled;
> My soul is in the sky.
>   Tongue, lose thy light;
>   Moon, take thy flight.
> Now die, die, die, die, die [5.1.296–302].

As Theseus notes, "With the help of a surgeon, he might yet recover, and yet prove an ass" (5.1.307–8). Indeed, he does recover, suggesting a rustic Bergomask dance to round the entertainment off in a more jolly vein.

The comparison between the mechanicals and the hobbits here is less than obvious. Apart from a reference to a Took who may have had a Fairy wife (though the reader is told that this is "of course, absurd" in *The Hobbit* [1.11]), there is no romantic relationship between a hobbit and an elf as there is between a mechanical and a fairy.[19] However, there is such a relationship hinted in the working manuscripts. Jen Stevens argues that Ovid's Pyramus and Thisbe, that same play performed by the mechanicals, inspired Tolkien's myth of the lovers Beren and Lúthien, a man and an elf. The myth appears in *LotR* when Sam begs Strider (Aragorn) to tell a story of Elves. He sings the tale of Tinúviel, Lúthien's other name (1.11.187). Strider himself is a man in love with an elven maiden, Arwen, who strikingly resembles Lúthien (2.1. 221). These lovers are also divided by race, family and doom, but in coincidence with the nuptials of *MND* are at the end, after their tribulations, reunited on the eve of Midsummer and wed upon a Midsummer Day, where the natural and supernatural meet.

Strider the Man, however, was originally Trotter, the Hobbit, and Strider, or Aragorn as he is later revealed, never completely shrugs off his draft origins. Shippey notes that "Tolkien remained strongly attached to this character" (*Author* 54). Indeed, although Trotter became Aragorn, he retains an innate sympathy and understanding with the hobbits that suggests beneath Aragorn son of Arathorn and heir of Isildur, Aragorn is still Trotter, described by Tolkien as a "wild hobbit: dark, long-haired, has wooden shoes" (*Author* 158).[20] In fact, Christopher Tolkien notes that from early drafts of the meeting in the Prancing Pony, "Trotter is at once so fully realized that his tone in this part of the narrative (indeed not a few of his actual words) was never changed afterwards" (*Return of the Shadow* 176). Strider the man still speaks the words of Trotter and has a Hobbit's appreciation of smoking. As king, he takes the name Strider, by which he is known by the hobbits, as the name for his royal house, thereby asserting his link to the Shire. It is thus that this hobbit-turned-man and King of Gondor weds the lady Arwen, an elf, discharging the tragic legacy of Pyramus and Thisbe/ Beren and Lúthien with a happy ending. Bottom, however, although briefly the paramour of a Fairy Queen, settles without regret for simply performing the role of Pyramus, enthusiastically simulating his wretched end, while the Fairy Queen gladly reunites with her Fairy King. The May-game dalliances and weddings echo in the resolutions of troubled romances: "the good catastrophe, the sudden joyous 'turn'" Tolkien identified as the Eucatastrophe of the fairy tale ("On Fairy-Stories" [OFS] 68). Like Bottom's Dream, with its Pauline influences, the ultimate romance of Trotter/Aragorn and Arwen, celebrated on Midsummer's day, fits Tolkien's definition of a happy ending, the Eucatastrophe that the author himself equates to Evangelium in offering a jubilant release or redemption from tribulation (OFS 71).

The Hobbits and mechanicals are not simple anachronisms set in fairy tales to translate and mediate the supernatural, whose happy fates provide spiritual and narrative resolution to the tales. They are themselves uncanny, a possibility of what could be on the unknowable journey into destiny. As Tolkien wrote: "All tales may come true ... as Man, finally redeemed, will be like and unlike the fallen that we know" (OFS 73). Thus patched, rag-tags, pieced together somewhat inelegantly, they can never be wholly explicable, wholly like the "us" we know. They are a little bit fey—an ancient prognostication written in hindsight, an imagined prospect premature and already bygone. They have no bottom, therefore they are Bottom's dream, they are the hobbits' road.

Notes

1. The mechanicals likely represent the guild-members of Shakespeare's youth. Montrose, for example, argues that "Bottom is primarily the comic representative of a specific socio-economic group with its own highly articulated culture," one "in whose artisanal, civic and guild-centred ethos Shakespeare had his own roots" (220). The mechanicals therefore reflect a unique English culture, one clearly distinguished from that of the mythological Greek figures and fairies.

2. Simon Schama, in his discussion of the culture of landscape, notes the ancient forests of England, including the Arden, with their "mythic memory of greenwood freedom" (140) were "the place where one found oneself" (141). Shippey identifies this same memory in Tolkien's work and *MND*, principally through similar chance encounters in Fangorn Forest and the woods outside Athens (*Road* 164).

3. Shakespeare lived in an age following on from the late Middle Ages, thus giving him a near perspective on traditions that still survived into Elizabethan England. Tolkien, on the other hand, lived some distance from the Middle Ages, but they were the object of much of his scholarship and interest.

4. C. L. Barber recounts the relationship between *MND* and traditional English May games and pageantry. Many qualities are echoed in Tolkien's Elvish cultures, which make merry in similar fashion, particularly in the earlier *Hobbit*.

5. Although Tolkien does rename tobacco "pipe-weed," these Hobbit crops date from the time after America became known to the British, meaning that they could never have been common in pre–Norman Middle-earth. Although there have been later attempts to undo these anachronisms, they remain an essential charm of the Shire, which, in the middle of great derring-do in the mists of myth, is curiously and provincially ahead of its time.

6. I have already indicated the commonality of feasting in Shakespeare and Tolkien, and Bottom's practical interest in the honey and hay provided by the fairies likewise parallels the Hobbits' crucial interest in eating and drinking. Jonathan Langford notes that the social component of Hobbit eating customs "is closest to our own," though "a testimony to their relative cultural shallowness and lack of spiritual knowledge" (128). As Langford continues, their "cultural openness ... reveals itself also in the ease with which hobbits are capable of adapting to the cultures and food habits of others" (129). Bottom likewise adapts readily, even to the provender of his later transformed self, and remains

sensitive to the social graces of eating and drinking, at least in respect to abstaining from garlic before performing at the wedding feast. Bottom can simply adjust his hunger to new cultures, because, as with the Hobbits, he views eating and drinking as principally social rather than as a physical need or spiritual ritual. Eating is indicative of the Hobbits and mechanicals' abilities to mediate socially with strange and foreign cultures and to likewise mediate between the ancient and fictional cultures and the culture of the reader: contemporary readers can easily relate to the Hobbits' love of mushrooms and beer, as with Bottom's hunger in Titania's bower.

7. Many critics, including Patrick Curry, have noted that Tolkien himself was against modernity, so it is not really surprising that the humor of his Hobbits should not find favor with modernism.

8. David Mikics, among others, also describes Bottom in terms of being "childlike," though this tends to relate more to his emotional range (116).

9. Langford, in recognizing this relationship, points out that the Hobbits also exert an influence upon the other races in "a setting in which a variety of cultural discourses are able to interact, largely through the influence of a hobbit culture that, while apparently subsuming itself to those discourses with which it comes in contact, actually establishes the ground upon which such exchanges take place" (133). Langford's analysis of *LotR* is based upon Mikhail Bakhtin's heteroglossia and thus focuses upon the dialogic, in particular noting that the Hobbits' eating customs, being social, insist upon "the common humanity of [their] participants" (129). It is a kind of culinary democracy.

10. To "gleek" actually indicates a joke, mirroring Merry's explanation of the Hobbits' habit of eloquence. Bottom thus calls less attention to the artistic merit of his voice, than to his ability to entertain with song.

11. Michael Holquist argues: "Bakhtin conceives existence as the kind of book we call a novel, or more accurately as many novels ... , for all of us write our own such text, a text that is then called our life. Bakhtin uses the literary genre of the novel as an allegory for representing existence as the condition of authoring" (30). Such allegory is embodied: *LotR* is ostensibly based on the Red Book, a collection of autobiography and biography of Bilbo, Frodo and other hobbits, and Bottom's life is bound up in Bottom's Dream and his role as Pyramus.

12. Mikics also argues the performance is "really about the mechanics of representation rather than its mechanical lovers" (118).

13. Likewise, after the destruction of the Ring, Sam muses upon his and Frodo's adventures, wishing that he could hear "the story of Nine-fingered Frodo and the Ring of Doom" as they had heard the story of Beren One-Hand at the Last Homely House (6.4.929). He has only a few pages to wait until the moment when, in Ithilien, a minstrel performs the song with that approximate title (6.4.933). It is not for Sam to put such wonders into song, but he himself has been part of his own discourse of wonders.

14. Shippey argues that though Hobbit poems "look unambitious" (*Road* 185), they nevertheless reveal a depth of Hobbit lore. Taking Sam's song in Minas Morgul, Shippey notes it reflects the Shire's particular poetics, including "a brave suggestiveness at once hopeful and sad" (*Road* 191). Sam's song is fitted to an old Shire melody and is inspired by his own feelings of dejection and despair, but it becomes a call to Frodo, who hears the song and replies, bringing the two hobbits back together in the midst of all their enemies. The song's recall of the Shire and the simple hopefulness of the hobbit is in itself enough to reverse the doom of all Middle-earth.

15. In initial drafts, Tolkien included the character of Trotter, a hobbit remarkable for wearing wooden clogs and wiser in the ways of the world. The ruin and deformity of his feet strangely indicates his wider experience, echoing the folk tradition of esoteric wisdom associated with a misshapen foot, and in the evolution of *LotR*, it is consequently Trotter who is transformed into Strider, the Ranger who becomes King. Although there is no mention of Strider having malformed feet, Trotter's earlier peculiarity disappearing, Strider's mystical powers, such as his ability to heal, and his great wisdom and compassion recall the Queen of Sheba, who was said to have had hairy legs or even hooves like an ass's (Warner 112). Ironically, the name of Strider is at last given to Frodo's pony, the one he rides to the Grey Havens on his final journey from Middle-earth. Strider is at last, indeed, hooved.

16. The Prologue to *LotR* states that Hobbits are not magical. Fey qualities, however, need not include only the magical, and the hairy feet of the Hobbits are quite enough to mark them out as supernatural.

17. Bottom's fate evokes Sam Gamgee's plea to Frodo not to allow Gandalf to translate him into something "unnatural" when he is caught listening in to their conversation (1.2.62).

18. C.L. Barber argues that in *MND*: "If Shakespeare were chiefly concerned with the nature of love, the clowns would be in love, after their fashion. But instead, they are putting on a play" (148). Barber suggests that the play is itself more about dramatic illusion than love and as such, the play within the play serves not as a discourse on star-crossed love, but on dramatic illusion, illustrated through the "invincibly literal-minded" crew of patches (148). In fact, Bottom the ass once again plays the paramour and once again, it is just an illusion.

19. In the actors' commentary of *The Fellowship of the Ring* DVD (Jackson), Dominic Monaghan and Billy Boyd, who play Merry and Pippin respectively, do however joke that the hobbits seduced many of the Elven maidens in Rivendell.

20. The name *Aragorn* also went through a dramatic reassignment. Aragorn was initially, possibly, a name for Gandalf's noble steed, Shadowfax (*Return of the Shadow* 351). Aragorn himself is somewhat of a patched, ragged creation, drawn out of multiple myths and kinds, to ultimately become the King.

Works Cited

Barber, C.L. *Shakespeare's Festive Comedy*. Cleveland: Meridian, 1963.

Curry, Patrick. *Defending Middle-earth: Tolkien, Myth and Modernity*. Boston: Houghton, 2004.

Elgin, Don D. *The Comedy of the Fantastic: Ecological Perspectives on the Fantasy Novel*. Westport, CT: Greenwood Press, 1985.

Hazlitt, William. "*A Midsummer Night's Dream*." (From Hazlitt's *Characters of Shakespear's Plays*.) In *The Romantics on Shakespeare*. Ed. Jonathan Bate. London: Penguin,1992. 471–72.

Holquist, Michael. *Dialogism: Bakhtin and His World*. London: Routledge, 1990.

Langford, Jonathan. "Sitting Down to the Sacramental Feast: Food and Cultural Diversity in *The Lord of the Rings*." In *Foods of the Gods: Eating and the Eaten in Fantasy and Science Fiction*. Ed. Gary Westfahl et al. Athens: University of Georgia Press, 1996. 117–41.

The Lord of the Rings: The Fellowship of the Ring. Special Extended DVD. Screenplay by Peter Jackson et al. Dir. Peter Jackson. New Line, 2002.

Mikics, David. "Poetry and Politics in *A Midsummer Night's Dream*." *Raritan* 18.2 (1998): 99–119.

Montrose, Louis A. "A Kingdom of Shadows." In *A Midsummer Night's Dream: Critical Essays*. Ed. Dorothea Kehler. New York: Garland, 1998. 217–40.

Mooneyham, Laura. "Comedy among the Modernists: P.G. Wodehouse and the Anachronism of Comic Form." *Twentieth Century Literature* 40.1 (1994): 114–38.

Schama, Simon. *Landscape and Memory*. London: Harper, 1995.

Shakespeare, William. *The Complete Works of Shakespeare*. Ed. David Bevington. 5th ed. New York: Pearson, 2004.

Shippey, Thomas A. *J.R.R. Tolkien: Author of the Century*. Boston: Houghton, 2001.

_____. *The Road to Middle-earth*. Rev. and exp. ed. Boston: Houghton, 2003.

Stevens, Jen. "From Catastrophe to Eucatastrophe: J.R.R. Tolkien's Transformation of Ovid's Mythic Pyramus and Thisbe into Beren and Lúthien." In *Tolkien and the Invention of Myth: A Reader*. Ed. Jane Chance. Lexington: University Press of Kentucky, 2004. 119–31.

Tolkien, J.R.R. *Letters of J.R.R. Tolkien*. Ed. Humphrey Carpenter. Boston: Houghton, 2000.

_____. *The Lord of the Rings*. 2nd ed. Boston: Houghton, 1994.

_____. "On Fairy-Stories." In *The Tolkien Reader.* New York: Ballantine, 1966. 3–84.

_____. *The Return of the Shadow.* Ed. Christopher Tolkien. The History of Middle-earth 7. Boston: Houghton, 1988.

Warner, Marina. *From the Beast to the Blonde: On Fairy Tales and Their Tellers.* London: Vintage, 1995.

"Perilously Fair"

Titania, Galadriel, and the Fairy Queen of Medieval Romance

ROMUALD I. LAKOWSKI

The two most famous representations of the figure of the Fairy Queen in English literature today are undoubtedly Shakespeare's Titania and Tolkien's Galadriel. Despite Tolkien's deeply ambivalent attitude to Shakespeare, it is not hard to find many profound connections between the two figures. Both Shakespeare's play and Tolkien's story deal with the meeting between the "Fairy Queen" and one or more mortals. In writing *A Midsummer Night's Dream* (*MND*), Shakespeare clearly drew on a wealth of medieval traditions about Fairy Land. There are many interesting parallels between Shakespeare's play and a number of surviving medieval romances.[1]

Tolkien (as a good medievalist) was deeply aware, like Shakespeare, of this rich medieval seriocomic tradition of stories involving love affairs between Fairies and Mortals. However, his treatment of this theme is purged of the grosser and more licentious elements to be found in Shakespeare's play. In many ways Tolkien's treatment of the Elves in *The Lord of the Rings* (*LotR*) (and *The Silmarillion*) can be seen as a very deliberate and self-conscious "revision" or rewriting of Shakespeare's treatment of the fairies in *MND*. Tolkien's Galadriel is just as clearly a "re-envisioning" of Shakespeare's Fairy Queen Titania.

Tolkien on Shakespeare

Before we turn to a comparison of Titania and Galadriel, it is necessary to at least briefly review Tolkien's well-known criticisms of Shakespeare's elves and fairies, which are to be found in his famous essay "On Fairy-Stories" (OFS) and elsewhere. One of Tolkien's major objections to Shakespeare's treatment of fairies and elves was their diminutive size, which in England was "largely a sophisticated product of literary fancy":

> I suspect that this flower-and-butterfly minuteness was also a product of "rationalization," which transformed the glamour of Elfland into mere finesse, and invisibility into a fragility that could hide in a cowslip or shrink behind a blade of grass [OFS 5–6].

Tolkien goes on to blame William Shakespeare and his near contemporary Michael Drayton for playing a part in this "literary business," and then gives a rather contemptuous summary of Drayton's *Nymphidia* ("one of the worst [fairy stories] ever written.... It would have been better if Lethe had swallowed the whole affair" [6–7]), a work itself inspired by Shakespeare's *MND*, in which the diminutive fairy knight Pigwiggen woos Queen Mab behind the back of her jealous husband Oberon. Tolkien argues that though Arthur, Guinevere, and Lancelot are not elves or fairies, "the good and evil story of Arthur's court is a 'fairy-story' rather than this tale of Oberon" (7). Although Shakespeare's treatment of the motif of the Fairy Queen in his plays is infinitely superior to Drayton's, it is not hard to see this as a veiled criticism of Shakespeare's treatment as well, especially of Mercutio's famous "Queen Mab" speech in *Romeo and Juliet* (1.4.53–94). Further on in the essay, Tolkien even seems to argue that Shakespearean drama and fantasy are completely incompatible (68).

The same views of Shakespeare's treatment of the Elves are expressed more succinctly in a couple of Tolkien's letters. In a footnote on Elves in his long letter to Milton Waldman in 1951, Tolkien explains that he is using the word in its ancient meaning, which continued down to Spenser: "a murrain on Will Shakespeare and his damned cobwebs" (Letters 143n). In another letter written in 1954, Tolkien expresses regret at having used the word "Elves" because of its disastrous debasement, in which "Shakespeare played an unforgivable part" (Letters 185).

Despite these statements, it is clear that Tolkien was very familiar with Shakespeare, and there are striking parallels between Shakespeare's plays, especially *Macbeth* (as has frequently been pointed out by Tom Shippey and others), and a number of plot elements in *LotR*. Indeed, Shippey himself has argued that Tolkien was "guardedly respectful" of Shakespeare and felt a kind of "fellow-feeling" for him: "After all, Shakespeare was a close countryman, from Warwickshire, in which county Tolkien spent the happiest years of his childhood, and which in

early drafts of his Lost Tales mythology he had tried to identify with
Elfland" (Shippey, *Author* 194–195).

Tolkien's and Shakespeare's Warwickshire

There are in fact many connections between Tolkien's and Shakespeare's Warwickshire. The modern city of Birmingham, where Tolkien
grew up, is now a separate metropolitan borough in England formed
from parts of the traditional English counties of Warwickshire, Staffordshire, and Worcestershire, but in Tolkien's day it was considered part
of Warwickshire. And Shakespeare's Stratford-upon-Avon in turn is only
about 20–25 miles from modern downtown Birmingham. Tolkien spent
the happiest years of his childhood in the village of Sare Hole, which
is now a suburb of Birmingham, but was then considered part of rural
Warwickshire. His fiancée, Edith Bratt, lived in the town of Warwick (8
miles from Stratford-upon-Avon) from 1913 to 1916, where Tolkien visited her often while studying at Oxford and later when he was doing
his military service in neighboring Staffordshire, and where they were
finally married on 22nd March 1916.

As Shippey points out above, in Tolkien's earliest creative writing
the heart of the Fairy Realm is identified with the English West-Midlands. In *The Book of Lost Tales* (*BoLT*), the earliest version of *The Silmarillion* (begun in 1916–1917), a human traveler, Eriol, visits the Elvish isle
of Tol Eressëa, which will later become England, and is welcomed by a
Fairy Queen, Meril-i-Turinqi, who is a forerunner of Galadriel. Her elves
then proceed to sing or tell Eriol the stories that will comprise *BoLT*.
According to Christopher Tolkien, in early jottings on Eriol Tolkien
clearly identified Kortirion, the capital of Tol Eressëa, with Warwick,
and the Elvish town of Tavrobel with Great Haywood in Staffordshire,
where Edith and J.R.R. Tolkien lived after their marriage (*BoLT* 1:25–26;
2:292–93).

Rather remarkably, we find in the earliest stages of the composition of *BoLT* that Tolkien (for all his criticisms of Shakespeare) included
a form of "Elfin diminutiveness." Though Elves were originally the same
size as men, they have faded: "in early notes Elves and Men are said to
have been 'of a size' in former days, and the smallness (and filminess
and transparency) of the 'fairies' is an aspect of their 'fading,' and
directly related to the domination of Men in the Great Lands" (1:32).
Though Tolkien soon abandoned the crude image of diminutive fairies,
the theme of the fading of the Elves runs through Tolkien's later writings and is echoed by Galadriel herself in her words to Frodo when she
sadly acknowledges that if the quest is successful, Lothlórien itself will

fade and the Elves "dwindle to a rustic folk of dell and cave, slowly to forget and to be forgotten" (*LotR* 2.7.356).

Despite Tolkien's apparent animosity toward Shakespeare, they clearly shared two deep bonds: a lifelong love for the countryside of the West-Midlands (especially Warwickshire, Staffordshire, and Worcestershire) and an affection for the language and dialect of the people among whom they grew up. The same very English Warwickshire countryside that is reflected in so many of Shakespeare's plays, also inspired Tolkien's description of the Shire (*Letters* 230, 235), and of the forests and trees for which both had such an affinity. Forest settings play an important role in a number of Shakespeare's comedies and romances: especially *MND, As You Like It* (*AYL*), *Two Gentlemen of Verona* and *Two Noble Kinsmen* (Saunders 196–203). In the case of *AYL*, Shakespeare's Forest of Arden is often identified not only with the Ardennes Forest in France but also with the English forest of the same name: "The fact that the Warwickshire Forest of Arden was so close to Stratford, coming in Shakespeare's day near to Shottery where Anne Hathaway lived, and that Shakespeare's mother's family name was Arden as well, has been irresistible to commentators" (Brissenden 41). In the same way, though *MND* may be nominally set in Athens, "the wood is in Warwickshire, with its brakes of sweet brier and beds of primroses and banks of wild thyme" (Briggs, *Puck* 44). The ancient Forest of Arden extended all the way to the eastern perimeter of Birmingham, and, though much of the forest was cleared in the Middle Ages, the area still remains quite woody today. Tolkien knew and loved these woods and forests at least as much as Shakespeare, and the woods and forests of Middle-earth are clearly modeled on those of the West-Midlands. Thus, it is not surprising to find parallels between the "Wood outside Athens" and Lothlórien, the Old Forest, and even (as Tom Shippey suggests) Fangorn (*Road* 164).

Medieval "Sources" and Analogues to A Midsummer Night's Dream

Despite Tolkien's criticisms of Shakespeare's fairies and elves, his engagement with *MND* was ultimately creative in that (as I will argue below) it led Tolkien to try and reconstruct the older medieval view of the "fairy world" from the evidence of a number of medieval romances. This reconstruction in turn inspired Tolkien's treatment of the elves in *The Silmarillion* and *LotR* (though not in *The Hobbit* to the same degree). There are a number of features of Shakespeare's treatment of the fairy world, especially of Titania, which have been neglected by the mainstream of Shakespeare criticism and that suggest that Shakespeare himself was familiar with the same medieval literary traditions, if not actual romances, that Tolkien drew on.

One of the major problems in approaching Shakespeare's *MND* is in reconstructing what the popular views of fairies were before Shakespeare's time. As Peter Holland comments: "Popular belief in fairies is notoriously difficult to document, in spite of the work of the two great scholars of Elizabethan fairies, Minor White Latham and Katharine Briggs" (22–23),[2] who are particularly unsatisfactory in their discussions of the figure of the Fairy Queen. Neither do the standard "Source Studies" of Bullough and Muir have much to offer. About the only source that Bullough includes in his collection of sources that reflects pre–Shakespearean fairy lore is the romance "Huon of Bordeaux" (389–94), and Muir has nothing at all to say about fairies. The only significant study of (non–Chaucerian) medieval models for *MND* is Frank Sidgwick's *The Sources and Analogues of* "A Midsummer-Night's Dream," published in 1908, which has been almost completely ignored by later scholars of the play.

There are a number of medieval romances and fabliaux involving relationships between fairy queens or brides and human lovers that shed light on the figures of both Titania and Galadriel. Common themes include the giving of a gift to the mortal lover, often a gift of prophesying or composing poetry or music, or a mortal already possessing these gifts gaining access to the Fairy world through them, as in the case of Sir Orfeo. Sometimes the fairy queen or fairy bride is transformed into a hideous hag as in *Sir Thomas of Erceldoune* (*Erceldoune*) and more subtly Chaucer's "Wife of Bath's Tale." Another common motif in these romances involves the mortal lover falling asleep beneath a tree and being abducted or carried off into the "fairy world," from which the lover can leave or escape only with great difficulty, and often only after a considerable passage of time.

As a scholar of Old and Middle English, Tolkien was thoroughly familiar with most of these tales of Faërie. One such romance was *Sir Orfeo*, a medieval retelling of the classical story of Orpheus and Eurydice, which Tolkien translated into modern English. In *Sir Orfeo*, the King of the Fairies abducts Dame Heurodis, King Orfeo's wife. Orfeo, after wandering for years through the wilderness in search of his wife, comes to the edge of the fairy realm and sees a great troop of fairy knights out hunting, but loses them. Shortly afterwards a bevy of fairy ladies passes him out hawking, with Heurodis among them. She and Orfeo recognize each other, but do not speak, and Heurodis is borne away by her companions. Orfeo, however, manages to follow them and by his boldness and great skill as a harper wins his wife back with the full consent of the Fairy King (Briggs, *People* 46–47).

Tolkien's familiarity with the poem dates back until at least 1921, when it was included in Kenneth Sisam's edition of *Fourteenth Century Verse and Prose,* for which Tolkien provided an extensive glossary. The conception of the Elves in *Sir Orfeo* is much more serious than Shakespeare's *MND,* and Tom Shippey at least has suggested that the twenty odd lines at the center of the poem dealing with the description of the hunting king (*Sir Orfeo* 281–302) are the "master-text" for Tolkien's own portrayal of the Elves (*Road* 57):

> He might se him bisides
> Oft in hot vndertides [mid-mornings]
> The king o fairy with his rout
> Com to hunt him al about,
> With dim cri and bloweing;
> And houndes also with him berking;
> Ac [but] no best thai no nome [caught],
> No neuer he nist [knew] whider thai bicome.
> And other while he might him se
> As a gret ost bi him te [drew near]
> Wele atourned [equiped] ten hundred knightes,
> Ich y-armed to his rightes [correctly],
> Of cuntenaunce stout and fers,
> With mani desplaid baners,
> And ich his swerd ydrawe hold,
> Ac neuer he nist whider thai wold [were going to].
> And other while he seighe [saw] other thing:
> Knightes and leuedis com daunceing
> In queynt [elegant] atire, gisely [skillfully],
> Queynt pas [steps] and softly;
> Tabours and trunpes [trumpets] yede [went] hem bi,
> And al maner menstraci [minstrelsy].[3]

The elves in the wilderness are seen repeatedly by Orfeo as he wanders mad and naked in search of his wife, but they remain elusive and shadowy, and there is an invisible barrier that Sir Orfeo cannot break through until he uses his skill in "minstrelsy" to gain access to the fairy kingdom.

Although there are many important differences between the medieval romance and Shakespeare's play, the powerful role of the King of Faërie in *Sir Orfeo* does provide a medieval prototype, along with Huon of Bordeaux, for Shakespeare's Oberon. The fairy king in *Sir Orfeo* for all his apparent cruelty (see especially the grisly description of the living "dead" at 387–402), honors his rash promise when Orfeo sings before him and gives him back his wife, Heurodis.

Most of these medieval romances involve an encounter between a fairy queen or maiden and a mortal figure, often a knight whom she takes as a lover. It was a genre popular enough for Chaucer to parody in his *Tale of Sir Thopas*, a tale well-known to both Tolkien (Rateliff 348) and Shakespeare, who has Feste adopt the name when he plays a false curate in *Twelfth Night*. What makes Chaucer's Sir Thopas a ridiculous figure is his belief that only an elf-queen would be good enough to be his lover:

> O Seinte Marie, benedicite!
> What eyleth this love at [against] me
> To bynde me so soore?
> Me dremed al this nyght, pardee,
> An elf-queene shal my lemman [lover] be
> And slepe under my goore [gown].
>   An elf-queene wol I love, ywis,
> For in this world no womman is
> Worthy to be my make [mate]
>   In towne;
> Alle othere wommen I forsake,
> And to an elf-queene I me take
> By dale and eek by downe! [Sir Thopas 784–796].

Sir Thopas's quest is, of course, a complete failure; only the Fairy Queen can initiate the relationship, though in some tales the human lover has quite an aggressive role.

Unlike Sir Thopas, Thomas the Rhymer or "True Thomas" is more successful in winning the love of the Fairy Queen. The story exists in two distinct forms: a medieval verse romance *Sir Thomas of Erceldoune*, surviving in five manuscripts, and ballad tradition first recorded in the nineteenth century in Walter Scott's *Border Minstrelsy* (1806).[4] There are important differences between the two ballad and romance versions, but in both Thomas has a meeting with the Fairy Queen:

> True Thomas lay on Huntlie bank;
> A ferlie [wonder] he spied wi' his ee;
> And there he saw a ladye bright,
> Come riding down by the Eildon tree [*Thomas the Rhymer* 1–4].[5]

In *Erceldoune*, before the Fairy Queen rides by, Sir Thomas is lying on Huntley Bank listening to various birds singing, including (depending on the manuscript) the "meryll" (blackbird), the jay, the "wode-wale" (wood-lark) and the "throstyll cokke" (song thrush) (29–31). There is a possible parallel here with the song of Bottom in *MND* (3.1.120–28), just before Titania wakes up. Among the list of birds mentioned by Bottom are the "ouzel cock" (cock-blackbird), the "throstle" and the "lark."

Rather comically, Thomas mistakes the lady for the "queen of heaven." (In an amusing reversal of this motif, when Bottom first awakens Titania by his singing, Titania cries out: "What angel wakes me from my flow'ry bed?" (*MND* 3.1.124). The Fairy Queen quickly corrects Thomas the Rhymer's mistake: "I am but the queen of fair Elfland, / That am hither come to visit thee" (15–16). She challenges him to kiss her: "And if ye dare to kiss my lips, / Sure of your bodie I will be" (19–20). After he kisses her, he comes under her power and she carries him off to fairy land for seven years.

The story in *Erceldoune* is much more explicit: Thomas insists on making love to the Fairy Queen, even though she warns him it will spoil her beauty. After they make love seven times the Fairy Queen is turned into a "hideous hag" (101–136). Thomas is so shocked that he tries to escape but she insists that he go with her: "This xii monthes thou most with me gone, / Middylle erthe thou shalt not se" (159–160). The Fairy Queen does eventually recover her beauty when they enter fairyland (233–244). She reveals to him that her transformation into the "hideous hag" was somehow necessary to prevent detection by her husband: "My lorde is so fers and fell, / that is king of this contre, / And fulle sone he wolde haue the smell, / of the defaute I did with the" (249–252).

In both *Erceldoune* (201–220) and *Thomas the Rhymer*, when the Fairy Queen carries him off, she tries to reassure Thomas that the fairy land is not evil:

> O see ye not yon narrow road,
> So thick beset with thorns and briers?
> That is the path of righteousness,
> Though after it but few enquires.
> And see ye not that braid braid road,
> That lies across that lily levin [lawn]?
> That is the path of wickedness,
> Though some call it the road to heaven.
> And see ye not that bonny road,
> That winds about the fernie brae [bank]?
> That is the road to fair Elfland,
> Where thou and I this night maun gae [must go]
> [*Thomas the Rhymer* 53–64].

Tolkien quotes these lines in his essay OFS with the comment: "The road to fairyland is not the road to Heaven; nor even to Hell, I believe, though some have held that it may lead thither indirectly by the Devil's tithe" (5). This is an important point: the fairy world is neither good nor bad in itself.

When the Fairy Queen takes True Thomas to the fairy land she warns him not to speak to anyone: "For, if you speak a word in Elflyn land, / Ye'll ne'er get back to your ain countrie" (*Thomas the Rhymer* 67–68). In *Erceldoune*, she warns him: "I pray the curtace man thou be;

/ And what any man to the say, / loke thou answere no man but me"
(226–228). Her reason is partly the fear that otherwise her husband will
detect her adultery: "Forsothe, Thomas, that is myn owne, / And the
kingis of this countre; / Me were as goode be hengyd or brent, / As he
wyst thou layst me bye" (221–224).

In both *Thomas the Rhymer* and *Erceldoune*, the Fairy Queen gives
Thomas a gift. In the Ballad it is the gift of truth speaking: "Syne they
came to a garden green, / And she pu'd an apple frae a tree—/ 'Take
this for thy wages, true Thomas: / It will give thee the tongue than can
never lee'" (77–80). In *Erceldoune*, she not only gives him the same gift
(317–320), but she also agrees to Thomas's request (341–348) to proph-
esy the course of future events. The rest of the text (349–700) is taken
up with a series of late medieval political prophecies, very closely related
in form and genre to the "Prophecies of Merlin" that Shakespeare par-
odied in *King Lear* (3.2.81–94).

The motif of the "Hideous Hag" that we saw in *Erceldoune* also
occurs in "The Wife of Bath's Tale." In Chaucer's tale, the unnamed
knight is returning home disconsolate having failed to find an answer
to the question Queen Guinevere had asked him, "what wommen love
moost" (985):

> And in his wey it happed hym to ryde,
> In al this care, under a forest syde,
> Wher as he saugh upon a daunce go
> Of ladyes foure and twenty, and yet mo;
> Toward the whiche daunce he drow ful yerne,
> In hope that som wysdom sholde he lerne [989–994].

As soon as the knight approaches them they vanish, and the knight
meets the "hideous hag" instead (995–999). That these dancing ladies
are fairies (and by implication the "hideous hag" also) is made clear
from the opening lines of the tale:

> In th'olde dayes of the Kyng Arthour,
> Of which that Britons speken greet honour,
> Al was this land fulfild of fayerye,
> The elf-queene, with hir joly compaignye,
> Daunced ful ofte in many a grene mede [857–61].

While Chaucer's knight is not carried off to fairy land, he is forced by
King Arthur to marry the hideous hag. Only when he, like Thomas of
Erceldoune, accepts her on her own terms, in the marriage bed, is she
transformed back into a beautiful young woman. In a cognate version
of the story, *The Wedding of Sir Gawain and Dame Ragnell*, the knight is
clearly identified as Sir Gawain, and Dame Ragnell turns out to have

been turned into a "hideous hag" by the enchantment of her step-mother. There is no magic in this version or any reference to the fairy world, except that Dame Ragnell is freed from her enchantment at the end by Gawain's acceptance of her in bed.

In the more distant cognate *Sir Gawain and the Green Knight*, which Tolkien both edited (with E.V. Gordon) and translated into modern English, there is no explicit reference to fairy land. However, it turns out that Sir Bertilak has been enchanted into the Green Knight by Morgan le Fey (Stanza #98). While there is no "hideous hag" as such, since Gawain's hostess is always young and beautiful, she does appear from time to time in the company of an old woman (Stanzas #41, 52), who is later revealed to be Morgan le Fay (Stanza #99). The theme of adulterous seduction, but this time successfully resisted, is the most important connection with the story in *Erceldoune*. There is even a strange parallel here with *MND*. Sir Bertilak willingly connives at his wife's attempted seduction of Gawain, just as Oberon is happy to make himself a cuckold in order to get revenge on his wife. This contrasts with the situation in *Erceldoune*, in which the fairy queen is afraid that her husband will discover her infidelity.

In another medieval romance, Marie de France's *Lanval*, originally written in Anglo-Norman French, and translated into Middle English as *Sir Launfal*, the knight Lanval is neglected by King Arthur, and goes off riding alone in the fields. He lies down to rest in a meadow when two beautiful girls approach and lead him off to meet their lady, who as the events of the story reveal is clearly a fairy. In the Middle English translation by Thomas Chestre, Sir Launfal's lover is clearly identified as "The kynges doughter of Olyroun [Avalon?], / Dame Tryamour that hyghte; / Her fadyr was Kyng of Fayrye, / of Occient [the West?], fer and nyghe" (*Sir Launfal* 278–281).

The knight and the lady make love, and she promises that he will never be in want and that she will appear to him in secret whenever he desires her, but she also lays upon him the injunction that he never talk of their love or else he will lose her. Eventually, Lanval blurts out his secret to Guinevere, who then goes to Arthur, accusing him of boasting that his love is more beautiful than she is. Lanval is condemned to trial by combat and is only spared when his love comes openly to Arthur's court and everyone recognizes the truth of Lanval's claim. In the end Lanval leaves Arthur's court and goes off with his lady to the fairy land of Avalon: "With her he's gone to Avalon—/ Or so say the poets of Breton—/ To the fair island far away / She ravished that noble youth" (*Lanval* 641–644).

A large part of the appeal of stories such as "True Thomas" and *Sir Launfal*, as Tom Shippey points out, is "elvish allure," in which desire

is mixed with danger (*Road* 59). After discussing Faramir's comment to
Sam in *The Two Towers* that Galadriel must be "perilously fair" (4.5.664),
Shippey goes on to comment: "One could say the same of Sir Launfal's
lady, or True Thomas's" (*Road* 59). Tolkien also makes the same point
in OFS:

> For the trouble with the real folk of Faërie is that they do not always
> look like what they are; and they put on the pride and beauty that
> we would fain wear ourselves. At least part of the magic they wield
> for the good or evil of man is power to play on the desires of his
> body and his heart. The Queen of Elfland, who carried off Thomas
> the Rhymer upon her milk-white steed swifter than the wind, came
> riding by the Eildon Tree as a lady, if one of enchanting beauty [8].

The Encounter with the Fairy Queen

At first sight the differences between Titania and Galadriel may
seem much more important than the similarities. Titania's relationship
with Bottom is clearly sexual, while Galadriel's relationship with Frodo,
Sam, Gimli and the other members of the Fellowship is more spiritual
than anything else. Titania tries to keep Bottom captive in the wood,
whereas the elves are initially reluctant to let the members of the Fellowship enter Lothlórien. Titania is clearly blinded by "lust" in pursuing Bottom, while Galadriel sees clearly and tests the hearts and the
minds of the members of the Fellowship. When she is tempted or tested
herself, it is the temptation to power, not lust, that she feels—if only for
a moment. Despite these differences there are a number of deep connections between the two fairy queens, which I will explore below.

As we have seen in the medieval romances discussed above the
meeting between the fairy queen (or king) and mortals often takes
place under a tree or in a forest (Saunders 132–162). Huon of Bordeaux
and his companions are riding through a forest and have just alighted
under a great oak, when the dwarf king of the Fairies Oberon rides by
(Bullough I:302). In *Sir Orfeo*, Heurodis is sleeping under a tree when
she is carried off by the King of the Fairies. Chaucer's Sir Thopas rides
through a forest and lies down to sleep on some soft grass where he
dreams about taking an elf-queen as his lover. In the *Ballad of Thomas
the Rhymer*, Thomas is lying on a bank when he spied "a ladye bright, /
Come riding down by the Eildon tree" (3–4). In *Erceldoune*, Thomas
and the Fairy Queen actually make love under the Eildon tree.

In Shakespeare's own *Merry Wives of Windsor* (*Wiv.*), Falstaff led
astray by his own lust is persuaded to meet Mistresses Ford and Page at
Herne's Oak in Windsor Forest disguised as Herne the Hunter with a

buck's horns on his head. Mistress Quickly then appears to him in the guise of the Fairy Queen and orders her "fairies" to dance around him and pinch him in punishment: "Corrupt, corrupt, and tainted in desire! / About him, fairies. Sing a scornful rhyme, / And, as you trip, still pinch him to your time" (5.5.90–92).

In *MND*, Peter Quince and Bottom tell the other mechanicals to meet "in the palace wood, a mile without the town, by moonlight. ... At the Duke's Oak" (I.2.92–3, 101). There Bottom, like Falstaff, acquires an animal head (at the hands of Puck), and there he also wakes Titania from her "flow'ry bed" (3.1.124) by his singing. In the case of *LotR*, the meeting takes place not so much under a tree but in it. The Fellowship have to ascend to a great flet at the top of a giant Mallorn tree to pay court to Galadriel and Celeborn.

There is often also a prohibition against speaking to the fairies. Huon of Bordeaux refuses to speak to Oberon lest he be bewitched. In *Wiv.*, when Falstaff sees the supposed Fairy Queen and her attendants, he says to himself: "They are fairies, he that speaks to them shall die. / I'll wink and couch; no man their works must eye" (5.5.46–47). Similarly, in *MND* (though the motivation is different), Titania instructs her fairies: "Tie up my lover's tongue; bring him silently" (3.1.196). Though there is no similar prohibition against speaking in Lothlórien, the various members of the fellowship often seem reluctant to speak, because of their grief at the loss of Gandalf and because most of the Elves did not understand the common tongue. In Peter Jackson's film version, the members of the Fellowship, especially Legolas, display a hushed and reverential spirit at this point (*Fellowship of the Ring* scene 38).

Even though the fairy world may seem both fair and perilous, it is essentially benevolent. In *Huon of Bordeaux*, when Huon denounces Oberon: "'I se the devyll who hath done us so myche trouble.' Oberon herde hym, and sayde 'frende, thou doest me injurey without cause, for I was never devyll nor yll creature'" (Brooks, Appendix I, p.146)—a point that is also made succinctly in *MND*. After Puck's warning that ghosts and "Damned spirits all, ... / Already to their wormy beds are gone," Oberon replies, "But we are spirits of another sort. / I with the Morning's love have oft made sport..." (3.2.382–89). Similarly in *LotR*, when Boromir objects that entering Lothlórien is perilous, Aragorn replies: "Perilous indeed ... fair and perilous; but only evil need fear it, or those who bring some evil with them" (2.6.329).

Even the Fairy King in *Sir Orfeo* eventually listens to Orfeo's plea and releases Dame Heurodis. Though Oberon can be both fierce and cruel until he gets what he wants from Titania, at the same time he shows genuine compassion for the lovers lost in the forest. Similarly, the king of the Wood Elves in *The Hobbit*, whom we first encounter while he is out hunting (in chapter 8), imprisons Thorin and company but in the end treats them with dignity and respect.

In the medieval romances discussed above, the fairies spend much of their time hunting, singing and dancing. In *MND*, Titania and Oberon do not themselves go hunting, but immediately after the reconciliation of Titania and Oberon in act 4.1, Theseus and Hippolyta (who in some productions are "doubled" with Oberon and Titania) appear onstage in the middle of a hunt. While the elves in *LotR* do not go hunting (except for Orcs), hunting is an important activity for the Elves in *The Silmarillion* and *The Hobbit.* Dancing and singing are both central activities in *MND*. When Titania and Oberon quarrel in act 2.1, Titania invites Oberon mockingly to "patiently dance in our round, / And see our moonlight revels" (2.1.140–41). When Titania and Oberon are reconciled, it is Oberon who this time in earnestness invites Titania to dance:

> Come, my queen, take hands with me,
> And rock the ground whereon these sleepers be.
> Now thou and I are new in amity,
> And will tomorrow midnight solemnly
> Dance in Duke Theseus' house triumphantly... [4.1.84–88].

While the Elves in *LotR* are never seen dancing, in *The Silmarillion*, when Beren first encounters Lúthien in the woods of Doriath, she is singing and dancing (165). And in Tolkien's last published work, *Smith of Wootton Major*, Smith Smithson dances with the Fairy Queen, without realizing who she is, on one of his visits to fairy land (160–161). Whenever we encounter the Elves in *LotR*, they seem to be singing. Galadriel herself sings twice for the members of the Fellowship as they are departing in the chapter, "Farewell to Lórien." Sometimes, it is the visitors to fairy land who sing. Sir Orfeo wins his wife back from the Fairy King through his skill at the harp, and when Bottom awakens Titania with his singing, she cries out: "I pray thee, gentle mortal, sing again. / Mine ear is much enamored of thy note" (3.1.132–33). Legolas unwittingly alerts the Galadhrim to the presence of the Fellowship when he sings "The Lay of Nimrodel" (2.6.330–32).

Entry to the fairy world is only possible at the will of the Fairy Queen or Fairy King. Often the human visitor is compelled to go to fairy land. Thomas the Rhymer is carried off to fairy land by the Fairy Queen. At the end of *Lanval*, Lanval is carried off to Avalon by his lady. Similarly, when Bottom tries to leave Titania's bower, Titania casts a spell on him:

> Out of this wood do not desire to go.
> Thou shalt remain here, whether thou wilt or no.

I am a spirit of no common rate...
And I do love thee. Therefore go with me [3.1.146–50].

In *LotR*, entry into Lothlórien is only possible by the will of the lady of the Golden Wood. It is by her special favor that even the dwarf Gimli is allowed to walk free in Lórien.

The encounter with the Fairy Queen has a profound effect on any mortal who meets with her. Whether as fairy wife (*Lanval*) or fairy lover (*Erceldoune*), the mortal that meets her becomes "captivated" by her beauty. However, the encounter with the mortal lover can also have a profound effect on the Fairy Queen as well, leading to her transformation into the "Hideous Hag" (*Erceldoune* and Chaucer's "Wife of Bath's Tale").

It is interesting to see how Shakespeare transforms the medieval tradition. Though Bottom seems willing enough to go along with Titania after she has cast her spell upon him, in practice he seems more concerned with eating and sleeping and getting the fairies to scratch his back than with making love. Much has been written on Shakespeare's use of Apuleius's *Golden Ass* (a work that Tolkien, no doubt, was also familiar with) as a source for Bottom's transformation, but there are medieval parallels too. Bottom's metamorphosis into an "Ass" is a comic reversal of the theme of the "Hideous Hag": it is the human lover instead of the Fairy Queen who is transformed: "My mistress with a monster is in love" (3.2.6). Although Titania herself is not literally transformed, there is nonetheless something very degrading about Titania's "lust," which Puck recognizes when he tells Oberon how he left "sweet Pyramus translated there, / When in that moment, so it came to pass, / Titania waked, and straightway loved an ass" (3.2.32–34). Oberon himself (in the end) takes pity on his wife:

> Her dotage now I do begin to pity.
> For, meeting her of late behind the wood
> Seeking sweet favors for this hateful fool....
> I then did ask of her her changeling child;
> Which straight she gave me....
> And, now I have the boy, I will undo
> This hateful imperfection of her eyes [4.1.46–62].

When Titania is released from her "dotage" by Oberon, she looks with loathing on her former lover: "My Oberon, / what visions have I seen! / Methought I was enamored of an ass... / How came these things to pass? / O, how mine eyes do loathe his visage now!" (4.1.75–77).

At first sight there is nothing comparable in *LotR*. Galadriel's appeal is on a very different, much more spiritual level than Titania's. She has a profound, sometimes disturbing effect on the members of the Fellowship because of her gift of reading hearts through which she tests each of their vocations to fulfill their quest. However, she herself is unexpectedly put to the test when Frodo offers her the Ring of power. She admits she has greatly desired it:

> "You will give me the Ring freely! In place of the Dark Lord you will set up a Queen. And I shall not be dark, but beautiful and terrible as the Morning and the Night! ... All shall love me and despair!" [2.7.356].

Galadriel recognizes that she is being put to the test, and renounces her desire for the ring even if it means she will in some way be diminished. In *LotR* Galadriel is threatened however momentarily with the possibility of being transformed into the "Hideous Hag"—the temptation here, however, is clearly not lust but the will to power. In the recent Peter Jackson film the transformation of Galadriel into the "Dark Queen" (*Fellowship* scene 39) is handled very crudely (like something out of a B-grade horror movie); in contrast, the Bakshi cartoon film manages very economically to portray Galadriel as being both beautiful and terrible at the same time (*Lord of the Rings* scene 22).

Another parallel between Galadriel and the Fairy Queen of the medieval romances (at least *Erceldoune*) has to do with her prophetic gift. As mentioned above, the second half of the "romance" of *Erceldoune* is taken up with a series of late medieval political prophecies supposedly made by the Fairy Queen to Sir Thomas. Galadriel fulfills a similar prophetic role in *LotR* when she lets Sam and Frodo look in her Mirror. However, she does warn them that it is very risky to be guided by prophecy, and that changing one's plans to prevent a prophecy from coming true may conversely cause it to be fulfilled (2.7.354). Bottom receives no prophetic insights from Titania, but he is left with a "most rare vision":

> I have had a most rare vision. I have had a dream, past the wit of man to say what dream it was. Man is but an ass if he go about to expound this dream.... I will get Peter Quince to write a ballad of this dream. It shall be called "Bottom's Dream" ... and I will sing it in the latter end of a play, before the Duke [4.1.203–215].

Like many before and since who have encountered the Fairy Queen, Bottom feels the need to put his experience into song, though as an "inarticulate poet" he must rely on the efforts of another songwriter. There is also just the faintest suggestion that Bottom's later thespian success draws its inspiration from the same source.

Like Bottom, Sam, whom we normally think of as rather a prosaic character (though he can recite poetry on occasion), is deeply touched by his encounter with Galadriel. He waxes lyrical, even though he claims he is not much good at composing poetry, in praising Galadriel to Faramir (4.5.664–65). It is Sam especially who is sustained by the memory of Galadriel on the journey to Mordor and remembers repeatedly to make use of the Lady's star-glass.

Frodo's reaction to Galadriel and Lothlórien is very different from Sam's. In many ways he seems to be overcome and rendered almost speechless by his experiences. After Galadriel has searched their hearts, he refuses to tell Boromir about what came into his mind. When he does sing it is to lament Gandalf's fall, but in the end he cannot bear to talk about it anymore. Unlike Sam, Frodo is not eager to look into Galadriel's Mirror initially. When he does so he feels overwhelmed and wishes the Ring had never been found and offers it to Galadriel because it is too great a matter for him. Galadriel herself recognizes that the tables have been turned and she herself is now being tested by Frodo. She in turn acknowledges the keenness of Frodo's inner vision. When the members of the Fellowship are finally preparing to leave Lothlórien and Galadriel gives Frodo her Phial, Frodo is overcome: he bows to her but is unable to find any words to speak. As they sail down the Silverlode, Frodo gazes at Galadriel's small and distant form. She is singing in Elvish, but Frodo does not understand the words: the music is fair, but does not comfort him.

It is Gimli's attitude, however, that is the closest to real love. When he meets Galadriel at first he glowers but he finds an unexpected welcome in her eyes: "it seemed to him that he looked suddenly into the heart of an enemy and saw there love and understanding" (2.7.347). His immediate response is to "fall in love" with her. When the Fellowship is departing Lothlórien and Galadriel asks him what he would like as a gift, all he can ask for is a single strand of her hair. When they depart, Gimli tells Legolas he has taken his deepest wound in parting from Galadriel. When Éomer suggests that Galadriel may be a sorceress, Gimli is ready to fight to the death in her honor.

The variety of very different responses by the various members of the Fellowship (and nothing has been said here about those of Aragorn, Boromir and Legolas) shows ultimately how ineffable the encounter with Tolkien's Fairy Queen. Bottom's experience is very similar. When he finally wakes up, he struggles very hard to recall his encounter with Titania the night before, but (in a brilliant parody of St. Paul's attempt to describe the ineffable nature of the "deep things of God" in 1 Cor. 2.9–10), he can only stammer:

> Methought I was—there is no man can tell what. Methought I was—
> and methought I had—but man is but a patched fool if he will offer
> to say what methought I had. The eye of man hath not heard, the

ear of man hath not seen, man's hand is not able to taste, his tongue to conceive, nor his heart to report, what my dream was [4.1.206–12].

Both Tolkien and Shakespeare react in complex ways to the heritage of the treatment of the Fairy Queen in the medieval romances. Both authors profoundly reshape the traditional materials they are working with. Each author ends up creating a vision of the Fairy World that is fresh and original, paradoxically because it is deeply rooted in older literary traditions about the Perilous Realm of Faërie. Though Shakespeare was criticized by Tolkien for trivializing fairy land, he cannot be blamed for the later excesses of English writers, starting with Michael Drayton. Tolkien's project of trying to "go behind" Shakespeare to reconstruct the medieval view of the Perilous Realm led ironically to the creation of a vision of Middle-earth (embodied in *The Silmarillion* and *LotR*) of startling originality, which has in many ways superseded Shakespeare's.

Notes

1. For the convenience of readers I have listed a number of online editions and translations of the medieval romances discussed in this paper. The quotations from *Lanval* and *Sir Launfal* in the paper are taken from them. The best introduction to the medieval view of the "High Fairies" is to be found in C.S. Lewis, *The Discarded Image*, ch. 6, "The Longaevi," 122–38. For an important recent study of the forest setting in the medieval romances discussed above (and of Shakespeare), see Corinne J. Saunders, *The Forest of Medieval Romance*, 57, 132–62, 197–203.

2. See the Heart of England Website, especially the webpage, "The Forest of Arden," and the webpages on Shakespeare and Tolkien.

3. Text taken from Kenneth Sisam's edition (pp. 22–23) with help from Tolkien's Glossary. Thorns have been silently modernized to "*th*," and yoghs to "*gh*" or "*y*" (1.301). Tolkien's own translation can be found in *Sir Gawain and the Green Knight, Pearl and Sir Orfeo*, p. 122. For the relationship between Tolkien's translation and Sisam's edition, see Christopher Tolkien's introduction, p. 13.

4. See Minor William Latham, *The Elizabethan Fairies*; K. M. Briggs, *The Anatomy of Puck, The Fairies in Tradition and Literature* and *The Vanishing People*.

5. Quotations from the *Ballad of Thomas the Rhymer* are taken from the Walter Scott text printed in James A. H. Murray's edition of *Thomas of Erceldoune*, pp. liii–lv. Quotations from *Sir Thomas of Erceldoune* are taken from the Lansdowne Manuscript, printed on pp. 1–47 of Murray's edition. Thorns have been silently modernized to "*th*."

Internet Resources

Chestre, Thomas. *Sir Launfal.* Ed. Anne Laskaya and Eve Salisbury. http://www.lib.rochester.edu/camelot/teams/launint.htm
_____. *Sir Launfal.* Trans. James Weldon. http://www.yorku.ca/inpar/launfal_weldon.pdf [Prose translation]
Drayton, Michael. *Nymphidia. The Court of Fairy.* http://www.luminarium.org/editions/nymphidia.htm

Heart of England Website. http://www.cv8lpl.freeserve.co.uk/default.htm
Marie de France. *Lanval.* Trans. Judith P. Shoaf. http://web.english.ufl.edu/exemplaria/
marie/lanval.pdf
Sir Gawain and the Green Knight. Ed. J.R.R. Tolkien and E.V. Gordon. http://www.hti.umich.
edu/cgi/c/cme/cme-idx?type=HTML&rgn=TEI.2&byte=6161184; http://etext.lib.
virginia.edu/toc/modeng/public/AnoGawa.html [Original text only]
Sir Orfeo. Ed. Anne Laskaya and Eve Salisbury. http://www.lib.rochester.edu/camelot/
teams/orfint.htm
Sir Orfeo. Retold by Linda Marie Zaerr. http://english.boisestate.edu/lzaerr/Sir%20
Orfeo.pdf [Prose Translation]
Thomas the Rhymer. Thomas Rymer. www.tam-lin.org/texts/thomas.html [Includes Walter
Scott Text (C) of *Thomas the Rhymer* and the Thornton Manuscript copy of *Sir Thomas
of Erceldoune* (not the Lansdowne MS, which I quote from Murray's edition above.)]
The Wedding of Sir Gawain and Dame Ragnell. Ed. Thomas Hahn. http://www.lib.rochester.
edu/camelot/teams/ragintro.htm
The Wedding of Sir Gawain and Dame Ragnell. Adapted by David Breedon. http://www.lone-
star.net/mall/literature/gawain.htm

Works Cited

Brissenden, Alan, ed. *As You Like It.* By William Shakespeare. Oxford World's Classics.
Oxford: Oxford University Press, 1994.
Briggs, K. M. *The Anatomy of Puck.* London: Routledge, 1959.
_____. *The Fairies in Tradition and Literature.* London: Routledge, 1978.
_____. *The Vanishing People.* London: Batsford, 1978.
Brooks, Harold F., ed. *A Midsummer Night's Dream.* By William Shakespeare. Arden Shake-
speare. London: Methuen, 1979.
Bullough, Geoffrey, ed. *Narrative and Dramatic Sources of Shakespeare.* Vol. 1: *Early Comedies,
Poems,* Romeo and Juliet. London: Routledge, 1961.
Chaucer, Geoffrey. *The Riverside Chaucer.* 3rd ed. Ed. Larry Benson. Boston: Houghton,
1987.
Holland, Peter, ed. *A Midsummer Night's Dream.* By William Shakespeare. Oxford World's
Classics. Oxford: Oxford University Press, 1995.
Latham, Minor William. *The Elizabethan Fairies.* New York: Columbia University Press,
1930.
Lewis, C.S. *The Discarded Image: An Introduction to Medieval and Renaissance Literature.* Cam-
bridge: Cambridge University Press, 1964.
The Lord of the Rings. Screenplay by Peter S. Beagle and Chris Conkling. Dir. Ralph Bak-
shi. Fantasy Films, 1978. DVD. Warner, 2001.
The Lord of the Rings: The Fellowship of the Ring. Special Extended DVD. Screenplay by Peter
Jackson et al. Dir. Peter Jackson. 2001. DVD. New Line, 2002.
Muir, Kenneth. *The Sources of Shakespeare's Plays.* London: Methuen, 1977.
Ratcliff, John D. "J. R. R. Tolkien: 'Sir Topas' Revisited." *Notes and Queries* 227 (1982): 348.
Saunders, Corinne J. *The Forest of Medieval Romance: Avernus, Broceliande, Arden.* Cambridge:
Brewer, 1993.
Shakespeare, William. *The Complete Works of Shakespeare.* Ed. David Bevington. 5th ed. New
York: Pearson, 2004.
Shippey, Thomas A. *J.R.R. Tolkien: Author of the Century.* Boston: Houghton, 2001.
_____. *The Road to Middle-earth.* Rev. and exp. ed. Boston: Houghton, 2003.
Sidgwick, Frank, ed. *The Sources and Analogues of "A Midsummer-Night's Dream."* London:
Chatto, 1908. [Includes modern spelling texts of the Thornton Manuscript of *Sir
Thomas of Erceldoune* and Drayton's *Nymphidia.*]
Sisam, Kenneth, ed. *Fourteenth Century Verse and Prose.* With a Glossary by J.R.R. Tolkien.
Oxford: Oxford University Press, 1921.
Thomas of Erceldoune. *The Romance and Prophecies of Thomas of Erceldoune.* Ed. James A.

H. Murray. Early English Text Society 61. London: Trübner, 1875. [Includes texts of *Thomas the Rhymer.*]

Tolkien, J.R.R. *The Book of Lost Tales.* Ed. Christopher Tolkien. 2 vols. Boston: Houghton, 1984.

_____. *The Hobbit.* 2nd ed. Boston: Houghton, 1966.

_____. *The Letters of J.R.R. Tolkien.* Ed. Humphrey Carpenter. Boston: Houghton, 2000.

_____. "On Fairy-Stories." In *The Tolkien Reader.* New York: Ballantine, 1966. 3–84.

_____. *The Lord of the Rings.* 2nd ed. Boston: Houghton, 1994.

_____. *The Silmarillion.* 2nd. ed. Boston: Houghton, 2001.

_____. *Smith of Wootton Major.* Boston: Houghton, 1978.

Tolkien, J.R.R., trans. *Sir Gawain and the Green Knight, Pearl and Sir Orfeo.* Ed. Christopher Tolkien. London: Unwin, 1979.

Tolkien, J.R.R., and E.V. Gordon, eds. *Sir Gawain and the Green Knight.* 2nd ed. Rev. Norman Davis. Oxford: Clarendon, 1967.

"The Wedding of Sir Gawain and Dame Ragnell." *The Romance of Arthur III.* Ed. James J. Wilhelm. New York: Garland, 1988. 99–116.

POWER

"We Few, We Happy Few"
War and Glory in Henry V *and* The Lord of the Rings

DANIEL TIMMONS

Since the Vietnam conflict, war as a subject and theme in art and literature has been suspect. After the terrorist attacks of September 11, 2001, the "war on terrorism" seemed to alter this prevailing attitude. However, some of the more vocal groups in opposition to the war in Iraq prove that a powerful sentiment against war *per se*, war of any kind, remains strong in both contemporary politics and criticism. Writing about the work of J.R.R. Tolkien, some commentators, such as Nick Otty, have condemned the perceived support for and celebration of war in *The Lord of the Rings* (*LotR*). Even fervent Tolkien supporters might shift uncomfortably when they read this description of the Rohirrim as they enter the fray before Minas Tirith:

> And then all the host of Rohan burst into song, and they sang as they slew, for the joy of battle was on them, and the sound of their singing that was fair and terrible came even to the City [5.5.820].

Our modern culture usually denounces this sort of outright praise of the glory of war, even though it may deem war necessary in certain circumstances.

Interestingly, though, *Henry V* (*H5*), despite its jingoistic tone and dubious pretence for war, remains one of Shakespeare's most admired plays. Henry calls his war upon France "this fair action" (1.2.310) even though the justification seems convoluted at best, corrupt at worst. Tolkien has been criticized for his battles and supposed "demonization" of the enemy to justify them, while Shakespeare remains free from such censure. This issue becomes particularly ironic because Tolkien—and not Shakespeare—actually *fought* in a bloody war and lived as citizen during another terrible conflict.

War in *LotR* is not a political intrigue designed to secure disputed territory or to assuage contentious factions, as it is in Shakespeare's *H5*. Tolkien does depict the brutal—and regrettable—nature of war. At the same time, he valorises honor and glory in battle because, unlike the Battle of Agincourt, the War of the Ring is a "just" cause. Strange as it may seem, Tolkien's fantasy book offers a more cogent perspective on war than Shakespeare's historical drama.

Before considering the treatment of war in *H5* and *LotR*, we should briefly review one major example of this cultural attitude against war. Niall Ferguson in *The Pity of War* sets out to deconstruct the reasons why England entered The Great War and the Allies imposed arguably harsh peace terms on Germany. Using the benefit of hindsight, Ferguson concludes that the costs, both in finance and in human lives, were too high to justify the result—namely, the security of Europe. As Ferguson notes, these issues are very complex (xli). My interest here is the attitude. The chapter titles in Ferguson's book indicate his bias: "The Myths of Militarism," "Britain's War of Illusions," "The Myth of War Enthusiasm," "'Maximum Slaughter at Minimum Expense,'" and so on. Ferguson positions himself as the "nay" voice, noting with some irony, "a surprisingly large number of historians" still insist the war "was not 'senseless'"(xxxiii). However, Ferguson has many more sympathizers than he implies in the above comment. I don't recall a storm of controversy when his book appeared. In fact, one of Canada's most respected journalists, Robert Fulford, supported Ferguson wholeheartedly.

Setting aside the offense to The Great War's deceased, survivors, and their descendants, Ferguson plaintively asks, "what were all these deaths—more than 9 million in all—really worth?" (xli). I have not the knowledge, experience, or, frankly, the desire to debate a renowned expert like Ferguson. I believe that England had to honor its treaty with Belgium, help keep France a sovereign nation, and repulse Germany's aggression and expansion. True, no one in the summer of 1914 could have foreseen the horror that would ensue, and if they could they might have striven harder to avoid it. However, the appalling battles and carnage transpired chiefly because Germany would not retreat within its legitimate borders. In any case, for critics like Ferguson and his supporters, war is plainly awful and avoidable. And, in particular, the death and destruction of The Great War was meaningless and not all heroic.

Given this common anti-war critical attitude, we might surmise Shakespeare's *H5* would be ripe for censure, or at least strong disapproval. After all, this play recounts the deeds of a king who, in God's name, invades a sovereign nation on a dubious premise, frightens and kills innocent civilians (however much he insists they be treated with care), slays prisoners, and claims the defeated nation's princess as his "capital demand" (5.2.96). However, relatively recent *Henry V* criticism and stage productions, even when they focus on the war issue, consider it a point of artistic exploration, not condemnation. Joan Hall observes:

> The play presents different aspects of warfare for our inspection, and we are left to decide whether war is a heroic enterprise or one that brings out the worst in its participants. If the theme can be summed up at all, it is that war has many faces [79].

A sound critical position, we may all agree. Yet it is not one that Ferguson and his ilk would take, I think. James Loehlin declares that productions "that condemn Henry whole-heartedly are *rare and rarely successful*" (my emphasis; 168). Loehlin claims the structure of the play requires "a two-sided view," meaning we may condemn war and killing, yet still admire and support "the construction of Henry's heroism" (168). The thin excuse for Henry's war and the resulting devastation does not, according to Loehlin, overshadow the valor and glory of the king and his warriors.

Even a post-modern critic, Robert Shaughnessy, in his review of recent productions of *H5*, encourages us to appreciate the play's war theme, rather than dismiss it. Shaughnessy remarks that the reviews of one production, which did have an anti-war message, display a "right-wing" bias, which indicates that apologists for Shakespeare remain many and active. Shaughnessy believes such reviewers are "nostalgic" for a bygone glorious Britain, one where her military prowess was a source of pride and self-identity. The play, then, becomes a forum to discuss contemporary *reactions to war*, rather than a work to disparage for the depiction of it. Shaughnessy states: "[T]he rhetoric of heroism and the rhetoric of realism—with neither term privileged over the other" resulted in one production that "was more concerned with representation of war than with 'war itself'" (58). If any critical target exists, Shaughnessy implies it is those who appropriate *H5* for patriotic or jingoistic purposes, not the play or its author.

Such critical objectivity is not evident in some commentary on *LotR*'s depiction of war. For example, Nick Otty claims that "War," that is, the concept itself, is celebrated in *LotR*:

> In 1983 [the year of Otty's paper], this model seems to match the foreign policy of both Downing Street and the White House.... *The Lord of the Rings* feeds Western ideologies of the Cold War, and whatever ideologies might be promulgated by the other side, the fact

that they are materialistic might limit their extension to a universal frame for the justified war [Colebatch 75].

As Hal Colebatch points out, it isn't easy to understand Otty's point.
Considering *LotR* was conceived and composed long before the Cold
War, we may wonder how the book could reflect the politics of this era,
whatever one's view of the subject. Otty tries to debunk the War of the
Ring by claiming authorial bias against understanding the motives of
"Sauron and Co." Colebatch wryly notes that it's not hard to see Sauron's
intention: to control and enslave all of Middle-earth. And to imply his
domain is some kind of cooperative, rather than a despotic realm,
appears willfully obtuse (Colebatch 75–77). Otty seems to dislike and
oppose the heroic ideal, exemplified in the Rohirrim passage cited at
the start; that is, some battles *are worth fighting* and one *should take joy*
in defeating a wicked adversary. By focusing solely on expressions of
epic heroism, rather than the root cause that gave rise to them, critics
like Otty bypass—and perhaps reject—the complex and difficult task of
actually deciding which wars can be justified.

John Goldthwaite also finds Tolkien's description and tone of epic
heroism both distasteful and reprehensible. Goldthwaite cites this scene
from "The Battle of Pelennor Fields." Aragorn, invoked by a litany of
his many names, sweeps up the river in the captured pirate ships to
turn the tide of battle. Goldthwaite declares: "Very seldom does one
encounter emotion this fraudulent and writing this bad in any genre"
(218). He is welcome to his opinion, but if we dismiss Tolkien because
of his elevated style and epic theme, then much of western literature,
from Homer through Milton to Tennyson, has to be discounted. More
astonishing is that Goldthwaite claims somehow Tolkien must have forgotten his own war experience and so offers a juvenile and sanitized
portrait in *LotR*:

> He regressed, it seems, into a compensatory dream of how a war
> ought to be fought, not with bodies piling up stupidly in trenches—
> that was all wrong, you see—but in the grand manner, with stirring
> rides and deeds of valor.... The irony must have escaped him that
> the make-believe swagger he was here honoring was precisely the
> kind of toy-soldiering that had led to the horrors of World War I to
> begin with [217–18].

Pretty strong stuff from a critic writing in 1996 in an era and a land in
which his heritage and institutions were largely preserved by the deeds
of men such as Tolkien, Lewis, and valiant souls who did not survive
The Great War. It would take a paper itself to refute Goldthwaite properly, but here is just one false implication: *The Lord of the Rings* doesn't

present bloody battles. If Goldthwaite closely and honestly read Tolkien's work, he would have noted this scene in "The Siege of Gondor":

> Shot and dart fell thick; siege-towers crashed or blazed suddenly like torches. All before the walls on either side of the Gate the ground was choked with wreck and with bodies of the slain; yet still driven as by a madness more and more came up [5.4.810].

As Barton Friedman observes, "it seems apparent that what [Tolkien's] generation knew as the Great War has left a discernible imprint on the encounters of his soldiers in the War of the Ring" (115).

To briefly recap here, my purpose is not to bury Shakespeare's *Henry V*. It is one of my favorite plays, and I enjoyed the Kenneth Branagh film. As well, I don't wish to overstate the critical belligerence to war in *LotR*. Two major studies of Tolkien and war from John Garth and Janet Croft have appeared in the last couple of years. Both books, using sound scholarship and critical objectivity, explore the complexity of Tolkien's war experience and how it is reflected in his creative works. And for every hostile voice, such as Otty and Goldthwaite, many exist, such as Colebatch, Friedman, Tom Shippey, and others, who eloquently and intelligently discuss Tolkien's treatment of war. Still, war, as a concept, has become so generic, divorced from any specific cause, process, or results that it's *presumed* to be wrong, in any and all circumstances. Again, the debate leading up to the war in Iraq is a perfect example. The anti-war protesters ignored Saddam Hussein's potential use of weapons of mass destruction, which he had produced and used in the past, or his threat to his neighbors, which he had attacked and invaded before, or the oppression and murder of his own citizens, which was well-documented. Social opposition to war is often echoed in art criticism. Thus, to celebrate the valor and strength of those fighting such battles appears, at the very least, antiquated, if not misguided. And while critics, directors, and audiences seem to accept and value *H5*'s depiction of war, *LotR* ultimately explores such issues in a more consistent and *universal* manner.

First of all, let's compare the cause of war in *H5* and *LotR*. The entire first act of *H5* is an exercise in finding a reason, any reason, for England to go to war against France. The clergy and nobles seem to be spoiling for a fight, not because France has threatened to attack England, but because of domestic political machinations. The Archbishop of Canterbury is worried about a piece of legislation that would deprive the clergy of much of their possessions; thus he encourages and offers to finance Henry's arcane claim to the throne of France. The Duke of Exeter also implores Henry to take up the battle: "Your brother kings and monarchs of the earth / Do all expect that you should rouse yourself / As did the former lions of your blood" (1.2.122–24). While Henry seems a bit more hesitant, lingering in his memory must be his father's words about busying "giddy minds" (i.e., domestic rebels) "with foreign quarrels" (*2H4* 4.5.212–13). And if Goldthwaite wants a text to denounce for grandstanding about war, he could hardly find one better than Henry's words after he was presented with the Dauphin's gift of tennis balls:

> And tell the pleasant Prince this mock of his
> Hath turned his balls to gunstones, and his soul
> Shall stand sore chargèd for the wasteful vengeance
> That shall fly with them, for many a thousand widows
> Shall this his mock mock out of their dear husbands,
> Mock mothers from their sons, mock castles down,
> And some are yet ungotten and unborn
> That shall have cause to curse the Dauphin's scorn [1.2.281–88].

What's this? A diplomatic insult is the justification for an invasion and the deaths of innocents?

Again, the point is not that we should condemn Shakespeare or Henry. But as Tolkien argues in his essay, "The Monsters and the Critics," fleeting disputes between kingdoms pale in comparison with the larger reality of the eternal war between good and evil. People may disagree that The Great War was such a conflict, but I doubt many think that World War II can be characterized any other way. The War of the Ring is a struggle between decent, though not perfect, free peoples and the enslaved armies of wicked tyrants. Although he is the prime agent to mobilize the forces of the West, Gandalf, unlike Henry, doesn't show any relish for the task: he knows that only the Ring can guarantee victory, but it cannot be used, and even if the war may be won, "much will be lost." Even the proud and eager warrior Boromir doesn't want to invade Mordor, but desires only to defend his city and fellow citizens, and mistakenly thinks the Ring could serve that noble purpose. Faramir also fights not with joy in the deed, but for his people and cultural heritage:

> I do not love the bright sword for its sharpness, nor the arrow for
> its swiftness, nor the warrior for his glory. I love only that which they
> defend: the city of the Men of Númenor [4.5.656].

This is why people go off to war against evil adversaries. It is not that they crave thrills or accolades, but to protect and preserve their homeland and way of life.

Furthermore, tyrants and megalomaniacs start wars—and, thankfully, often sow the seeds of their own defeat in the process. Sauron's grave mistake, as Gandalf observes, is that he should have bent all his guile to finding the Ring, rather than engage the West in battle. This tactic blinded him to the true quest, eventually to his own destruction. Tolkien's work is a "fantasy" tale, but anyone with a passing knowledge of war history can see parallels in the Punic Wars, the invasions of Genghis Khan, and, of course, the war machine of Hitler and the Nazis. The war in *H5* may represent general issues of men in battle and clashes between nations. But the War of the Ring is a microcosm of the universal struggle between the forces of evil and good, which many people argue is going on in the world today.

Obviously, much more could be said about Shakespeare's depiction of war. There is the wonderful scene when Henry walks in disguise amongst his troops and engages a few soldiers in conversation about whether the king is responsible for the souls of his men if indeed the "cause" is not "just" nor the "quarrel honourable" (4.1.127–28). Every man's "soul" is his own, as Henry states, but we may sympathize with the poor soldiers who wonder if their deaths will be meaningless if the king ransoms himself after their throats are cut. But, again, the complexity is in the specific political situation: Henry going after a kingdom upon which he has only a weak, and maybe false, claim. With his rejection of compromise and rousing battle speeches, Henry seems determined to see his purpose, however tenuous, go forward, largely to his own personal gain and glory.

We can contrast Henry's approach to war with Gandalf's. At various stages, Gandalf rejects a compromise from the enemy, not because he enjoys war, but because it would be a bargain with the devil. Saruman tries to convince Gandalf he has only two choices—to submit to him or fall to Sauron—but Gandalf defiantly insists there is a better way. We should neither dismiss, as Tolkien does in the Foreword to the second edition, nor fully endorse the possibility that the War of the Ring is analogous to World War II. Still, Gandalf sounds like an anti–Neville Chamberlain in the scenes where Saruman urges a compromise with the enemy. As Saruman attempts to persuade Gandalf to join him, even after the ruin of all his own plans, we may wish our real life political leaders could speak with Gandalf's frankness: "Understand one another? I fear I am beyond your comprehension. But you, Saruman, I understand now too well" (3.10.568). And perhaps there is an echo of Churchill when Gandalf rejects the Mouth of Sauron's offer at the very gates of Mordor, turning down the harsh terms of occupation and refusing to negotiate with Sauron's mere mouthpiece. In addition to revealing that some causes are worth fighting and dying for, the War of the Ring dramatizes the historical truth that embracing certain terms of "peace" may end up being far worse.

Finally, even people who are willing to admit that some wars are unavoidable may still feel that one should never feel joy or take glory in them. Recall that Rohirrim passage about warriors singing for the joy of battle. One could say, "all right, fight and kill, if you must, but only a misguided fool—or worse—would take pleasure in such deadly deeds." One doesn't have to be a narrow-minded pacifist to hold such a view. Indeed, Henry insists that his soldiers express no self-satisfaction in their incredible victory:

> Come, go we in procession to the village:
> And be it death proclaimèd through our host
> To boast of this, or take that praise from God
> Which is his only [4.8.113–16].

The Chorus reports that even back in London, Henry, "being free from vainness and self-glorious pride" (5.0.20), demands a low-key celebration. The irony is rich here because in order to rally his troops before fighting, Henry waxes mightily on the honor, glory, and indeed joy of the battle:

> But if it be a sin to covet honor
> I am the most offending soul alive.
> ...
> We few, we happy few, we band of brothers.
> For he today that sheds his blood with me
> Shall be my brother;
> ...
> And gentlemen in England now abed
> Shall think themselves accurst they were not here,
> And hold their manhoods cheap whiles any speaks
> That fought with us upon Saint Crispin's day! [4.3.28–67].

Without the lure of fame and glory, Henry might never have roused his men to face such odds in battle, in a foreign land, where the cause was hardly known or even irrelevant to them. In the end, the king wins his foreign kingdom, gains his bride, and achieves great renown, while his brave and war-weary soldiers go back to England and resume their mundane lives.

In *LotR*, the stakes are far higher and the cause much nobler. The joy that Rohirrim, the Men of Gondor, and their valiant leaders experience goes beyond having poems written about them. True, this is the heroic ideal, found in works such as *Beowulf*, where achieving everlasting fame is a motive of a warrior. Théoden urges his soldiers to fight to achieve great deeds that may be remembered in song. Following in the epic tradition, Tolkien provides a poem after victory in the Battle of Pelennor Fields, citing the fallen great, such as Théoden, King of

Rohan. But none of the expressions of joy and glory seems gratuitous. There is never any boasting, overt bravado, or exulting in the fallen or defeated. After the victories at Helm's Deep and Minas Tirith, mercy and care are shown towards the wretched allies of Saruman and Sauron. There is joy in a victory over evil, not in death and destruction. As with Armistice Day and Victory in Europe Day, the celebrations are for the *end of war*. The glory achieved is well-deserved because the cause was just. Joy in battle might disturb modern sensibilities. But, clearly, in *LotR*, no true-hearted warrior kills chiefly for pleasure. The Orcs and cruel Haradrim do, and this mindset contributes to their demise. As is often the case, the soldiers who win the war are those most committed to enjoying the fruits of victory: peace and sanctity.

In the end, *LotR* does give us a vision of a world without war. The annihilation of Sauron, the fall of Mordor, the return of the rightful King, all usher in an earthly paradise. At the close of *H5*, the Chorus grimly reminds us that Henry's victorious reign was relatively brief, and those that came after him "made his England bleed" (Epilogue 12). Shakespeare's last statement on war might seem more realistic than Tolkien's. Disputes between nations and peoples might go on and on, and elusive, lasting peace shall remain a "fantasy." But Tolkien also has Gandalf remind everyone that evil may come again. To reject the need to face it, to dismiss any cause of war as worthy or just, or to disparage the glory of those who fight and die to preserve our homelands and ways of life, seem superficial and shameful. Tolkien offers a view of war more powerful and profound than the great Bard. Éowyn, the one who first embraced and then learned the limits of the heroic ideal of dying in battle, in the Houses of Healing rightly refutes the Warden's simplistic pacifism:

> "It needs but one foe to breed a war, not two, Master Warden.... And those who have not swords can still die upon them. Would you have the folk of Gondor gather you herbs only, when the Dark Lord gathers armies?" [6.5.937].

Would Fergusson? Would Otty? Would we?

Note

An earlier version of this paper was presented at The Mythopoeic Society annual conference in San Francisco in 2001.

Works Cited

Colebatch, Hal. *Return of the Heroes:* The Lord of the Rings, Star Wars *and Contemporary Culture.* Perth: Australian Institute for Public Policy, 1990.

Croft, Janet Brennan. *War and the Works of J.R.R. Tolkien.* Westport, CT: Praeger, 2004.

Ferguson, Niall. *The Pity of War.* New York: Basic Books 1999.

Friedman, Barton. "Tolkien and David Jones: The Great War and the War of the Ring." *Clio* 11.2 (1982): 115–36.

Garth, John. *Tolkien and The Great War: The Threshold of Middle-earth.* Boston: Houghton, 2003.

Goldthwaite, John. *A Natural History of Make-believe: A Guide to the Principal Works of Britain, Europe, and America.* New York: Oxford University Press, 1996.

Hall, Joan Lord. *Henry V: A Guide to the Play.* Westport, CT: Greenwood Press, 1997.

Loehlin, James N. Henry V. Shakespeare in Performance. Manchester: Manchester University Press, 1996.

Otty, Nick. "The Structuralist's Guide to Middle-earth." In *J.R.R. Tolkien: This Far Land.* Ed. Robert Giddings. London: Vision, 1983. 154–77.

Shakespeare, William. *The Complete Works of William Shakespeare.* Ed. David Bevington. 5th ed. New York: Pearson, 2004.

Shaughnessy, Robert. "The Last Post: *Henry V,* War Culture, and the Postmodern Shakespeare." *Theatre Survey* 39.1 (1998): 41–61.

Shippey, Thomas A. *J.R.R. Tolkien: Author of the Century.* London: Harper, 2000.

Tolkien, J.R.R. *The Lord of the Rings.* 2nd ed. Boston: Houghton, 1994.

The Person of a Prince

Echoes of Hamlet *in J.R.R. Tolkien's*
The Lord of the Rings

KAYLA MCKINNEY WIGGINS

We write, in great measure, to explain our world, to make sense of the chaos. We read, at least in part, to find answers, to make meaning. The great works of literature serve as mirrors for our own realities, and our own personalities. They comment on the human condition, offer us hope, or define our hopelessness. They shape our identities and give us "counsel for the peril of the world" (*The Lord of the Rings* [*LotR*] 2.2.236). Writing almost four centuries apart and in different mediums, Shakespeare and Tolkien created characters of heroic stature who are touchstones for our most fundamental sense of self-awareness. As readers, we are surer of our own humanity, of our own worth, of the possibilities and the tragedies of human existence because we have known Hamlet and Aragorn, Faramir, Frodo and Sam. Heroes of different worlds and different means of expression, they represent the best in all of us—the potential in life and death and dreaming—just as their foils, Boromir and Fortinbras, Claudius and Denethor, represent our limitations.

Tolkien on Shakespeare

J. R. R. Tolkien says of his schooldays that, apart from Shakespeare, which he "disliked cordially," his only exposure to English poetry was in translating it to Latin (*Letters* 213). In the same passage, he notes that his primary studies were in Latin and Greek, with exposure to English language and history but not to "English Literature." What is most inter-

esting about this passage is the distinction Tolkien makes among genres, placing Shakespeare's writings under the heading of English poetry,
as distinct from English literature and English language studies.
Schooled in the Classics, the budding philologist and medievalist was
attracted to antiquity, to the foundations of his Anglo-Saxon heritage.
This same attraction apparently accounts for some of his negative
response to Shakespeare. In his writings, Tolkien primarily objects to
those works by Shakespeare that attempt—in his view inadequately—to
express the fantastic, objecting primarily to Shakespeare's treatment of
the elves and to his misuse of the marching trees in *Macbeth* (*Letters* 185,
143n, 212n). For Tolkien, the magic of theatre—the recreation of life
on stage—is a difficult enough slight-of-hand without adding the
difficulty of fantasy as a second level of magical effect: "To be dissolved,
or to be degraded, is the likely fate of Fantasy when a dramatist tries to
use it, even such a dramatist as Shakespeare" ("On Fairy-Stories" [OFS]
50).

Thus, Tolkien's problem with Shakespeare is not so much a problem with the writer or the written product as with the genre, and in particular, with the critical response to the genre. In Tolkien's view, it "is
a misfortune that Drama, an art fundamentally distinct from Literature,
should so commonly be considered together with it, or as a branch of
it" (OFS 49). As Tolkien rightly notes, plays, intended to be performed,
are a different kind of expression than novels or epics, intended to be
read. He takes exception with critics who depreciate "Fantasy" in favor
of "the forms of literature or 'imagination' that they themselves, innately
or by training, prefer" (49). He complains that "criticism in a country
that has produced so great a Drama, and possesses the works of William
Shakespeare, tends to be far too dramatic. But Drama is naturally hostile to Fantasy" (49). So, drama cannot do fantasy well, and in terms of
critical appreciation, fantasy is forced to take a backseat to drama.

Beyond his commentary on the failure of theatrical fantasy, Tolkien
has little to say of Shakespeare in his letters. He does comment on a
1944 production of *Hamlet* in admiring tones, although he concludes
that the proper place of Shakespeare is in the theatre and not in the
study, something Shakespeare himself would probably have approved:

> But it emphasized more strongly than anything I have ever seen the
> folly of reading Shakespeare (and annotating him in the study)
> except as a concomitant of seeing his plays acted. It was a very good
> performance, with a young rather fierce Hamlet; it was played fast
> without cuts; and came out as a very exciting play. Could one only
> have seen it without ever having read it or knowing the plot, it
> would have been terrific [*Letters* 88].

Tolkien's own writings share with Shakespeare's this quality of excitement. The two authors also share an affinity for writing characters who become a part of our consciousness, who echo our essential humanity. They also have in common a body of criticism that takes exception with, among other things, the author's medium.

Genre in Hamlet *and* The Lord of the Rings

Hamlet is part of a tradition in Renaissance theatre known as Revenge Tragedy. Based in the works of the Roman playwright Seneca, Revenge Tragedy included melodramatic trappings like ghosts, madness, suicide, horrific speeches, and, of course, revenge. Much of the early critical attention to *Hamlet* centered on the prince's personality and his supposed failure to act, with scholars rejecting Hamlet's avowed reasons for delay as untruths and excuses. It seems curious to me that generations of scholars have agreed to disbelieve the text itself and to conclude that the dramatic expectations of its form or its source material are irrelevant to an understanding of the play. In much the same way, early critical responses to Tolkien's *LotR* seemed more concerned with the debate between reality and fantasy than with the actual qualities of the work.

Shakespeare's *Hamlet* harks back to several historical and dramatic sources, including a lost play known as the *Ur-Hamlet,* which had been performed by 1589. The "favorite choice for authorship of the *Ur-Hamlet* is Thomas Kyd, whose *Spanish Tragedy,* c. 1586, in common with Shakespeare's *Hamlet,* contains a ghost, a revenge motif, simulated madness, a play within a play, and a 'faithful' Horatio" (Satin 381). While this is the accepted view in Shakespearean scholarship, Harold Bloom concurs with Peter Alexander in crediting Shakespeare with the authorship of the *Ur-Hamlet* (Bloom 383). This speculation, if it were true, would make Shakespeare the author of the earliest known Revenge Tragedy, and would account at least in part for the depth and complexity of *Hamlet* since it would mean that the author was engaged intellectually with the subject matter of the play for more than a decade.

The themes of *Hamlet* are large ones—life and death, good and evil—and the story concerns enlightened men struggling to redress wrongs and establish balance in a world grown inexpressibly corrupt. *The Lord of the Rings,* indeed all high fantasy, shares the same concerns. Like Shakespeare, Tolkien has created characters of transcendent power in a work that dominates its genre. Nevertheless, much of the early critical writing on *LotR* seemed more concerned with the nature of the work than the quality of it. Like the scholars who complained that

Beowulf included too much fantasy and not enough history, early critics of Tolkien's work lamented his lack of realism in a world dependent on reality. Roger Sale, for example, saw Tolkien's work as flawed and located the flaw in what he saw as Tolkien's withdrawal from the modern world: "The old terms for the struggle of good against evil—courage, loyalty, honor, magnificence, fortitude—are mostly irrelevant now" (Sale 53). Later scholars disagree, however. Tom Shippey argues that the "dominant literary mode of the twentieth century has been the fantastic" (*Author* vii). Shippey groups Tolkien with a group of "traumatized" twentieth-century authors writing fantasy in response to the issues of the modern world (*Road* xvii). Verlyn Flieger sees Tolkien as a modern thinker "dipping into the past for the stuff of his story but reworking it for the age in which he lived," noting that a story does not "have to have a contemporary setting in order to mirror contemporary thought" (8). Tolkien was writing high fantasy in the epic tradition, and realism as a twentieth-century literary concept was simply not the point. Epics are not realistic whatever insights they may bring regarding the individual cultures that created them. Is *Beowulf* realistic, with its tale of monsters and underwater battles? Is *Gilgamesh* realistic, with its journey to a land beyond death? Closest to realism, perhaps, would be *The Iliad*, but the siege of Troy with its euphemistic arrows of Apollo and its godly/priestly dictates thinly veiling the disease and tensions of camp life is still literature utilizing the fantastic mode. Tolkien uses fantasy not to depict reality but to echo it, as he struggles with the large issues and messages of the human condition. Like Shakespeare, he depicts the conflict between good and evil, life and death as it is played out within the confines of a world growing rapidly corrupt and in danger of being consumed by wickedness. Also like Shakespeare, he embodies good in the person of "princes" who struggle with evil and, in time, overcome.

The Person of a Prince

The prototype for Shakespeare's Hamlet, for "all Hamlets," is a legendary Danish prince named Amleth, the subject of a twelfth-century "mythical hero story" by Saxo Grammaticus (Satin 382). The *Historica Danica* recounts the tale of the open murder of a king by his own brother, incestuous marriage between the wife of the murdered king and the murderer, feigned madness on the part of the prince in an attempt to protect himself from his deadly uncle, attempted seduction and rape, spying leading to a brutal murder, a journey to England, and—finally—horrific revenge. The tale was retold in a slightly more sophisticated form by the French author Beleforest in 1582, and this work probably served as the source for both the *Ur-Hamlet* and Shakespeare's final version of the Amleth story (Satin 382). Whatever the nature of the *Ur-Hamlet*, and whoever the author, Shakespeare's final conception makes a sophisticated and infinitely rewarding use not only of the source material but of the conventions of Revenge Tragedy, centered in the person of the prince.

Harold Bloom calls Hamlet "the most aware and knowing figure ever conceived" (404), but also "as ambivalent and divided a consciousness as a coherent drama could sustain" (387). Hamlet is larger than life, emotionally, intellectually, and spiritually. He is all of us, and none of us. Harold Goddard, echoing Emily Dickinson, says that we see ourselves mirrored in Hamlet, "that everyone admits finding something of himself in the Prince of Denmark" (95). Yet it is equally true, as Harold Bloom says, that Hamlet transcends his play, that he is beyond us, beyond any character in literature, and has "usurped the Western literary consciousness" (385, 422, 413). In his seminal work, *Shakespearean Tragedy*, A.C. Bradley notes that Hamlet has "exerted a greater fascination" and "been the subject of more discussion" than any other character in "the whole literature of the world" (74). That this discussion is problematic goes without saying. It is our very identification with Hamlet, says Harold Goddard, that dooms *Hamlet* criticism "to go on being what it has always been: a sustained difference of opinion" (95). For centuries, this difference of opinion has centered on the nature of the play and the nature of the prince, as scores of critics have found the two at odds.

That Hamlet's most decisive actions result in the deaths of others— Polonius, Rosencrantz and Guildenstern, Claudius, and Laertes directly, and Ophelia indirectly—is also a source of dissatisfaction among critics. It is hard to reconcile a man who encompasses all humanity with the negative energies of revenge. Yet the form of the play demands that there must be revenge, that someone must take that revenge, and that he must die in consequence. The perceived conflict between the qualities of the prince and the demands of the medium led T. S. Eliot to declare *Hamlet* "an artistic failure" (98), but Bradley points out that Hamlet himself never doubts that he should take revenge, if Claudius proves guilty (80); neither do audiences and readers. Claudius deserves to die and die he must, but when we look into the mirror that is the character of Hamlet, some of us may feel just the slightest discomfort with the image of revenge staring back at us. Why put this courtier, soldier, scholar, this "paragon of animals" (2.2.308) at the center of such a play? Why put the sword in his hand? Why take his life at the end? One reason, of course, is because the form of the play and the morals of the time demanded it; beyond that, however, this story, like Tolkien's epic, serves to remind us that there is death in the world and there is evil, but there is also life, and good to counter the evil. Perhaps Shakespeare and Tolkien wrote to show us that there are consequences for every action, even if those consequences are sometimes turned back on the good and the innocent. Northrop Frye in *Fools of Time* comments that the tragic quality of drama comes from the heroic element, "a capacity for action or passion, for doing or suffering, which is above ordinary human experience" (4–5). Frye places *Hamlet* among Shakespeare's social tragedies in which an order figure (King Hamlet) is destroyed by a rebel-figure (Claudius), and a nemesis (Hamlet) must kill the rebel and restore order (17).

In much the same way, Tolkien echoes the tradition of the world's great epics in which a hero ventures forth on a quest of renown and returns to his world after hardships and adventures, trials and discoveries as a figure of order and hope, but never without a painful twist. Gilgamesh seeks eternal physical life but finds instead enduring fame as a good king. After restoring order to the Danish kingdom by defeating Grendel and his mother, Beowulf eventually becomes king of the Geats and ultimately sacrifices himself for his people, restoring order— albeit temporary—out of the chaos of the dragon. Odysseus returns to Ithaca to restore his rule and his family but with a twenty-year gap in his happiness. The company of the Ring also restores order out of chaos in *LotR*. Frodo and Sam fulfill their negative quest, destroying the Ring and ensuring the triumph of good over evil. They rebuild their world, from the top down, restoring the rightful king to the throne and bringing order to Gondor, Rohan, and the Shire. But the cost is a high one— most of the magic of their world is lost to the new order. The new world is the world of Man; Wizards and Elves will diminish or retire.

Harold Goddard says that Hamlet was a light-bearer, that his "mind was focused on philosophy, on religion, and on art" (107). As a student in Wittenberg, the most famous center of learning in the Renaissance world (Johanyak 203) and a center of religious study, Hamlet could hardly have avoided confronting the deepest issues of the human condition. That he did so is borne out in the seven great soliloquies that debate life, death, hope, despair, and destiny. Even without poetry, Hamlet's mind and soul reach the heights of human expression:

> "What a piece of work is a man! How noble in reason, how infinite in faculties, in form and moving how express and admirable, in action how like an angel, in apprehension how like a god!" [2.2. 304–8].

Hamlet dies, but he has the opportunity to restore order; he is a tragic hero not because of a supposed flaw but because of his intractable situation (Summers 146). Hamlet is perhaps the most balanced character in literature, demonstrating a capacity for action, a range of emotion, and a depth of spiritual reflection that echoes his own description of the puzzling glory that is a man, and the Greek precepts of "Know Thyself" and "Nothing Too Much."

Tolkien's noble "princes" embody the same qualities of nobility, intellect, and decency exhibited by the Prince of Denmark. Aragorn is perhaps the most obvious prince of the story, destined as he is to be king of the West. Aragorn fits the classic model of the mythological hero. Though born to royalty, his is a line of kings in exile. He is raised in obscurity and not told his true identity until he reaches adulthood. He then serves a long apprenticeship that includes countless journeys as he secretly both protects his kingdom and trains to rule, learning skill with arms while serving with the men of Rohan and of Gondor and learning wisdom from Gandalf and his studies in ancient lore and legends. He falls in love but cannot act upon his feelings, beyond plighting his troth, until he has proven himself and recovered his kingdom. Like Hamlet, he is a man of wit and wisdom, courage and fortitude. He balances physical prowess—he is a warrior and woodsman, capable of phenomenal feats in war and incredible endurance in trials—with intellect and learning demonstrated in his knowledge of the history and lore of his people. His spiritual depth is indicated by his ability, like medieval kings, to heal the sick and dying; by his successful wrestling of the *palantír* away from Sauron's influence; and by his keen awareness of the emotions of others. Aragorn is a leader—commanding love and loyalty from all who follow him—but he is also a guide, giving of himself to others even at the risk of his life and his ultimate happiness (Kocher 127). There are few more moving sequences in literature than the long race of Gimli, Legolas, and Aragorn across the plains of Rohan, and the dark journey on the paths of the dead in a desperate race to come to the aid of the besieged inhabitants of Gondor. In both these instances, the others are held on course by the strength of Aragorn's will and their love for a leader who asks no more of them than he asks of himself, and who would ultimately give his all to save them.

> In Aragorn, Tolkien presents an ideal king, proven worthy by his long *cursus honorum* and by his battlefield experience; an able and responsible leader, without hubris or the overmastering desire for conquest and power. Aragorn claims the throne he knows is his by right of birth, but he has no quarrel with being required to prove himself worthy of it [Croft 91].

While we share Hamlet's thoughts through his soliloquies, Tolkien achieves his successful portrait of a man of balanced humility and power in part by showing him from the outside, through the perspectives of the hobbits and the authorial narrative. We come to know Aragorn through his actions and his words; his thoughts are his own. Those actions and words are telling enough, but there is a sense always of greater depth that we are not privy to. In the inn at Bree during our first introduction to Aragorn, we see a range of reactions to his encounter with the hobbits: his wry regret at not being taken on his own merit, his terrible knowledge of the Ringwraiths, and his commanding—though still hidden—force: "If I had killed the real Strider, I could kill you. And I should have killed you already without so much talk. If I was after the ring, I could have it—NOW!" (1.10.168). We also see the depth of his spirit, willing as he is to sacrifice all for others and his world: "I am Aragorn son of Arathorn; and if by life or death I can save you, I will" (ibid.). This is just our first introduction to this mysterious figure who is feared by Butterbur and trusted by Gandalf. Over the course of the story, we will come, like the hobbits, to know him much better and to love him, though we will never know the total sum of this remarkable man. Aragorn was a surprise even to Tolkien himself; in the early evolution of the character, even his author did not anticipate his identity as the hereditary heir of the West (*Letters* 216).

Two other hereditary rulers are the brothers Boromir and Faramir. Though they are not technically princes, being the sons of Denethor, the Steward of Gondor, they come from a long line of rulers, functional kings governing Gondor in the absence of the hereditary king. Many writers have noted the antithetical nature of these two brothers. In *Following Gandalf*, Dickerson notes that Faramir sees the value Gondor places on war as a sign of the decline of a great civilization while Boromir sees war as an opportunity to win personal glory (60). Boromir is modeled on Beowulf and the warrior of ancient and medieval epic. Faramir is a Renaissance prince, enlightened and schooled, a man who would prefer peace although he accepts the necessity of war. He is no less talented than his brother, though his father sees him as the lesser of the two. He is quick and resourceful in battle, though his leadership style, like Aragorn's and Hamlet's, is predicated on careful thought and deliberation, the mark of a true leader. He is an intellectual, having studied the history and lore of his people, in part under the tutelage of the wizard Gandalf. He knows the history of the Ring, and its dangers. He rejects all thought of taking or using it, saying, "I would not take this thing, if it lay by the highway. Not were Minas Tirith falling in ruin and I alone could save her, so, using the weapon of the Dark Lord for her good and my glory" (4.5.656). He demonstrates his spiritual depth in his tribute before eating when he and his men rise and face west, observing a moment of silence: "'So we always do,' he said, as they sat down:

'we look towards Númenor that was, and beyond to Elvenhome that is, and to that which is beyond Elvenhome and will ever be'" (4.5.661). Tolkien himself identified with Faramir, though he said he lacked the courage of his characters (*Letters* 232n).

While the hobbits of Tolkien's story are closer in kind to modern people and smaller in stature than the great with whom they associate and are associated, they all exhibit some degree of princely attributes. The actual contributions Merry and Pippin make to the War of the Rings may seem few in number, especially compared to the military prowess of Aragorn, Faramir, Legolas, and Gimli, but they loom large in terms of the successful completion of the war. Merry and Pippin engineer their own escape from the Orcs, and they are the catalyst that brings the Ents into the battle. Pippin saves the life of both Faramir and Beregond, and Merry not only saves the life of Éowyn but destroys the chief of the Ringwraiths. By the time they return to the Shire to free their homeland of evil, they have grown princely indeed; as Gandalf says, they are "among the great" (6.7.974). In later days they become literally the hereditary rulers of the Shire, as near to princes as their democratic world can boast. While they remain soldiers of Rohan and Gondor, the king's representatives in the Shire, Merry also becomes the Master of Buckland and Pippin the Took the Thain; Sam is elected mayor seven times (App.B.1071–72).

Sam is an intriguing character, beginning the tale as (apparently) a simple-minded gardener who hires on as companion and man-of-all-work to Frodo, and becoming the most unexpected hero of all. Sam's love of elves, lore, and stories reveals a surprising depth to him from almost the very beginning. His exposure to the great and near-great of his times only serves to strengthen his sturdy good sense, and his loyalty and determination raise him to their level. Sam's growth occurs, particularly, during the final stages of his journey with Frodo, after they have crossed into Mordor and Sam has rescued Frodo from the Orcs. He becomes the viewpoint character at this stage of the journey and it is his spiritual depth as indicated in his nearly indomitable hope, his physical prowess as indicated in his ability to endure almost limitless hardship, and his emotional depth as indicated in his love and compassion for Frodo that really foster the success of the quest. Frodo is so consumed by the fire of the Ring that he can no longer share the narrative with us. Only Sam's will carries the quest on to its conclusion, just as his voice completes the story. Tolkien seems to have felt a great affinity for Sam, particularly as the story progressed. He says in his letters that Sam is "the most closely drawn character," that Frodo is not as interesting because he is high-minded and has a vocation (105), even though he also says that Frodo gave everything to the quest, and that probably no one else could have achieved it (253). In a rather vague, passing reference in the midst of a discussion of Aragorn's love for Arwen, Tolkien seems, in fact, to call Sam the chief hero of *LotR* (161). This is clearly not accurate if we regard hero as synonymous with protagonist. Frodo is without question the main character; he is the one with the quest to accomplish. However, he would not have accomplished it without the contributions of the many other "heroes" who people the narrative. He and Sam deserve Tolkien's designation of them as the "princes of the west" (*Letters* 308).

Vengeance and Justice, Betrayal and Loyalty

Modern sensibilities are at the core of the critical debate over both *Hamlet* and *LotR*. In the modern world, we do not believe in ghosts that command revenge, nor do we believe it is right to deliberately take the life of another. Consequently, it is difficult for us to envision the noble mind and spirit of Hamlet accepting the need, the necessity, indeed the imperative, of killing an unarmed man, or characters as noble and selfless as Aragorn and Faramir living lives predicated on the necessity of daily violence and warfare. But Hamlet—for all that he may be a mirror for all people at all times and echo Renaissance ideals—is based on an ancient model. And Aragorn and Faramir inhabit a world not as far removed from our own as we might want to believe, a world where the presence of evil all too often demands a response from good that counters violence with defensive violence.

The plot of *Hamlet* inverts the Greek story of Orestes, which chronicled the movement of a society from personal vengeance to justice. Ultimately, Orestes is vindicated in the first court of law for his murder of his mother and her lover in retaliation for the slaughter of his father. In his search for justice, however, Hamlet cannot count on society or law because the state of Denmark mirrors the corruption of its leader. "For if the sun breed maggots in a dead dog" (2.2.181), Hamlet says, using the common Renaissance metaphor of the sun for the ruler. Claudius is the sun, and he is breeding maggots in the dead body of Denmark. In the absence of justice, vengeance must rule. The end of the play, however, presupposes a reestablishment of order, significantly through storytelling and renewed nobility. Horatio will tell Hamlet's story, Hamlet will be honored in death as he never had a chance to be in life, and Fortinbras will return the throne of Denmark to its former status. Ironically, he will be a king much like King Hamlet, a warrior and a man of action, seemingly having little in common with the complex and philosophical Prince Hamlet.

In much the same way, the characters of Tolkien's epic must reestablish order out of chaos. In a world never far removed from the possibility of evil—much like our own—they have carved out civilizations of tenuous peace: the domesticated Shire existing unawares on the edges of Wilderland; the tribal culture of Rohan; the last bastion of the men of Westernesse in the far-flung realm of Gondor; and the carefully isolated, consciously distanced realms of the elves. But unbeknown to many of the inhabitants, ultimate evil exists both within and without these sheltered realms. When it erupts, it is up to the leaders of these separate groups to step forward and to potentially sacrifice all to reestablish balance. The actions they take, and the sacrifices they make, restore their world, but nothing can ever completely banish evil from the mortal realm.

Machiavellian Rule

Hamlet's inaction has been blamed for the multiple deaths in the play, but in reality Claudius is to blame. His political and personal machinations set in motion the horrific sequence of events that cost the royal court of Denmark both of its leading families. Claudius exhibits the more obvious qualities of a Machiavellian prince, representing the new order of the Renaissance in its negative capacity even as Hamlet represents Renaissance humanism in its positive intellectual and spiritual incarnation.

Dealing as it did with a new kind of political figure, a "new" prince for a new time, Machiavelli's *The Prince* became "the intellectual property of every well-read European during the sixteenth century, and garnered a reputation as a handbook for tyrants" (Bonadella and Musa 17–18). Machiavelli's work "defines man as a selfish animal ruled by the insatiable desire for material gain and driven by the principle of self-interest" (25), a perfect description of Claudius. While Machiavelli does give some good advice to prospective rulers, he is like Polonius in that even his good advice is self-serving. He counsels rulers to model themselves on the ancients, but also urges social conflict as a positive force (26). While he cautions rulers to not alter the laws or taxes of a conquered people, he also suggests that the best way to maintain control in such circumstances is to destroy the hereditary line (Machiavelli 82). Even while assuring the would-be successful prince that he must have the support of the people—that nobles can always be created or destroyed—he suggests that the best way to maintain the loyalty of the populace is by making sure they always need the assistance of the state (108, 110). He cautions rulers to never rely on mercenaries and to give their thoughts to the strategies of war (116, 124). He says that "it cannot be called skill to kill one's fellow citizens, to betray friends, to be without faith, without mercy, without religion; by these means one can acquire power but not glory" (104), but he also suggests that an effective ruler must at times be cruel in order to keep his subjects loyal since mercy can lead to greater disorders (130), that it's better to be feared than loved (131), and that the strongest princes are not afraid to break promises when the need arises (133). A prince, says Machiavelli, "and especially a new prince, cannot observe all those things by which men are considered good, for in order to maintain the state he is often obliged to act against his promise, against charity, against humanity, and against religion" (135). Claudius does not adhere perfectly to the Machiavellian principles: he avoids war in favor of politics, he uses mercenaries, and he does not seem to court the favor of the common people, but he does break the line of succession, and he doesn't hesitate to manipulate others to his own ends, encouraging Rosencrantz and Guildenstern, Polonius, Ophelia, and Gertrude to act as spies on his behalf, and urging Laertes to kill for him. Even murder is not beyond Claudius' range; he does not hesitate to commit fratricide and even less to plot against the life of his nephew on two separate occasions.

Beyond the clear and absolute evil of Sauron, two characters in *LotR* could be said to be Machiavellian princes. Saruman does not hesitate to corrupt and pervert those around him in order to achieve his goals of conquest, even going so far as to torture and pervert nature to achieve his ends. He destroys the natural beauty of Orthanc, does extreme damage to Fangorn Forest, and breeds a race of half Men/half Orcs that are a perversion of both species. He corrupts or attempts to corrupt others, completely destroying Wormtongue, attempting to convince Gandalf to join in his self-serving plots against the free peoples of Middle-earth, and even manipulating Treebeard into releasing him. Saruman's corruption is made worse by the fact that he is a being of a higher order; he is not a Man, but a Wizard, and the highest among the Wizards of Middle-earth.

Denethor, too, is among the highest figures in Middle-earth, descended as he is from the line of the West. Though in name only a steward and not literally a king, he is in function the ruler of Gondor and its empire, the avowed enemy of Sauron. While not ignoble, he is nonetheless unyielding to the point of cruelty, and so self-absorbed that his ability to judge men, even his own sons, is severely impaired. Ultimately, when faced with the return of his king, he fails both in his faith and in his charge, sending his only surviving son to almost certain death in battle and, later, seeking death himself through suicide. Evil rulers in Middle-earth, however, are ultimately the stooges of the ultimate evil,

Sauron. They are the pawns and he is the chess master, controlling them through the remaining *palantíri* of Middle-earth, in much the same way Théoden, a good king, is controlled by Saruman through the lies of Wormtongue.

Machiavelli suggests that a new prince can come to power through evil or through the election of his peers (103); Claudius has done both. He has emptied the throne by murder and snatched it away with the support of the nobility from Hamlet, who is the rightful heir, facilitated by Hamlet's apparent absence. Because it seems odd that a thirty-year-old prince, the only son of an ageing father, would still be at school studying religion or philosophy, A. C. Bradley speculates that Hamlet was not away in Wittenberg at all when his father died, but living in the Danish court (361). This seems unlikely, though, since Hamlet would almost certainly have inherited had he been present when his father died. Harold Bloom has suggested, curiously, that Hamlet, in essence, is twenty at the beginning of the play and thirty at the end (393). It seems much more likely that Hamlet, although not still a student in Wittenberg when his father dies, is away from court, never expecting such a tragedy, and that his response to his grief and, especially, his mother's remarriage is to want to return to the university and the comfort of his studies in religion and philosophy. The Machiavellian prince creates the appearance of goodness while choosing always the most advantageous path; Hamlet, on the other hand, is the essence of goodness attempting to find the right course of action in the face of overarching corruption and evil, a course denied to him by his scheming uncle.

In *Hamlet*, Claudius has violated two other principles of Machiavellian rule, and these lead directly to his downfall. Machiavelli advises rulers to keep their hands off their subjects' property and women so as to not be hated (132), and to surround themselves with good advisers since princes are judged by the qualities of the people with whom they surround themselves (154). Claudius takes his brother's property and his brother's wife, engendering the hatred, at least, of his nephew. His chief adviser is Polonius, a foolish man who is at least as corrupt as Claudius himself. Our first extended contact with Polonius shows him in fatherly discourse with his departing son, treating Laertes to a lengthy lecture on the proper behavior of a young gentleman. This speech is justifiably famous for its wisdom, but in the space of two scenes—two months' time in the court at Elsinore—Polonius gives it the lie by sending a servant to spy on his little-trusted son; even Reynaldo is shocked. After sending Laertes to France, Polonius orders Ophelia to guard her virtue and never speak to Hamlet again only to turn around within two months and command her to speak to Hamlet as the bait for a trap, endangering her immortal soul by placing a prayer book in her hand

and forcing her to participate in lies and duplicity while giving the appearance of a spiritual exercise. Perhaps the most famous line from Polonius' advice to his son underscores the emptiness and corruption at the center of the Danish court: "This above all: to thine own self be true, / And it must follow, as the night the day, / Thou canst not then be false to any man" (1.3.78–80). If Polonius is telling Laertes to know himself and always be genuine with others, it is ironic that he almost immediately believes in Laertes' dishonesty and corruption. If he is advising his son to put himself first—in the Machiavellian model—it does not follow that this will always lead to honest treatment of others, just to the appearance of such treatment.

Saruman is perhaps the best example of this kind of verbal manipulation in Tolkien's work. Renowned for the power of his speech into which he seems to have invested a great deal of his magic, he seems capable, or at least believes himself capable, of verbally manipulating anyone. He even tries to control Gandalf in this way, proving that although his powers may be great, his perceptions of others, like Polonius', are severely limited. Urging Gandalf to join with him in complicity with the new order, he says:

> We can bide our time, we can keep our thoughts in our hearts, deploring maybe evils done by the way, but approving the high and ultimate purpose: Knowledge, Rule, Order; all the things that we have so far striven in vain to accomplish, hindered rather than helped by our weak or idle friends. There need not be, there would not be, any real change in our designs, only our means [2.2.253].

This is a prime example of the end-justifies-the-means misreading of Machiavellian principles, and Gandalf recognizes it for what it is: an agenda for betrayal. A member of the highest order of life in Middle-earth, Saruman proposes abandoning his obligation to preserve and nurture this world; he suggests betraying its peoples to further his own selfish ends. Although other betrayals also occur—Boromir betrays his oath to the company, Denethor betrays his rule and his son, Wormtongue betrays his king and his people—the inhabitants of Middle-earth are largely loyal and betrayal is an aberration most often associated with Sauron and the lure of the Ring of Power. Indeed, ambition for power seems to be at the heart of all betrayal in the realm of Middle-earth, as perhaps it is in life.

Betrayal is the primary mode of behavior in the rotten state of Denmark, stemming perhaps from this same ambition. Polonius betrays both his children and dies pursuing his own political and social advancement. Gertrude betrays her dead husband and her living son. Ophelia betrays her lover; Laertes, his prince, choosing—like his king—poison as his means to murder. Rosencrantz and Guildenstern betray their childhood friend—ironically, for the motive they assign incorrectly to Hamlet, ambition—and are betrayed in return. Claudius betrays everyone: brother, nephew, courtiers, queen, and—ultimately—state. Even King Hamlet betrays his son by commanding revenge, guaranteeing Hamlet's death since morally an avenger could not be allowed to survive. Only Horatio remains true to Hamlet. "Give me that man / That is not passion's slave, and I will wear him / In my heart's core, ay, in my heart of heart" (3.2.70–72) says Hamlet, little thinking, perhaps, that he is not only describing Horatio but also himself.

This kind of devotion is much less rare in Middle-earth. Indeed, it is friendship, and the loyalty growing out of friendship, that nurtures and sustains the members of the company as they endure an impossible quest. Deep bonds are established among these people as they face the greatest challenges of life and death together, so that Merry will always be a man of Rohan no matter how far he journeys in life, and Pippin of Gondor, not only because of oaths sworn but because of friendships forged with Denethor and Éowyn, with Beregond and his son, Bergil. The old Ent Treebeard will never forget them, or they him. Frodo is sustained by the friendship of Sam, his own Horatio, and in a twisted, stunted way, even by the friendship of Gollum. Indeed, without this strange three-way relationship, the quest would not have been achieved. The hobbits come to love Aragorn, as he does them, and even that most solitary of wanderers is nurtured in need by the friendship and loyalty of those who follow him and fight beside him: the Dúnedain and the sons of Elrond, Legolas and Gimli, Éomer, and even Gandalf. Perhaps the greatest example of friendship in Middle-earth, beyond that of Sam and Frodo, is the curious friendship that evolves between the elf Legolas and the dwarf Gimli. Beginning as hereditary enemies, they share the hardships and dangers of the journey and the distrust of others. Along the way, they become congenial competitors and eventually lifelong friends.

Fate and Fatalism, Chaos and Order

Fatalism seems to be the dominant mode of feeling for both Hamlet and Frodo as they face their separate trials. In his most famous soliloquy, Hamlet questions the very efficacy of human life: "To be, or not to be, that is the question" (3.1.57). Faced with his father's death, his mother's remarriage, and his uncle's wicked duplicity, even death offers a dubious comfort: "To die, to sleep; / To sleep, perchance to dream" (3.2.65–66). On Mount Doom, and indeed long before in his dark journey across Mordor, Frodo sees death as the inevitable outcome of his quest. He tells Sam, "I am glad that you are here with me. Here at the end of all things" (6.3.926). Sam, too, draws on the metaphor of sleep but as a comfort, assuring Frodo that after the quest is fulfilled, an outcome he at least never truly doubts, "we can have some rest and some sleep" (4.8.697). Sam's enduring hopefulness foreshadows the ultimate message of these two great works, the belief that however dark the journey, there is purpose in living, there is a plan in operation no matter how little of it we are capable, in our limited human capacity, of understanding. In the dark moments before he faces his own death, when he has finally accepted that he must be an avenger and almost certainly die in the attempt, Hamlet assures Horatio that "There is special providence in the fall of a sparrow" (5.2.217–18) just as Elrond assures the gathering in Rivendell before the advent of the quest, "You have come and are met, in this very nick of time, by chance as it may seem. Yet it is not so. Believe rather that it is so ordered that we, who sit here, and none others, must now find counsel for the peril of the world" (2.2.236).

Though he goads himself to passion, Hamlet is a thinking, moral, rational being who finds himself in conflict with an irrational world. Called—in fact commanded—to restore order, he does so by the only avenue open to him: through private revenge. This violates our modern sensibilities; it does not violate Hamlet's once he is convinced of its rightness. While he wanted revenge, if possible, without sacrificing his life (Bradley 80), by the time he returns after his aborted trip to England, he has given up hope of achieving that end. Hamlet spends the first three acts of the play questioning the necessity of existence, and championing life reluctantly as the better alternative to the unknown country of death; after the killing of Polonius, his mood and his discourse change. He is made abruptly aware of the inevitability of death and the equality of humanity; we are all in the same boat, and it is shipping water. When he returns from England, his mood has changed again. By this time, he has held Claudius' letter ordering Hamlet's execution and altered that letter so as to engineer the deaths of Rosencrantz and Guildenstern. He knows finally the depths to which corruption can go, but he also knows that an operative providence exists; how else would he have found that letter in time? "There's a divinity that shapes our ends, / Rough-hew them how we will" (5.2.10–11). He will not survive the vengeance he must take—how could he?—but there is a higher plan and Denmark, somehow, will be saved. "Heaven will direct it" (1.4.90), since heaven has chosen Hamlet to be "their scourge and minister" (3.4.182).

Frodo shares affinities with both Aragorn and Hamlet, with their identities intersecting in their roles as tragic or epic heroes. Northrop

Frye in *Anatomy of Criticism* lists five designations for heroic character. The first level is the level of myth, where the character is a divinity, superior in kind to other men and the environment (33). The second level is the level of romance, where the hero is superior in degree to other men and his environment; romance posits a world where the ordinary laws of nature are suspended. The fourth level in Frye's classification is that of the hero who is not superior to the environment or other people; the hero, thus, is one of us and the story is realistic; the final level is the ironic mode with its hero who is inferior in power or intelligence to others (34). At the third level, the medial category, the hero is superior in degree to other men but not the environment, making the hero a leader and the story a tragedy or an epic (33–34). Hamlet's tale is clearly a tragedy; Aragorn's is clearly an epic. I believe that Frodo's journey falls into both categories. While *LotR* is a fantasy and, as such, may share some affinities with romance, the supernatural elements of the world of Middle-earth belong only to the Wizards, who are beings of another order. Every other element of this world, however foreign to our own, is explained as a natural phenomenon. While some might argue that Frodo's character falls more naturally into the fourth category, I would argue that in his role in the Shire, particularly before the quest, Frodo showed himself superior to his peers. He was learned, artistic, and in touch with the deeper realities of his world.

Frodo shares affinities with Aragorn in his role as epic hero: "A hero ventures forth from the world of common day into a region of supernatural wonder: fabulous forces are there encountered and a decisive victory is won: the hero comes back from his mysterious adventure with the power to bestow boons on his fellow man" (Campbell 30). Aragorn's entire adult life has been his venturing forth, culminating in his kingship and marriage at the end of the final book, with the restoration of order implied by the return of the King. Frodo's quest to destroy the Ring is his venturing; while his quest is to destroy something rather than to acquire something, the boon he brings back to Humankind is the gift of free will, unburdened by a world-dominating evil. According to Joseph Campbell:

> The composite hero of the monomyth is a personage of exceptional gifts. Frequently he is honored by his society, frequently unrecognized or disdained. He and/or the world in which he finds himself suffers from a symbolical deficiency. In fairy tales this may be as slight as the lack of a certain golden ring, whereas in apocalyptic vision the physical and spiritual life of the whole earth can be represented as fallen, or on the point of falling, into ruin [37].

Again, both Aragorn and Frodo fulfill these expectations. Each has exceptional abilities, according to his station in life, and his training.

Aragorn has lived a life of purposeful obscurity, but his heritage and potential future are well recognized in some circles. Frodo is one of the chief members of his society and is revered by others for his willing assumption of the burden of the Ring. Ironically, he falls into obscurity upon his return to the Shire, after he and Aragorn and the others have rescued their world from its spiritual decline. As the heroes of monomyth they achieve regeneration of their society and the result is "the unlocking and release again of the flow of life into the body of the world" (Campbell 38, 40), symbolized by the recovery of the white tree of Gondor and the glorious flowering of the Shire.

Just as Frodo shares with Aragorn characteristics of the epic and mythic hero, he shares with Hamlet characteristics of the tragic hero. In *Fools of Time*, Northrop Frye says that a tragic hero exhibits "a capacity for action or passion, for doing or suffering, which is above ordinary human experience" (4–5). Anyone who witnesses the tormented soliloquies of Hamlet or the phenomenal suffering of Frodo on the plains of Mordor would concur with this designation. Frye goes on to say that "The fact that an infinite energy is driving towards death in tragedy means that the impetus of tragedy is *sacrificial*" (5). The members of two entire households are dead by the end of *Hamlet* and the prince has sacrificed his life in the interest of righting a personal, familial, and societal wrong. Although Frodo remains alive at the end of *LotR*, he is no less a sacrifice. He is too deeply wounded to live at peace. He tells Sam: "'I tried to save the Shire, and it has been saved, but not for me. It must often be so, Sam, when things are in danger: some one has to give them up, lose them, so that others may keep them'" (6.9.1006). He will go into the West, to the undying lands, for a time, but eventually he will die, as all mortals must (*Letters* 411).

In Tolkien, as in *Hamlet*, hope and fate are operative forces. Throughout *LotR*, the characters continue to hope against all odds. Only those who are under the influence of the enemy—Denethor and, for a time, Théoden—give in to despair. Fate, too, is emphasized over and over throughout the work, a higher operative order masquerading as chance and free will, from the "chance" of the Ring coming to Bilbo and Frodo to the "chance" of Gollum falling into the abyss. The night before they leave Lórien, Galadriel comforts the company with the hope of providence: "Maybe the paths that you each shall tread are already laid before your feet, though you do not see them" (2.8.369). While Hamlet comes to believe in the operation of providence, his hope for personal survival dies. In the world of tragedy—focused as it is on the struggles of an individual life caught in the net of destiny—life may go on after the end of the play, but it will never be the same and it hardly seems to matter. In the world of epic, with its larger scope, there is always someone to continue the journey. Sam says, "Well, I'm back" when he returns from the Havens, vocalizing and embodying the hope of stable continued existence; life goes on, in essence as in fact (6.9.1008). If the impulse of tragedy is toward death, the impulse of epic is toward regeneration, whatever the consequences for the individual hero.

Works Cited

Bloom, Harold. *Shakespeare: The Invention of the Human.* New York: Riverhead, 1998.
Bondanella, Peter, and Mark Musa. "Introduction: An Essay on Machiavelli." In *The Portable Machiavelli.* New York: Penguin, 1979. 9–40.
Bradley, A. C. *Shakespearean Tragedy.* 3rd ed. New York: St. Martins, 1964.
Campbell, Joseph. *The Hero with a Thousand Faces.* New York: MJF, 1949.
Carpenter, Humphrey. *Tolkien: A Biography.* Boston: Houghton, 1977.
Croft, Janet. *War and the Works of J. R. R. Tolkien.* Westport, CT: Praeger, 2004.
Dickerson, Matthew. *Following Gandalf: Epic Battles and Moral Victory in* The Lord of the Rings. Grand Rapids, MI: Brazos, 2003.
Eliot, T. S. *The Sacred Wood: Essays on Poetry and Criticism.* London: Methuen, 1920.
Flieger, Verlyn. *A Question of Time: J. R.R. Tolkien's Road to Faerie.* Kent: Kent State University Press, 1997.
Frye, Northrop. *Anatomy of Criticism.* Princeton: Princeton University Press, 1957.
_____. *Fools of Time: Studies in Shakespearean Tragedy.* Toronto: University of Toronto Press, 1967.
Goddard, Harold. "Hamlet." In *Major Literary Characters: Hamlet.* Ed. Harold Bloom. New York: Chelsea, 1990. 95–121.
Johanyak, D. L. *Shakespeare's World.* Upper Saddle River, NJ: Prentice Hall, 2004.
Kocher, Paul. *Master of Middle-earth.* New York: Ballantine, 1972.
Machiavelli, Niccolo di Bernardo. "The Prince." In *The Portable Machiavelli.* New York: Penguin, 1979. 77–166.
Satin, Joseph. *Shakespeare and His Sources.* Boston: Houghton, 1966.
Sale, Roger. "Tolkien and Frodo Baggins. In *J. R. R. Tolkien.* Ed. Harold Bloom. Philadelphia: Chelsea, 2000. 27–63.
Shakespeare, William. *The Complete Works of William Shakespeare.* Ed. David Bevington. 5th ed. New York: Pearson, 2004.
Shippey, Thomas A. *J. R. R. Tolkien: Author of the Century.* Boston: Houghton, 2000.
_____. *The Road to Middle-earth.* Rev. and exp. ed. Boston: Houghton, 2003.
Summers, Joseph H. "The Dream of a Hero: *Hamlet.*" In *Major Literary Characters: Hamlet.* Ed. Harold Bloom. New York, Chelsea, 1990. 139–55.
Tolkien, J. R. R. *The Letters of J.R.R. Tolkien.* Ed. Humphrey Carpenter. Boston: Houghton, 2000.
_____. *The Lord of the Rings.* 2nd ed. Boston: Houghton, 1994.
_____. "On Fairy-Stories." In *The Tolkien Reader.* New York: Ballantine, 1966. 3–84.

How "All That Glisters Is Not Gold" Became "All That Is Gold Does Not Glitter"

Aragorn's Debt to Shakespeare

JUDITH J. KOLLMANN

Shortly after the hobbits meet Strider/Aragorn for the first time in The Prancing Pony, Butterbur the Innkeeper gives Frodo a letter Gandalf had written him. In it he finds a verse Bilbo had composed regarding Aragorn and which opens with the line "All that is gold does not glitter" (1.10.167). That Tolkien loved old folk sayings and used many in The Lord of the Rings (LotR) is well known. As Tom Shippey points out in J.R.R. Tolkien: Author of the Century (195, 203), such sayings are both common and ancient; perhaps it is only coincidence that both Shakespeare and Tolkien used a few of the same old saws. Still, Tolkien did little "by accident," and "All that is gold does not glitter" remains stubbornly evocative of Shakespeare's "All that glisters is not gold" (Merchant of Venice 2.7.65). Moreover, Tolkien has done something odd with it: he has inverted it. It is this inversion which is applied to Aragorn. No doubt Tolkien was amused at his joke; however, as Neil Isaacs has stressed,

> Oblique references, sardonic suggestions, and off-color incongruities are all part of the repertoire of Tolkien as humorist: but it is important to realize that no joke is present just for its own sake ... invariably there will be some overriding tonal or thematic significance to the humor [Isaacs 9–10].

Others have also noticed that Tolkien frequently rewrites Shakespeare. Tom Shippey observed that Tolkien rewrote a stanza from the concluding "Song" of *Love's Labour's Lost* (5.2.910–14), and attributes its composition to Bilbo (2.3.266); moreover, Sam's Cirith Ungol song

> ends, "I will not say the Day is done,/nor bid the Stars farewell." ... They ... repeat, but strongly contradict, a famous Shakespeare passage from *Anthony and Cleopatra,* in which Cleopatra says to her handmaiden, "Our bright day is done, / And we are for the dark" [*Author* 203].

Perhaps such sayings derive from common ancestors in ancient folk maxims; however, scholars have found several of these teasing allusions in *LotR,* and some of these are less elusive. In them Tolkien deliberately left enough of the original so that the reader is inevitably reminded of Shakespeare. Two well-known examples, both derived from *Macbeth,* occur: the first when Éowyn and Merry confront the Lord of the Nazgûl, and the second when Tolkien transformed the "walking" of "Great Birnam Wood" into the march to war of the Ents and Huorns.

Aragorn and Henry V

The line "All that is gold does not glitter" becomes a hint, a pointer inviting us to examine the possibility that Tolkien adapted Shakespeare more widely than simply borrowing a few sayings or motifs. Since the line specifically applies to Aragorn, the hint is that Aragorn himself might owe a debt to a Shakespearian character. And if one seeks a Shakespearian analogue to Strider/Aragorn, one character springs forcefully to mind: Prince Hal/Henry V of the *Henry* tetralogy (*Richard II* [*R2*], *1* and *2 Henry IV* [*1H4, 2H4*], and *Henry V* [*H5*]). In part, the similarity stems from a common literary ancestry in medieval romance, but also derives from a shared intellectual affiliation—a fascination with the concept of a sweeping history of kings embedded within a matrix of dynasty and destiny, and above all, a fascination with the qualities of kings that lead to monarchic greatness or to failure.

Others have dealt with sagas of kings. There were at least four works Tolkien had read containing evaluations of kingly qualities, monarchic successes and failures: the Old Testament (1 and 2 Samuel; 1 and 2 Kings); *Beowulf;* Snorri Sturluson's *Heimskringla Saga;* and Shakespeare's plays (notably, in addition to all the history plays, *Macbeth* and *King Lear,* although *Hamlet* also deals with these issues). Of these, the Old Testament was too religious for Tolkien's purposes; it evaluates monarchic greatness in terms of the degree to which the kings are faithful and obedient to God. Sturluson's *Saga* embraces Viking values, which are pragmatic rather than ideological. *Beowulf* has a greater tragic sense, but is narrow in its definition: a great king is one who protects his people, does not kill needlessly, and is generous in gift-giving. Only Shakespeare shares Tolkien's breadth and depth of perspective. And predictably, they came to different conclusions because Tolkien established a different historic context, and, while using Hal/Henry as a template for Strider/Aragorn, Tolkien created a completely different personality.

Both Shakespeare and Tolkien examined the leadership and temperament traits kings must have and what they must not be or do; they evaluated issues of princely power; and, finally, dealt with two conundrums peculiar to princes. The first of these is the question whether princes can afford personal authenticity; the second is the realization that there is a fundamental contradiction inherent in kingship: kings cannot afford to be human; yet, inevitably, they cannot escape their humanity. The greatest kings are those who somehow achieve balance between the office and the man. As far as the question of authenticity is concerned, Shakespeare seems to conclude that masks become part of the ceremony surrounding a king and are a necessary element of the "place, degree and form / Creating awe and fear in other men" (*H5* 4.1.244–45). Tolkien's implicit argument is that a king can be what he seems. As far as the issue of balance is concerned, Shakespeare and Tolkien created two kings in Henry V and Aragorn who are among a very few monarchs in English literature who achieve and maintain it throughout their reigns, but they achieve it in somewhat different ways.

Of course the two characters share a common literary ancestry in medieval romance and in fairy tale. Verlyn Flieger described Aragorn as "the traditional disguised hero, the rightful king ... who steps from the shadows into the limelight when his moment comes.... He is buried in obscurity until the moment comes for him to step forward and announce himself by word or deed" (Flieger 43, 45). This description applies equally well to Hal: when we first meet each character, he is disguised; each is heir to a kingdom; each steps forward and unmasks himself; each achieves his kingdom and princess. That is the generalized formula; but in the specific applications of these elements there are a number of similarities coupled with significant differences that are remarkably similar to Tolkien's methods when he dealt with other Shakespearian allusions. In this case Aragorn appears to be a careful inversion of Hal's less desirable traits. The first line of Aragorn's poem indicates the key difference: the ambiguity of Hal's character versus the clarity of Aragorn's. "All that is gold does not glitter" immediately implies disguise, for gold that does not shine has to be hidden in some way; nevertheless, it remains gold, as does Aragorn. However, the line is also an allusion to Hal's difficult monologue at the end of act I, scene ii of *1H4* because it contains an implicit paraphrase of a major metaphor in Hal's speech:

> I know you all, and will awhile uphold
> The unyoked humor of your idleness:
> *Yet herein will I imitate the sun,*
> *Who doth permit the base contagious clouds*
> *To smother up his beauty from the world,*
> *That when he please again to be himself,*
> *Being wanted he may be more wondered at*
> *By breaking through the foul and ugly mists*
> *Of vapors that did seem to strangle him.*
> ...
> So, when this loose behavior I throw off
> And pay the debt I never promisèd,
> By how much better than my word I am,
> By so much shall I falsify men's hopes;
> *And like bright metal on a sullen ground,*
> *My reformation, glitt'ring o'er my fault,*
> Shall show more goodly and attract more eyes
> Than that which hath no foil to set it off
> [*1H4* 1.2.189–209; italics mine].

Hal uses two pieces of figurative language; the first is a personification, the second a simile. The personification is that of the sun, a golden object, which allows himself to be covered, or disguised, by that which is dull and ugly. In the simile, Hal compares his reformation to "bright metal on a sullen ground ... glitt'ring." Hal begins by implying that he is as the sun, a magnificent golden object, deliberately obscured, but suddenly springing forth to bring light and life to his people. This is a version of "all that is gold does not glitter." However, by the end of the speech he is using more ambiguous language about himself: "Shall I falsify men's hopes." He next uses a simile that compares his reformation to "bright metal on a sullen ground ... glitt'ring" that inevitably reminds the reader of "all that glitters is not gold" since the variety of "bright metal" is not specified; it merely lies on "sullen ground." Shakespeare suggests, therefore, that all that glitters in Hal is not gold; something in him "falsifies." As Ellen Caldwell maintains,

> In fact, what Hal promises seems to contradict authentic reformation. The "loose behavior" is a ruse to be thrown off. He accepts no culpability for his actions, though he does so later in well-crafted public speeches to his father (3.2) and the representatives of the Percies' army (5.1). Hal's reformation will glitter o'er his fault, not erasing or atoning for the fault, but simply covering it with the pretense of yet another act. It's a work of theater, rather than of authentic reform [n.p.].

The falsification becomes more apparent when one examines the ways in which the two characters use disguise. When we meet each character, he is disguised; each bears a familiar, common name: "Hal" and "Strider"; and each has made himself peripheral to his greater society. Hal's is not a physical disguise, but a behavioral mask or image. Although he is the Prince of Wales, he does not attend to any heir-apparent duties unless specifically summoned by his father. Instead, he hobnobs with commoners at inns, apparently seeking only amusement. Aragorn's disguise is physical, extending not only to his clothes but to his face, so he bears the marks of his disguise on his body. Whereas "Hal" is a diminutive form of Henry (one which implies a trivialization of person), "Strider" is explicitly descriptive, suggesting strenuous, purposeful activity. He is also called a Ranger, a wanderer who perhaps has peacekeeping or exploratory functions. Distrusted by the Bree folk who look down upon him, he is a figure of cloaked potentiality whose appearance emits ambiguous signals: he is "strange-looking"; his cloak is of good quality, but "travel-stained," and his "high boots" are made "of supple leather that fitted him well, but had seen much wear and were now caked with mud" (1.9.153). He listens to, and watches, the hobbits "intently"; his face is "overshadowed"; yet he manifests signs of comfort, and therefore the possibility of fellowship, with his tall tankard on the table before him, and his long-stemmed pipe. However, this initial ambiguity, once resolved, also dissolves the issue. Aragorn will always be trustworthy; what he says he will always mean.

Each character has a poetic description applied to him—Hal's monologue in *1H4* (quoted above) and Aragorn's poem. In each case, the verse serves as descriptor of the character's fundamental self. Hal's speech presents us with the essential ambiguity of his character, raising the question whether a prince can possess and manifest personal authenticity, or whether he must always present images or masks to his world. The difficulty with Hal is that, whether he is prince or king, we can never be quite sure of him. He accomplishes great deeds and administers impartial justice. But these, too, might be "a work of theater" as he manipulates those around him.

Aragorn's poem was, as the reader learns at the Council of Elrond, composed for him by Bilbo, so from the start Tolkien removes the egocentricity that pervades Hal's monologue:

> All that is gold does not glitter,
>   Not all those who wander are lost;
> The old that is strong does not wither,
>   Deep roots are not reached by the frost.
> From the ashes a fire shall be woken,
>   A light from the shadows shall spring;

Renewed shall be blade that was broken,
The crownless again shall be king [1.10.167].

Hal's monologue emphasizes what he seems to be, and, perhaps, that he will merely move from mask to mask; Aragorn's explains what he is: the thesis statement of the poem as a whole is that he is, unquestionably, gold. The initial four lines also point out that he is not lost, and he is strong, enduring, and even thriving. The second quatrain becomes a prophecy, applying two metaphors to him: he will become fire and light for his people (would it be reaching to suggest there is an additional allusion to Hal's speech here?) and concludes with the promise that he will indeed become king. The complete poem stresses his integrity, even as it simultaneously embraces his present, in his wandering; his past, in his already-lengthy lifespan and in his lineage; and his future as reviver and king of his people.

Princes and Power

Shakespeare and Tolkien were also both deeply concerned with princely power—the right to it, the usurpation of it, its right and its wrong uses, and the effect of power upon its wielder. Shakespeare returned to this again and again, but nowhere with greater sustained intensity than in the *Henry* series. Richard, in *R2*, has become king by the accepted mode—dynastic inheritance. His family line goes back through an unbroken chain of eldest sons to Henry II Plantagenet, whose dynasty ascended the throne in 1154; further, Richard is a descendant (via Henry II's mother) of William the Conqueror. Beyond this, however, Richard is the exemplar of everything a monarch should not be: impulsive and arbitrary, he chooses his friends based entirely on his personal preferences. Consequently he listens to poor counsel and ignores sound advice; as a result he was probably involved in the murder of his uncle, the Duke of York, and is persuaded to plunder the Duchy of Lancaster, which is in his care during the exile of the heir, Henry of Bolingbroke.[1] These poor decisions result in his abdication and, eventually, murder. Henry IV, on the other hand, has excellent leadership qualities, but, as the usurper of the throne, sits shakily upon it. The result, in *1H4* and *2H4*, is that his reign is constantly threatened by rebellion. *Henry V* is the story of a man who is the second of his family to rule—not a lengthy precedent, but better than being the first. Moreover, he is also (via the House of Lancaster) a lineal descendant of Henry II.

To a peaceful accession he adds exemplary leadership abilities which are demonstrated by the act of removing the mask of the indolent prince and assuming that of the responsible king even as he lays the foundations for his reign. This occurs immediately prior to his coronation and immediately following it in a sequence of four actions. First, he secures his family by assuring his brothers of their safety: "Brothers, you mix your sadness with some fear. / This is the English, not the Turkish court; / Not Amurath an Amurath succeeds, / But Harry Harry" (*2H4* 5.2.46–49). Second, he places impersonal justice on a firm footing when he turns to the Lord Chief Justice, who at some point in Prince Hal's dissolute career had had him incarcerated and who now expects to lose his position. Instead, Henry reconfirms him in his office and adds:

> You shall be as a father to my youth.
> My voice shall sound as you do prompt mine ear,
> And I will stoop and humble my intents
> To your well-practiced wise directions [5.2.118–21].

Third, he summons parliament in order to choose his council from among the great Lords, thereby establishing sound and methodical government:

> Now call we our high court of Parliament.
> And let us choose such limbs of noble counsel
> That the great body of our state may go
> In equal ranks with the best-governed nation [5.2.134–37].

His fourth action, which follows his coronation, is to reject Falstaff and thereby to banish dissipation and levity from his court: "I know thee not, old man. Fall to thy prayers. / How ill white hairs becomes a fool and jester!" (5.5.47–48). He may seem to be a moral prig, but one must put this into its historic context: Richard was no paragon, and Henry IV's reign was turbulent because he had been an opportunist who seized power and because he had arranged for Richard's murder. To his credit, Prince Hal always supports his father (saving Henry's life at the Battle of Shrewsbury) and, as his monologue addressed to his father's crown (that "troublesome a bedfellow" [4.5.22]) demonstrates, he is not eager for power, although he will not shirk the responsibility when it comes.

Nevertheless, Henry V is aware that he is benefiting by means of his father's sins, and is assailed by guilt on the morning of the Battle of Agincourt, fearing that God will demonstrate His displeasure in the House of Lancaster by destroying Henry and his army on the field of battle:

> Not to-day, O Lord,
> Oh, not to-day, think not upon the fault
> My father made in compassing the crown!

He describes the penance he has already paid in lieu of his father:

> I Richard's body have interrèd new;
> And on it have bestowed more contrite tears
> Than from it issued forcèd drops of blood.
> Five hundred poor I have in yearly pay
> Who twice a day their withered hands hold up
> Toward heaven, to pardon blood; and I have built
> Two chantries, where the sad and solemn priests
> Sing still for Richard's soul. More will I do... [*H5* 4.1.290–300].

Aragorn, son of Arathorn, on the other hand, descends directly from Elendil through thirty-nine generations extending over 2,933 years (App.A.1014); nor has any member of his house ever seized a throne. Like Henry V, however, Aragorn forbears from grasping any kingly power until he is offered it. He first declares his true identity publicly to Éomer and the Rohirrim on the Plains of Rohan: "Aragorn threw back his cloak. The elven-sheath glittered as he grasped it, and the bright blade of Andúril shone like a sudden flame as he swept it out. 'Elendil!' he cried. 'I am Aragorn son of Arathorn, and am called Elessar, the Elfstone, Dúnadan, the heir of Isildur Elendil's son of Gondor'" (3.2.423). However, the first acknowledgment of his right to rule comes from Gandalf when Gandalf asks him "to take the Orthanc-stone and guard it" (3.2.580). Once the offer is made, Aragorn is quick to assert who he is and his right to this symbol of kingly power:

> "Dangerous indeed, but not to all," said Aragorn. "There is one who may claim it by right. For this assuredly is the *palantír* of Orthanc from the treasury of Elendil, set here by the Kings of Gondor. Now my hour draws near. I will take it."
> Gandalf looked at Aragorn, and then, to the surprise of the others, he lifted the covered stone, and bowed as he presented it.
> "Receive it, lord!" he said: "in earnest of other things that shall be given back. But if I may counsel you in the use of your own, do not use it—yet! Be wary!"
> "When have I been hasty or unwary, who have waited and prepared for so many long years?" said Aragorn.
> "Never yet. Do not then stumble at the end of the road" [3.2.580].

Tolkien was as fascinated with the artifacts symbolic of majesty as was Shakespeare, and in this passage he created a deliberate contrast in action between Hal and Aragorn. When Hal believes is father is dead, he addresses the crown in terms that make clear he knows what responsibilities of its wearer are symbolized by it. And then he reaches out and takes it. There are no witnesses. There is nothing wrong with his action but it underscores Hal's character: he takes it; he does not wait for someone to give it to him. Aragorn knows what the *palantír* is; he claims it verbally, stating "I will take it," but he makes no motion to do so. And Gandalf (who will later place the crown on Aragorn's head—after Aragorn has also requested that Frodo carry the crown to Gandalf) formally presents the Stone to its owner. The implication is that the symbols of majesty belong not only to the king but also to the greater community. The House of Lancaster takes, even before acknowledgment of the right to do so is made; Aragorn will always wait for the acknowledgment. The degree of opportunism is radically different. One consequence is that Aragorn is not conflicted as is Hal, for Aragorn's right to rule and his willingness to do so thus become unquestionable; he has worked single-mindedly to this end for decades, and the prospect of the crown will not trouble his sleep.

Aragorn not only proclaims his identity in this passage but, although he listens to Gandalf's counsel, he does something he has never done before: he contravenes the advice, and, following his own judgment, looks into the *palantír*, declares himself to Sauron and wrestles control of it from his enemy. Aragorn has begun to take initiative, and thereby take power. When the next morning he informs Legolas and Gimli that he has looked into the stone, Gimli overreaches himself, becoming critical of Aragorn as well as inquisitive:

> "You have looked in that accursed stone of wizardry!" exclaimed Gimli with fear and astonishment in his face. "Did you say aught to—him? Even Gandalf feared that encounter."
> "You forget to whom you speak" said Aragorn sternly, and his eyes glinted. "Did I not openly proclaim my title before the doors of Edoras?
> "What do you fear that I should say to him? ... Nay, my friends, I am the lawful master of the Stone, and I had both the right and the strength to use it, or so I judged. The right cannot be doubted. The strength was enough—barely" [5.2.763].

These three passages mark the beginning of Aragorn's transition into kingly behavior: first, he unmasks himself by word and gesture to his allies and to his enemy; second, he begins to make decisions independent of his trusted counselors; and third, he speaks sharply to Gimli for criticizing him. On each occasion he adopts an imperious manner and his language is elevated accordingly. But then he descends again to equality, friendship, and colloquial speech. He is not yet King in Gondor.

Even when he is invited after the Battle of the Pelennor Fields to

enter Gondor and claim his throne, he chooses not to do so, inform-
ing Prince Imrahil: "I fear that if I enter it unbidden, then doubt and
debate may arise, which should not be while this war is fought. I will
not enter in, nor make any claim, until it be seen whether we or Mordor will prevail" (5.8.843). When he does go into the City, it is as a
healer, simply "one cloaked in grey" (5.8.844) even though he is aware
at this point that Denethor is dead and the strife he feared will not take
place. He heals, and then, although all Gondor has become aware that
"'The King is come again indeed!' ... he cast his cloak about him, and
slipped out of the City.... And in the morning the banner of Dol Amroth
... floated from the Tower, and men looked up and wondered if the coming of the King had been but a dream" (5.8.853). Although Aragorn
summons the princes of Gondor and Rohan to a council in the morning, the meeting takes place in his tent and not in the Citadel of Minas
Tirith.

Authenticity and Unmasking

By the conclusion of *LotR*, Aragorn is as perfect as a human being
can be. And by the conclusion of *H5*, so is Henry. In Aragorn, Tolkien
has eliminated Hal's calculating, ambiguous quality along with Hal's
love-hate attitude toward the crown, but perhaps the most significant
element that he revised was the effect of the disguise upon the disguised. Both characters assume disguises that make them seem less and
other than what they truly are—"all that is gold does not glitter." Both
consort with and are comfortable among common men; Aragorn enjoys
a tall tankard and a good pipe in The Prancing Pony, while Hal's best
times are in The Boar's Head with Falstaff. But when Hal becomes King
Henry V he leaves this mask of the fun-loving prince behind him along
with his sobriquet of Prince Hal. The only element of this experience
that he will take with him into kingship is his ability to communicate
with the common man.

The issue of the authenticity of the prince is central to *1H4* and
2H4, where it is manifested both in Hal's assumption of his disguise of
his "true" character and his awareness of the uses to which he puts it,
and in assessing his character the reader is left with a few doubts: to
what degree is this man sincere? When, if ever, does one see the real
person? One can never be sure. What we do know is that deception runs
in the family.

Henry Bolingbroke maintains, in *R2,* that he has returned from
exile only to take back the lands of his dukedom that have been plun-
dered by Richard and his friends; but he forces Richard to surrender.

When Richard offers to abdicate, he does not refuse, and finally he arranges for Richard's murder. At the Battle of Shrewsbury he has a number of his men go into battle wearing his coat of arms—another form of disguise—which is both clever and ruthless, and is a useful ploy to safeguard himself. As Bevington notes, "as usual in Shakespeare, the perspective seems many-sided and delicately balanced" (737), and concludes that Shakespeare tacitly "acknowledg[es] ... a special kind of morality pertaining to kingship" (737).

Aragorn, on the other hand, takes "Strider" with him; from the beginning he has two names, two selves, two manners: one low, the other high. But instead of becoming an issue of image, or of a divided personality, the disguise becomes simply two facets of the same person. Tolkien uses it to promote greater moral integrity in, and unity of, Aragorn's character, for Tolkien would never have accepted the concept of "a special kind of morality pertaining to kingship." Rather, as Aragorn says to Éomer, "Good and ill have not changed since yesteryear; nor are they one thing among Elves and Dwarves and another among Men. It is a man's part to discern them" (3.2.428). We never, once past our introduction to Strider, doubt his sincerity or his integrity, and Aragorn himself fuses his personality into one seamless fabric.

It is interesting to see how Tolkien accomplishes this. Gandalf, in a conversation with Frodo, alludes to Aragorn long before Frodo meets him. But when Frodo first sees Aragorn in the Prancing Pony, he asks Butterbur who the stranger is, and therefore it is Butterbur who gives him a name: "he is one of the wandering folk—Rangers we call them.... What his right name is I've never heard: but he's known round here as Strider. Goes about at a great pace on his long shanks" (1.9.153), and when Frodo approaches him he introduces himself: "I am called Strider" (ibid.), emphasizing that, like "Ranger," "Strider" is a descriptive appellation that, while accepted by him, has been bestowed upon him by others. It is Gandalf, in his letter to Frodo, who writes a reference for Aragorn as "a friend of mine ... a Man, lean, dark, tall, by some called Strider." In his second postscript Gandalf adds, "Make sure it is the real Strider. His true name is Aragorn" (1.10.166–67). There is an interesting modulation in these passages: from "by some called Strider" to "the real Strider" and finally to "his true name is Aragorn." The name "Strider" may have been given by others, but it is real; still, he has a true name. From this point until the Field of Cormallen in *The Return of the King*, the hobbits call Aragorn "Strider" exclusively. The only exception is Bilbo, who always calls him "The Dúnadan." Gandalf and most of the other characters call him Aragorn. Even Frodo, who knows Aragorn's true identity, continues to use "Strider," for Strider is, indeed, their friend and guide. When Aragorn declares himself to the Rohirrim, however, he announces himself by all his names except two: the first, Strider, and the last, Telcontar. When he is reunited with Pippin and Merry at the gates of Orthanc and chooses to have lunch with the hobbits rather than with "the great ones," Aragorn wraps himself in his elvish cloak, thus covering his chain mail, lights his pipe, looking much as he did at The Prancing Pony, and Pippin says "Look! ... Strider the Ranger has come back!"

> "He has never been away," said Aragorn. "I am Strider and Dúnadan too, and I belong both to Gondor and the north" [3.9. 549].

And, finally, when he is reunited with Pippin in Gondor after the Battle of Pelennor Fields, Pippin speaks up again:

> "Strider! How splendid! Do you know, I guessed it was you in the black ships. But they were all shouting *corsairs* and wouldn't listen to me. How did you do it?"
> Aragorn laughed, and took the hobbit by the hand. "Well met indeed!" he said. "But there is not time yet for travelers' tales."
> But Imrahil said to Éomer: "Is it thus that we speak to our kings? Yet maybe he will wear his crown in some other name!"
> And Aragorn hearing him, turned and said: "Verily, for in the high tongue of old I am *Elessar*, the Elfstone, and *Envinyatar*, the Renewer": and he lifted from his breast the green stone that lay there. "But Strider shall be the name of my house, if that be ever established. In the high tongue it will not sound so ill, and *Telcontar* I will be and all the heirs of my body" [5.8.845].

Aragorn no longer wears a disguise, not only because he has proclaimed himself openly, but because the disguise has ceased to be a mask: it has been assumed into the person of Aragorn. The first name has indeed become the last, and the lowest has been united to the highest. Thus his several names reflect the integration of self; they are not a series of images behind which a real person might, or might not, exist.

When Hal becomes king he leaves "Hal" behind; there is, however, another option for a name, one that lies between the too-common "Hal" and the formality of "Henry," and that is "Harry," the name his father uses for him. While Hal will turn away from the thieves and will no longer consort with common folk of questionable ethics, he nevertheless takes a little of his experience among the folk into his kingship: he can speak with them, he can listen to them, and he can understand them. He will never again consort with them in the inns of England, but he will bring them together into one united "band of brothers" that will include not only Englishmen but also Scots, Welsh, and Irish men, and when he walks among them unrecognized on the night before Agincourt he is able to give them "a little touch of Harry in the night" (4.0.47). He banters with his knights, debates the ethics of wars and kings with his soldiers, and bolsters the morale of his generals. He can communicate across all ranks. At the same time, as the audience discovers, this, too, is a mask, but it is one which his officers recognize and approve, for it disguises fears that he cannot allow his men to glimpse. Instead, his rhetoric embraces them and lifts them up as brothers:

> We few, we happy few, we band of brothers.
> For he today that sheds his blood with me
> Shall be my brother; be he ne'er so vile,
> This day shall gentle his condition [4.3.60–63].

Henry, too, has found his métier.

War and Politics

Much has been written concerning Hal's integrity, or the lack of it; opinions vary across the spectrum because Hal's "historic" world is more complex than Aragorn's Middle-earth. Each Shakespearian character is a compound of traits and motives that result in a rich, if frustrating, ambiguity that is lacking in Tolkien's characters, who are more polarized along an axis of good and evil: there are heroes and villains in Middle-earth, whereas there are few real villains in the Henry tetralogy and (perhaps), at the end, one traditionally heroic figure in Henry V. In the tetralogy every major character is pursuing his own concept of the Good, although most of them equate "good" with their personal agendas—Hotspur with his honor; Falstaff with his life, wealth and comfort; the great lords with their power. Insofar as there is any selfless desire for right rule it rests in the hands of two persons: the Lord Chief Justice, who is the most altruistic character in the plays, and with Henry V (and this is not to say that Henry's motives are not compounded with self-interest as well). Still, these two are the best individuals in a flawed world. Insofar as he may, Hal/Henry possesses integrity: given the lawlessness of Richard and his father, a king professing moral rectitude is undoubtedly wise.

Interestingly, Aragorn and Henry share political scope of vision. Aragorn states he "belongs to Gondor and the North." He intends to unify what was split long ago into two kingdoms and subsequently fragmented further into small cultures or countries into one united kingdom. Similarly, in *H5* Henry perceives the unification of the British Isles into one country, and desires to annex France into the union (as it once nearly was). Neither Hal's nor Aragorn's view is one of empire-building, but rather that geographic units having historic and cultural affinities with one another should be joined. These perspectives resonate more in accord with the vision of Alfred the Great, the first medieval king to conceive of a unified England, than with the Caesars.

However, before each hero can unify kingdoms, he must win a war. For Henry, it is a war to conquer France, a war that he must start, and therefore one he must justify. The opening two scenes of *H5* establish exactly that. In the first the audience discovers, as the Archbishop of Canterbury and his assistant are on their way to the King's Council, that the Church is eager to deflect Henry's attention from the wealth of the Church, and therefore will support turning his attention to a war with France. In the second, we discover that the current French monarchy bases its right to rule on Salic Law (that only males can inherit the throne); however, the churchmen argue that, via his maternal line, Henry has a better claim, and precedent demonstrates that in the past the French acknowledged inheritance through the female line. Henry and his Council then meet with the French delegation, which gives him the Dauphin's insulting gift of tennis balls. Thus, if there is a villain, it is the Catholic Church; the king has been provided with legal grounds for starting the war, and, finally, a French insult has been added to the injury of having been by-passed for the French crown in the first place. One must justify an act of aggression with every possible argument. Henry leads a small army to France, and after a moderately successful summer season he is intercepted by the French as his army is marching to winter quarters. Outnumbered five to one, the English had no hope of winning the Battle of Agincourt, but they did. Shakespeare did not describe Henry's brilliant military tactics; instead, the English seem to win because they have greater valor and by a miracle of God. As Henry says, "O God, thy arm was here! / And not to us, but to thy arm alone, / Ascribe we all" (4.8.106–8). The victory at Agincourt becomes a eucatastrophe.

As Sauron made the first act of aggression in *LotR*, Aragorn's councilors after the Battle of the Pelennor Fields do not have to worry about justifying their actions; thus, their motives lack self-seeking. In order to protect Middle-earth, their best strategy is to draw Sauron's attention away from the interior of Mordor and the Ring-bearer. Beyond justification, however, the two battles, of Agincourt and the Black Gate, are very similar: both Henry's and Aragorn's armies are vastly outnumbered, and neither army ought to have a chance of winning; yet they do. Additionally, both *H5* and *The Return of the King* emphasize an extended period of rejoicing after the battles. Henry engages in badinage with his men, and when Fluellen the Welshman notes that Henry is not shy of wearing a leek in his cap "on Saint Tavy's Day" Henry affirms this, saying "I wear it for a memorable honor, / For I am Welsh, you know, good countryman" (4.7.103–4). Subsequently, when he meets the French royalty, Henry woos and wins the Princess Katharine's consent to their marriage. During this charming scene, Henry first imitates courtly love tradition, then abandons it because he is "such a plain king that thou wouldst think I had sold my farm to buy my crown" (5.2.126– 28). However, he speaks better French than Katharine does English, and employs just the right touch of flattery co-mingled with passion: "You have witchcraft in your lips, Kate. There is more eloquence in a sugar touch of them than in the tongues of the French council" (5.2.278–80). Henry shifts his masks swiftly, but he has also grown comfortable in his role as king, perhaps because he is convinced that his victory at Agincourt is proof that God has confirmed the legitimacy of his reign. He now wears ceremony easily, with authority over it, recognizing that "nice customs curtsy to great kings.... We are the makers of manners, Kate; and the liberty that follows our places stops the mouth of all find-faults" (5.2.271–75). Henry has found his balance; the man is comfortable as king.

Aragorn has always possessed balance. He is crowned, hailed as "The King Elessar," and enters Minas Tirith for the first time as its monarch. Like Henry, he takes command, establishing the foundations of his reign by dispensing justice, first with mercy to the men who served Sauron—the Easterlings, the people of Harad, the slaves of Mordor, and, second, with honor, to Beregond, the Guard of the Citadel; then he secures his ally, Éomer, saying, in words that echo Henry's to Fluellen: "'Between us there can be no word of giving or taking, nor of reward; for we are brethren'" (4.5.948). And he marries his princess, Arwen, who had been wooed—and won—many years ago.

Henry and Aragorn seem to be ultimate expressions of the fairy tale hero, and one expects both Shakespeare and Tolkien to write the traditional statement at the end of their stories: "and they lived happily ever after." *Henry V* reminds the audience that Henry died in war and all his achievements were frittered away:

> Small time, but in that small most greatly lived
>   This star of England. Fortune made his sword,
> By which the world's best garden he achieved,
>   And of it left his son imperial lord.
> ...
> Whose state so many had the managing,
>   That they lost France and made his England bleed [Epilogue 5–12].

Predictably, Tolkien revises this. Aragorn reigns for a long time ("six score years" [App.A.1037]). He, too, has a son, Eldarion, but he "is a man full-ripe for kingship," and Aragorn dies, not by violence but because he has "the grace to go at my will, and give back the gift" (ibid.). Shakespeare does not mention Katharine in his Epilogue, but Tolkien makes Arwen's grief at her loss a poignant moment. For her, a hundred and twenty years is too short. She is still vibrant, and her death of grief for losses of husband, father, and the High Elves of Lothlórien is perhaps the most bitter moment in *LotR*. So Tolkien and Shakespeare end in the same place: with the affirmation of the brevity of life and the inevitable loss of everything.

Conclusion

Tolkien was a very deliberate and thoughtful writer, very familiar with Shakespeare, and did nothing by accident. This is most obvious when we consider Aragorn as a response to Henry V.

Aragorn has many points in common with Hal and yet these have often been so completely inverted that one cannot help but consider them to be deliberate. Hal is completely human; initially, at least, possessing conflicting emotions or rather undesirable character traits. He wants to be king and yet feels it an imposition, a payment of a "debt I never promised"; he is calculating, manipulative, probably callow; when he becomes king he is guilt-ridden by the means through which he gained his position; and finally, although he becomes a hero-king who does achieve harmony between his person and his office, we never do know how much of what we see is the genuine man or merely a series of performances.

Aragorn, on the other hand, becomes a perfect man and hero: he has few internal divisions and no ambiguities; and although in the earlier sections of the story he occasionally demonstrates a reluctance to lead, or a lack of confidence in his own decisions, or advises caution before venturing into the unknown, these seeming insecurities or weaknesses become paradoxically commendable as the reader discovers their sources lie in Aragorn's wisdom, humility, and caution, for subsequent events establish he possesses courage without brashness and pride without hubris. The most significant change is that Tolkien simplified Hal's character, straightening out the ambiguities, establishing the integrity of the character, so that Aragorn, without the loss of his humanity, becomes, in Joseph Campbell's terms, the perfect hero-king, hero-lover, and the redeemer (in a secular sense) of his people. In his last action, he accomplishes what Campbell has called the final act of the true hero: "reconciliation with the grave" (356). And, in all of this, Tolkien modernized him.

Shakespeare had taken a medieval king and transformed him into a Renaissance prince, thereby modernizing him. It was here that Tolkien found an excellent paradigm for the creation of a hero who is also founded on medieval motifs—but is simultaneously Númenorean. As Samwise says of Faramir, another of Tolkien's most heroic characters, one can discern the "air of Númenor" in Aragorn's nature and his quality is of "the very highest" (4.5.667). In the "Akallabêth: the Downfall of Númenor," Tolkien identifies Númenor with "Atalantë" (*Silmarillion* 318). Aragorn is the descendant, therefore, of the most perfect human beings and of Middle-earth's (and, as Atlantis, our world's) first, and most highly advanced human civilization. There could be no civilization in which people attained greater perfection, and that must mean (among other things) that those Númenóreans who chose to do so, could achieve not only great art and technology but also personal maturity and wholeness. Interestingly, Joseph Campbell observes that "The modern hero-deed must be that of questing to bring to light again the lost Atlantis of the co-ordinated soul" (388). It is at this point that the alpha (Númenor/Atlantis) and the omega (Middle-earth/our world) meet: Aragorn embodies the yearning of the modern psyche for the wholeness of the human being, the synthesis of all the masks, the possibility "for men and women to come to full human maturity through the condition of contemporary life" (Campbell 388). Aragorn achieves this by setting aside his own agenda in the interest of his world. No doubt this seems far-fetched; however, it is rooted in the reality of human behavior: times of extreme crisis bring out the finest (as well as the worst) in humanity. In recent events we have witnessed the behavior of those who loot, rape and destroy subsequent to a catastrophe; we have also observed those who risk themselves to save others. These last are nobly heroic, in Aragorn's manner, and undoubtedly Tolkien witnessed many cases of selfless heroism during World War I. There were uncounted cases of it during the Blitz as well. Notable examples include putting out bombing fires at St. Paul's Cathedral by old men and boys; the saving of the stained glass windows of York Minster by farmers who hid the dismantled glass, packed in barrels, on their farms; and, in London, the rescue of strangers trying to walk home in blackout and fog by residents who reached out of their homes and pulled them to safety. The reward for Aragorn's altruism is the achievement of his greatest hopes. And he has become one of Tolkien's postmodern heroes, paradoxically modern because he is Númenorean and because he offers hope. After all, his disguise-name while growing up in Rivendell was "Estel, that is 'Hope'" (App.A.1032).

Notes

1. Shakespeare clearly valued sound counsel as highly among his characters as Tolkien did among his (see Kollmann).

Works Cited

Bevington, David. "The Life of King Henry the Fifth." In *The Complete Works of Shakespeare.* Ed. Hardin Craig and David Bevington. Rev. ed. Glenview, IL: Scott, 1973. 736–38.

Caldwell, Ellen. "'Banish All the Wor(l)d': Falstaff's Iconoclastic Threat to Kingship in *1 Henry IV*." Fortieth International Congress on Medieval Studies. Kalamazoo: Western Michigan University, May 6, 2005.

Campbell, Joseph. *The Hero with A Thousand Faces.* 2nd ed. Princeton: Princeton University Press, 1968.

Clark, George. "J.R.R. Tolkien and the True Hero." In *J.R.R. Tolkien and His Literary Resonances.* Ed. George Clark and Daniel Timmons. Westport, CT: Greenwood Press, 2000. 39–52.

Flieger, Verlyn. "Frodo and Aragorn: The Concept of the Hero." In *Tolkien: New Critical Perspectives.* Ed. Neil D. Isaacs and Rose A. Zimbardo. Lexington: University Press of Kentucky, 1981. 40–62.

Isaacs, Neil. "On the Possibilities of Writing Tolkien Criticism." In *Tolkien and the Critics.* Ed. Neil D. Isaacs and Rose A. Zimbardo. South Bend, IN: University of Notre Dame Press, 1968. 1–11.

Kollmann, Judith. "Elisions and Ellipses: Counsel and Council in Tolkien's and Jackson's *The Lord of the Rings.*" In *Tolkien on Film: Essays on Peter Jackson's The Lord of the Rings.* Ed. Janet Brennan Croft. Altadena, CA: Mythopoeic, 2004. 149–74.

Shakespeare, William. *The Complete Works of William Shakespeare.* Ed. David Bevington. 5th ed. New York: Pearson, 2004.

Shippey, Thomas A. *J.R.R. Tolkien: Author of the Century.* Boston: Houghton, 2000.

Tolkien. J.R.R. *The Lord of the Rings.* 2nd ed. Boston: Houghton, 1994.

___. *The Silmarillion.* New York: Ballantine, 1977.

"The Shadow of Succession"

Shakespeare, Tolkien, and the
Conception of History

ANNALISA CASTALDO

There is absolutely no doubt that the creation of Middle-earth was influenced by J.R.R. Tolkien's work as a medieval scholar. Tolkien was an Oxford-trained linguist of rare ability, and his work on *Beowulf* and *Sir Gawain and the Green Knight* remains relevant today. His letters reveal his fascination not just with works from England's past, but those of Norway and Finland as well. To cite just one example of how directly Tolkien borrowed from his medieval sources, Bilbo's stealing of Smaug's cup replicates in many ways the cup stealing incident in *Beowulf*, in which a dragon guarding a hoard of gold and jewels is roused to fury by a thief.

> In the grave on the hill a hoard it guarded,
> in the stone-barrow steep. A strait path reached it,
> unknown to mortals. Some man, however,
> came by chance that cave within
> to the heathen hoard. In hand he took
> a golden goblet, nor gave he it back,
> stole with it away, while the watcher slept [2212–2217].

The parallels to Bilbo's adventure are so close it is clear that Tolkien had the passage in mind as he wrote.

But what of Shakespeare? It is much less obvious what influence, if any, Shakespeare had on Tolkien's imagination as he created *The Lord of the Rings* (*LotR*). Humphrey Carpenter's biography cites only two references to Shakespeare by Tolkien, both negative (30, 45), which strongly suggests that Tolkien deliberately rejected Shakespeare and the version of magic and fairies in plays like *Macbeth* and *A Midsummer*

Night's Dream. And yet, in England at the beginning of the twentieth century, there was no more highly regarded literary figure than Shakespeare. Even those artists who at least partially rejected Shakespeare, like Tolkien and George Bernard Shaw, had to grapple with his enormous legacy. It is possible to see traces of the plays in Tolkien's work, and in particular, Shakespeare's conception of the history play influenced and modeled a way of presenting history that Tolkien could have found in few other places. Neither the medieval myths nor the early 20th century conception of history suited the structure of the story that Tolkien wanted to tell; Shakespeare's history plays, however, did.

This is not to suggest that the few direct correlations between Shakespeare's plays and *LotR* are what matter; any such connections are minor and end up demonstrating how great writers all use certain themes and motifs, rather than Tolkien's direct reference to Shakespeare. For example, as Frodo and Sam climb the stairs of Cirith Ungol, Sam gains heart by looking beyond present and even future dangers, to the moment when their completed adventures will be "put into words, you know, told by the fireside.... And people will say: 'Let's hear about Frodo and the Ring!'" (4.8.697). This is the same way Henry V rallies his small army in the face of overwhelming odds:

> This story shall the good man teach his son;
> And Crispin Crispian shall ne'er go by,
> From this day to the ending of the world,
> But we in it shall be rememberèd [*Henry V* (*H5*) 4.3.56–59].

The speeches are similar, even though the similarities do not suggest any specific attempt to echo or allude to Shakespeare's famous speech (very famous when Tolkien was writing *The Return of the King* because of the phenomenon of Laurence Olivier's 1944 *Henry V* film).[1] It is not direct correlation that is important, but similar treatment of the theme of hope as temporally based.

In fact, only twice in his writings does Tolkien seem to be alluding to Shakespeare directly. Both reference magical moments in *Macbeth* which Tolkien felt were poorly handled—the moving forest is recast as the Ents and the witches' prophecy that "none of woman born / Shall harm Macbeth" (4.1.80–81) becomes the Nazgûl's overconfident claim that no man can stop it. But these are only two direct references, and both are corrective rather than respectful. Clearly, Tolkien had no conscious interest in Shakespeare as a positive model.

Yet Shakespeare's influence must have had some effect on the man who wanted to create a unified body of myth that was specifically for England. The traditional myths of England—King Arthur and Robin Hood—Shakespeare sidestepped as neatly as Tolkien. Instead, Shakespeare shaped history to mythologize both a certain time (although he rejected what we would now call historical accuracy) and themes important throughout his writing—the use and misuse of power, the interlocking of fate and individual effort, and the ambiguity of choice. These are themes that Tolkien embraced as well. Moreover, Tolkien wished to create the intricate layering of a true mythology, to provide a sense of weight and realism in his world in order to support his linguistic experiments. In the Appendices, *The Silmarillion* and the stories of the "past" injected into the main narrative, Tolkien created history rather than simply story, and it is in this creation of a full-fledged world that he could have found Shakespeare his most useful model.

Shakespeare did not invent the history play, but he certainly perfected it. No other major playwright of the period devoted as much energy to the history of England, and while Shakespeare borrowed much from earlier folk plays like *The Troublesome Reign of King John*, he was the first to understand that historical events needed to be shaped just like fictional ones, if they were to be more than episodic spectacle. This was a gradual realization; Shakespeare's first three history plays— the three parts of *Henry VI*—are episodic and sprawling, with dozens of characters, many of whom appear only once. From these plays Tolkien may have gained a sense of how to compact the sweep of time and cover months or even years in a brief time while spending pages on a single incident. But these plays were unpopular with the public and not highly valued by scholars, so it is more likely that Tolkien's knowledge was based on *Richard III* (*R3*), *H5*, and the two parts of *Henry IV* (*1H4, 2H4*). In these plays, Shakespeare shifted his stories away from the history of the chronicles he used as sources and shaped the events by marrying them much more strongly to individual characters.

History had much need of shaping, as far as the government was concerned. Henry VII won the English throne by conquest, and his claim was extraordinarily shaky, based on being the great-great grandson of the uncle of Richard II, the king whose overthrow in 1399 led to almost a century-long battle for the throne. Tudor propaganda legitimized Henry's claim by demonizing the last Plantagenet, Richard III, and claiming that God had sanctioned Henry's invasion, but in reality he succeeded because almost all the other claimants were dead. One of the methods Henry VII used in an attempt to shore up his claim was to commission Polydore Vergil, around 1501, to write a history of England, and to link the current Tudor line to King Arthur. Vergil's work was actually based on sound scholarship and therefore did not advance the Tudor claims, but nonetheless, historical writing became increasingly popular in the following decades and remained linked to politics throughout the sixteenth century. The chronicle histories of

Edward Hall, *Union of the Two Noble and Illustre Famelies of Lancastre and York,* and Raphael Holinshed, *The Chronicles of England, Scotland and Ireland,* both approached history as an exercise in nation building. It is not that these writers altered facts to deliberately mislead their audience—that conception of history is a modern invention. Rather they conceived of the very notion of telling their nation's past as a way of explaining and celebrating the glorious procession of history towards Protestantism, the Tudor line, and especially the peaceful and prosperous reign of Elizabeth I.

Shakespeare seized this idea of history as national propaganda and advanced it, creating a new kind of mythology. The two linked tetralogies—cycles of four linked plays—that span the reigns of Richard II to Richard III create an epic cycle of plays that function on their own, and yet are closely linked together. The plays contain an overarching view of history as part of God's master plan, but this is only subtly suggested; most of the emphasis is on the individual and his decisions and character. The death of Richard II, a legitimate king, begins a train of events that results in civil war and divine punishment, culminating in the outright evil of Richard III, who climbs to the throne over a pile of bodies. His defeat marks the end of the divine punishment and the beginning of a new period of history. Although Shakespeare wrote two other English histories—*King John* and *Henry VIII*—and a number of other plays based on the chronicles, such as *Macbeth* and *King Lear,* it is these eight plays people think of first when they think of Shakespeare's history plays, and this sequence is the one that shows the greatest kinship with Tolkien's sense of history.

Certain links to Tolkien's work are suggestive. One of the key elements of Tolkien's ethical structure is that all the characters in *LotR* have a choice in their moral decisions. In a key moment in *The Two Towers,* Gandalf offers the defeated Saruman (whose ability to manipulate others with his voice perhaps echoes Richard III, who is so persuasive that he can win a woman's heart after killing her husband) a second chance, promising to protect him if only Saruman will freely choose a new path. It is only after Saruman rejects this opportunity that Gandalf breaks his staff and casts him from the Council. Likewise, time and again in Shakespeare's history plays, characters are presented with options, and must rely on their own judgment to choose the correct one. While they may be intimidated, manipulated, or influenced, they are never puppets, not even to God, and often the choice is not clear. In *R3,* for example, Richard sends two men to murder his brother Clarence. The two characters are never on stage again, and historically there is no doubt that Clarence will die in the scene, but while both are at first comfortable with murdering a prince for money, one discovers his conscience and tries vainly to save Clarence. Nor is this change an unmotivated one; Clarence tries to persuade them both to let him live, using a variety of reasons both logical and emotional.

> 1st Murderer: What we will do, we do upon command.
> 2nd Murderer: And he that hath commanded is our king.
> Clarence: Erroneous vassals! The great King of kings
> Hath in the table of His law commanded
> That thou shalt do no murder [1.4.196–200].

The plea almost works with the Second Murderer, but he is not fast enough to warn Clarence against the First Murderer's attack. History continues as it must, but there is a moment when the audience is shown that things could have happened differently, if men made different choices.

This emphasis on the ambiguous choice is a hallmark of the humanist thinking of the Renaissance. In the early medieval tales on which Tolkien based much of his work, choice was hard, but it was rarely ambiguous. Beowulf can choose not to fight the dragon he knows will kill him, but to do so would be to abandon everything he is, to not be the hero. "All gloomy his soul, / wavering, death-bound. Wyrd full nigh / stood ready to greet the grey-haired man" (*Beowulf* 2419–21). The idea that fate is certain appears in the story of Frodo's journey to Mount Doom. When he first promises to take the Ring to Mordor, Elrond claims that the task is "appointed" to Frodo and only he can succeed. Unlike Beowulf, there is no clear single God who creates this fate, but this only makes the inevitability of the task more poignant. Throughout his journey, Frodo refers to his fate as the Ring-bearer: "I must carry the burden to the end. It can't be altered" (6.1.891) and "It is my burden and no one else can bear it" (6.3.916). Here Tolkien is most closely following the medieval models of the hero, appointed by fate or God and echoing *Beowulf* almost directly: "The fight is not yours / nor meet for any but me alone" (2532–33). The burden of history (here as real as the history Shakespeare conceived) is inescapable; the hero can only succeed or fail, not chose a different path.

But when Tolkien turns to men, choice suddenly comes to the fore-front, choice which is based on flawed mortal beliefs. Denethor under-values his son, Faramir, just as Henry IV undervalues his son, Hal, because both are blinded by an apparently more heroic choice. Despite the fact that Shakespeare's characters are locked into their historical actions, by emphasizing their internal struggles, he makes their choices seem more like choices than those of the fictional characters in medieval tales, just as Tolkien does. When Boromir tries to convince Frodo to give him the Ring, he uses reason first, rather than force, because his judgment, his view of the world, tells him he is right. He sees the Ring as a gift that fate has given them to use against Sauron, a perfectly reasonable belief for a warrior used to handling dangerous weapons. In much the same way, Henry V insists upon a long council to determine whether his claim to the throne of France is legitimate and worth a war, and at one point asks the Archbishop of Canterbury point blank, "May I with right and conscience make this claim?" (*H5* 1.2.96). Both Shakespeare and Tolkien present the choices of individuals as important but ambiguous, with good motives at times leading to disaster and evil to peace. Most striking is Gollum's fateful recovery of the Ring and his subsequent fall into the fires of Mount Doom, which turns out to be the only way the Ring can be destroyed, just as Richard III's rise to the throne through murder and treachery turn out to be the only thing that can unite the warring nobles and bring about peace.

Another important link between Shakespeare and Tolkien's conception of history is its continuous nature. *The Lord of the Rings* has connections to the early Finnish and Norse myths in that it describes the passing away of the Third Age, and the final disappearance of Elves from the world of Man. In that sense, Tolkien is referencing a climactic finale, such as Ragnarok, but rather than an apocalypse leading to the end of everything, the end of the Third Age marks the commencement of the Age of Man—in a sense, the beginning of our own history. In much the same way, Shakespeare chose not to write about King Arthur, but about the period that gave birth to his own age—the Tudor period. And just as the final speech of *R3* looks forward to the more peaceful, if less heroic future, so Tolkien ends his tale not with the passing of the Elves and Frodo, but with Sam returning home to his family.

Another characteristic of epic is a clear-cut and definitive victory—the complete defeat of evil and suitable rewards for all heroes. Tolkien avoids this simplistic kind of ending when the defeat of Sauron is followed by the need to free the Shire from Saruman/Sharkey, Frodo's inability to return to his old life, and Sam's feeling of being torn in two. This ending, which follows the more conventional triumphant ending of Aragorn's crowning and marriage to Arwen, is a key factor in the depth and emotional power of *LotR*, precisely because Tolkien is brutally honest about what losses victory always requires. Frodo tells Sam, "It must often be so, Sam, when things are in danger: some one has to give them up, lose them, so that others may keep them" (6.9.1006). Frodo has been too damaged to live comfortably in the Shire, and even the recognition for saving it goes, as Sam painfully notes, to Merry and Pippin rather than Frodo.

Many scholars have pointed to Tolkien's own experiences during World War I as the cause of this awareness. While I do not doubt that,

I would also point to Shakespeare's ordering of his history plays. Rather than follow chronology, and begin with the overthrow and death of Richard II, Shakespeare began in the exact middle, with the crowning of Henry VI. That play opens with the nobles mourning over the coffin of Henry V "too famous to live long" (*1H4* 1.1.6). And the final play Shakespeare wrote in the cycle was the triumphant tale of *H5*, which ends with the conquest of France, the union of Henry and Catherine, Princess of France, and the establishment of peace. But the last word belongs to the Chorus, who reminds the audience what they have recently seen performed on the stage—the loss of all Henry has achieved when his son becomes king at the age of nine months, "[of] Whose state so many had the managing / That they lost France and made his England bleed" (Epilogue 11–12). The more simplistic celebration of Henry VII's defeat of Richard III belongs to an earlier play, and is over-shadowed by the reworked structure Shakespeare imposes. The plays thus contain an awareness of sadness and loss at their moments of greatest triumph. Tolkien seems to have echoed this structure and incorporated history as a cycle when he added the Appendices, telling the history of the First and Second Ages only after the end of the Third Age. Both writers, then, begin their stories *in media res* (as historical chronicles must inevitably begin) and end looking back to the past and forward to a future that is for the audience, also the past.

Finally, it seems to me that Tolkien must have used Shakespeare as a model in perhaps the most important element of his story. The epics of the Middle Ages had no interest in the common man; heroic deeds, by their very nature, were performed only by heroes, and heroes were of noble or even divine birth and upbringing. Peasants or workers make almost no appearance in early medieval literature. For example, *Beowulf* is almost completed before a man who is not a warrior appears, and then he has no name, but is defined only by his action of stealing a cup from the dragon's hoard. Even in the Finnish *Kalevala*, where heroes such as Wainamoinen work at sowing seeds, there are no societies of workers. Wainamoinen is a hero because he has the wisdom and magic to grow all types of seed; they do not grow simply from hard labor, nor does Wainamoinen require the aid of other, ordinary men. And even when heroes appear to come from common stock, it inevitably turns out that they were only disguised until the proper moment, as when Arthur is revealed to be the son of a king when it is time to pull the sword from the stone. Yet Tolkien gives the task of destroying the Ring not to Aragorn or Gandalf, not to a hero or a mighty wizard, but to a Hobbit, one of the "little people" who succeeds through the homely virtues of determination, hope and loyalty. While Frodo is recognized as somewhat special or "queer" (half Brandybuck, after all), he is never other than a Hobbit, and Sam's very strength comes from his ordinary Hobbit nature. Further, Tolkien separates the most typical heroic fighting from Frodo. Despite a few dramatic fights (especially against Shelob), most of what Frodo and Sam endure is endless walking, hunger and thirst, fear and despair. Frodo bears the additional burden of actually carrying the Ring, but this does not ennoble him in the traditional, epic fashion; he becomes more passive and helpless, until finally Sam must carry him toward Mount Doom. Even in the end, when Saruman destroys the Shire and even tries to kill Frodo, Frodo tries to let him go, a most unheroic choice in light of medieval epics.

Where would Tolkien have found a model for centering a heroic tale on the most unlikely, unheroic character? Shakespeare did not center his plays around the common man—his plays were mainly about kings and other nobles—but he did introduce quasi- or non-historical characters who were not noble into the drama, and made their actions important to the unfolding of events. In the early plays, these characters are minor and work mainly as emblems. As Janis Lull points out, Saunder Simpcox's bogus miracle of recovered sight neatly points up how blind the truly religious Henry VI is to events surrounding him (93). However, in the later plays, which would have been much more familiar to an early twentieth century audience, these quasi-historical characters take on increased importance and value. In *H5*, King Henry walks through his camp in disguise the night before battle, and finds himself engaged in a debate about the king's responsibilities with three rank and file soldiers. While there is no changing Henry's mind, Williams especially presents his arguments powerfully enough to make the audience question this king's devotion to war. Tolkien may well have had this scene in mind when he repeatedly staged scenes of Hobbits questioning or even disobeying those in power, even after, as with Merry and Pippin, they have taken oaths of loyalty. In *Henry V* loyalty does not mean unquestioning obedience, no more than it does in *LotR*.

And then there is Sir John Falstaff. Created as a companion for Prince Hal in *1H4*, Falstaff immediately broke the bonds of the history play, becoming more important to the drama than the central political issues of rebellion and civil war. Interestingly, Falstaff resembles Hobbits in many ways. He is not small, but he has a round stomach and a love of good food and wine. He craves comfort, but in dangerous situations he always comes out on top. He is cleverer with his words than his sword, and while he appears to be a mischief-maker, on closer inspection he is revealed to be a sort of jester, one who reveals important truths in folly. In his most famous speech, he questions the point of honor. "What is that 'honor'? Air. A trim reckoning! Who hath it? He that died o'Wednesday" (*1H4* 5.1.134–35). While Frodo is not nearly the trickster or coward Falstaff is, he shows his ancestry when he voices the wish that he had not been born in such a time. In the end of *2H4*, the rejection of Falstaff takes on the mantle of tragedy, making him more central than the newly crowned King Henry V.

While I would not argue that Shakespeare is solely responsible for Tolkien's ability to conceive of a hero who is not an aristocratic warrior, it is clear that of all the literary models he might have had, only Shakespeare provided this element. Tolkien would not have found it in the medieval epics he loved,[2] or in his experience of World War I, which resolutely rejected the notion of heroism as an answer to anything. While Tolkien did not consciously turn to Shakespeare, the history plays could have provided the unconscious model for many of the elements that are most engaging in *The Lord of the Rings*.

Notes

1. Olivier's film was released, to critical acclaim and box office success, in November of 1944. Tolkien wrote the quoted passage sometime between May 12, 1944, and November 29, 1944, when he sent Christopher an outline of Book Five, which mentions tying the dialog on the nature of stories to the never-used final chapter of Sam reading to his children (*War* 219). Tolkien seems to have revised the chapter in late 1946, perhaps as a result of seeing Olivier's film.

2. Tolkien's commentary on his Beorhtnoth play shows that he was well aware that medieval epics could not provide a model for the common man's heroism in modern day warfare.

Works Cited

Beowulf. The Oldest English Epic: Beowulf, Finnsburg, Waldere, Deor, Widsith, and the German Hildebrand. Trans. Francis B. Gummere. New York: Macmillan, 1909. 1–158.

Carpenter, Humphrey. *Tolkien: A Biography*. New York: Ballantine, 1977.

Lull, Janis. "Plantagenets, Lancastrians, Yorkists and Tudors: *1–3 Henry VI, Richard III, Edward III*." In *The Cambridge Companion to Shakespeare's History Plays*. Ed. Michael Hattaway. Cambridge: Cambridge University Press, 2002. 89–105.

Shakespeare, William. *The Complete Works of William Shakespeare*. Ed. David Bevington. 5th ed. New York: Pearson, 2004.

Tolkien, J.R.R. *The Letters of J.R.R. Tolkien*. Ed. Humphrey Carpenter. Boston: Houghton, 2000.

_____. *The Lord of the Rings*. 2nd ed. Boston: Houghton, 1994.

_____. *The War of the Ring*. Ed. Christopher Tolkien. The History of Middle-earth 8. Boston: Houghton, 1990.

West, Richard C. "Setting the Rocket Off in Story: The *Kalevala* as the Germ of Tolkien's Legendarium." In *Tolkien and the Invention of Myth*. Ed. Jane Chance. Lexington: University of Kentucky Press, 2004. 285–94.

"The Rack of This Tough World"

The Influence of King Lear *on* Lord of the Rings

Leigh Smith

Tolkien's famous claim to have "disliked" reading Shakespeare as a student and his annoyance at some of Shakespeare's devices, e.g. "his damned cobwebs" (*Letters* 143n), have led many readers to believe that he was hostile to the playwright's work in its entirety. However, a close look at the content of his criticism reveals that what he disliked was Shakespeare's use of the fantastic: the fairies, witches, and moving forests, which he believes either fall flat or draw back from their own implications. He contends that "Drama is naturally hostile to Fantasy" and that no stage-effects, no matter how well-created, can alter this fact ("On Fairy-Stories" 49). But Shakespeare did not, of course, always use the fantastic. In *King Lear,* as critics have often noted, the references to "gods" are belied by a depressingly naturalistic, character-driven plot-line, in which those who look to the supernatural to set the world right are bitterly disappointed (Greenblatt 120). *Lear* has none of the fantastic elements to which Tolkien objects in *Macbeth.* And not only does Tolkien never express dislike for *Lear,* but as Michael Drout points out, he actually refers to it when he needs an example of a great work of art originating (as *Beowulf* does) from a folk-tale (Drout 141). Indeed, for Tolkien, the high quality of *Lear* is too obvious to require argument. He asks, rhetorically, "Are we to refuse '*King Lear*' either because it is founded on a silly folk-tale (the old naif details of which still peep through as they do in *Beowulf*) or because it is not '*Macbeth*'? Need we even debate which is more valuable?" (Tolkien, *Beowulf* 55). Both Drout

137

and Shippey have demonstrated that Tolkien was intimately familiar with *Lear* (including its origins in Layamon's *Brut*), thought highly of it, and adapted images and syntax from it in his own fiction (Drout 5; Shippey, *Author* 186–7).

Drout's analysis, in particular, offers the most detailed examination to date of the ways Tolkien makes use of *Lear*. Focusing mostly on specific passages in *Return of the King*, Drout shows that much of Tolkien's seemingly archaic or "non-standard" wording and syntax actually derives from *Lear* (Drout 153) and that this derivation offers a useful clue to interpreting Tolkien's work. I wish now to take the next logical step and explore more fully the influence of *Lear* on Tolkien, specifically *The Lord of the Rings* (*LotR*). I hope to show that Tolkien made use of *Lear* on almost every level: in his creation of major and minor characters, in his depiction of feudal and family relationships, in his use of plot devices such as disguises, and in his presentation of *LotR*'s overriding theme, the relationship between good and evil.

Fathers, Sons, and Daughters

King Lear, upon meeting Edgar in the filthy and destitute guise of Mad Tom, immediately asks, "Didst thou give all to thy daughters?" (3.4.48). He cannot imagine that any force in the universe other than ungrateful daughters could bring a man to such misery. Ironically, Edgar is suffering from the mirror image of Lear's malady. Like Cordelia, he is the good child, rejected by his father because of a greedy sibling's lies. In *The Two Towers*, Tolkien creates a double plotline of the same type. His Théoden and Denethor are also self-deceived fathers who reject good children until almost too late.

When Théoden first appears in "The King of the Golden Hall," he is in much the same condition as Lear at the beginning of the play: both kings feel older than they are. Lear has gathered his family and closest advisors to announce his intention "To shake all cares and business from our age, / Conferring them on younger strengths while we / Unburdened crawl toward death" (1.1.38–40). Yet he later realizes, through bitter experience and self-analysis, that his infirmity was probably not the result of his age, but of the cozening of his elder daughters, who stood to profit from his infirmity. Regan, for example, tries to silence him by reminding him that anyone "Must be content to think you old" (2.4.237), implying that he should follow her directions. In a moment of clarity, he tells Gloucester, "They flattered me like a dog and told me I had white hairs in my beard ere the black ones were there" (4.6.96–98).

Théoden also has been made old before his time, not by a child of his, but by a trusted counselor who stands to gain from the king's weakness. Gríma Wormtongue, under orders from Saruman, has clearly been exerting the same kind of flattery and control over Théoden as Goneril and Regan have exerted over Lear. When Théoden is first described, he is prematurely stooped and shrunken with age, and we soon discover the reason. Wormtongue constantly urges the king not to strain himself, to let others handle his affairs; like Goneril and Regan, Wormtongue pretends to care only for the king's interests, but he first coaxes, then demands, that Théoden dismiss those who are truly loyal (Éomer and Gandalf). After regaining his power and self-respect, Théoden realizes that Wormtongue's flattery and cozening would soon "have had me walking on all fours like a beast" (3.6.508). This statement recalls Lear's willingness to "crawl toward death"; in both cases, a king's aging, stripped of its dignity and turned into a beastlike crawling, is only one consequence of flattery.

A potentially worse consequence is to place both Lear and Théoden almost beyond help by causing them to reject a good child. Cordelia, especially when married to the king of France, could have protected Lear against his enemies, as Éomer (a nephew in the role of a son) would have protected Théoden. While Goneril and Regan do not exactly talk their father into disowning Cordelia, their phony, glib responses to his love test make possible his outraged rejection of their honest sister. Had neither of them been willing to "profess / Myself an enemy to all other joys" and "alone felicitate / In your dear Highness' love" (1.1.72–76), Cordelia's "Nothing" would not appear an insult to Lear, as it does not to Kent or any other impartial observer. Even Goneril and Regan know that their father has acted with "poor judgment" (1.1.294–95), but they acknowledge this fact only to each other, as it increases their share of the spoils and gives them a freer hand by removing both Cordelia and Kent from Lear's side. For a similar reason, Wormtongue, with the same oily, courtier-like glibness, convinces Théoden to throw Éomer into prison. Like Goneril and Regan, Wormtongue wishes to weaken his master to gain the spoils of his defeat. As Gandalf deduces, Wormtongue has been promised his pick of Rohan's treasure and women whenever the city falls to Saruman.

This parallel goes further, as both *Lear* and *LotR* depict a second father who mistakenly turns against a good child. Like Gloucester, Denethor has two sons, rejects a good son, and becomes suicidal when he realizes the extent of his mistake. However, Drout rightly equates Denethor's madness and despair with Lear's, observing that "[k]ings are not permitted to despair," and neither are stewards (Drout 146).

Furthermore, both Lear and Denethor have rejected good children for the same reason: for speaking too plainly. Cordelia, when asked to flatter her father with a profession of love, says "nothing." Faramir, when criticized by his father for excessive lenity, which could lead to defeat, answers, almost as simply, "So be it" (5.4.794). Lear, outraged at his daughter's refusal to play the game her sisters play, tells her, "Better thou / Hadst not been born than not t'have pleased me better" (1.1.2237–38). Denethor, outraged at Faramir's refusal to bring him the Ring, questions his loyalty and claims to wish that Faramir had died in Boromir's place.[1]

Yet, when Denethor believes Faramir is dead, he reacts much as Lear does to the death of Cordelia. Both express the same guilt, the same vain hope that their rejected children will live long enough to forgive them. Carrying Cordelia's body, Lear cries, "I might have saved her, now she's gone for ever! / Cordelia, Cordelia, stay a little. Ha? / What is't thou say'st? Her voice was ever soft" (5.3.275–77). Denethor, lingering by a (seemingly) dying Faramir, recalls how he sent his son "unthanked, unblessed, into needless peril" and insists on staying by his side, hoping he will speak before he dies (5.4.805). Denethor's madness seems to have the same source in guilt and despair as Lear's has. And like Lear's, it could be cured only if his wronged and dying child would speak.

Drout also identifies in both Lear and Denethor the sin of "wanhope," or despair of God's mercy, the gravest of all faults in a ruler whose realm is under attack (Drout 147). Nevertheless, I would suggest that Denethor's guilt about his son is at least as influential as his despair for his city in the suicidal madness to which he finally succumbs. On this point, the parallel between Denethor's words and Lear's, as well as the words others use in describing them, are especially revealing. Referring to Cordelia, Lear says, "my poor fool is hanged" (5.3.311). The resemblance to Denethor becomes clearer if we remember that both Cordelia and the Fool alternately serve the function of forcing Lear to hear the truth (Hawkes 56; Guilfoyle 120; McFarland 117). Although both make him furious, he eventually comes to listen more closely to their judgments than to the flatterers he once preferred. With this in mind, Denethor's statement that "The fool's hope has failed" (4.4.805) evokes Lear. While Lear means Cordelia and Denethor means Gandalf (not Faramir), both grieving fathers refer to an absent "fool" who is closely linked with their dying children. Both "fools" are far from foolish, and both fathers might have avoided much pain by listening to their counsel.

As they do not, the breaking of mind and will that Denethor suffers is similar to that of Lear and Gloucester. Upon witnessing Lear's madness, Gloucester calls him a "ruined piece of nature" (4.6.134). At Lear's death, Kent says "He hates him / That would upon the rack of this tough world / Stretch him out longer" (5.3.319.21). Likewise, the blinded Gloucester, who seems more tortured by his own misjudgment of Edgar than by anything Cornwall has done to him, also becomes suicidal, claiming that he cannot "bear it longer" (4.6.37). And indeed, when he learns that Edgar is alive, "his flawed heart ... burst smilingly" (5.3.200–203). These images of breaking and ruining, as on a torture rack, are also applied to Denethor, who tells Pippin, "my life is broken" (5.4.807). Pippin has already seen that "something had snapped in his proud will, and his stern mind was overthrown" (5.4.805). Both kings have been overthrown, not by rebellious subjects or foreign invasion, but by their own guilt and despair.

Admittedly, my comparison between them has limitations. I would not do Boromir such injustice as to compare him to Edmund, especially since Tolkien is careful to indicate that the brothers love each other and never become rivals for their father's favor (App.A.1032). Further, Lear loves Cordelia best, but Denethor does not love Faramir best. Though he prefers Boromir, Faramir most closely resembles his father, with his shrewd understanding of human nature and his clear kinship to his Númenorean ancestors. But Gandalf must reassure Faramir that his father does love him and will eventually remember this fact. By the end, Denethor might easily say, with Gloucester, that his elder son is "no dearer in my account" (1.1.20–21).

Kingship and Identity

These conflicts within the self contribute, in both texts, to the larger theme of identity. How one identifies the king—and how he identifies himself—is an especially burning issue in both *Lear* and *LotR* because it, in turn, determines what constitutes legitimate authority. In *Lear*, the question of whether the outcast king remains the king determines the way we judge the moral choices of almost everyone else, especially those (Gloucester, Kent, Albany, and Edgar) who aid a foreign invasion and would seem therefore to be traitors. In *LotR*, when Théoden and Denethor are (like Lear) not in their perfect minds, the identity of the king (or steward) has similar moral implications for those under his command. Furthermore, Aragorn's identity as the king, and his legitimacy to rule Gondor, turns out to mean much more than his lineal descent from Isildur. It requires a self-knowledge that kings in *LotR*, as in *Lear*, must gain to rule effectively.

First, for both authors, legitimate kingship requires a ruler in full possession of his decision-making abilities and able to exercise authority. Tolkien and Shakespeare linguistically connect kingship with identity as they track Lear and Théoden through their initial abandoning of authority (and with it, identity) back to legitimate kingship. Kent refers to Lear as "old man" when trying to make him see his folly, "Lear" when giving up on doing so, "King" when departing into banishment, and "master" when resolving to continue his service. By the end, Kent kneels to him again and calls him "my good lord." In Théoden's hall, the narrative voice reveals the true situation. Initially, Théoden is referred to as "the old man," then as "Théoden." Only when he vows to lead his troops into battle himself is he called "the king." Both kings recognize their loss of authority and seem to connect it with a loss of identity. Lear responds to Goneril's disrespect with an immediate question about identity: "Does any here know me? ... Who is it that can tell me who I am?" (1.4.223–27). Théoden, urged by Gandalf to grasp his sword again, feels for it in vain. Vaguely remembering that he gave away this symbol of his power, he wonders aloud where Gríma may have hidden it. An alert reader who remembers *Lear* ought to wonder what would have happened, had Théoden regained sufficient sense of purpose to call for his sword without the presence of his powerful guest. Clearly, a king not in possession of his will leaves the same power vacuum as a mad king.

For this reason, a mad king in both *Lear* and *LotR* ceases to be a king. Madness in a king is obviously dangerous, and even a steward such as Denethor can ill afford it (Drout 145–6). Even before Lear relinquishes power, the legitimacy of his rule is in serious question. The everloyal Kent, who has always "honored [Lear] as my king" (1.1.140) sees his rejection of Cordelia as a sign of madness. He declares "Be Kent unmannerly / When Lear is mad" (1.1.145–46). This is when he calls Lear "old man" instead of "king" and defies his command to keep silent. Likewise, Pippin disobeys Denethor when he sees that the steward has lost his sanity. When asked who is in charge of the city, Denethor or Gandalf, Pippin answers, "The Grey Wanderer or no one, it would seem" (5.4.808). Kent and Pippin are both dismissed, against their wills, from their rulers' service, but refuse to leave. Their disobedience is based upon the view that a mad ruler's commands are not binding.

The greatest danger of mad kings is that they expose the realm to tyranny. When the king is not truly in command, there are always self-interested people such as Lear's daughters and Gríma Wormtongue ready to step into the vacuum. Soon enough, serving the nominal king, as loyal subjects do, becomes treason against the new power. Gloucester conspires with the French invaders, who, prompted by Cordelia, seek to place Lear back on the throne; Éomer continues to fight Saruman's orcs, preventing his uncle's kingdom from falling completely into the hands of its dangerous neighbor. Therefore, both are called traitors, a charge which means torture for Gloucester and prison for Éomer. Such dangerous times require figures of rare nobility, such as Albany and Gandalf, to assume power temporarily and "the gored state sustain" (5.3.326). Gandalf frequently finds himself forced to command in the absence of a legitimate ruler. He assumes command in Meduseld only long enough for Théoden to recover his judgment, at which time Gandalf immediately returns authority to the king, offering his own services as a counselor. In Minas Tirith, he is willing to give power back to the legitimate authority, as soon as one is available. But few people with Gandalf's ability to seize power are willing to surrender it so easily. Also, Gondor is more fortunate than Lear's England because Gondor's mad ruler is not a king, but a steward, and a sane, legitimate king is available, in the person of Aragorn. Yet Tolkien continually calls the reader's attention to the danger of tyranny in which Gondor constantly stands. Like Denethor, Aragorn has looked in the *palantír* and shown himself to Sauron. Had he also collapsed into despair and madness, Gondor would have fallen to Sauron, an even worse tyrant than the villains of *Lear.*

For both Shakespeare and Tolkien, a tyrant is never a legitimate ruler. True kings are identified by the justness of their rule and their willingness to put aside personal desires, as well as personal safety, and rule in the interest of the governed. In the initial "love test," Lear behaves like an arbitrary dictator, disowning his daughter for a word, banishing a loyal retainer for disagreeing with him, and otherwise making decisions that affect the entire realm according to his personal whims. He becomes "every inch a king" (4.6.107) only after being stripped of his power and forced to "feel what wretches feel" (3.4.34). Ironically, at the time he declares himself "every inch a king," he has exchanged his golden crown for one of leaves and flowers. Yet, his right to call himself king seems clearer than ever before. He has developed empathy with his subjects, urging his Fool to enter the shelter before him and realizing that Gloucester can "see how this world goes with no eyes" (4.6.149–50). In a moment of startling clarity, he condemns the hypocrisy of those in power (presumably including himself) and laments that "a dog's obeyed in office" (4.6.158–59). With such humility and insight, he would surely make a much better king now than he ever was in the days of his power. But of course, it is now too late. Nor do we need to wonder what kind of government has established itself in Lear's absence. Not only do we see the extrajudicial torture of Gloucester, but Albany recognizes that the French invasion has found friends in England "whom the rigor of our state / Forced to cry out" (5.1.23–24). Clearly, tyranny invites rebellion and thus does not even offer the stability it often claims as its chief advantage.

Tolkien makes the same observation even more graphically than does Shakespeare. First, his legitimate kings, Théoden and Aragorn, fight beside their troops, while his tyrants, Saruman and Sauron, hide in fortified towers, letting their slaves do battle for them. Théoden's men are suddenly hopeful of victory when they learn that the Lord of the Mark will lead them himself, and Aragorn inspires many to follow when he vows to march to Mordor, distracting Sauron and aiding Frodo in his mission. Second, Théoden and Aragorn recognize noble motives and reward loyalty. Théoden's doorward Háma allows Gandalf to enter Meduseld with his staff and brings a sword to Éomer; Beregond leaves his post to prevent the death of Faramir. While a tyrant would punish both of them, Théoden sends Háma to fetch Éomer from prison, and Aragorn sends Beregond to Ilthilien, so he may continue serving Faramir. As their disobedience is prompted by loyalty, their kings allow them to continue serving their beloved captains. Had Lear done likewise, anyone who threatened him would have had to contend with a fully-armed Kent, whose "life [he] never held but as a pawn / To wage against thine enemies" (1.1.156–57).

Third, Tolkien's' legitimate rulers care more about the safety of their realms and subjects than about their own power. For this reason, Théoden, restored to his full strength and authority, withstands Saruman's attempt to flatter him, recalling the "torches at Westfold and children that lie dead there" (3.10.566). For the same reason, Aragorn chooses not to enter Gondor and claim the kingship until the war is over, so as not to jeopardize the city's unity. Indeed, his concern is well-founded, as Denethor—who, significantly, is not a king—seems unable to distinguish between his own interests and those of Gondor. When he says, "the rule of Gondor, my lord, is mine and no other man's, unless the king should come again" (5.1.741), it is difficult to imagine him easily granting Aragorn's claim. It is equally difficult to imagine Denethor pardoning, as Aragorn does, the Easterlings who fought against Gondor. But Aragorn's willingness to put the good of the country and its allies before his own pride seems to be precisely the quality that makes others wish to follow him, as many do on the (apparent) suicide mission to Mordor. Éomer surely speaks for many when he says, "Aragorn succored me and my people, so I will aid him when he calls" (5.9.862). Likewise, Théoden's courage and kindness prompt Merry, out of love, to vow service to him.

In this, Aragorn and Théoden, who inspire others freely to serve them, contrast sharply with Saruman, who forces Gríma to follow him when Frodo offers better choices, and with Sauron, who has "few servants but many slaves of fear" (6.1.880). Interestingly, whatever their pretensions to world domination, neither Saruman nor Sauron calls himself a king, and the defeat of each seems a natural result of their inability to understand loyalty and self-sacrifice, such as the legitimate rulers demonstrate and inspire in others. Even Denethor, who has much greatness about him and is hardly to be compared with Tolkien's villains, is not loved as the true kings are loved. Beregond's devotion is to his captain, Faramir, not to the steward, and when Pippin makes his vow of service, he is not prompted by love but by wounded pride at the disdain in Denethor's voice.

As this example shows, Shakespeare and Tolkien take great care to present the identity of the king as obvious even without his official signifiers. The blinded Gloucester, who fails to recognize his son Edgar's voice, does recognize his king and tries to kiss his hand. At this point, Lear is crowned again, albeit with leaves and flowers: a sad parody of crowned kingship, but a natural crown. Lear declares himself "every inch a king," and Tolkien offers a parallel image that seems to argue for the truth of Lear's claim. By the road to Osgiliath, Frodo sees a beheaded, abused statue of a king. As with Lear, the "years had gnawed it and violent hands had maimed it" (4.7.687). But Frodo finds the statue's head lying near the road, crowned by nature with a white-flowered vine and golden moss, and this fleeting glimpse of unconquered majesty gives him new strength and much-needed hope. For Tolkien, as for Shakespeare, this natural crown appears to tell a more basic truth than the golden one. Restoring this truth to the political realm will not be easy in either text, and this moment of illumination dissolves into darkness. Yet it offers a hope for the future whose realization will require not only war and strife, but also a king's search for identity.

The king who must replace the fallen statue is, of course, Aragorn. Tolkien tracks the development of Aragorn's identity through his various names, as well as tokens associated with the kingship, until he, too, is "every inch a king." After the death of his father, Aragorn has a lineal right to the throne of Gondor, but that throne is, as yet, too dangerous for him to claim. The elves protect him by concealing his lineage and calling him "Estel" or "hope," and that concept becomes an important part of his identity. He is the exiled king, of the same archetype as King Arthur, whose triumphant return will bring a new golden age of peace and prosperity.[2] Therefore, when Elrond reveals to Aragorn his "true" identity, he gives him the broken sword Narsil and the ring of Barahir (their common ancestor), but not yet the Sceptre of Annúminas. In this way, Elrond presents the kingship as an honor to be earned, not simply as a lineal right, and Aragorn will spend the next few decades earning it. Years later, when he reappears as counselor to Denethor, he is called "Thorongil," meaning "eagle of the star" (App.A.1030). At this point in his life, he is developing and proving not only his physical and mental abilities, but also his willingness to act for the good of his city. He is persuaded that he can, for the time, better serve Gondor's interests as a counselor than by asserting his claim to the kingship. During his many years as a Ranger, an unknown and mostly unregarded protector of Westernesse, he becomes the Strider who offers help to the four hobbits at Bree. Later, at the Council, Elrond gives Aragorn his proper name, publicly. This renaming is Aragorn's first clear step toward the throne of Gondor, as it reveals his descent from Arathorn and thus from Elendil. Reaffirming his readiness to take this step, he brings Narsil—reforged as Andúril—with him on the Quest.

Although the primary goal of this Quest is to destroy the One Ring, it resembles more traditional quests such as the Quest of the Holy Grail in one respect: it reveals the character, and therefore the identity, of everyone who undertakes it. For Aragorn, this means one more change of name, as he finally accepts the crown and the other signifiers of kingship. The exiled king returning to his own country to claim his patrimony is a common feature of quest-romance, and Aragorn assumes this role as Elessar, or "Elfstone." Literally, this name comes from the green stone that Arwen sends him through Galadriel, but it also marks him as the predestined heir to the House of Elendil. Nevertheless, he does not call himself by this name until nearly the end of *Return of the King*, when he is also ready to assume the crown and scepter.

Thus, in both *Lear* and *LotR*, legitimate kingship belongs only to one with a lineal right to it, but that lineal right is not enough. The claimant must also undergo trials that develop him as a person and as a ruler. He must prove his worth and fitness to rule until he—and those he rules—recognize him as king, with or without the royal signifiers. On this point, we should note that Faramir, awakening in the Houses of Healing, recognizes his king as easily as the blinded Gloucester. Because this process may take longer than the king and country can afford, Lear's life ends tragically, as Théoden's and Aragorn's do not. Nevertheless, Shakespeare and Tolkien develop their kings with the same qualities: physical and political courage, concern for the governed, and knowledge of their own identity that others can easily recognize. Since no one is born with these qualities, both writers show their kings taking a long time to mold. But once they are molded, even a blind man can identify them.

Disguises

Given the importance of identity in *Lear* and *LotR*, we should not be surprised to see both Shakespeare and Tolkien using disguises for similar purposes, as various characters reveal and conceal different aspects of themselves. Although disguise appears to be one of Shakespeare's favorite devices, he employs it mostly in the comedies; in fact, *Lear* is the only one of the great tragedies in which he employs it at all. There, we find a faithful retainer, Kent, concealing his rank and identity to continue serving the master he loves. We also find a young knight, Edgar, transforming himself into a mad beggar, first to escape his father's anger, then to protect his father. And of course, we find a king traveling incognito until he can safely reveal himself. Not only does Tolkien use disguises in *LotR* that correspond to these, but he uses no others. Éowyn, disguised as Dernhelm, parallels Kent; Frodo and Sam, disguised as orcs, parallel Edgar; and Aragorn, traveling incognito, parallels Lear.

The comparison between Éowyn and Kent is partly an implication of the resemblance, first discussed by Drout, between Lear's "Come not between the dragon and his wrath," which is said to Kent (1.1.122), and the Lord of the Nazgûl's "Come not between the Nazgûl and his prey," which is said to Éowyn (5.6.823; Drout 144–45). Drout also notes a similarity between Lear's holding a looking-glass up to Cordelia's face to see if any breath mists the glass and Imrahil's holding a polished vambrace up to Éowyn's face (5.6.827; Drout 139). While the comparison between Cordelia and Éowyn is a natural one, I would argue that she more closely resembles Kent. Just as Kent refers to Lear as his king whom he has "Loved as my father" (1.1.141), Tolkien's narrator tells us that Éowyn/Dernhelm "had loved his lord as a father" (5.6.822). This similarity of diction becomes especially telling if we remember that Éowyn is not Théoden's daughter, but a kinswoman and retainer, whom Théoden trusts to lead the Eorlingas in his absence. Second, Kent and Éowyn are in a similar situation when they are told "Come not between the dragon / Nazgûl and his prey / wrath." Kent is trying to protect Lear from his own folly, much more than he is trying to protect Cordelia. Lear is the one who urgently needs protection—from himself. When he threatens Kent "on thy life" to stop contradicting him, Kent responds, "My life I never held but as a pawn / To wage against thine enemies, nor fear to lose it, / Thy safety being motive" (1.1.156–58). Éowyn, threatened with death by the Nazgûl, shows no fear, vowing to protect her king if she can.

Third, Kent and Éowyn disguise themselves for the same purpose: to continue serving their beloved lords. The banished Kent is expressly defying Lear's orders so that "thy master, whom thou lov'st, / Shall find thee full of labors" (1.4.6–7). Éowyn disguises herself as Dernhelm so as to follow her lord when he has ordered her to remain in Rohan. Like Kent, she stays close to her king. She even recognizes in Merry's face a similar desire to follow wherever Théoden leads, and her collaboration with Merry might reasonably be compared to Kent's collaboration with the Fool. Although the Fool appears to see through Kent's disguise, as Merry does not see through Éowyn's, he recognizes "the face of one without hope who goes in search of death" (5.3.785). In a sense, Éowyn *is* Dernhelm: like many of Shakespeare's disguises, this one tells something about the wearer. Just as Kent is also "your servant Caius" (5.3.288), nothing is said of Dernhelm that is not also true of Éowyn.

A very different type of disguise protects the innocent Edgar from his father's wrath and the equally innocent Frodo and Sam from Sauron's. When Edgar fears for his life, he chooses "the basest and most poorest shape / That ever penury, in contempt of man, / Brought near to beast" (2.3.7–9). Mad Tom, whose face he can cover with dirt and from whom passers-by will instinctively avert their eyes, offers a convenient persona, not only for hiding Edgar's identity, but also for begging sustenance. Like Edgar, Frodo and Sam disguise themselves as the lowest of the low, so as not to be noticed. Although Tolkien is less likely than Shakespeare to treat being "near to beast" as worse than the alternatives, his orcs do have numerous beast-like associations, being frequently described as hairy and snarling and wearing garments made of animal hide, which Frodo dons in Mordor to conceal his identity.

Tolkien's orcs even exhibit some qualities of Mad Tom's insanity, or more accurately, of Edgar's construction of insanity. As Shakespeare's audience would expect, Mad Tom is possessed by a "foul fiend" who has led him "through fire and through flame" (3.4.51).[3] Sauron does the same to his orcs. Indeed, the comparison between Sauron and the devil is easy to make, and Tolkien makes it himself, describing Morgoth as a fallen angelic spirit, like Lucifer (*Letters* 243). This would make Sauron equivalent to a demon, like the angels seduced by Lucifer. Tolkien's orcs, like madmen possessed by the devil, are also described in terms of damage: they are "ruined" and "twisted" elves (6.1.893), as the insane Lear is a "ruined piece of nature" (4.6.134). And when Sauron withdraws his attention from them, they are no longer able to function. This suggests that they have never had wills of their own but have been driven by Sauron's will. Like Mad Tom, they are essentially possessed by a demon.[4]

The final disguise that appears in both texts is the near-proverbial one of the king dressed as a commoner. When kings in literature conceal their identity, they typically do so for one of two reasons: to avoid danger or to gain information. Both Lear and Aragorn first travel incognito for the former reason, but the latter quickly becomes more important. At first, these two may seem unusual subjects for a discussion of disguise. Unlike the examples treated earlier, Lear and Aragorn do not choose their disguises. Others, trying to protect them, take them away from their palaces and conceal them until they can safely return to their thrones. Also, neither of them is exactly in costume and masquerading, as Dernhelm and Mad Tom are doing. Nevertheless, both of them do without the trappings by which subjects would expect to know their king. Thus, their royalty is concealed, and they have to live as "unaccommodated man" (3.4.105–6), with only the affection, respect, and charity they can draw to themselves.

As a result, they learn who their real friends and enemies are. Lear could have used this information earlier than he has it, but he seems to be a better man and a better king for knowing that Cordelia and Kent are his friends. His former outrage at the disrespectful treatment he receives is long gone, and he accepts the prospect of prison as calmly as any philosopher—as long as Cordelia is with him (5.3.8–18). And he receives the banished Kent without anger or surprise. Aragorn, as a result of his own time in disguise, will never need to wonder whether his vassals are truly devoted to him or only seek the royal favor. When he is not only without a crown, but without much prospect of living long enough to acquire one, his companions follow him, as Éowyn says, "because they would not be parted from thee—because they love thee" (5.2.767). For the same reason, Kent and the Fool follow the unaccommodated Lear. Both Shakespeare and Tolkien present the chance to know who is really devoted as a rare and valuable opportunity for a king—and as a major benefit of disguise.

Relationship Between Good and Evil

In *J.R.R. Tolkien: Author of the Century*, Shippey presents two seemingly incompatible concepts of evil and shows that Tolkien employs both in *LotR*. The basic distinction is this: in the "Boethian" view, evil is merely a lack or absence of good and has no independent existence; in the "Manichean" view, evil is an outside force which must be actively opposed (*Author* 128–35). I agree that Tolkien uses both ideas in his presentation of evil and would argue that Shakespeare, in *King Lear*, provides him with a model for doing so. Further, I contend that Shakespeare presents a third concept of which Tolkien also makes use. We might consider this one the opposite of the Boethian view: good as dependent upon evil.

Most noticeable in the language of *Lear* is the "Boethian" view of evil as absence. Shippey quotes C.S. Lewis, who speaks of God "without whom Nothing is strong" (qtd. in Shippey, *Author* 127). This recognition of the grim banality of evil is one of the features that, according

to Shippey, mark Tolkien as an author of the twentieth century. While
Shippey is correct that this view of evil is a noticeable feature of
twentieth-century literature, I would argue that a model for it already
exists in *Lear*, almost in its twentieth-century form.

If the modern view is that evil is not irresistible temptation, but a
hollowed-out, soulless "nothingness," then the modern view is certainly
present in *Lear*, where the word "nothing" appears twenty-nine times,
and evil appears, not in terms of sin or pain, but as lack and deprivation. Since Lear believes, like Aristotle, that "nothing will come of nothing" (1.1.90), Cordelia's answer of "nothing" in her father's love-test
leads to her dowry's becoming "nothing" (1.1.245). He tries to punish
her by taking away, not realizing that he is punishing himself doubly
through the sacrifice of his land and his daughter. The profit from
Lear's surrendered land becomes "nothing," and he is slowly divested
of everything else, culminating in his encounter with Mad Tom, when
he tears off his clothes (Kermode 1299). Likewise, Gloucester suffers
through loss of both his son and his eyes. The horror that descends on
him after his blinding is not pain, but lack: "I have no way and therefore want no eyes" (4.1.18). Thus, the evil characters in *Lear* have been
called "nihilistic" in their desire to tear down all the restraints of civilization and live in a state of graceless naturalism (Kermode1301–2).

In *LotR*, evil operates through precisely this type of stripping, of
paring-away, of what Shippey calls "wraithing."[5] Sauron is completely
without physical form, the Ringwraiths are without real bodies, Gollum
is "shrunken" and "starved" (4.8.699), and even Bilbo, after years with
the Ring, feels "thin, sort of *stretched*" (1.1.32). In Mordor, Frodo and
Sam's suffering is presented, like Lear's, in terms of deprivation: of
water, of food, of protection against the elements. And Frodo's greatest torment appears not to be the wounds left by the orcs' whips, but
the "blind dark" of Mordor. He tries to picture scenes of his happier
days in the Shire, but he "cannot see them" (4.3.916). For Frodo, as for
Gloucester, all is "dark and comfortless" (3.7.88). The word "nothing"
appears less often in *LotR* than in *Lear*, but when it does, it has the same
power and substance. Gandalf will do "nothing" to Saruman (3.10.568–
69), and the punishment could hardly be greater, as Saruman resents
mercy more than punishment. Gollum probably believes what he tells
Faramir: he has "done nothing" (4.6.674). When he "sneaks" away, on
the stairs of Cirith Ungol, and Sam asks what he has been doing, he
says, "Nothing, nothing" (4.8.699). And his "nothing" proves as dangerous as any positive evil when he abandons Frodo to Shelob, telling himself that "he [Gollum] won't hurt Master" (4.9.709).

Tolkien's presentation of the Manichean view of evil also seems to
owe much to *Lear*. Gloucester, saved from suicide, has good reason to

believe both in "ever-gentle gods" (4.6.219) and in gods "like wanton boys [who] kill us for their sport" (4.1.36–37). Some see these two viewpoints as progress in Gloucester's thinking (Kermode 1300), but the time that passes between the two references, even in the telescoped world of tragedy, seems hardly enough to produce a real philosophical shift. Like many people, Gloucester sees his gods as cruel or merciful, depending on his circumstances. As he knows better than most, Lear's evil daughters and his own evil son represent tyranny and injustice which cannot be called "nothing" and disregarded. Those on the side of good must fight, as Cordelia does in the French invasion, as Edgar does in killing Oswald and Edmund. Yet, because of the strength of evil, the fight against it has a feeling of hopelessness about it. Even at the end, when the good and wise are back in control, the future appears "desolate and drained of meaning" (Kermode 1302). Albany and Edgar are good men, worthy of the power that descends on them, but their victory is far from absolute or permanent and brings them no satisfaction. Lear and Cordelia are dead. Kent departs, apparently to commit suicide, and no one thinks of stopping him. Edgar's final speech is not about the triumph of good over evil, but the "weight of this sad time" (5.3.329).

This same sense of heaviness, of "weight," lies over what should be the happy ending of *LotR*. As critics have often noted, Tolkien was acutely aware of the transitory nature of happiness, that "[n]othing was safe. Nothing would last. No battle would be won for ever" (Carpenter 31; Flieger 3). Evil has appeared, not only in lacks and absences, but in armies that must be fought, tyrants that must be resisted (Shippey, *Author* 134). At the end of *LotR*, Sauron is defeated, Aragorn is king, and the Shire is saved. The representatives of good have won, but not completely or permanently. The glory of Lothlórien will now fade, and the elves will now leave Middle-earth, taking with them all of the beauty and magic they have made and come to represent. As Saruman tells Galadriel, "You have doomed yourselves, and you know it" (6.6.961). Frodo has completed his task and survived, but he is now too damaged to enjoy the future he helped secure. The task of rebuilding the Shire and sustaining the "gored state" falls to the new Mayor, Sam, as the task of rebuilding a devastated Gondor falls to Aragorn. Thus, in his dual presentation of evil as both the "shadow of the good" (Shippey, *Author* 133) and as an outside force that can never be completely defeated, Tolkien seems not only to agree with Shakespeare, but to use the same devices for presenting it.

In addition to these, there is a third dimension to the relationship between good and evil in *Lear* and *LotR*. Not only is evil dependent upon good, but good is disturbingly dependent upon evil. In both texts, the need to struggle against evil has undeniably good effects: it develops silly, irresponsible characters into heroes. At the beginning of *Lear*, Gloucester is a bigger fool than the Fool, chattering about Edmund's illegitimacy right before his face and attributing all human failings, including Edgar's supposed disloyalty, to the stars (1.2.106–7). Especially given his early tendency to talk too much and too carelessly, the grandeur of his refusal to speak under torture is matched only by his compassionate restraint when Lear mistakenly observes that "Gloucester's bastard son / Was kinder to his father than my daughters / Got 'tween the lawful sheets" (4.6.114–16). Considering the extent of his own anguish, his pity for Lear shows a generosity of spirit that few people can claim and which, sadly, seems to come only from great suffering.

I have already discussed Lear's own growth as a king and as a human being. Let us now notice the amount of pure evil that is necessary to effect such a change in him. Before he suffers from the cruelty of his daughters and other forces of nature, he is not only petty and self-indulgent, but misjudges those he ought to know best, mostly because he refuses to see the situation from anyone else's viewpoint. He believes Cordelia must be "untender" and Kent "recreant" because he cannot see how his love-test looks to them. Yet, when he has a chance to "feel what wretches feel" (3.4.34), he learns to imagine everyone's motives, from the beadle, who lashes the whore all the harder because of his own lust, to Cordelia, in whose forgiveness and failed attempt to save him he now sees a sacrifice upon which "the gods themselves throw incense" (5.3.21). Suffering has taught him both pity for others and better understanding of their motives.

In *LotR*, the personal growth that various characters undergo in the struggle against evil is even more marked and pervasive. At the outset, the most foolish character in the fellowship is probably Pippin. He is the one who loudly and humorously calls Frodo the "Lord of the Ring," much to Gandalf's dismay (2.1.220). This childish inability to grasp the seriousness of the situation causes him later to drop the stone into the well at Moria, by which time Gandalf's "Fool of a Took" is already a familiar characterization. Yet Pippin is the one who has all the workable ideas for getting himself and Merry away from the orcs and whose quick thinking saves Faramir's life on the Pyre of Denethor. Even more telling, I think, is his self-restraint outside the Black Gate of Mordor, when Gandalf refuses the terms offered by Sauron to save Frodo. Especially considering his earlier tendency to talk too much, the fact that he "mastered himself" and resolves "to die soon and leave the bitter story of his life, since all was in ruin" (5.10.873) shows not only growth in his character, but a personal progress from silliness to heroic courage and self-sacrifice that is strikingly similar to Gloucester's.

Indeed, the personal growth that readers often note in Merry and Pippin, symbolized by the effects of the Ent-water, results directly from the greatest evil Tolkien knew: war. The once-popular view that Tolkien glorified war or ignored twentieth-century experience with it has been effectively refuted in recent books by John Garth and Janet Croft, who demonstrate that Tolkien's own war experience, including the "animal horror" of trench warfare (*Letters* 72), influences all his fiction. When Tolkien pictures war, he pictures total war, complete with sophisticated propaganda and industrial mechanization, war that devastates the landscape and consumes everyone who comes within its reach, combatants and non-combatants alike. Near the end of World War II, he writes to his son Christopher about the physical and spiritual waste of war and the sad impossibility of doing away with it (*Letters* 75). There should be no question that Tolkien saw war as one of the greatest evils of the fallen world. Yet, he also dared to depict another aspect of war, one that many of his contemporaries refused to acknowledge. Bernard Knox, explaining the mixture of glory and horror in Homer's battle scenes, observes that war has "its own strange and fatal beauty" (29), which depends, paradoxically, on its equally real horror. Knox goes on to remark "how clear and memorable and lovely is every detail of the landscape" to a soldier going into battle because he "fears he may be seeing [them] for the last time" (30). Tolkien's warriors, like Homer's, are sometimes intoxicated by what Homer would call "the dusty joy of battle." His Rohirrim "sang as they slew, for the joy of battle was on them" (5.5.820), and the younger hobbits discover in themselves the same "resources of endurance, courage and self-sacrifice" (Knox 29) that war has always brought out in men. Thus, Tolkien shows that the greatest evils often produce the greatest virtues.

Even Frodo, whose nature is far from the shallow self-absorption of King Lear, has, at the outset, a good deal to learn about empathy and compassion, as well as courage. When he learns that Gollum has probably given Sauron all the information he needs to link the One Ring with the Shire and the Bagginses, his first reaction is dismay that Bilbo chose not to kill Gollum. When Gandalf tries to explain the importance of pity and mercy in resisting evil, Frodo is understandably afraid and cannot feel sorry for Gollum. Of course, as Gandalf predicts, he does feel pity when he actually sees Gollum, but not only because of Gollum's wasted, tormented appearance. If this were the only factor, it would also move Sam, who is hardly incapable of pity. Frodo seems to understand Gollum's agony in a personal way that eludes Sam until he sees Gollum for the last time on Mount Doom and is somehow unable to hurt him. By this time, Sam also has worn the Ring, undergone intense suffering, including hunger and thirst, and "now dimly he guessed the agony of Gollum's shriveled mind and body" (6.3.923). Like Lear, they have learned from experience to sympathize with "Poor naked wretches" (*Lear* 3.4.28), and their compassion for this "forlorn, ruinous, utterly wretched" (*LotR* 6.3.923) creature saves not only them, but Middle-earth. Tolkien says as much when he writes that "the 'salvation' of the world and Frodo's own 'salvation' is achieved by his previous *pity* and forgiveness of injury" (*Letters* 234). Nor is his understanding and compassion confined to the particular torment of bearing the Ring. In "The Scouring of the Shire," he shows pity even to Saruman and Gríma, to which Saruman grudgingly observes, "You have grown, Halfling" (6.8.996).

By the time the Ring goes into the fire, even Frodo's fear is gone. He has grown so accustomed to believing that there is no possibility of surviving the destruction of the Ring that he consents to move further away from the exploding mountain only to oblige Sam. As Tolkien demonstrates, this kind of heroic despair is often all that courage means. It certainly corresponds closely to Pippin's feelings at the opening of the Black Gate, Merry's when he helps Éowyn slay the Nazgûl, and Théoden's when he emerges from the caves at Helm's Deep. One might argue that the world would be a better place if the evils that render such virtues necessary did not exist. What is beyond argument is that the virtues we value most depend upon evil, not just to be appreciated, but for their very existence. Shakespeare and Tolkien are among the few writers who have had the intellectual courage to confront this paradox directly, to admit that evil might be not just inevitable, but necessary.

Conclusion

Thus, the images and phrases in *LotR* that critics have traced back to *Lear* point to a source whose influence on Tolkien's work is more important and pervasive than Tolkien himself probably realized. In *LotR*, Tolkien follows patterns established in *Lear*, not only in isolated rhetorical devices, but in his presentation of the most significant themes in his work. First, Tolkien borrows elements of the basic plot of *Lear* by presenting a pair of fathers who are deceived into rejecting a good child. He continues to follow this plot when one of his fathers realizes his folly too late, and, believing his child dead, becomes suicidal in his guilt.

Second, Tolkien uses the same definition of good kingship that Shakespeare uses in *Lear*. Since this definition is not unique to Shakespeare, Tolkien's agreement on it need not in itself indicate influence. However, Tolkien teaches his kings (especially Aragorn) this definition through a specific lesson plan that includes exile from the palace and a lengthy search for identity. While the disguised king returning to claim his title is a common enough plot device that Tolkien need not have taken it from *Lear*, the two authors employ that device in a way that is not common. For both kings, the key scene is not their crowning—Lear never gets his crown back, and Aragorn gets his after the suspense is long over. Instead, each one has a defining moment in which he (and his subjects) know, even without the symbols of his office, that he is "every inch a king." Whether this fact becomes official reality is almost beside the point. This approach to the plot of the exiled king is rare enough that we should at least give serious consideration to the possibility that Tolkien takes it from Shakespeare.

Third, Tolkien's use of disguise is very similar to Shakespeare's. Éowyn disguises herself as Dernhelm, just as Kent disguises himself as Caius, in order to follow a feudal lord who has been like a father to her, but who has forbidden her to follow. Then, Frodo and Sam disguise themselves as the lowest of the low to avoid attracting attention, the same reason Edgar does so. While orcs are not mad beggars, they have a good deal in common, especially if one takes the Elizabethan view, as Edgar does, that madmen are possessed by demons. And of course, the two kings travel incognito for their own safety, and in the process learn much about kingship.

Fourth, Tolkien presents the complex relationship between good and evil precisely as Shakespeare does in *King Lear*. As other critics have shown, he defines evil in two ways: as a failed attempt at good and therefore dependent upon good for its meaning (the Boethian view) and as an independent force that exists separately from good and must be actively resisted (Manichean view). This dual view is also present in *Lear*, where evil repeatedly appears as "nothing" but nevertheless must be fought. Shakespeare and Tolkien also deal forthrightly with a frightening paradox: just as evil depends upon good, good also depends upon evil. Both writers connect their characters' personal growth with the need to resist evil. Even the specific virtues they develop—courage and compassion—result directly from their experiences with cruelty, deprivation, and war.

Some of these similarities may indeed result from coincidence, rather than influence. However, the number and extent of them, along with the fact that we know Tolkien regarded *King Lear* as a great work of art, makes it seem reasonable to believe that Tolkien's writing was affected by it. In *LotR*, he not only agrees with *Lear* in his view of major issues, but employs similar methods in presenting them.

Notes

1. As a result, supporting characters fall into the same roles. Gandalf, like Kent, tries to assure the insulted father that he is better off without the gift his honest child has refused to give. Predictably, given the pride and inflexibility of Lear and Denethor, neither succeeds, and both Gandalf and Kent must try to save the kingdom without the blessing of its ruler. Only Théoden supplies an example of the wiser choice. Letting Éomer out of prison, he acknowledges that "Faithful heart may have froward tongue" (3.6.510). Lear and Denethor suffer largely because they are late in learning this fact. (Editor's note: The edition of *LotR* used as the standard for this book has "forward tongue." I have chosen to use the corrected quotation from later editions.)

2. Tolkien might also be recalling that Henry VI, during the Wars of the Roses, referred to Henry Tudor, Earl of Richmond, as "England's Hope." Certainly, the Tudor Age came to be seen as a golden age, when England finally put the bloody rivalry between York and Lancaster safely in the past. But Henry Tudor, like Arthur (and King Horn and many another medieval romance hero) could not simply claim his throne. He had to earn it, not only by fighting, but also by forging alliances and proving himself to be the one who can unite the country.

3. Numerous studies connect madness in Shakespeare with Elizabethan and Jacobean views of madness as demonic possession. For example, see Joanna Levin's "Lady Macbeth and the Daemonologie of Hysteria."

4. Tolkien himself associates Poor Tom with Mordor, drawing from his mock-insane babble the image of the Dark Tower (Shippey, *Road* 208).

5. In his essay "Orcs, Wraiths, Wights," Shippey makes an intricate argument about the wraithing process in *LotR*, whose details need not be rehearsed here. The examples that follow are those that seem analogous to events in *Lear* and may have their source in it.

Works Cited

Carpenter, Humphrey. *Tolkien: A Biography*. Boston: Houghton, 1977.

Croft, Janet Brennan. *War and the Works of J.R.R. Tolkien*. Westport, CT: Praeger, 2004.

Drout, Michael. "Tolkien's Prose Style and Its Literary and Rhetorical Effects." *Tolkien Studies* 1.1 (2004): 137–63.

Flieger, Verlyn. *Splintered Light: Logos and Language in Tolkien's World*. Rev. ed. Kent, OH: Kent State University Press, 2002.

Garth, John. *Tolkien and the Great War: The Threshold of Middle-earth*. Boston: Houghton, 2003.

Guilfoyle, Cherrell. "The Redemption of King Lear." In *Shakespeare's Play within Play: Medieval Imagery and Scenic Form in* Hamlet, Othello, *and* King Lear. Kalamazoo: Western Michigan University Medieval Institute, 1990. 111–27.

Greenblatt, Stephen. "Shakespeare and the Exorcists." In *After Strange Texts: The Role of Theory in the Study of Literature*. Ed. Gregory Jay and David Miller. University: University of Alabama Press, 1985. 101–23.

Hawkes, Terence. "Something from Nothing." In *King Lear*. Plymouth, U.K.: Northcote, 1995. 52–57.

Kermode, Frank. Introduction to *King Lear*. In *The Riverside Shakespeare*. 2nd ed. Gen. ed. G. Blakemore Evans. Boston: Houghton, 1997.

Knox, Bernard. Introduction. *Iliad*. By Homer. Trans. Robert Fagles. New York: Viking, 1990.

Levin, Joanna. "Lady Macbeth and the Daemonologie of Hysteria." *ELH* 69.1 (2002): 21–55.

McFarland, Thomas. "The Image of the Family in *King Lear*." In *On King Lear*. Ed. Lawrence Danson. Princeton: Princeton University Press, 1981. 91–118.

Shakespeare, William. *The Complete Works of William Shakespeare*. Ed. David Bevington. 5th ed. New York: Pearson, 2004.

Shippey, Thomas A. *J.R.R. Tolkien: Author of the Century.* Boston: Houghton, 2000.
_____. "Orcs, Wraiths, Wights: Tolkien's Images of Evil." In *J.R.R. Tolkien and His Literary Resonances.* Ed. George Clark and Daniel Timmons. Westport, CT: Greenwood Press, 2000. 183–98.
_____. *The Road to Middle Earth: How J.R.R. Tolkien Created a New Mythology.* Rev. Ed. Boston: Houghton, 2003.
Tolkien, J.R.R. *Beowulf and the Critics.* Ed. Michael D.C. Drout. Medieval and Renaissance Texts and Studies. Vol. 248. Tempe: Arizona Center for Medieval and Renaissance Studies, 2002.
_____. *The Letters of J.R.R. Tolkien.* Ed. Humphrey Carpenter. Boston: Houghton, 2000.
_____. *The Lord of the Rings.* 2nd ed. Boston: Houghton, 1994.
_____. "On Fairy-Stories." In *The Tolkien Reader.* New York: Ballantine, 1966. 3–84.

Shakespearean Catharsis in the Fiction of J.R.R. Tolkien

Anne C. Petty

"Tragedy is an imitation of an action that is serious, complete, and possessing magnitude ... effecting through pity and fear [what we call] the *catharsis* of such emotion" (Aristotle, *Poetics* 50). As Shakespearean scholar John Briggs has observed, "Aristotle's well-known and enigmatic definition of catharsis in the *Poetics* does not specify whether the phenomenon occurs within audiences, characters, or plots, or within some combination of all three. We know that in tragedies it is supposed to be a movement of pity and fear" (Briggs 83). The term *catharsis* is problematic: it can be translated as purification or purgation, but in the purely literary sense is often understood to mean the experience of what Aristotle termed "tragic pleasure." That is, our vicarious sharing of a character's pain, terror, loss, and redemption brings a sense of emotional cleansing. Aristotle says, somewhat in passing, that catharsis can apply to both tragedy and comedy, but unfortunately whatever he might have written regarding comic catharsis has never been found. About the effects of tragedy, however, he had a good deal to say.

Of special importance is the requirement that action within the tragic plot be believably motivated and proceed from discernible causes. Accidents, simple bad luck, or simply the two-dimensional machinations of a completely evil character do not constitute an authentic tragic experience; the tragic events must have meaning beyond mere physical misery. Whether this cleansing effect through the momentary experience of pity and fear applies to the fictional characters or to those experiencing the creative work by reading or watching it, the sensation of poignant catharsis marks the work as tragedy.

As critic Harold Bloom explains in his massive study, *Shakespeare: The Invention of the Human*, "Shakespeare was the poet of loneliness and of its vision of mortality" (727). In this sense, Tolkien's instinct for tragedy was as profound as Shakespeare's, and his creation of the atmosphere of doom looming large over his heroines and heroes in the great tapestry of Middle-earth has moved many readers to anxiety, sorrow, and bittersweet relief. Tolkien's ability to induce catharsis in his readers is consistent with the tragic vision found in such plays as *King Lear, Hamlet, King Richard III*, and *Macbeth*. According to Bloom, "the pain Shakespeare affords us is as significant as the pleasure" (11), which easily describes any sympathetic reader's experience with *The Lord of the Rings* (*LotR*) or *The Silmarillion*.

The ultimate question I want to ask is this: Did Tolkien as a fiction writer create plots and characters that produce catharsis of a Shakespearean magnitude, and is there any evidence of inspiration for this tragic sensibility from the plays themselves? We know from his letters that Tolkien experienced moments of catharsis during the writing of his fiction: "I remember blotting the pages (which now represent the welcome of Frodo and Sam on the Field of Cormallen) with tears as I wrote" (321). Following this lead, I believe we can find a surprising number of instances where cathartic situations in *The Hobbit, LotR*, and *The Silmarillion* have resonances within the great tragedies of Shakespeare. To find these instances, we must look for the three elements Aristotle lists as being the most effective means of evoking tragic catharsis: reversal, recognition, and suffering. These elements are the stock in trade of Shakespearean tragedy.

Historical Perspectives

To discover this influence in Tolkien's narratives, we begin with the evolving interpretation of catharsis in literature: Aristotle's original theory of tragedy, the Renaissance rediscovery of the *Poetics*, and modern ideas about vicariously experiencing the personal tragedies of literary protagonists.

According to translator James Hutton, Aristotle's *Poetics* was not highly revered or even widely known during the classical or medieval eras. As a small work comprising twenty-six very short chapters or sections, it is commonly considered to be a collection of his lectures on poetry. In fact, Hutton claims we should really consider the *Poetics* "a modern book, called into life and activity by the needs of Renaissance and modern literature" (29). The Renaissance revival of Aristotle began in Italy in the sixteenth century with imitation of the great masters of

ancient literature followed by a tremendous amount of inquiry into the
nature of poetry, with the *Poetics* "supplying the major topics of discussion" (29) according to Hutton. Imported to England by the Renaissance Humanists in the early 1600s, the *Poetics* and its notion of catharsis
took on a certain moral connotation in which the tragic fall of noble-
men and kings provided lessons for ethical behavior. Although the term
catharsis appears nowhere in Shakespeare's writings, it seems too conservative to assume he was not aware of the concept when contemporaries such as Ben Jonson "absorbed a good deal of it" (Aristotle 31)
and tragedies such as *Macbeth, King Lear,* and *Hamlet* vividly demonstrate its effects.

In *Making Shapely Fiction,* critic Jerome Stern defines literary catharsis as figuring out "how to make unhappy endings work" (95). In other
words, the writer's challenge is to lead the audience (or readership)
through a range of draining emotions that will ultimately bring them
to recognition of "the inevitable sufferings of all humanity" (94). Such
modern interpretations of *catharsis* include, and indeed focus on, the
Willy Lomans (or Frodos) of the world, the humble everyman. However, Shakespeare's tragic characters, following Aristotle's model, were
elevated in status: kings, queens, and nobles. In our search for Shakespearean influence, then, we must look to Tolkien's elevated leaders
rather than his homely Hobbits. For the limited scope of this essay, my
target examples are three noble leaders of Middle-earth: a Dwarf lord,
a Steward of Men, and an Elf prince, namely, Thorin Oakenshield,
Denethor of Gondor, and Fëanor, patriarch of the Noldor.

How, then, to find the bridge between Shakespeare and Tolkien?
Tolkien's overall annoyance with Shakespeare is well known. His letters
are sprinkled with derogatory references to the Bard, the most often
quoted being his mention of having to study Shakespeare ("which I disliked cordially") as an adolescent at King Edward's School (*Letters* 213).
He strongly objected to Shakespeare's treatment of fairies ("damned
cobwebs" in his letter-essay to Milton Waldman [143n]) and Elves, about
which Tolkien held his own very specific opinions, famously expounded
in his essay, "On Fairy-Stories" (OFS). Such protests notwithstanding,
there is evidence that he knew the plays well, went to see performances
of them, and could be moved by well-acted presentations. In a 1944 letter to his son Christopher, he described a performance of *Hamlet* acted
by a "young rather fierce Hamlet" as a "very exciting play" (88). In OFS,
while acknowledging *King Lear*'s source in earlier folklore plots, he
emphasizes that it is the author's individual style, the "general purport
that informs with life the undissected bones of the plot" (19), that matters most.

Echoes of Shakespearean language, character motifs, themes, and larger plot devices are scattered throughout his novels and stories. Anyone needing to be convinced of how readily these references can be discovered need only read Michael Drout's essay, "Tolkien's Prose Style and Its Literary and Rhetorical Effects." T. A. Shippey also has much to say about Shakespearean resonances in *LotR*, exploring obvious parallels (the Nazgûl Lord's demise at the hands of a woman) as well as more subtle resonances (Anglo-Saxon alliteration littering the dialogue of *Macbeth* and echoed by Gandalf in phrases such as "If we fail, we fall") (Shippey 182–84).

But to discover catharsis, what kind of evidence are we looking for? First, we want to identify the elevated status of each protagonist in order to gauge how far each has fallen by the end of his tale. Arousal of pity and fear—or, in more modern terms, sympathy and terror or foreboding—is accomplished best through tragic interaction between characters with strong ties of family, love, or friendship. By tragic interaction, I mean those plot points so often quoted from the *Poetics*: reversal (change of fortune that brings about a fall from status or happiness), recognition (discovery of the source or cause of the fall), and suffering (loss and desire for redemption). In addition, we must look for traits within the characters themselves that allow these situations to develop. Thus, my study refers to both literary catharsis (that experienced by the characters) and personal catharsis (emotional and intellectual responses evoked in readers and audiences).

Thorin Oakenshield, Denethor, and Fëanor all demonstrate Tolkien's subtle understanding of what makes Hamlet, Lear, Richard III, and Macbeth such compelling characters. Through vicarious experience of their complicated lives, whether on stage or the printed page, readers (and theatergoers) become emotionally and intellectually engaged with their fulfillments and disappointments, unexpected reversals of fortune and redemptions, and especially with the confrontation of death and mortality.

The internal aspect of catharsis is difficult to prove or dissect, because who can tell what readers or theatergoers are feeling as they experience a work? However, the literary aspect of catharsis is easily documented—a character sheds tears, rails against fate, regrets bloody deeds, commits suicide. These overt demonstrations of catharsis give those who apprehend the work clues as to how to feel about what they are reading or seeing. In that respect, literary catharsis triggers the personal release of emotional tension and brings a new way of thinking about the subject. Shakespeare's plays, whether read or experienced in the theater, provide ample cathartic triggers, and, I hope to show, Tolkien's fiction does as well.

Thorin Oakenshield

The Hobbit may seem an unlikely place to begin a study of catharsis. After all, if it is a children's book, it should not contain tragedy strong enough to provoke strong catharsis in characters or readers. The truth, however, is that The Hobbit begins in the shallows and descends gradually, but surely, into darker waters. While its structure has been described (and denigrated) as episodic, it also presents a single, well-structured account of leadership gone wrong. Thorin Oakenshield's personal journey of revenge turns to blind greed, delusions of former grandeur, and willful disregard of good advice and the safety of his companions. His fall is both predictable and deserved, but there is much more to his story than merely reaping what he has sown. His death at the end of the Battle of Five Armies is an early demonstration of the sort of tragedy that so suited Tolkien as a writer, and its Shakespearean overtones are many.

Consider where Thorin begins his journey. At the outset of the adventure, he is described as an "enormously important dwarf, in fact no other than the great Thorin Oakenshield himself" (Hobbit 1.18). Among the hoods hung in Bilbo's hallway, his is the only one with a long silver tassel. Like many Shakespearean heroes, he enters the tale in a position of power and respect. The opening scene of Macbeth, for example, presents the protagonist as a respected leader and fighter whose bravery under siege inspires both awe and fear. The same could be said of Thorin, whose leadership is unquestioned. Like Shakespeare's treatment of his Scottish general, Tolkien gradually reveals Thorin's true colors.

Through his interactions with Bilbo, Gandalf, and the other dwarves during preparations for their quest to regain the dragon-usurped treasure under the Lonely Mountain, he is shown to be "very haughty" and disdains to offer an "At your service!" to Bilbo, unlike the other dwarves (Hobbit 1.19). He is likewise too self-important to pitch in with cleaning up the hobbit's kitchen after dinner and takes the best bedroom for himself, ordering breakfast specially cooked his way, without so much as a word of thanks to his host. He is clearly in charge of the physical expedition and expects the others to obey him without argument. From this, we have the first indications that he could be tempted by power, especially where it concerns regaining his grandfather Thror's lost kingdom. The possibility that he could become a bloodthirsty tyrant like Macbeth or Richard III seems unlikely at this point, but as The Hobbit darkens toward its denouement, those comparisons become more appropriate.

At the touch of Thorin's golden harp, the dwarves' song of lost riches and thieving dragons reveals to Bilbo "a fierce and a jealous love, the desire of the hearts of dwarves" (1.24). And when Gandalf explains that he acquired Thror's map of the Lonely Mountain from Thorin's father Thrain, who had been held and tortured by the Necromancer, Thorin momentarily shifts his sights from dislodging a dragon to taking on a much greater adversary until Gandalf admonishes him not to be ridiculous. These inclinations toward potentially disastrous self-aggrandizement are not unlike Macbeth's initial reaction to the prediction that he would take on the role of both thane and king. "Glamis, and Thane of Cawdor! / The greatest is behind" (1.3.116–17) he muses, realizing that the first part of the witches' prophecy has already come true. The idea that he could indeed go further comes to him as he considers his future: "Two truths are told, / As happy prologues to the swelling act / Of the imperial theme" (1.3.128–29).

Thorin echoes this proclamation of titles as he makes his grand entrance into the great hall of Lake-town: "'I am Thorin son of Thrain son of Thror King under the Mountain! I return!'" (10.209). Townsfolk make songs in the honor of the Mountain-king's return, and the Master of Lake-town seats Thorin in his own chair of office, further inflating his ego. "Thorin looked and walked as if his kingdom was already regained and Smaug chopped up into little pieces" (10.211). Lady Macbeth echoes these sentiments as she welcomes Macbeth's return after his elevation to higher status by King Duncan, proclaiming him "Great Glamis! Worthy Cawdor! / Greater than both, by the all-hail hereafter!" (1.5.54).

From Thorin's pride and its resonance in *Macbeth*, we turn now to the effect the Dwarvish treasure hoard exerts after Smaug is dispatched. All the dwarves fall under its spell, and Thorin especially, as he assumes the title of King Under the Mountain in both word and deed. As I discussed in *Tolkien in the Land of Heroes*, by playing the tyrant, Thorin "oversteps his power as leader of the expedition to the Lonely Mountain when his lust for the heirloom of his house, the Arkenstone, clouds his judgment" (171). It blinds him to the reality of the situation and isolates him from the goodwill of others. What follows next is to find where his reversal of fortune occurs, the scene for its appearance having now been set up.

In answer to parlays from representatives of Men and Elves claiming a share of the treasure, Thorin makes his stance clear with warlike songs. He refuses all claims on the hoard, no matter how reasonable or fair-minded, commanding the hosts to move away from the Mountain's entrance and to consider themselves "foes and thieves." Here Thorin makes a rash and foolish decision that estranges him from those who could be allies and endangers the lives of those closest to him. In a fit of fury, he shoots an arrow into the shield of one of the heralds, commanding him to "'Begone now ere our arrows fly!'" (15.278). This adamant refusal to see reason or change his edict mirrors the stubbornness of King Lear when he abjures Kent in the same way: "If on the tenth day following / Thy banished trunk be found in our dominions, / The moment is thy death. Away! By Jupiter, / This shall not be revoked" (1.1.179–82).

Once war becomes reality and the mountain put under siege by the armies of Mirkwood and Lake-town, Thorin's fortunes begin a downward spiral. As one wry messenger observes, the dwarves might have possession of all the gold, but it won't be edible once they begin to starve. This echoes Macbeth's tenacity in defending his citadel against impossible odds and in spite of dire warnings from scouts in the field. Tension is further heightened by Thorin's refusal of advice from the old raven Roäc, who predicts that the treasure will be his death. Roäc warns of "winter and snow" coming with the approaching hosts, and asks "How shall you be fed without the friendship and goodwill of the lands about you?" (16.279). Likewise, Macbeth snaps at one of his officers, "Our castle's strength / Will laugh a siege" to scorn: here let them lie, / Till famine and the ague eat them up" (5.5.2–4). The sense of stalemate is taut, but readers know that something must snap soon.

This impasse means that Thorin must sacrifice his life for a wrong cause. When the Arkenstone is revealed to be in the hands of his enemies, thanks to Bilbo's burglary skills, Thorin's greatest reason to defend the hoard evaporates. This is the checkmate move that forces him into agreeing to divide the treasure. Calling down curses on all involved and refusing to admit the error of his decision in spite of the odds against him, Thorin appears doomed, and we are filled with foreboding over how the axe will fall. Gandalf offers a foreshadowing of the catharsis to come when he chides Thorin for not being a very good King under the Mountain, adding, "'But things may change yet'" (17.288).

Further resonance with the final act of *Macbeth* is clear as Tolkien's story moves toward the Battle of Five Armies. Macbeth prepares to fight the encroaching English forces, believing all the while that he cannot lose because of the prophecies that say, "none of woman born / Shall harm Macbeth" and "Macbeth shall never vanquished be until / Great Birnam wood to high Dunsinane Hill / Shall come against him" (4.1.80–94). But to his great shock, the battle takes an unthinkable turn as both prophecies turn out to have loopholes. Likewise, when Dain's army prepares to attack the forces of Men and Elves, the conflict changes unexpectedly when the sudden attack of goblins and wargs forces them into an emergency alliance. In both cases, emotional tension is stretched to its snapping point—Macbeth confronts his mortal enemy, Macduff, who was "from his mother's womb / Untimely ripped" (5.8.15–16), and Thorin leaps into battle at last, fighting Orcs alongside his sworn enemies.

Thorin's impending death from his wounds creates the perfect situation for tragic catharsis. The requisite moment of recognition comes in his final meeting with Bilbo. Remember that for tragedy to work, the ending must transfigure the sadness and horror of the events so that readers (and viewers) experience catharsis rather than depression. Jerome Stern's explanation of the proper outcome of tragedy (meaningful, pleasurable release from the building tension of the play or novel, rather than emotional manipulation that only leaves you with a feeling of emptiness and disappointment) applies to both Shakespeare and Tolkien.

The death scene of the protagonist is critical: what is lost and what is gained, and how is order restored to the realm in which the action occurs? Sometimes revelatory catharsis is achieved through the point of view of the tragic character, but it can also come through the words of someone important to the protagonist. Although Macbeth faces death alone and friendless, damned beyond all redemption, he musters a last surge of courage, telling his avenging adversary, "Yet I will try the last. Before my body / I throw my warlike shield. Lay on, Macduff, / And damned be him that first cries, 'Hold, enough!'" (5.8.32–34).

Likewise, Thorin's death is crafted so that he voices his own truth, expressing regret by wishing he could take back his hateful actions. Readers are encouraged to feel compassion for Thorin as he painfully acknowledges what Bilbo has tried to tell him, namely that if "'more of us valued food and cheer and song above hoarded gold, it would be a merrier world'" (18.301). Bilbo's tearful reaction at his passing, where we are told that he cried his eyes out and lost his voice from weeping, models the bittersweet release that "gave him more sorrow than joy" (ibid.). As in *Macbeth*, order is restored by command passing to a more worthy commander, in this case Dain, Thorin's cousin, who deals out the treasure fairly and ensures that Thorin is entombed with honor. As a symbol of unity restored, Bard places the stolen Arkenstone on his breast and the Elvenking lays Thorin's Elvish sword Orcrist atop the tomb. It is an emotional yet satisfying end to Thorin's tragic story. Closure is provided by Bilbo's sense of resignation; he has come face to face with death and loss, and is a sadder but wiser Hobbit for having known the great Thorin Oakenshield.

Denethor

We read in the *Poetics* that one of the greatest opportunities for tragedy derives from estrangement or deadly conflict involving parent and child. Nowhere in Shakespeare is this theme more poignant than in *King Lear*. Whether Lear's character is seen as sympathetic or deplorably self-destructive, it is virtually impossible to come away from the play emotionally untouched. I believe that Tolkien's creation of Denethor in *The Lord of the Rings* reflects this impact of *Lear* in a number of ways. In addition, there are instances in *Richard III* and *Macbeth* where we can see models for Denethor's prideful, dangerous nature and flawed vision of the world.

Tolkien presents Denethor as having the genetic potential to be like the great kings of old. His heritage is that of a nobleman, but his arrogance and need for power reduce him to cruelty and madness. The reader's catharsis at his suicide derives from relief for Faramir and regret at the way in which the last Steward's life shriveled to bitterness and needless death. Like Shakespeare, Tolkien uses a noble character to illuminate the universal theme of the use and abuse of power. The issue of stewardship, especially the consequences of leaders renouncing their responsibilities, is what drives both Denethor and Lear toward ruin. Both lose their command and eventually even their human dignity. Examining the fall of Denethor in the light of Lear gives added insight into Tolkien's sense of tragedy and his ability to touch readers' emotions revolving around family, duty, and loyalty.

Denethor is not an easy character to feel sympathy toward. We first perceive him through his son Boromir's words at the Council of Elrond, where he is described as being a strong leader and loremaster, but Gandalf's follow-up to Boromir's speech offers a slightly different slant on the Steward that suggests an imperious and dismissive nature more cunning than Boromir recognizes. Denethor's haughty words to Gandalf, "'you will find naught that is not well known to me, who am master of the lore of this City'" (2.2.246) reflect an attitude shared by both Lear and Richard III. Richard describes himself as "subtle, false, and treacherous" (1.1.37), and as Lear prepares to hand power over to his daughters and their husbands, he commands them with arrogance to say who loves him most in order to receive the best reward. The makings of *hubris* (exaggerated pride calling for retribution) are clearly marked in these characters, and, as readers, we know that pride goes before a fall.

To identify Denethor as a potentially tragic figure, one who can make us fear his actions and feel sorrow at their consequences, we need to discern the point at which he makes his fatal error in judgment. Wise as he seems at first, Tolkien allows him to make mistakes, even greatly harmful ones. His arrogance is easily documented. Denethor imagines himself wiser than mere mortals because of his Númenórean heritage, but more to the point, he possesses a *palantír.* It could be argued that his first obvious mistake in *LotR* is to allow Boromir to go to Rivendell instead of Faramir, who is much more diplomatic, with the intuitive gifts of the ancient Númenóreans. Faramir, as we know, refused the lure of the Ring when he encountered Frodo in Ithilien; who knows how the journey of the Nine Walkers would have proceeded if he had been a member of the Fellowship instead of his easily tempted brother?

The real problem, however, is Denethor's decision to use the *palantír.* It allows him to see far and wide over his territory, but it also allows him to touch the mind of Sauron, leaving him vulnerable to the primary source of evil in Middle-earth. Filling the Steward's mind with visions of doom and destruction, Sauron is able to confuse Denethor's perception of reality, pushing him to the breaking point. "'And even now the wind of thy hope cheats thee and wafts up Anduin a fleet with black sails,'" (5.7.835), he cries. This echoes Macbeth's wrong interpretations of the visions shown him by the three witches and their prophecy-intoning apparitions. The fact that both Macbeth and Denethor would even accept as tenable any information coming from such clear sources of evil reveals their flawed personalities.

To further fuel the catharsis to come, both Tolkien and Shakespeare set their royal fathers against their offspring through rashly made decisions based on misreading the personalities of those offspring. Both Faramir and Cordelia have genuine love for their misguided fathers, but refuse to mouth the flatteries and follow the selfish orders demanded by those fathers. "'Your bearing is lowly in my presence,'" Denethor tells Faramir, "'yet it is long now since you turned from your own way at my counsel'" (5.4.794). The arrogant Lear demands, "Which of you shall say doth love us most" and, when Cordelia refuses to play sycophant, he cautions her, "Mend your speech a little, / Lest you may mar your fortunes" (1.1.94–95).

Denethor's reversal of fortune from stern ruler to demented, broken old man has numerous resonances within *Lear.* For Lear, the actual point of reversal comes when both false daughters refuse to take him in, forcing him to spend the night in a terrible storm. At this point, his royalty is in tatters and his sanity cracking. In the company of his Fool, Lear laments his hateful daughters: "Is there any cause in nature that makes these hard hearts?" (3.6.76–77). A similar point of reversal for Denethor is most vividly brought home in *The Return of the King,* when Faramir is carried to him half-dead from the battlefield. This sends Denethor to his private tower to face a different kind of raging storm.

What he sees when he consults the *palantír* is his breaking point, and we are told that when he returned to sit by Faramir's bed, "the face of the Lord was grey, more deathlike than his son's" (5.4.803).

In *King Lear*, our initial feelings toward Lear are outrage at his shallow and irrational treatment of Cordelia. We desperately want him to acknowledge the mistake he's made and to reconcile with her in some way, even though he repeatedly throws away opportunities to do so. The same can be said for Denethor's cruel treatment of Faramir. Whose heart does not ache when Faramir asks if he should have died in his brother's place and his father replies, "'Yes, I wish that indeed.... For Boromir was loyal to me and no wizard's pupil.... He would have brought me a mighty gift'" (5.4.795). This is a clear echo of Lear's hateful words to Cordelia: "Go to, go to, better thou hadst not been born than not to have pleased me better" (1.1.237–38).

Denethor's recognition of his love for Faramir comes as he sits by his son's bedside, refusing to be parted from him. This reversal is overshadowed, however, by his growing madness and despair that sees only the end of the world. Like Lear, the immensity of his suffering breaks his mind; both shed tears for their lost children and both harbor fleeting hope that each still lives, giving readers a brief hope that disaster can be avoided. The situation between Denethor and Faramir is similar to Lear's rejection of Cordelia, but with a Tolkienian twist. Denethor pushes Faramir away, denying him the father's love he deserves; however, Denethor dies on his pyre without his much-abused son—Faramir is given a second chance to fulfill his potential, this time under the worthy kingship of Aragorn.

Gandalf frames the cathartic experience for us, commenting on both death and life to Beregond: "'So passes Denethor, son of Ecthelion.... And so pass also the days of Gondor that you have known; for good or evil they are ended'" (5.7.836–37). In *King Lear*, the exchange between Kent and Edgar at Lear's death repeats these sentiments, as Kent says, "Vex not his ghost. Oh, let him pass! ... The weight of this sad time we must obey; / Speak what we feel, not what we ought to say" (5.3.319–30).

When Lear's moment of recognition comes—that Cordelia's love was genuine and remained true to him even as he spurned it for the false loyalty of his elder daughters—it is too late for him to be healed by its catharsis. Her death followed by his completes the tragic cycle of outrage, fear, sorrow, and release. For the audience or reader, the ordeal is tragic, but it is also satisfying in its completeness and worth the experience of witnessing Shakespeare's representation of familial love rejected and repaid.

In *LotR*, Denethor's outcome is equally bittersweet. "'Ill deeds have been done here; but let now all enmity that lies between you be put away,'" Gandalf tells Denethor's stunned retainers (5.7.837), echoing the pronouncement of the Earl of Richmond at Richard III's violent death: "Proclaim a pardon to the soldiers fled / That in submission will return to us ... we will unite the white rose and the red" (5.5.16–19). Order is restored, but at what price? Senseless death has cast its long shadow over the world for Lear, Richard III, and Denethor, and what has been done will not easily be undone. And yet—although Denethor has not died a good death, Faramir lives to refresh the fading line of high Númenóreans beside his rightful king. Fear and sorrow have been replaced by hope.

Fëanor

We come at last to Fëanor, arguably the most well-conceived, complex character in *The Silmarillion*. Here Tolkien has drawn a portrait of the best and brightest of the Firstborn, one who should have been a shining example of his kind, but instead allowed *hubris* to destroy everything that should have been his glory. His pride in creating the Silmarils and his ensuing madness when they are stolen dooms not just Fëanor but the entire line of Noldorin Elves. So much suffering and loss occurs in *The Silmarillion* because of him that when his cursed life is finally brought to an end, tears are appropriate for everyone touched by it, readers included. Because Tolkien was so emotionally engaged with the Silmarillion mythos, his own sorrow at so much beauty and promise laid low is visceral, and highly Shakespearean, as we'll discover.

The death of a parent, feelings of displacement, obsession for revenge, ruin of a once exalted leader along with those who inherit his self-inflicted curse—these plot elements are the stuff of high tragedy. References to *King Lear, Hamlet, Macbeth,* and *Richard III* are strewn in Fëanor's wake in a broad path through *The Silmarillion.* The way in which these parallels lead up to the cathartic resolution of his fate constitutes this final section of my study. When we read that before "the Valar were aware, the peace of Valinor was poisoned" (68), we are immediately reminded of that famous line spoken by the soldier Marcellus in *Hamlet,* "Something is rotten in the state of Denmark" (1.4.90), and it is the way in which this poison flows through the plot toward death that brings such poignant catharsis.

Like all the truly great Shakespearean tragic figures who reap in spades what they sow, Fëanor squanders his many gifts to the anguish and grief of those around him (as well as readers who become emotionally invested in his bright beginning). If any one line from Shake-

speare could set the tone for Fëanor, it would be the opening line from
King Richard III, "Now is the winter of our discontent" (1.1.1), for it is
Fëanor's inability to be content that fuels his fiery nature and sets the
tension for the tragedies to come. Although Fëanor does not kill his
way to the throne, as do Richard, Macbeth, and Hamlet's uncle
Claudius, he comes close. Hamlet-like, he hates his father's second marriage and the perceived advancement of the sons of that union. He
threatens his half-brother Fingolfin at sword point with angry words:
"Get thee gone, and take thy due place! ... Try but once more to usurp
my place and the love of my father, and maybe it will rid the Noldor of
one who seeks to be the master of thralls" (70). Compare King Richard's
angry outburst, "Why, Buckingham, I say I would be king.... Shall I be
plain? I wish the bastards dead, / And I would have it suddenly perfor-
m'd" (4.2.12–18).

Fëanor defiantly refuses wise counsel until he meets his death far
from his homeland and bereft of all friends but his sons, who are bound
by oath to defend him. It is painful to watch the gradual but relentless
advance into the darkness of one who outshone those around him with
his physical beauty, tremendous personal power, and ability to create
objects of great wonder. Tolkien gives readers many emotional clues and
triggers for the impending fall, with cathartic tension building relentlessly as the banished Noldor pursue their doom. The terrible Kinslay-
ing at Alqualondë where the Eldar slaughter their own kind and
Mandos's cold, terrifying pronouncement of doom in the aftermath
bring feelings of fear, foreboding, and sorrow to a peak.

Where can we say that Fëanor definitively falls into error, making
that critical wrong decision or taking a crucial wrong action that
solidifies the tragedy? There are many clues along the way that such a
moment is inevitable, from his sad childhood deprived of a mother's
love, to his resentment at his father's remarriage, to his jealousy of his
half-brothers. We can also point to his secretive nature that hides the
motivations for his actions and hoards the Silmarils. I believe the telling
moment, however, is when he draws his sword against Fingolfin over
the issue of supremacy. From this act flow (1) his banishment as well as
that of King Finwë, his father, from Tirion, (2) the summons to give up
his sacred Silmarils against his will to save the Two Trees defiled by
Ungoliant and Melkor, and (3) the Noldorin rebellion that drives him
and most of his kin out of the Blessed Realm and into Middle-earth
where death awaits.

He makes other disastrous decisions and commits rash acts with
increasingly evil results (swearing the oath that dooms his House and
entire line, killing his Elvish kinsmen in order to steal the Swan ships
at Alqualondë, deserting most of the remaining Noldor in the ice fields

of the Helcaraxë). All these events, however, are the result of that initial warlike challenge to his half-brother, where his true nature is revealed and words are said that change the course of his life. Once he openly draws a weapon in the Blessed Realm with murderous intent, his course, like that of Macbeth, is set. We cannot help but feel both horror and sadness for Macbeth as he voices the reality of his situation: "I am in blood / Stepped in so far that, should I wade no more, / Returning were as tedious as go o'er" (3.4.137–39). Fëanor's bloody theft of the ships at Alqualondë puts him in the same hopeless situation.

Fëanor's reversal of fortune is both gradual and swift, which makes for an emotional ride. Let me explain this. With mounting dread, we watch as he makes one damaging move after another, knowing the outcome cannot be positive. The emotional tension Tolkien weaves into Fëanor's gradual ruin comes from the conflicting emotions Fëanor himself feels about his situation: he resists the dictates of others and wants the knowledge Melkor has to offer, but at the same time hates the dark Vala more than anyone. He creates the most beautiful objects in all Valinor, the Silmarils, but the pride and greed that consume his heart prevent him from sharing them willingly with the Valar and Eldar. He wants to be acknowledged for his great skill, yet at the same time he pushes everyone further away as Melkor poisons his intellect and passions.

That is the gradual part that is so difficult to watch. In the blink of an eye, however, the gradual slide becomes an avalanche when Melkor slays Finwë and steals the Silmarils. This is not simply bad luck or happenstance; the jewels have cast their spell over Melkor as well as Fëanor. His desire to have them at all costs is as strong as Fëanor's is to hoard them. It is no surprise that in a blind fury Fëanor swears revenge for their theft; what is surprising is the level of deranged venom that forms the oath. Fëanor's curse, called down on Melkor and the heads of anyone else who might have designs on the jewels, is the most Middle-earth–shattering oath any of its inhabitants have ever witnessed. The language in which Tolkien couches the famous oath is some of his most Shakespearean in weight and cadence. Fëanor and his seven sons lift swords together, swearing to hound "to the ends of the World Vala, Demon, Elf or Man as yet unborn, or any creature, great or small, good or evil" (83) who obtains a Silmaril. This scene calls to mind the ghost's emphatic command, "Swear," as Hamlet demands repeatedly that his followers take an oath on his sword to keep secret the apparition's appearance.

This is the moment of absolute reversal, from which neither Fëanor nor his immediate kin will ever recover. One of the strongest emotional triggers for poignant catharsis is the revelation that great Manwë, highest of the Valar, sheds tears when Fëanor refuses to abort his decision to take the Noldorin host out of Aman and into the untamed world of Middle-earth. The prophecy of doom spoken by Mandos, grim as it is, is simply the final stage of the reversal initiated by Fëanor. Tolkien tells us that Fëanor "hardened his heart" and vowed to carry on with his disastrous plan, much like King Richard in his determination to sweep away all obstacles to his power: "But I am in / So far in blood that sin will pluck on sin; / Tear-falling pity dwells not in this eye" (*R3* 4.2.63–65), nor in the eye of Fëanor the Firstborn.

As a plot device with tremendous emotional value, Fëanor's oath frames the history of the Noldor from this point forward. The visceral experience of doom and foreboding released by those words is hard to resist—the Noldor recoil from it, modeling what readers may also be feeling. The indication that Fëanor is headed for a bad end cannot be ignored, especially once he burns the stolen Swan ships on the shore of Middle-earth, recalling Kent's words of warning to Lear about what happens when "majesty falls to folly." Kent pleads, "Reserve thy state, / And in thy best consideration check / This hideous rashness" (1.1.150–52). Likewise, Fëanor's act of defiance has literally and symbolically burned his bridges behind him. There can be no return.

Tolkien carefully develops the remaining stages of Fëanor's demise to maximize the emotional tension and release that is imminent. Fëanor's foolish pursuit of skirmishing orcs, fueled by fury rather than reason, has been set up all along, and we recognize this to be consistent behavior. With dread, we read how, surrounded and outnumbered, he is horribly wounded. But rather than allowing him to die at that moment, Tolkien prolongs the agony for one more paragraph, letting his sons rescue him from the attack and bear him back toward their base camp on the plains of Mithrim, stretching the tension further like a bent bow.

The release comes when Fëanor asks them to halt, providing what we recognize as a moment of cathartic revelation: "with his last sight he beheld far off the peaks of Thangorodrim, mightiest of the towers of Middle-earth, and knew with the foreknowledge of death that no power of the Noldor would ever overthrow them" (107). The manner of his death fulfills our expectations, occurring in a sudden fiery exit that incinerates his body to ashes and smoke.

The moment when Fëanor realizes that all the grim determination and cruel ruthlessness with which he has pursued his enemy Morgoth has been in vain is possibly the single most poignant aspect of his troubled tale. Here, Tolkien creates the so-called bittersweet pleasure of catharsis through tragic irony; after such a long and harrowing struggle to arrive across the ice and sea to Middle-earth, Fëanor dies in a surprise orc raid before his first camp is established. Shakespeare couldn't have written a better scene himself, although the desperate ending of *Macbeth* comes close.

Macbeth, who in the early hours of the siege of his castle boasts, "Till Birnam wood remove to Dunsinane, / I cannot taint with fear" (5.3.2–3) and "I'll fight, till from my bones my flesh be hack'd" (5.3.32), models Fëanor, who chases after the retreating orcs with no heed for his own safety. But when told by a messenger that "the wood began to move" (5.5.35), Macbeth sees, as did Fëanor, "with the foreknowledge of death," that his ambitions are doomed and his enemy cannot be overcome. "If this which he avouches does appear," cries Macbeth, "There is nor flying hence nor tarrying here. / I 'gin to be aweary of the sun, / And wish th'estate o'th' world were now undone" (5.5.47–50).

In *The Silmarillion*, the coda of reconciliation and restoration of order comes somewhat later when Fingon, son of Fingolfin, rescues Fëanor's son Maedhros from Thangorodrim. Although the doom of the curse is far from being extinguished, forgiveness between the two houses of Fingolfin and Fëanor allows a respite from bloodshed. Richmond, at Richard III's death, voices a similar sentiment of reconciliation when he says, "Now civil wounds are stopped, peace lives again" (5.5.40).

Conclusion

"Endings," wrote Steven Winn on New Year's Day 2005 for the *San Francisco Chronicle*, "define and disappoint, gratify and frustrate. They confer meaning and confirm the structure of what's come before" by providing a kind of punctuation mark to a slice of life. The successful artistic ending is "both startling and inevitable, mysteriously certain. It clarifies even as it complicates, crystallizes and expands" (2). We can easily see how this applies to the endings we've been discussing where catharsis clarifies the deaths of Thorin Oakenshield, Denethor, and Fëanor, as well as Lear, Macbeth, Hamlet, and Richard III.

In the final analysis, the experience of catharsis gives fresh insights into human nature, where disaster as well as redemption is possible. Recall that in his theory of tragedy Aristotle remarked that the downfall of the protagonist occurs through some mistake, either of judgment or action; by this we see that tragic heroes are neither all good nor all bad, neither black nor white, dark nor light, but rather some shading of gray. They are intermediates, with layers and depth that allow for change and revelation.

Shakespeare instinctively knew this to be true, which is superbly demonstrated in his depictions of the intellectual Hamlet obsessing over the right course of action and the passion-driven Lear railing against the elements of wind and rain. As Harold Bloom expressed it, "What Shakespeare invents are ways of representing human changes, alterations not only caused by flaws and by decay but effected by the will as well, and by the will's temporal vulnerabilities" (2). Tolkien, I believe, absorbed these truths from his encounters with Shakespeare—the evidence lies before us in the lives (and deaths) of a Dwarf, a Man, and an Elf.

Works Cited

Aristotle. *Poetics*. Trans. James Hutton. New York: Norton, 1982.

Bloom, Harold. *Shakespeare: The Invention of the Human*. New York: Penguin, 1998.

Briggs, John C. "Catharsis in *The Tempest*." *Ben Jonson Journal* 5 (1998): 115–32.

Drout, Michael. "Tolkien's Prose Style and Its Literary and Rhetorical Effects." *Tolkien Studies* 1 (2004): 137–63.

Petty, Anne. *Tolkien in the Land of Heroes: Discovering the Human Spirit*. New York: Cold Spring, 2003.

Shakespeare, William. *The Complete Works of William Shakespeare*. Ed. David Bevington. 5th ed. New York: Pearson, 2004.

Shippey, Thomas A. *The Road to Middle-Earth*. Rev. and exp. ed. Boston: Houghton, 2003.

Stampfer, Judah. "The Catharsis of King Lear." *Shakespeare Survey* 13 (1960): 1–10.

Stern, Jerome. *Making Shapely Fiction*. New York: Norton, 1991.

Tolkien, J. R. R. *The Hobbit*. 2nd ed. Boston: Houghton, 1966.

___. *The Letters of J.R.R. Tolkien*. Ed. Humphrey Carpenter. Boston: Houghton, 2000.

___. *The Lord of the Rings*. 2nd ed. Boston: Houghton, 1994.

___. "On Fairy-Stories." In *The Tolkien Reader*. New York: Ballantine, 1966. 3–84.

___. *The Silmarillion*. 2nd ed. Boston: Houghton, 2001.

Winn, Steven. "Endings Are a Catharsis." *San Francisco Chronicle*, 1 January 2005. Retrieved 22 December 2005 at http://www.sfgate.com/cgi-bin/article.cgi?f=/c/a/2005/01/01/DDG7VAJAL81.DTL&hw=winn&sn=011&sc=859

MAGIC

Prospero's Books, Gandalf's Staff

The Ethics of Magic in Shakespeare and Tolkien

NICHOLAS OZMENT

When Prospero wanted something done, he opened his books and called upon the beholden spirit Ariel. When Gandalf was in a bind, he lifted his staff and called upon "the Secret Fire." These two characters, along with Merlin, have probably had the most influence in shaping our present-day conceptions of wizards. Yet though they share that mantle, they are remarkably different in both the source and nature of their power. Nonetheless, Tolkien and Shakespeare held strikingly similar ideas in differentiating between types of magic and in portraying magic's inherent dangers. In this chapter, I explore those affinities by comparing and contrasting Prospero and Gandalf. This comparison will illuminate a further distinct kind of magic in Tolkien absent in *The Tempest*: a kind of white magic that has much in common with the miracles of the saints and angels in Judeo-Christian myth and scripture. This chapter will also demonstrate that the ethics of magic was more than an ancillary concern for both writers.

Tempests Old and New: A Storm of Controversy

"Burn those wicked books!"

That is not just the cry of early Massachusetts Puritans, or of contemporary Taliban leaders. It is a cry that can be heard now in PTA meetings and church luncheons across the United States, and it is raised by parents who allege they are only trying to protect their children. What sort of books have gained such notoriety for veiling wickedness, coiled like serpents under dust-jackets? Pornography? Books that promote drug use or terrorism or suicide? No: Harry Potter books, in fact—books that promote magic, which no one even believes in anymore, presumably. Yet according to Mark West, a professor of English with a specialty in children's literature at the University of North Carolina at Charlotte, "They [opponents of the Harry Potter series] don't see it as fantasy. They see it as real. A small group of Americans can't accept fantasy that way" (qtd. in Dunne). Equating the mere mention of a witch or a magic spell with evil, this small but vocal group made the Harry Potter books the most challenged literature of 1999, according to the American Library Association, with twenty-six separate attempts to ban them from bookshelves in sixteen states (Dunne). Potter author J.K. Rowling's magical subject matter puts her in company with Shakespeare and Tolkien, both of whose works have also been banned at one time or another. We can add several other authors to this list, including Ursula Le Guin, C.S. Lewis, and Madeleine L'Engle. Ironically, the latter two authors, like Tolkien, are professed Christians. Shakespeare is also assumed by many to have been a Christian, although he left no autobiographical statement. Still, this is no defense in the judgment of religious fundamentalists, who perceive any such trucking with magic to be a violation of biblical admonishments.

That books which concern themselves to some extent with the workings of magic continue to draw criticism and attack should indicate that magic is not a dead issue. Of course, it was treated as a non-issue by critics through much of the twentieth century (that is to say, it was rarely treated at all); as Donald Keesey observes, "the philosophical and ethical problems of white and black magic that concerned the Elizabethans are largely unavailable to modern readers, most of whom do not believe in magic of any kind" (181). In deference to this perceived irrelevance of magical themes to a modern audience, Ole Martin Skilleås draws an analogy between Prospero and a modern scientist. This reader-response critical approach draws applications from the play to a modern reader's concerns with issues of nuclear arms and other technologies by which scientists exercise great power over others and over the natural environment:

> Much has been made of Prospero as magician, even "white magician" in contrast to Sycorax's black magic. However, no matter what colour one attributes to his magic, it cannot be expected of the modern audience that it will interpret the character of Prospero in this way. The thought-world in which magic is a serious option is one which it takes great mental effort to enter. To relate to the pow-

ers of Prospero, and appropriate the themes of the play for present concerns, it seems more fruitful to see him as [a] proto-scientist [183].

It is interesting to note that this same tack has been used by critics who draw parallels between Tolkien's Ring and the atomic bomb, though Tolkien defiantly protested any such allegorical connection in his Foreword to the Second Edition. It may be granted that Tolkien— and no doubt Shakespeare—would have had no qualms with a modern audience using "applicability" (Tolkien's preferred term to "allegory") to draw moral lessons from their stories and apply them to present concerns, or, as Skilleås describes it, to reconcile "topical" and "perennial" themes. However, one of Skilleås's premises is wrong on its face— namely, that the mental effort required to enter "the thought-world in which magic is a serious option" is too great to be expected of a modern audience. The rise in popularity of the fantasy genre in recent decades alone should put that assumption to rest (the Harry Potter books are now running neck-and-neck with *The Lord of the Rings* [*LotR*] as the best-selling books of all time next to the Bible). And the distinction between the "Dark Arts" and good magic is still as prevalent at Hogwarts as it was in Middle-earth or on Prospero's island.

One might be tempted to amend the contention of critics like Skilleås—that the ethical use of magic is a dead issue—by saying (with that snobbish air of the literati) it is only an issue for the young and the uneducated. It is this attitude which has barred Tolkien from serious literary studies until recent years. When works of fantasists like Tolkien or Le Guin have received critical scrutiny, it has usually been with the approach adopted by Skilleås toward *The Tempest*: an approach which seems to say, "We can't seriously discuss these antiquated topics without likening them to something else and discussing *that* instead." In other words, by giving them a veneer of allegory we can get something useful out of them. In the case of *The Tempest*, it may be the modern (allegorical) reading of Skilleås, the psychological reading of Bernard Paris, or the political (colonial) reading of Paul Brown; what they all have in common is a notable disregard for the magic which is the crux of Shakespeare's story. That is not to say any of these applications are not valid; they all offer insights in their respective contexts. However, reading these various treatments it is easy to forget that magic is at the heart of the story Shakespeare wanted to tell, as it is at the heart of Tolkien's story. And, of course, Tolkien was neither young nor uneducated. An Oxford professor in the modern era, he was every bit as concerned with the ethics of magic in his work as a pious Elizabethan would have been.

Abjuring Rough Magic

It is noteworthy that the logic (what little there may be of it) under-lying the arguments of the anti–Potter crowd is congruent with the logic underlying Prospero's need to break his staff and drown his book(s) of magic; the theological principle that informs both is one and the same. Consequently, the present controversy serves as an illustration, helping to usher modern readers into the supernatural worldview that held cen-ter stage—literally—in Elizabethan England.

Magic and the occult appear in most of Shakespeare's plays, often mentioned in passing, but sometimes providing a driving element of the plot: the ghost in *Hamlet*, the witches in *Macbeth*, Puck in *A Midsum-mer Night's Dream*, the magician presiding over *The Tempest*. Modern Shakespeare studies have tended to take these elements in stride merely as tropes, elements kept by Shakespeare when he adapted legends, fairy tales, and earlier "histories" for his plots. Viewed in this way, as little more than extra baggage, these elements can be dismissed (or rele-gated to a place of minor importance) as part of the overall supersti-tion that pervades pre–Enlightenment literature. However, in recent years scholars have begun to reevaluate the importance of these motifs, restoring them to prominence in medieval and Renaissance studies. Examples of this trend in the past few years include the New Perspec-tives on Witchcraft, Magic, and Demonology series edited by Brian P. Levack of The University of Texas, and the Magic in History series pub-lished by Pennsylvania State University Press. But we can go back to the Oxford History of English Literature series of the 1950s to find the first sounding of this modern critical blind spot, when Oxford professor C.S. Lewis contended that

> the medieval author seems to write for a public to whom magic, like knight-errantry, is part of the furniture of romance: the Elizabethan, for a public who feel that it might be going on in the next street. Neglect of this has produced strange readings of the *Tempest*, which is in reality no fantasy (like the *Midsummer Night's Dream*) and no allegory, but Shakespeare's play on *magia* as *Macbeth* is his play on *goeteia* or the *Merchant of Venice* on usury. Shakespeare's audience believed (and the burden of proof lies on those who say Shake-speare disbelieved) that magicians not very unlike Prospero might exist [8].

Michael D. Bailey notes that "belief in witchcraft quickly became nearly universal in late medieval and early modern Europe, and the image of the witch that first appeared in the early 1400s endured as a figure of fear and persecution for many centuries" (2). When considering the audience of *The Tempest*, our awareness of this belief in supernatural forces, coupled with a belief that certain men could interact with and control them, is crucial if we are to proceed with a clear understanding.

No less a figure than Shakespeare's patron King James wrote his own treatise on the dark arts, *Daemonologie* (1597), in which the proclamation that such practices should be "most severely punished" (xi) was made by the man with the most power to enforce it. That James supported the Globe is a happy fact for future generations—his successors were not so tolerant, and the puritanical sect of English Protestants, when they came into power shortly thereafter, saw to it that the theatre was shut down for decades. They found offense with both its alleged promotion of lasciviousness and its fascination with witchcraft and the occult. The suspicion or outright condemnation of magic by his contemporaries surely tempered Shakespeare's work: "[Prospero's] speech of renunciation, sometimes taken as an autobiographical confidence by the poet, was to them [Shakespeare's audience] necessary in order that the ending might be unambiguously happy" (Lewis 8).

We have thus far spoken of magicians and witches in the same breath, but there is a further distinction here, clearly found in Shakespeare's work, which reflects learned thinking of the time. Richard Kieckhefer distinguishes between "magia" and "sorcellerie" and "witchcraft" (80). While there is some overlapping of the usage of these terms, three distinctions can be made, which will shed light on the cognitive sense with which Elizabethan writers approached this subject. For the present treatment I will denote them as natural magic, Platonic magic, and witchcraft. We will see all three at work in *The Tempest*, and one (for further illustration) at work in *Macbeth*. When we turn to *LotR* we will find these distinctions intact, with a further variant exemplified by Gandalf.

Natural magic has often been related by scholars to the sciences, and indeed they grew in tandem: practitioners of one often practiced the other. Both had as their aim control of the natural world. Sometimes described by Elizabethan writers as "high magic" to distinguish it from witchcraft (considered "low magic"), natural magic rested on the belief that there were forces in nature that could be manipulated. It shared, then, the same goals as science, and stood with science against astrology—an early form of determinism that declared fate was beyond humankind's control, destined as it was by the movements of planets and stars. Alchemists were never able to turn lead into gold, but they did give birth to chemistry. Prospero produces storms with the magical aid of his servant Ariel—today storms can be produced with technology by releasing pellets of a certain chemical composition into clouds to accelerate condensation. Would an Elizabethan see any material distinction? Clarke's Law, attributed to science fiction writer Arthur C. Clarke, states that "Any sufficiently advanced technology is indistinguishable from magic." Many scholars and historians therefore equate the early practitioner of natural magic with the modern scientist, arguing that science outlived its sibling only because one worked and the other didn't. Both share the same roots and reach for the same ends: to exercise dominance over the natural order. Patrick Curry notes that "the appropriation of magic and its transformation into modern science is one of the most important events (and closely-guarded secrets) of the past three centuries" (63). Tolkien himself was keenly aware of the connection, noting in a letter both the interrelated motives and attendant temptations of magic and technology:

> He [the sub-creator who becomes deluded by his abilities into wanting more control and to possess that over which he exercises dominance] will rebel against the laws of the Creator—especially against mortality. Both of these (alone or together) will lead to the desire for Power, for making the will more quickly effective,—and so to the Machine (or Magic). By the last I intend all use of external plans or devices (apparatus) instead of developments of the inherent inner powers or talents—or even the use of these talents with the corrupted motive of dominating: bulldozing the real world, or coercing other wills. The Machine is our more obvious modern form though more closely related to Magic than is usually recognized [*Letters* 145–46].

The Elves of Lórien may be placed in the tradition of natural magic, using as they do the power of the Elven Rings to keep their woods artificially unchanging for millennia—a kind of "green" magic, used to preserve rather than to remake. However, Prospero does not appear to be of this ilk: he does not tap into natural energies but commands sprites like Ariel to do his bidding. This brings us to Platonic magic. And this is where, for a Christian Elizabethan audience, things begin to get problematic.

The philosophy of late-medieval Europeans had two primary influences: Christianity and Platonism. The adaptation and interweaving of the two has been coined neo–Platonism, and it comprises a complex worldview, but only one element of neo–Platonism concerns us here. According to Lewis, the Platonists (with pious intent, as they were often monks and priests) drew on pagan sources to populate the cosmos with all manner of spiritual beings:

> In their task of defending what they thought a spiritual cosmology they raked together all that the late pagan sources ... could tell them about the invisible population of the universe. They readmitted all those "middle spirits ... betwixt th' Angelical and Human

kinde", which St. Augustine is labouring to expel all through the
eighth and ninth books of the *De Civitate Dei*.... But our unambigu-
ous friends and foes, ministering angels and seducing devils, occupied the center of the stage. Now the imagination is filled with
spirits of "another sort": the *aërii homines* with whom Cardan's father
conversed, Prospero's Ariel, [etc.] [11–12].

As a result, "this mass of mysterious but not necessarily evil spirits creates the possibility of an innocent traffic with the unseen and therefore
of high magic or *magia*" (12).

The tension lies in the fact that many devout Christians in Shakespeare's audience (including King James himself) would not allow such
a distinction between neutral and evil spirits—if they were not angels,
then they were demons. Perhaps a sufficiently pious and disciplined
magician could command them as one would Hessian mercenaries—
using destructive forces for good ends—but this was generally not tol-
erable.

That Prospero considers Ariel just such a neutral spirit is clear:

> Thou, my slave,
> As thou report'st thyself, was then her [Sycorax's] servant;
> And, for thou wast a spirit too delicate
> To act her earthy and abhorred commands,
> Refusing her grand hests, she did confine thee,
> By help of her more potent ministers
> And in her most unmitigable rage,
> Into a cloven pine [1.2.272–79].

Ariel would not carry out Sycorax's more abominable commands, and
was consequently imprisoned by other spirits under her control—evil
spirits with whom Prospero has no traffic. This distinction—between
Sycorax and Prospero—brings us to the final magic we find in Shakespeare: witchcraft or "black magic."[1]

The line of demarcation between the powers of Prospero and Sycorax can be drawn in various ways—genteel and educated/savage and
barbarous; male/female; spiritual/earthy. However, we are primarily
concerned with the distinction between high magic and witchcraft, in
both their ends and means. Sycorax's ends are presumably destructive,
whereas Prospero's are remunerative and restorative. Sycorax commanded evil spirits; Prospero commands neutral spirits. Sycorax traf-
ficked with demons; indeed, Prospero declares that her son Caliban is
the offspring of an incubus: "Thou poisonous slave, got by the devil himself / Upon thy wicked dam" (1.2.322–23). It is important to note that
Prospero is not speaking metaphorically: such unions between mortals
and spirits were once considered possible, though we are far removed

from the day when Heinrich Kramer, in his highly influential *Malleus Maleficarum* ("The Hammer of Witches") could seriously address a whole section to "Whether the Relations of an Incubus Devil with a Witch are always accompanied by the Injection of Semen" (198). Nonetheless, we still see the motif appear in modern literature (Ira Levin's *Rosemary's Baby*, not to mention some evangelical Christian fiction concerning the Anti-Christ). This view of Caliban, incidentally, may muddy some recent colonial interpretations, since he may not technically be a native, but rather a partly supernatural being.

Another example of low magic or witchcraft (the designations "white magic" and "black magic" did not come into vernacular use until later) can be found in *Macbeth*, not only with the three witches but with Lady Macbeth herself when she speaks the incantation, "[U]nsex me here / And fill me from the crown to the toe top-full / Of direst cruelty! Make thick my blood; / Stop up th' access and passage to remorse" (1.5.41–44). Many in Shakespeare's audience would have seen the practices of Lady Macbeth, the Weird Sisters, and Sycorax as "a species of treason" (Carroll 305) because they invoke infernal spirits to reverse the natural order. This view goes back to biblical injunctions:

> When thou art come into the land which the LORD thy God giveth thee, thou shalt not learn to do after the abominations of those nations. There shall not be found among you *any one* that maketh his son or his daughter to pass through the fire, *or* that useth divination, *or* an observer of times, or an enchanter, or a witch, Or a charmer, or a consulter with familiar spirits, or a wizard, or a necromancer. For all that do these things *are* an abomination unto the LORD [Deut. 18:9–12].

Levitical law enforced capital punishment on such practices: "Thou shalt not suffer a witch to live" (Exodus 22:18). These injunctions were propagated by Christian missionaries as they came in contact with pagan cultures. In a story recounted in the book of Acts, new converts in one town disposed of their magical tools:

> Many of them also which used curious arts brought their books together, and burned them before all *men*: and they counted the price of them, and found *it* fifty thousand *pieces* of silver [19:18–19].

Prospero echoes this renunciation when he declares, "But this rough magic / I here abjure, ... I'll break my staff, / Bury it certain fathoms in the earth, / And deeper than did ever plummet sound / I'll drown my book" (5.1.50–57).

Prospero clearly must do this, if he (and Shakespeare) are to be pardoned by the audience (including that most intimidating audience member, the King of England). When we comprehend the underlying assumptions, it is not hard to understand why this should be so. A belief in angels and demons, coupled with a rejection of the Platonic view of neutral spirits, leaves Prospero in league with demons (for angels, in this worldview, cannot be controlled by humans for personal ends). The infamous witch-hunter Cotton Mather would certainly label Prospero a practitioner of witchcraft as guilty as Sycorax, for "the Doing of Strange ... Things by the help of evil Spirits." Mather also declared, in 1689, that "there are wonderful Storms in the great World, and wonderful Wounds in the little World, often effected by these evil Causes" (368). Prospero effects both—Mather's contention could serve as a synopsis of Prospero's major actions in the play. Mather would, furthermore, distinguish them from miracles (which are effected by divine Providence), contending that the ends, here, do not justify the means (trafficking with spirits).

Armed with this brief overview of Elizabethan conceptions of magic, we can now add how Tolkien discerned between types of magic and where Prospero might fall in his estimation. Tolkien generally distinguished between two kinds of magic: *magia*, which exercises power to more quickly achieve its ends; and *goeteia* or *enchantment*, which can be either illusion or (in the Elvish sense) sub-creative Art. Tolkien does not make a blanket judgment about one being inherently good and the other inherently evil: though elves by their nature exercise *goeteia*, they also use the Elven Rings, which are a type of *magia* forged with noble purpose and used to good effect. Sauron, too, uses both *magia* and enchantment: "But his *magia* he uses to bulldoze both people and things, and his *goeteia* to terrify and subjugate" (*Letters* 200). When we consider how we would classify Prospero's use of magic, we find ourselves dealing with a mixed bag. He condemns Sycorax's exploitation of Ariel for her own wicked purposes, reminding Ariel that when he refused to comply she imprisoned him in the tree. Yet when Ariel grumbles or so much as questions his master, Prospero threatens to reimprison him in the same tree! Also, though Prospero's ostensible motivation is to restore himself to his rightful dukedom, to put wrongs to right and to see justice done—healing and restoration—there is no small amount of revenge at play here. He cannot help but enjoy seeing his enemies— and even his future son-in-law—squirm. Bernard Paris makes a good argument for this cruel streak in Prospero, a vindictiveness which is off-putting to some modern readers (Paris). We may reasonably speculate that had Prospero not drowned his magic book and broken his staff, his magic would have continued to bring out this vindictive side of him, and what would have started with noble intentions might ultimately twist him into a sadistic monster little better than Sycorax.

This may remind us of the corrupting power of the Ring, and the warning of another wizard:

> Do not tempt me! For I do not wish to become like the Dark Lord himself. Yet the way of the Ring to my heart is by pity, pity for weakness and the desire of strength to do good. Do not tempt me! I dare not take it, not even to keep it safe, unused. The wish to wield it would be too great for my strength [1.2.60].

Gandalf Unveiled

Proceeding ahead three-and-a-half centuries, we come to an Oxford Professor of Philology who pens an epic romance which draws upon a Platonic view of reality (and which does to some extent reflect the professor's own "anachronistic" worldview). We are now in a position to consider how Tolkien expanded on medieval conceptions of magic, and to see how he sidestepped Prospero's "rough magic" dilemma. In comparing Prospero and Gandalf, what interests me here is the *source* and *substance* of their respective powers. The most elementary difference between the two wizards is that Prospero is a mortal man and Gandalf is an altogether different order of being. Were we simply comparing the wizards' feats, we would quickly be struck by the disparity between their displays of power. Prospero exercises his magic more impressively in seventy pages than Gandalf appears to do throughout Tolkien's more than 1,000-page epic. Prospero further exercises direct manipulation over people and events; Gandalf is reticent to use such power.

Indeed, Gandalf uses his magic quite sparingly, and when he does use it, the effects are usually unostentatious—making fireworks in the Shire, kindling wet firewood, lighting his staff in the Mines of Moria. He lets loose a bit in Eregion, routing a pack of Wargs, and at the Council he alludes to the night he held the Riders at bay: "Such light and flame cannot have been seen on Weathertop since the war-beacons of old" (2.2.257). In the battle with the Balrog his true mettle is on full display, though its outcome takes place offstage. What brings us back to Gandalf's peculiar nature is this: though his magic generates few shockwaves on the material plane, his magic is simultaneously operating on another plane. When he confronts Théoden, for instance, this is a showdown between himself and the spirit of Saruman, who, through Wormtongue, has in a sense possessed the King of Rohan. Here Gandalf asserts himself:

> He raised his staff. There was a roll of thunder. The sunlight was blotted out from the eastern windows; the whole hall became sud-

denly dark as night. The fire faded to sullen embers. Only Gandalf
could be seen, standing white and tall before the blackened hearth
[3.6.503].

After Gandalf's exhortation, "slowly Théoden left his chair," and
the ensuing change in the king's demeanor seems to be nothing less
than an exorcism. Such confrontations in which there seems to be more
going on at an unseen, spiritual level occur throughout the books: when
Gandalf confronts Saruman, Denethor, the Witch-king of Angmar, not
to mention the encounters of various characters (Saruman, Pippin,
Denethor, Aragorn) with the mind of Sauron through the *palantíri*.
   This brings us to the most important distinction between Gandalf
and virtually any other wizard of myth, legend, and literature: a fundamental difference in his true nature. Perusal of the Appendices, as well
as *The Silmarillion*, reveals clues only hinted at in *LotR*. But Tolkien was
much more explicit in his letters about the nature of his Wizards. In a
letter he never sent, Tolkien commented parenthetically on the fact
that Treebeard does not know the true nature of the Wizards: "though
I do, even if exercising my subcreator's right I have thought it best in
this Tale to leave the question a 'mystery', not without pointers to the
solution" (190). By following these pointers we learn, in fact, that Gandalf is Olórin, wisest of the Maiar, who are servants of the Valar (*Silmarillion* 30; *Letters* 411). And who are these mysterious immortal beings?
We may, for shorthand, draw this analogy: the Valar are like demigods
or archangels, the Maiar their angelic servants. Tolkien's mythology is
monotheistic—there is one Supreme Creator, Ilúvatar. The Ainur—the
Valar to whom Ilúvatar gave the privilege of creating the universe—sang
the world into existence, but had no part in making Men or Elves.
   In fact, though Tolkien drew mainly upon northern European
myths, his creation story is most congruent with the Judeo-Christian
creation myth. Tolkien scholar Joseph Pearce gives an excellent sum-
mation of Tolkien's creation story, simultaneously explaining how it
remained consistent with Tolkien's own private belief:

> "amid all the splendours of the World, its vast halls and wheeling
> fires," Ilúvatar chose a place for the habitation of his Children "in
> the Deeps of Time and in the midst of innumerable stars." Thus,
> in a feat of ingenious invention, or sub-creation, Tolkien not only
> distinguishes Men and Elves as being made directly "in the image
> of God," essentially different from the rest of Creation, but at the
> same time accommodates the theory of evolution. The evolution
> of the cosmos was simply the unfolding of the Music of the Ainur
> within which the One places his Children in a habitation prepared
> for them.... In a similar feat of ingenuity, Tolkien explains that the
> Valar, the angelic powers given the responsibility of shaping the

cosmos, have often been called "gods" by Men. In this way he manages to accommodate paganism as well as evolution within his mythology, making both subsist within Christian orthodoxy [Pearce 90–91].

The Maiar were given stewardship over Middle-earth by the Ainur, and they were able to take physical form in this task. As Gandalf tells Denethor:

> [T]he rule of no realm is mine, neither of Gondor nor any other, great or small. But all worthy things that are in peril as the world now stands, those are my care. And for my part, I shall not wholly fail of my task, though Gondor should perish, if anything passes through this night that can still grow fair or bear fruit and flower again in days to come. For I also am a steward. Did you not know? [5.1.741–2].

Gandalf is one of the Wizards or *Istari* sent to Middle-earth in the Third Age to aid in the resistance against Sauron (*Letters* 207). Two other Istari appear in *LotR*, Saruman the White and Radagast the Brown, and two Blue Wizards are mentioned in *Unfinished Tales*. In several of his letters Tolkien described Gandalf as an "incarnate" angel, explaining that by incarnate he meant the Istari "were embodied in physical bodies capable of pain, and weariness, and of afflicting the spirit with physical fear, and of being 'killed,' though supported by the angelic spirit they might endure long, and only show slowly the wearing of care and labour" (202).

Thus exploring the origins of the wizards, we come to a startling conclusion: *they are not wizards at all* in the sense that Prospero is a wizard, or Merlin, or Dumbledore, or any other example of our popular conceptions of a wizard. Why, then, did Tolkien call them wizards, especially given the "shady" associations of that term in western culture? Tolkien writes in defense: "But 'wizards' are not in any sense or degree 'shady'. Not mine." He then offers this explanation for his word choice (and recall that we are dealing with a master linguist): "I am under the difficulty of finding English names for mythological creatures with other names, since people would not 'take' a string of Elvish names, and I would rather they took my legendary creatures even with the false associations of the 'translation' than not at all" (207).

When Gandalf performs magic, then, he is drawing upon his own innate "angelic" powers, though it may be added that he also practices natural magic as a bearer of Narya, the Elvish Ring of Fire. Therefore, when Gandalf exercises magical power, he most closely parallels not Prospero but *Ariel*. That is, his powers are innate, though he is akin to an angelic power whereas Ariel would be identified as a "middle spirit" in medieval Platonic cosmology.

Tolkien once described Gandalf as an "Odinic wanderer" (*Letters* 119). Curry cleverly makes a point here by providing the following descriptive passages: "'a bearded stranger seeming in long cloak larger than life,' 'an old wanderer glancing up from under a shadowy hood or floppy-brimmed hat ... with a gleam of recognition out his one piercing eye,' whose chief skill was 'as a wizard or sorcerer or *vates*,' in his 'usual disguise of wide-brimmed hat, blue cloak, and tall staff.' He usually appeared as 'a tall, vigorous man, about fifty years of age ... clad in a suit of grey, with a blue hood, and ... a wide blue mantle flecked with grey ... on his finger or arm he wore [a] marvelous ring'" (101). Any reader will readily recognize this character, but then Curry springs the surprise that these are descriptions of Wodan (Norse Odin). Curry adds that even Gandalf's trick on the trolls in *The Hobbit*—keeping them preoccupied until the sun turns them to stone—has an exact precedent in tales of Odin competing with giants in a riddle game, with the same stiffening results. Bradley J. Birzer points out yet further parallels: "Throughout northern mythology, Odin serves as one who inspires certain heroes. Like Gandalf, Odin not only gives them courage, but he also gives them powerful, supernatural gifts as aids in their exploits. And like Gandalf, Odin has a supernaturally endowed horse" (79).

Yet Gandalf is not to be conflated with a god or deity. The resonance from the poetic echoes of Norse myth are intentional, but with this caveat: the Valar and the Maiar are created beings, having as their source the one uncreated being, Ilúvatar. Tolkien explained this theological side-stepping in a letter giving a synopsis of *The Silmarillion* to a potential publisher. Therein he noted that his myth reveals "God and the Valar (or powers: Englished as gods).... These latter are as we should say angelic powers, whose function is to exercise delegated authority in their spheres" (146). In another letter he added that the Valar are "of high angelic order we should say, with their attendant lesser angels—reverend, therefore, but not worshipful" (193). By creating this hierarchy, Tolkien hoped to achieve this effect: "On the side of mere narrative device, this is, of course, meant to provide beings of the same order of beauty, power, and majesty as the 'gods' of higher mythology, which can yet be accepted—well, shall we say baldly, by a mind that believes in the Blessed Trinity" (146). *The Silmarillion* records that "Men have often called [the Valar and Maiar] gods" (25). Tolkien believed this to be not far from the truth in human history: "After all, I believe that legends and myths are largely made of 'truth,' and indeed present aspects of it that can only be received in this mode" (*Letters* 147). Though some men of a primitive age mistook the Valar for gods, Tolkien added in a footnote to another letter that "for help they ['good' peoples] may call on a *Vala* (as *Elbereth*), as a Catholic might on a Saint, though no doubt knowing in theory as well as he that the power of the Vala was limited and derivative" (193n).

The salient points about Gandalf as *wizard*, then, are these: First, he is an immortal spirit in human guise—*The Silmarillion* records that in the First Age he moved among the elves: "[T]hough he loved the Elves, he walked among them unseen, or in form as one of them, and they did not know whence came the fair visions or the promptings of wisdom that he put into their hearts" (31). In the Third Age he still performs his mission in a veiled way, as Gandalf the Grey, a peculiar, eccentric old "wizard."

Second, his power is finite; there are other, malevolent powers in the world stronger than he. Like Ariel imprisoned, Gandalf is imprisoned atop the Tower of Orthanc by Saruman. His physical body can be slain, as the Balrog seems to do in its own death throes. Though wise, he is fallible; he is mistaken for several years about Bilbo's Ring, and Saruman's treachery takes him completely by surprise. He, too, can be corrupted, like Saruman, who was lured by the promise of "Knowledge, Rule, Order" (2.2.253) into studying the Enemy's arts.

Third (to expound on the first point), he is a Maia incarnated in human form. There are numerous precedents for this idea in the Old Testament, with messengers of the Lord visiting, conversing, and even dining with such patriarchs as Abraham and Lot. Particularly resonant with Gandalf is a passage in Daniel that tells the story of Shadrach, Meshach, and Abednego, who are thrown into a "burning fiery furnace" for refusing to worship King Nebuchadnezzar. The furnace is stoked so fiercely that it consumes the soldiers appointed to throw them in, yet the three young men do not burn. Further, Nebuchadnezzar is shocked to see a fourth in the midst of the fire: "Lo, I see four men loose, walking in the midst of the fire, and they have no hurt; and the form of the fourth is like the Son of God" (Daniel 3:25). Gandalf seems to serve essentially the same purpose as this enigmatic fourth figure: to sustain and uphold, in the midst of tribulation, those who refuse to bow to the Dark Lord.

Fourth, and most important though most overlooked, Gandalf is a servant of the Secret Fire. When he confronts the Balrog, he declares defiantly, "You cannot pass.... I am a servant of the Secret Fire, wielder of the flame of Anor" (2.5.322). Tolkien confided to Clyde Kilby that the Secret Fire was the Holy Spirit (Kilby 59). Gandalf's power, then, comes directly from Ilúvatar, or Tolkien's mythical conception of God. Seen in this light, Gandalf's battle with the Balrog bears closer scrutiny.

The Balrogs were also Maiar, servants of Melkor, a literary equivalent to Lucifer. Here Tolkien is also drawing on the Hebraic myth of Lucifer's fall in which he brought with him a host of fallen angels. The battle of Gandalf and the Balrog finds an interesting parallel with a story in the book of Daniel. After having fasted and prayed for three weeks, Daniel has a vision in which he is visited by an angel sent to give him a prophecy. As to the three-week wait, the angel explains that he had been held up: "But the prince of the kingdom of Persia withstood me one and twenty days: but, lo, Michael, one of the chief princes, came to help me" (10:13). This enigmatic aside has been interpreted by most scholars in a spiritual context: the prince of Persia being a demonic spirit who holds some form of dominion over Persia. This spiritual battle between the angel and the prince of Persia is thus echoed by the battle between Gandalf and the Balrog. The parallel, for Tolkien, would have been almost exact. Michael is an archangel in the Hebraic hierarchy; the arrival of Michael would be the equivalent of the intervention of Manwë—and Tolkien has suggested in letters that it was Manwë or Ilúvatar who sent Gandalf the White back to fulfill his calling.

The wide chasm between Gandalf and Prospero should now be clear, and consequently the reason why Tolkien, despite his deeply held reservations against any meddling with the occult, did not believe that the magic of his wizards morally compromised them. Tolkien shared many of the same biases towards magic—at least a certain kind of magic, or magic used for a certain end—as did Shakespeare's Elizabethan audience. However, his wizard Gandalf did not have to renounce his magic because it came from Ilúvatar and was a manifestation of angelic power guided by wisdom, tempered by humility, and restrained toward the goal of stewardship—preserving that which is good against the machinations of Sauron. Even when he returns as Gandalf the White, "[h]e is still under the obligation of concealing his power and of teaching rather than forcing or dominating wills, but where the physical powers of the Enemy are too great for the good will of the opposers to be effective he can act in emergency as an 'angel'—no more violently than the release of St Peter from prison" (*Letters* 202–3). Yet in a sense Gandalf did abdicate his own power when his mission was fulfilled, by removing himself. Tolkien conceived of the Third Age as being the last age of myth, when spirit beings could still walk among mortals. As Birzer observes:

> His job accomplished, Gandalf's immense and direct holy power can no longer be permitted to linger in Middle-earth. There is a danger that he will distort the inhabitants' free will in choosing the good because of his virtue and charisma as an incarnate Maiar. The world of myth allows for such beings to walk the earth. The world of history rarely abides such intrusions [78].

Tolkien, Magic, and Orthodoxy

Tolkien's stories of Middle-earth encompass different kinds of magic—the enchantment or "natural" magic inherent in the Elves; the black magic of Sauron and the bent Saruman; the magic of Gandalf, which rather than simply being "white magic" can be said to have a kinship with the miracles of the saints and prophets or the Hebraic angels. This distinction was a crucial one for Tolkien, a strict Roman Catholic. It is an issue that still resonates today in the cultural clash between conservative Christians who object to virtually anything that smacks of sorcery or witchcraft, and the rest of society, most of whom will root for the witches as long as they're ostensibly playing for the right team.

Tolkien believed that such powers exist, and are still present in Middle-earth—our Earth—today, though if they once took physical form they do so no longer, interacting rather on a spiritual plane, influencing the course of human events through wicked men. About "that ruddy little ignoramus Hitler," Tolkien noted in a letter that "the odd thing about demonic inspiration and impetus is that it in no way enhances the purely intellectual stature: it chiefly affects the mere will" (55). Though the forces of darkness may no longer approach world leaders in the way that the Weird Sisters approached Macbeth, in Tolkien's view they still bend men's wills to pride, envy, and greed, often with the enticing promise: "Knowledge, Rule, Order." In numerous other letters Tolkien alluded to the spirit of Sauron or Mordor or Saruman at work in modern politics—fascist movements and insatiable consumer-capitalism alike.

Yet one of Tolkien's hopes (as he elaborated in "On Fairy-Stories") was to reclaim a certain kind of magic, the magic of Faerie, for his own time:

> I have not used "magic" consistently, and indeed the Elven-queen Galadriel is obliged to remonstrate with the Hobbits on their confused use of the word both for the devices and operations of the Enemy, and for those of the Elves. I have not, because there is not a word for the latter (since all human stories have suffered the same confusion). But the Elves are there (in my tales) to demonstrate the difference. Their "magic" is Art, delivered from many of its human limitations: more effortless, more quick, more complete (product, and vision in unflawed correspondence). And its object is Art not Power, sub-creation not domination and tyrannous reforming of Creation [*Letters* 146].

Prospero, literary forerunner to modern scientists—with Dr. Frankenstein as an intermediary link (recall that Frankenstein began his unhallowed pursuit by studying the works of Paracelsus and Cornelius

Agrippa)—gains his power through the study of books. His staff, we may presume, was fashioned according to these esoteric texts, whereas Gandalf's staff seems almost an extension of himself, a conduit and amplifier of his innate power. Tolkien, like many in Shakespeare's audience, would have disapproved of the methods of Prospero, seeing him as a "shady" wizard using his power to manipulate nature and to coerce wills. As Shakespeare undoubtedly intended for his audience to do, Tolkien may have sympathized with Prospero's plight, but seen in his good intentions the seeds of ruthlessness, domination, and lust for power.

Even Sauron started out sympathetically—just ask the men of Númenor or the Elves of Eregion who helped him forge the rings to restore the parts of Middle-earth that had been ravaged by Morgoth. Tolkien noted in a letter that "at the beginning of the Second Age he was still beautiful to look at, or could still assume a beautiful visible shape—and was not indeed wholly evil, not unless all 'reformers' who want to hurry up with 'reconstruction' and 'reorganization' are wholly evil, even before pride and the lust to exert their will eat them up" (190). In this Sauron reminds us of another angel of light who fell. Tolkien made the allusion explicit:

> Satan fell. In my myth Morgoth fell before Creation of the physical world. In my story Sauron represents as near an approach to the wholly evil as is possible. He had gone the way of all tyrants: beginning well, at least on the level that while desiring to order all things according to his own wisdom he still at first considered the (economic) well-being of other inhabitants of the Earth. But he went further than human tyrants in pride and the lust for domination, being in origin an immortal (angelic) spirit [*Letters* 243].

Morgoth, and Sauron, and Saruman are echoes of that ancient story of the corrupting influence of pride and lust for power, which might even turn a Galadriel into a bloodthirsty earth goddess, or a Gandalf into a "self-righteous" tyrant (*Letters* 333). This has always been the danger of the allure of magic.

Which brings us back to the present day, when one of our most popular stories is about a young wizard who is admonished not to use his powers to influence Muggles, and to resist the temptations to strive for power and immortality of the sort which creates a Voldemort. That these themes still resonate may be explained metaphorically by critics like Skilleås, with magic standing in for the technology that holds out similar promise. Tolkien would have agreed with many conclusions which can thereby be drawn, but with this subtle difference: Tolkien saw technology not as a substitution but as a *continuation* of magic. It is not merely an analogy; it is the offspring. In any case, the questions raised are the same: In an age when modern alchemists have grown a human ear on the body of a mouse, when our insatiable lust for more speed and convenience create catastrophic changes in the environment, when we have the capability to wipe out the human race several times over with the push of a button, at what point will our wonder-workers recoil from the side-effects of their work and abjure their rough magic? Will they be wise enough to know when to drown their books, bury their staffs, throw the ring back into the fire? Will it be too late?

Notes

The author wishes to gratefully acknowledge Gabriel Dybing and Frederic S. Durbin for their critiques. Thanks also to Linda Pepper for her support. Finally, a special thanks to Melissa for her constant encouragement.

1. Practicing modern-day Wiccans object to this one-on-one correlation between "witchcraft" and "black magic," often making a case for their practices being congruent with the former two types of magic—"green magic" of the natural type, or Platonic magic, calling upon benevolent and beneficent spirits. It is a compelling case, if one is willing to go beyond Skilleås et al. and concede that these distinctions are anything but antiquated nonsense. For the strict materialist, a distinction such as whether one casts hexes by calling upon demons or casts healing spells using earth magic is a moot one, since all of it is play-acting and therefore meaningless (except insofar as it may reveal something psychologically about the practitioner).

Works Cited

Bailey, Michael D. *Battling Demons: Witchcraft, Heresy, and Reform in the Late Middle Ages.* Magic in History. University Park: Penn State University Press, 2003.
The Bible. Authorized King James Version. Oxford World's Classics: Oxford University Press, 1997.
Birzer, Bradley J. *J.R.R. Tolkien's Sanctifying Myth.: Understanding Middle-earth.* Wilmington, DSE: Intercollegiate Studies Institute, 2003.
Carroll, William C., ed. "Witchcraft and Prophecy." In *Macbeth: Texts and Contexts.* Boston: St. Martin's, 1999. 300–307.
Clark, Stuart. *Thinking with Demons: The Idea of Witchcraft in Early Modern Europe.* Oxford: Clarendon, 1997.
Curry, Patrick. *Defending Middle-earth: Tolkien: Myth and Modernity.* 1997. Rev. ed. Boston: Houghton, 2004.
Dunne, Diane Weaver. "Look Out, Harry Potter!—Book Banning Heats Up." *Education World.* 10 April 2000. retrieved 22 December 2005 at http://www.education-world.com/a_admin/admin157.shtml
James I, King of England. *Daemonologie.* 1597. Ed. G.B. Harrison. Elizabethan and Jacobean Quartos. New York: Barnes & Noble, 1966.
Keesey, Donald, ed. *Contexts for Criticism.* 3rd ed. Mountain View, CA: Mayfield, 1987.
Kieckhefer, Richard. "The Specific Rationality of Medieval Magic." In *Demonology, Religion, and Witchcraft.* Vol. 1 of *New Perspectives on Witchcraft, Magic, and Demonology.* Ed. Brian P. Levack. New York: Routledge, 2001. 59–82.

Kilby, Clyde S. *Tolkien and The Silmarillion.* Wheaton, IL: Shaw, 1976.
Kramer, Heinrich, and Jacob Sprenger. *Malleus Maleficarium.* 1487. In *Witchcraft in Europe 400–1700.* Ed. Alan Charles Kors and Edward Peters. Philadelphia: Penn Press, 2001. 180–229.
Lewis, C.S. *English Literature in the Sixteenth Century.* Oxford History of English Literature. Ed. F.P. Wilson and Bonamy Dobrée. London: Oxford University Press, 1954.
Mather, Cotton. "A Discourse on Witches." 1689. In *Witchcraft in Europe 400–1700.* Ed. Alan Charles Kors and Edward Peters. Philadelphia: Penn Press, 2001. 367–70.
Paris, Bernard. "*The Tempest*: Shakespeare's Ideal Solution." In *Bargains with Fate: Psychological Crises and Conflicts in Shakespeare and His Plays.* New York: Plenum, 1991. 261–77.
Pearce, Joseph. *Tolkien: Man and Myth.* San Francisco: Ignatius Press, 1998.
Shakespeare, William. *The Complete Works of William Shakespeare.* Ed. David Bevington. 5th ed. New York: Pearson, 2004.
Skilleås, Ole Martin. "Anachronistic Themes and Literary Value: The Tempest." In *Contexts for Criticism.* Ed Donald Keesey. 3rd ed. Mountain View, CA: Mayfield, 1987. 181–89.
Tolkien, J.R.R. *Letters of J.R.R. Tolkien.* Ed. Humphrey Carpenter. Boston, Houghton, 1981.
_____. *The Lord of the Rings.* 2nd ed. Boston: Houghton Mifflin, 1994.
_____. "On Fairy-Stories." In *The Tolkien Reader.* New York, Ballantine, 1966. 3–84.
_____. *The Silmarillion.* 2nd ed. New York: Houghton, 2001.

Merlin, Prospero, Saruman and Gandalf

Corrosive Uses of Power in Shakespeare and Tolkien

FRANK P. RIGA

In his portrait of Gandalf and Saruman, Tolkien does not make specific reference to Shakespeare's figure of Prospero in *The Tempest*. Nevertheless, there is a telling connection. Both writers draw on themes surrounding a common source: the many legends and tales associated with Merlin, the most ubiquitous wizard figure in Western culture. Born the son of a virgin and a demon, Merlin in his many incarnations has remained an ambiguous figure, poised between good and evil (Vadé 796). Prospero, like Merlin a magician, is just as ambiguous and complex as his wizard predecessor. Surprisingly, the Merlin-Prospero connection has all but escaped critical notice, perhaps because Prospero has so long and frequently been viewed as a positive figure, a benign patriarch who practices "white" magic and who gains power only to renounce it, a figure modeled, so many have argued, on the Bard himself. Furthermore, the connection between Shakespeare's enchanter and Tolkien's wizards has been almost completely neglected, with comments about the connection limited to a few words made in passing. No critical studies have dealt in any depth with the above connections. This paper will explore the complex interrelationship between Merlin, Prospero, Gandalf, and Saruman and will demonstrate how the Merlin/ Shakespeare connection sheds new light both on Shakespeare's magician and Tolkien's wizards.

Shakespeare was certainly aware of the Merlin tradition. In his plays, Shakespeare mentions Merlin by name twice and refers to wizards on four different occasions.[1] Merlin was also a widely known figure in Shakespeare's time, especially in the version presented by Geoffrey of Monmouth. In "*The Tempest* and King James's *Daemonologie,*" Jacqueline Latham notes: "Geoffrey of Monmouth's *Historia Regum Brittaniae,* incorporating Merlin's prophesies, was popular Tudor propaganda" (n.p.). Geoffrey's account, among others, would have been well known to Shakespeare and his contemporaries. More specifically, Geoffrey Bullough indicates that the *History* is among the possible sources for two of Shakespeare's plays (3.7–11; 8.273–81). In 1610, one year before Shakespeare's *The Tempest* was performed at Whitehall Palace, a masque by Ben Jonson featuring Merlin material was also presented at Whitehall. The occasion was the investiture of King James's 15-year-old son as Henry, Prince of Wales. In the masque, Merlin lists all the great kings of Britain up to and including James I (Stewart and Matthews 149). In addition, William Rowley claimed to have collaborated with Shakespeare before the latter's death on a farce entitled *The Birth of Merlin or The Child Hath Found His Father* (Stewart and Matthews 159). Shakespeare would also have been acquainted with the widespread reputation of historical Renaissance figures who were frequently compared to Merlin in his mage incarnations (Stewart and Matthews 120, 159).

The Merlin Tradition

A brief overview of the Merlin figure as he appears in literary texts, from Geoffrey of Monmouth's *History of the Kings of Britain* through the Renaissance, provides a good indication of the material that would have been familiar to Shakespeare and his contemporaries. Merlin, whose dual nature derived from his virgin mother and demon father, was above all an ambiguous figure whose positive and negative attributes were stressed in differing degrees, depending on the agenda of the writer.

Geoffrey of Monmouth depicts Merlin essentially as a folkloric hero with great gifts of prophecy and magic who is able to control human beings at will, to influence the destinies of kings. In Geoffrey's mythology surrounding the founding of Britain, Merlin plays a deciding role in the establishment of the royal succession to the British throne. To Merlin is attributed the founding of the Round Table, and on Merlin depends the successful defense of the Britons against invaders. But, while his divine origins predominate, the demonic aspect of his birth continues to haunt him and his access to supernatural power allows for deceit and abuse. In Geoffrey's account of King Arthur's conception, for example, Merlin uses his power to create illusions which help Uther Pendragon act on his adulterous longings for another man's wife, the

Duchess Igerna. In a tale echoing Zeus's deception of Amphitryon and rape of Alcmena (Morford and Lenardon 354), Merlin deceives the Duchess into believing that she is in bed with her husband when she is actually being impregnated by Uther.

As Peter Goodrich indicates, Geoffrey's account "became so popular throughout Europe that it established the primary features of the legend and started a vogue for Arthurian literature with Merlin as a permanent fixture" (5). Merlin figures after Geoffrey retain the moral ambiguity imparted by their demonic/divine origins. Some accounts, however, stress his beneficent nature as a great mage, while others feature his demonic tendencies and predilections. Written during the thirteenth century, Robert de Boron's *Merlin* transforms Merlin into a Christ figure whose childhood parallels medieval legends about the childhood of Christ and whose aims are fully reconciled with Christian teleology. As Goodrich notes, "Robert's conception of the mage makes Merlin a Christian spokesman of the divine will" (11). In the *Suite Post Vulgate*, by contrast, Merlin's diabolical nature is foregrounded. A lecher, a seducer, and an evildoer, he is finally hoisted with his own petard as the young woman he desires, and to whom he teaches his magic, imprisons him in a tomb and leaves him to an ignominious death (Berthelot 169).

From medieval times until the Renaissance and beyond, Merlin was to retain his double-sided nature and potential (Goodrich 18). During the Renaissance, Merlin frequently appeared as the epitome of the Renaissance scholar and mage. Notable is the fact that throughout the tradition, whatever his nature, he seldom renounced his power willingly. During the sixteenth century, numerous translations and reworkings of the Merlin material appeared in France and Great Britain (Vadé 803; Stewart and Matthews 120). The Merlin prophecies, like Geoffrey's *History*, enjoyed a kind of vogue which lasted well into the eighteenth century. This material would therefore have been familiar and readily available to Shakespeare and would be the logical point of departure for his portrait of a powerful enchanter. Given the ubiquity of this figure, it is surprising that Geoffrey Bullough, in his magisterial eight-volume compendium of the narrative and dramatic sources of Shakespeare's plays, does not mention the Merlin figure as a possible source or model for Prospero. If we recognize the figure of Merlin with his shifting and ambiguous moral stance as a previously overlooked source for Shakespeare's Prospero, we can account for a similar ambiguity in Prospero, an ambiguity that has continued to concern and puzzle critics and directors to the present.

Prospero and Merlin

Critical studies of Shakespeare's *The Tempest* are divided for the most part by two antithetical interpretations of Prospero. On the one hand, Prospero is presented as a beneficent, kindly figure modeled on Shakespeare himself, a larger-than-life enchanter in the sense of the Renaissance mage. On the other hand, he is interpreted as a negative figure, an abusive and vengeful tyrant who enslaves Caliban, the savage yet hapless inhabitant of the island which Prospero has stolen from him.

One of the earliest traditions views Prospero as a positive, beneficent, almost god-like figure who brings divine retribution, revelation, and conversion to the evil characters and beings in the play, including not only Prospero's political enemies, but also Caliban. William Hogarth's eighteenth-century painting, *Scene from* The Tempest (ca. 1735–40), is representative. In this sentimentalized version, as Stephen Orgel has suggested, Prospero resembles "a Rembrandt rabbi" who "watches benignly as a courtly Ferdinand in ermine and gold embroidery salutes a classically draped Miranda, a magic book at her feet and a garlanded lamb at her side" (6). The iconography of the picture derives, as Robert Simon has noted, from traditional paintings of the nativity and the annunciation (qtd. in Orgel 6). The idealized view of Prospero was further elaborated in 1838 by Thomas Campbell, the first critic to introduce the autobiographical interpretation of Prospero as an allegory of Shakespeare saying farewell to the stage (Vaughn and Vaughn 105). Writing in 1875, Edward Dowden epitomizes the autobiographical view. For Dowden, "the grave harmony of [Prospero's] character, his self-mastery, his calm validity of will, his sensitiveness to wrong, his unfaltering justice, and with these a certain remoteness from the common joys and sorrows of this world, are characteristic of Shakspere [*sic*]." Like the bard, "Prospero has reached not only the highest levels of moral attainment, he has also reached an altitude of thought from which he can survey the whole of human life, and see how small and yet how great it is" (qtd. in Craig 1248). This view is seconded by editor Harden Craig in his 1951 introduction to *The Tempest* (1248).

The Prospero-Shakespeare identification continues to find numerous representatives in Shakespearean scholarship. In 2004, Stephen Greenblatt reiterates the claim that Prospero is a metaphoric rendition of Shakespeare. Richard Monette's 2005 stage presentation of *The Tempest*, the farewell performance of a well-known Shakespearean actor, William Hutt, now in his 80s, continues the tradition, suggesting by implication that Prospero is a lordly self-portrait of Shakespeare taking his final leave after a long and distinguished career of magical illusions in the form of his art (*The Tempest*, Program Notes). Viewing Prospero as an allegory of the playwright Shakespeare often results, however, in a non-critical interpretation of Prospero, since to criticize Prospero is to criticize Shakespeare. Such an approach disregards the questionable and even negative aspects of Prospero that have emerged in a completely different strand of Shakespeare criticism.

This negative view of Prospero is not a recent phenomenon, as one might expect. Instead, it predates post-colonial theory by almost 150 years, demonstrating that this approach is not simply an offshoot of late twentieth-century theoretical models. For the most part, this interpretation arises from a more sympathetic understanding of Caliban which implies a less positive assessment of Prospero (Vaughn and Vaughn 105). In this reassessment of Caliban, the earliest positive note is struck by Coleridge in an 1811 lecture which describes Caliban as "a noble being" (Vaughn and Vaughn 103). In 1818 William Hazlitt argued that the island belongs by right to Caliban, not to Prospero, so that Prospero is, by implication, a thief and usurper (Vaughn and Vaughn 104). As Jonathan Bates notes, William Hazlitt was "the first to read *The Tempest* in terms of Imperialism" (144). *The Enchanted Isle* (1848), a satirical comedy written by William and Robert Brough, portrays Caliban as a revolutionary, a hereditary bondsman, and the equivalent of a slave. With the success of the satire, "the idea of Caliban as a republican and as a 'native' was established as a strand in nineteenth-century interpretations of the Shakespearean character" (Griffiths 42). In 1892, in an article written for *Harper's New Monthly Magazine*, Andrew Lang clearly states the relationship between Prospero and Caliban in terms of the colonizer as opposed to the colonized:

> [Caliban] was introduced to the benefits of civilization. He was instructed. The resources of his island were developed. He was like the red men in America, the blacks in Australia, the tribes of Hispaniola. Then he committed an offence, an unpardonable offence, but one that Caliban was fated to commit. Then he was punished. Do we not "punish the natives" all over the world, all we civilized powers? ... All this appears to be as inevitable as it is odious, and all this occurred in Caliban's island. My own sympathies have always been with "the natives," with Caliban.... If Caliban wants to kill Prospero, as he does, can one blame him? Prospero had taken his land, had enslaved him, had punished him cruelly [qtd. in Griffiths 45–46].

Andrew Lang's comments clearly point to a line of criticism that emerged more fully in the twentieth century. In a 1944 essay, W.H. Auden states, "we cannot help feeling that Prospero is largely responsible for his corruption, and that, in the debate between them, Caliban has the best of the argument" (58).

Octave Mannoni's influential study, *Prospero and Caliban: The Psychology of Colonization* (1956), expands the argument, making the relationship between Prospero and Caliban analogous to the position of the colonizer and the colonized in Madagascar. Prospero, whom Mannoni sees as identical to Shakespeare, is a tyrant who controls Miranda, Ariel, and Caliban with the same "paternal omnipotence" (105). To Miranda, his daughter, Prospero gives orders that are "absurd and quite unwarranted" and he "even goes so far as to threaten her with his hatred" (105). In the case of Ariel, "Prospero has promised him his liberty but fails to give it to him" (105). Mannoni points out that "there is little logic" to Prospero's argument that Caliban deserves his treatment for the offense of attempting to violate Miranda's honor. According to Mannoni, Prospero's claim, "you tried to violate Miranda, therefore you shall chop wood, belongs to a non-rational mode of thinking" (106). Mannoni compares Prospero's attitude, which he sees as identical to Shakespeare's, to that of the colonizer who attempts to justify his domination and enslavement of others with non sequitur arguments. From the 1970s onward, critical studies expanding on Mannoni's observations have reassessed both Prospero and Caliban, noting numerous areas in which Prospero, the wise, beneficent patriarch, emerges as the irrational, abusive, imperialist tyrant (see also Orgel 24–25 and 24n1).

The view of Prospero as a tyrant and imperialist, then, is almost as old as the tradition that he is a beneficent mage. Stephen Orgel provides a telling summary of the two conflicting views of *The Tempest* which have remained unresolved until the present:

> *The Tempest* is a text that looks different in different contexts, and has been used to support radically differing claims about Shakespeare's allegiances.... We have seen Prospero as a noble ruler and mage, a tyrant and megalomaniac, a necromancer, a Neoplatonic scientist, a colonial imperialist, a civilizer [11].

Such antithetical views—both drawing evidence from the text—demonstrate that there is no single, easy interpretation of Prospero, either as irrevocably evil or almost unambiguously good. But these conflicts in interpretation do not mean that the text is simply indeterminate. If we recognize that Prospero is grounded in the Merlin tradition, we discover that the opposing characteristics attributed to him in critical studies are not only understandable, but inherent in Prospero himself.

The resemblance of Prospero to Merlin plays an important role in our understanding of Shakespeare's mage. The critical neglect of the Merlin-Prospero connection is surprising, especially if one considers the many parallels and resemblances between Merlin figures and Shakespeare's mage. Like Merlin, Prospero is a magician and enchanter who possesses extraordinary powers. He not only raises storms, but he claims even to have raised the dead. Similar to Geoffrey's and Robert's Merlin, Prospero claims to use his power in positive ways, especially to punish those who, like Antonio, deserve punishment for their evil deeds and to enslave Caliban, a "bestial" creature whom Prospero views as evil incarnate. He also uses his magical powers to arrange a marriage between his daughter, Miranda, and Ferdinand, the son of his enemy, the King of Naples. He thereby attempts to bring about a peaceable resolution to a difficult political situation by controlling the succession. In this, too, he resembles Merlin, who arranges magically for the succession of Arthur to the throne.

Like Merlin, he has a different, darker side that is inextricably bound up in all his actions. Geoffrey's Merlin uses dubious means to carry out objectives which, ostensibly, are ethically sound. He also abuses his power in many of the accounts, severely punishing those who oppose him, and enslaving the will of King Uther Pendragon whom he purports to be advising. Prospero, too, abuses his magical power. He is able to dispossess Caliban in the name of civilizing him, and when Caliban counters his expectations, Prospero enslaves and tortures him. His magical powers allow him to keep Ariel imprisoned, forcing him to do the enchanter's bidding even though Ariel had been promised his freedom. Magic also allows him to take revenge on his enemies. Even though—as he repeatedly states to Miranda—he has no intention of harming them physically, he tortures them mentally. His power allows him, through Ariel, to set up a situation where he entraps Antonio into plotting treason and murder against the King of Naples. In other words, Prospero, as Stephen Orgel has noted, creates a situation that permits him the possibility of blackmailing Antonio later in the play.

By incorporating the two Merlins of tradition—the divine and the demonic—Shakespeare creates a double-voiced character whose overt claims and intentions are contradicted implicitly by many of his actions and words, as well as by the comments of others.[2] Shakespeare thus puts into question the beneficence of Prospero's stance. The civilized, highly educated Prospero engages in violence, invective, tyranny, and injustice. At the same time, he deceives himself by maintaining, through self-serving rationalizations, that his actions are justified. Prospero is not an evil man. He has the "best" of intentions. But his intentions do not make him a beneficent mage. He is rather a man who is blind to the "savageries" he commits or condones while decrying the savageries of others.

In his doubled presentation of Prospero, Shakespeare draws on the strategies of reversal used by one of his sources, Michel de Montaigne's *Of Cannibals* (1580). Montaigne's essay has been seen primarily as the source for Gonzalo's description of a utopian fantasy when he first arrives on the island (2.1.150–71). But critics have neglected a key aspect of Montaigne's essay; namely, the reversal of perspectives and the resulting doubled vision which provide a key to Shakespeare's doubled vision of Prospero. Montaigne does not maintain without reservation that the cannibals are noble savages. On the contrary, he notes that they eat their fellow human beings, a custom that Europeans consider savage. But, in comparing the culture of the savages to that of the civilized, Montaigne argues that the civilized, despite their claims to the contrary, are in some ways just as savage, if not more so, than those they condemn. What is worse, he asks—to eat one's fellow creatures, who are already dead and can suffer no pain, or to torture human beings to death on the rack, to draw and quarter them, and to commit other atrocities as civilized Europeans are wont to do to? As Montaigne states, "We may well call these people Barbarians" (85), according to rational thinking, but not in comparison to the civilized "who surpass them in every kind of barbarity" (86). Montaigne recognizes the irony of the fact that while "judging their faults so clearly, we should be blind to our own"(85).[3]

Prospero, in a like manner, while claiming to be civilized, engages in savageries he fails to recognize. Caliban (an anagram of Can[n]ibal) is no noble savage, since his violent impulses clearly undermine such a claim. But Prospero is able, because of his superior (magical) powers, to become an abusive tyrant and slave master to Caliban and a less abusive but no less tyrannical slave master to Ariel. Caliban is hurt physically and verbally abused with names such as "poisonous slave," "most lying slave," "abhorrèd slave," "savage," "hagseed," "malice," "misshapen knave," and "thing of darkness."[4] Prospero abandons all attempts to correct or civilize him because Caliban has disobeyed Prospero's injunctions and behaved in a non-civilized way. Ariel only escapes Prospero's punishments because, even if he objects to his enslavement, he is invariably compliant to Prospero's demands. Like Montaigne's portrait of the civilized, Prospero is sensitive to the faults of others and ready to condemn their machinations and crimes, all the while remaining blind to his own reprehensible behavior. He fails, throughout much of the play, to recognize his own self-contradictions. He renounces his power over Caliban and Ariel, but only after he has no more need of them. He releases his hold over his enemies, choosing virtue rather than revenge, but only after he has punished them psychologically. He recognizes their claim to his pity, but only after Ariel prompts him.

Numerous critics have supported the beneficent mage tradition by referring to the revelation, the conversion, and the harmonious tying up of loose ends at the end of the play in order to demonstrate that

Prospero has exercised an unambiguously beneficial, even divinely sanctioned, influence on the various players involved in the events. But given the numerous contradictions, the conclusion of the play is not a return to harmony, as many critics have argued. Instead, as Stephen Orgel observes, it leaves many issues unresolved[5]:

> The concern with repentance, forgiveness, reconciliation, and regeneration is one that is voiced often throughout *The Tempest*. But a much less clear pattern is the one that is acted out: repentance remains, at the play's end, a largely unachieved goal, forgiveness is ambiguous at best, the clear ideal of reconciliation grows cloudy as the play concludes. And in this respect, the play is entirely characteristic of its author and genre: Shakespearean comedy rarely concludes with that neat and satisfactory resolution we are led to expect, and that criticism so often claims for it [13].

Orgel provides an excellent discussion of the many contradictions inherent in the ending, demonstrating that harmony only appears to have been restored, but numerous questions remain unanswered. Miranda and Ferdinand appear as less than ideal lovers, Antonio is forced to give up the kingdom by a form of blackmail, Prospero only renounces his magic once he has achieved his ends by ensuring the succession, and the masque, with a rape at its center, is less than harmonious.[6] All of these contradictions underscore the doubled vision of Prospero, who makes claims for harmony, forgiveness, and renunciation on the surface, but whose actions are at odds with these claims.

Prospero's final words to the audience have puzzled critics.[7] But Prospero's comments are less puzzling if we see them in the context of the doubled vision of the civilized man who ostensibly represents all that is most prized in civilization—scholarship wisdom, power through mental achievement—but who, at the same time, commits acts that do not harmonize with these professed ideals. The words of the epilogue, where Prospero speaks "not [as] an actor in a play but [as] a character in a fiction" (Orgel 55), reflect a self-knowledge that Prospero has never admitted throughout the play. In the epilogue, the enchanter recognizes implicitly that, depending on how members of the audience read his character and judge which of his two voices appears to dominate the play, they will either view him positively and applaud him for his good intentions, or view him negatively and condemn him for his less than ethical deeds. Prospero's final words are therefore a plea to the audience not to condemn him for his actions but instead to reward his good intentions by pardoning him. He begins by asking the audience to make a decision:

> Now my charms are all o'erthrown
> And what strength I have 's mine own,
> Which is most faint. Now, 'tis true,
> I must be here confined by you
> Or sent to Naples [Epilogue 1–5].

The audience is asked to decide his fate: is he to be "confined" on the island, or can he go to Naples and be free? He continues by asking the audience not to punish him by leaving him on this isolated island:

> Let me not,
> Since I have my dukedom got
> And pardoned the deceiver, dwell
> In this bare island by your spell [Epilogue 5–8].

Here he explains why he ought to be forgiven, since he has "pardoned" those who deceived him. However, the notion that we should forgive him because he has now reacquired his position of power ("Since I have my dukedom got") may be a practical argument, but it has little to do with forgiveness. We find a similar false logic here to that pointed out by Mannoni: You attempted to rape my daughter, therefore you must be my slave. Here he argues, I now have my dukedom back, therefore I should be forgiven.

Given the illogic of the statement, and the fact that he has only pardoned Antonio after compelling him to give up the dukedom, it is probably not surprising that Prospero fears the audience might still judge him negatively, and by their "spell"—that is, in their negative response to his character—doom him to continued exile on the island. He therefore intensifies his plea:

> But release me from my bands
> With the help of your good hands.
> Gentle breath of yours my sails
> Must fill, or else my project fails,
> Which was to please. Now I want
> Spirits to enforce, art to enchant,
> And my ending is despair,
> Unless I be relieved by prayer,
> Which pierces so that it assaults
> Mercy itself, and frees all faults.
> As you from crimes would pardon'd be,
> Let your indulgence set me free [Epilogue 9–20].

He has wished to "please." Generally, the word "please" is interpreted as referring allegorically to Shakespeare wishing to please the audience with his plays. But literally, it refers to the claims of Prospero who wishes to please the audience by convincing them of the goodness of his intentions. The audience could just as easily judge him, at best, as a tainted hero whose moral ambiguity is his most prominent trait. The critical reception of Prospero certainly corroborates this self-evaluation, since critics have either praised or condemned him, and continue to do so.

In the next part of the epilogue, Prospero admits in a rather radical statement of self-incrimination that his faults are so severe that only prayers to Mercy itself would be adequate to absolve him from "all faults." Furthermore, the audience is requested to forgive him, not as they would have their faults forgiven, but as they would have their crimes forgiven. Prospero does not refer to his own deeds as "crimes," but he suggests that the audience might judge them to be analogous to crimes. This plea for forgiveness suggests that he finally has a true insight into his own character. He has finally come to the rather agonizing recognition that he is not a blameless, beneficent patriarch, justified in all of his actions, but that instead he is a man in need of forgiveness. If there is a revelation in the play, then these words indicate that Prospero may finally have seen himself clearly and may have recognized that, for all his self-justifications, he has been, following Montaigne's argument, no less barbarous than the barbarian he has mistreated and enslaved. His other deeds, including his psychological revenge, his manipulation of his daughter and Ferdinand, and his failure to give Ariel his liberty may also need forgiveness if we are to see his "reward"— the return to Naples—as justified. Like Merlin, then, Prospero is a man poised between good and evil. But unlike any of the past Merlins, he has become conscious of his own equivocal nature, has reflected on it, and has recognized the problems inherent in the power he has wielded.[8]

Prospero, Saruman, and Gandalf

Tolkien did not admit to direct influence by Shakespeare. However, like most well-educated Englishmen of his time, Tolkien was steeped in Shakespeare.[9] Furthermore, like Shakespeare, Tolkien was working in the Merlin wizard tradition, so that both writers were drawing from similar sources in which the uses and abuses of power are explored in relation to a powerful enchanter. The link between Prospero and Gandalf has been recognized but has not been examined beyond a few words in passing. For example, Tom Shippey notes that Prospero was "a model of sorts for Gandalf," adding, "at least in his shortness of temper" (196), but he does not go further than this brief but suggestive observation. An exploration of the Prospero-Gandalf connection, however, points toward a far more complex picture. It is true that Gandalf may well be modeled in part on Prospero, but he embodies the positive side of Prospero, the benign yet powerful patriarch whom critics have so often seen in Shakespeare's magician. Indeed, one could almost argue that Gandalf is the figure many critics have traditionally described in their positive assessment of Prospero. Prospero's tyranny, his abuse of power, and his victimization of Caliban, on the other hand, find no counterpart in Gandalf's nature. Instead, the potential for tyranny and abuse which are the corrosive side-effects of the supernatural power exercised by both Merlin and Prospero are embodied in the figure of Saruman. Thus, in Tolkien, instead of a single, complex and ambivalent figure, we have at least two different figures, each one representing a different aspect of Merlin and Prospero. Saruman represents the dark, negative, evil tendencies, while Gandalf embodies the positive aspects.

SARUMAN

The link with Prospero's "dark side" is particularly evident in the figure of Saruman. As Tolkien tells us in his *Unfinished Tales* (*UT*), Saruman was one of the Istari, or emissaries from the Valar, as is Gandalf. They have been sent to Middle-earth to counter the growing power of Sauron, a Maia who has set up an evil kingdom in Mordor and whose mission it is to enslave the peoples of Middle-earth. Saruman, formerly known as Curunir, is considered the leader of the Istari. When Saruman appears before the Valar to be sent to Middle-earth, he proves to be "of noble mien and bearing with ... a fair voice" (*UT* 389). He is "clad in white" (389). In other words, he looks on the surface much like the benevolent critical representations of Prospero. During his sojourn on Middle-earth, Saruman resembles Prospero in many ways. Like Prospero, he is a scholar who prides himself on his great learning and on his studies into necromancy and magic. He also resembles Prospero in his isolation. By the time period represented in *The Lord of the Rings* (*LotR*), at the end of the Third Age, Saruman has become a solitary who has retreated to his "island," the fortress tower of Orthanc, a small world that he controls entirely. Like Prospero, he controls the wills of others. Just as Prospero has a minion, Ariel, who does his bidding, so Saruman has Wormtongue. Ariel deceives and controls the courtiers, while Wormtongue, with the help of Saruman's magical powers, deceives, controls, and enslaves the will of Théoden, reducing him to an abject creature who is only released from his thrall by Gandalf's intervention.

Both Prospero and Merlin imprison those who have wronged or defied them. Prospero imprisons and enslaves Caliban for attempting to rape Miranda, while Saruman imprisons Gandalf in Orthanc when Gandalf refuses to help Saruman wrest power from Sauron and become

a joint ruler of Middle-earth. Prospero indicates that he has learned how
to raise the dead (5.1.48–50); Saruman breeds a new race of fighting
Uruk-hai to carry out his will and to fight his battles. Prospero creates
powerful illusions which cause those whom he has enthralled to see
things contrary to reality. Similarly, during the confrontation at
Orthanc, after he has lost the battle at Helm's Deep, Saruman speaks
in a voice that controls the perceptions and responses of his listeners.
Thus, when Saruman argues with Gandalf, the others who are listening
hear only "the gentle remonstrance of a kindly king with an erring but
much-loved minister" (3.10.567). Believing this illusion, the others conclude that Gandalf will make an alliance with Saruman and betray them.
The illusion is only broken when Gandalf bursts into laughter (3.10.
568). While Shakespeare's enchanter takes revenge on his enemies who
have deprived him of his power and threatened his life, Saruman devastates the Shire to take revenge on the Hobbits, whom he sees as instru-
mental in bringing about his downfall.

    Yet, Prospero is not an evil man, nor has he chosen evil consciously.
The faults he has are the byproduct of the power and control he uses
to effect his revenge. Nor does Saruman begin as evil. When he arrives
on Middle-earth, Saruman, like the other Istari, takes human form, and
so even if his intentions are good, he may choose methods that align
him with the forces of evil, represented by Sauron. Thus, he could "fall
away from [his] purposes, and do evil, forgetting the good in the search
for the power to effect it" (*UT* 390). Initially, like Prospero, Saruman
has good intentions. He proposes to save Middle-earth from enslavement to the Dark Lord. But his desire for the power to effect these ends
seduces him into using the *palantír* or Seeing Stone, which puts him in
the power of Sauron.

    Although Saruman resembles Prospero in many ways, one decid-
ing factor causes Saruman's trajectory to differ radically from Prospero's. This factor is Prospero's choice to renounce his revenge and,
subsequently, his magical powers. He recognizes, through Ariel's empathetic comments, that his victims are deserving of his pity. As Ariel states,
"Your charm so strongly works 'em / That if you now beheld them your
affections / Would become tender" (5.1.16–19). Thereupon Prospero
makes his decisive shift, renouncing his revenge, for, he states, "the
rarer action is / In virtue than in vengeance" (5.1.27–28). In this choice,
he begins to recognize the cruelty that grows out of an unrelenting
demand for revenge. Just as important as his renunciation is his further recognition, expressed in the play's epilogue, that, while claiming
to be justified, he has committed acts reprehensible enough to warrant
possible audience disapprobation and to require forgiveness. Saruman,
by contrast, is offered the choice to renounce his power and thoughts

of revenge and to join the peoples of Middle-earth in their fight against Sauron. Gandalf reports: "I gave him a last choice and a fair one: to renounce both Mordor and his private schemes" (3.10.570). But, unlike Prospero, Saruman flatly refuses. The difference between the two wizards is underlined by the fate of their staffs. Prospero promises voluntarily to break and bury his staff deep in the earth and to drown his magic book in the sea (5.1.54–47). Saruman has his staff forcibly removed from his hands and "split asunder" by Gandalf, who thereby expels him from the Order of the Istari and the White Council (3.10.569). Saruman does not voluntarily relinquish the *palantír* which links him to Sauron. Instead, he loses it through the thoughtless and angry gesture of Wormtongue, who flings it out of the tower in a fit of rage (3.10.569–70).

Saruman is the example of a figure who realizes in all its negative implications the evil potential of both Merlin and Prospero. Saruman's choices lead to his own progressive degradation, of which he seems unaware. He declines from a leader of the free peoples to a plotter bent on ruling Middle-earth, to a self-serving demagogue with his own new-bred army of monsters. In his final act of revenge on the Shire and the Hobbits, the supernatural powers and desire for revenge, which link him with Prospero, are seen in their meanest and most petty light. Murdered by his own henchman, Saruman is reduced to little more than skull and bones: "Frodo looked down at the body with pity and horror, for as he looked it seemed that the long years of death were suddenly revealed in it, and it shrank, and the shriveled face became rags of skin upon a hideous skull" (6.8.997). The human pity felt by Frodo here is the same kind of pity that caused him and Bilbo to spare Gollum and thus to bring about the final act that saves Middle-earth from the power of the Ring. This kind of pity, too, saves Prospero, allowing him to recognize his own "savageries."

GANDALF

Just as Saruman embodies the dark side of both Prospero and Merlin, so Gandalf represents the beneficent aspects of Prospero and the heroic qualities of Merlin as a wise counselor, strategist, and leader in battle. Gandalf, like Prospero, is a scholar, an enchanter, and a teacher, as well as a political strategist who works to ensure the succession to the throne. For Merlin, it is King Arthur, for Prospero, Miranda and Ferdinand, and for Gandalf, Aragorn, the heir of Isildur. But Prospero's scope is far more limited than Gandalf's, both in his motivations and his area of action. Prospero's primary motivations throughout most of the play are revenge, control, and dynastic ambition. Gandalf's primary motives are, by contrast, altruistic: concern for the peoples of Middle-earth, the desire to protect them from coercion and enslavement by the Dark Lord, and the hope to reestablish the royal claims of Aragorn rather than to guarantee his own—Gandalf's—succession. Gandalf's altruism even extends to self-sacrifice when he "dies" in his battle to protect fellowship members from the Balrog at Khazad-dûm.

Both Prospero and Gandalf, like Merlin, are teachers. But Prospero's teaching tends to be hortatory. His lecture to his daughter, Miranda, is punctuated by commands urging her to pay attention. When he no longer wishes her to hear, he uses magic to put her to sleep. As Miranda's comments to her father suggest, he has frequently withheld information and refused to answer her questions. His purpose is not to awaken Miranda to knowledge and independence, but to control and limit her perceptions of reality. During the play, he wishes to create a situation that will guarantee the succession, so that his approach to her is manipulative rather than pedagogical. Gandalf does appear to resemble Prospero in small ways. He withholds information and fails to answer questions. Indeed, in what could be seen as a parody of Prospero's lecture to Miranda, Tolkien pokes fun at the tiresome lecturer by having Pippin fall asleep during the ride to Gondor, while Gandalf lectures him about the history and customs of the people of Gondor. But the main purpose of Gandalf's teaching is not to control and manipulate. Instead, while he often remains mysterious about his doings, he differs from Prospero in that his teaching is designed to teach the free peoples of Middle-earth how to become independent and how to protect themselves from evil when he is no longer there. Gandalf, then, is a facilitator rather than a mere purveyor of knowledge.

Prospero's powerful abilities as an enchanter are more than matched by Gandalf's magical capabilities. Both share this power with Merlin figures. But, unlike Gandalf, Prospero is initially seduced and corrupted by the power of magic. He only renounces his revenge and the magical powers once he recognizes their corrosive influence. Gandalf is quite unlike Prospero in this area. He renounces the corrosive uses of power—represented by the Ring—from the outset. He recognizes the danger inherent in the powers the Ring represents. He therefore refuses to take or even touch the Ring when it is offered to him by Bilbo (1.1.34) and Frodo. When Frodo asks, "Will you not take the Ring?" Gandalf cries, "No ... with that power I should have power too great and terrible. And over me the Ring would gain a power still greater and more deadly." By using such powers, no matter how good his intentions, Gandalf knows that he would "become like the Dark Lord himself" (1.1.60). Gandalf knows immediately what Prospero only discovers after using magic to manipulate and enslave: that even if one's intentions are good and just, the power represented by magic is corrosive, not because it is magical, but because of its great potential for controlling both the elements and other human beings. It therefore corrupts even those who mean to use it well. Gandalf has access to considerable magic power aside from the Ring, but even this magic is used sparingly, and on singular occasions when the powers of the peoples of Middle-earth would be insufficient to deal with a supernatural menace. His purpose is to allow his students with non-magical powers to become independent and to carry on without him after he has gone. Prospero, by contrast, does not evince such altruistic motives in leaving Caliban on the island. Merlin, in some versions, desires to make his pupil, King Arthur, independent, while in others, he enslaves Arthur's will.

While Prospero's island represents the narrowness of his arena, Gandalf's arena includes not only the whole of Middle-earth, but also the supernatural realm of the Valar. Gandalf's sphere of activities and expertise has a far wider range than Prospero's. Gandalf resembles Merlin as the heroic warrior and counselor of kings. Gandalf counsels and advises Aragorn, heir to the throne, and he leads the men of Gondor in battle when the steward, Denethor, abdicates his authority and responsibility when they are under attack. Furthermore, while Prospero lost his kingdom because he retreated into his studies of magic, Gandalf's studies make him sensitive to the political situation, so that he helps guide the peoples of Middle-earth through his knowledge of the Ring, its nature, and its means of destruction. Prospero is the academic who lacks the political interest and acumen to keep his kingdom together, delegates his own responsibility to his brother, and leaves himself open to be deposed. Gandalf is the scholar who uses his knowledge to grapple with rather than retreat from political and social realities.

Gandalf, like Saruman, could be considered Tolkien's response to Prospero and Merlin. Saruman is Prospero as he could have been, had he failed to renounce his powers. Gandalf is Prospero as he might have been: an altruistic leader and educator, a counselor and companion, a strategist and battle leader who embodies all the qualities of a statesman and a philosopher. Like the Merlin of *Suite Post Vulgate*, Saruman's choices lead to isolation and death, and like Robert's Merlin, Gandalf's choices lead to a new beginning and life.

This study opens up new ways of seeing Prospero, Saruman, and Gandalf, both in relation to one another and in relation to the Merlin figure from which they derive. A key to the mutually illuminating qualities of these characters lies in the ambiguous nature of Merlin himself, poised as he is between good and evil. Shakespeare's doubled portrait of Prospero, drawing both on the Merlin tradition and the strategies of Montaigne, is highlighted in the epilogue, where the two sides of Prospero are specifically described. Prospero—and Shakespeare—leave the answer to the questions raised in the epilogue open to the audience. Is Prospero an evil Merlin figure worthy of punishment and further confinement on the island? Or is he a well-intentioned, if somewhat misguided, mage who should be rewarded for renouncing magic and its corrosive uses? The paradox of Prospero's vision as the civilizer engaged in "savagery" is particularly poignant in these last words on stage.

By the same token, Saruman and Gandalf are not simply schematic antitheses—the evil Merlin as opposed to the good Merlin. Instead, seen in relation to Merlin and Prospero, their predecessors in the wizard tradition, they reveal multiple layers of complexity and ambiguity which allow Tolkien, like Shakespeare, to highlight the role of choice in the trajectories they follow. Against the backdrop provided by Merlin and Prospero, Saruman's potential for good as well as his choice of evil and its dire consequences are all the more clearly etched. Gandalf's character, too, is highlighted as we see more distinctly the path he could have taken had he, like Saruman, been seduced by the temptation of the Ring and its promise of power.

Notes

1. For Merlin, see *Henry IV, Part One* (3.1.144–6) and *King Lear* (3.2.95). For "wizard," see, for example, *Henry VI, Part Two* (1.4.15).

2. I am using the concept of a double-voiced character in a sense derived from Mikhail Bakhtin's concept of a text that "expresses simultaneously two different intentions" (324). These two voices overlap each other, representing different, conflicting aspects of Prospero's character, so that they are "dialogically interrelated" (324).

3. See also Montaigne's comment: "Each man calls barbarism whatever is not his own practice; for indeed it seems we have no other test of truth and reason than the example and pattern of the opinions and customs of the country we live in" (77).

4. Line references to the above are, respectively, 1.2.322, 347, 354, 358, 368, and 370; 5.1.268 and 275.

5. Prospero seems to forgive Antonio, but he blackmails him with his reminder that he could—but does not choose to—reveal Antonio's treasonous plot to murder the King of Naples.

6. Orgel demonstrates that Ferdinand and Miranda, for example, "play out, at chess, a brief game of love and war that seems to foretell in their lives all the ambition, duplicity, and cynicism of their elders" (29). Furthermore, reconciliation is not achieved: "Alonso is penitent, but the chief villain, the usurping younger brother Antonio, remains obdurate" (51). Even the acts of renunciation are only promised after Prospero has actually achieved his ends (53), while Antonio is compelled to give up the kingdom (53). Orgel concludes, "The sense of unfinished business is finally the life of the play" (56).

7. Stephen Greenblatt notes the contradictions in the epilogue, but he reframes them, shifting them into the arena of aesthetics by viewing them as Shakespeare's statements about his art (375–77).

8. Greenblatt recognizes that Prospero feels guilt, but does not refer the guilt to Prospero, whom he absolves of any possible crime: "For Prospero, whose morality and legitimacy are repeatedly insisted upon, this guilt does not make entire sense, but it might have made sense for the playwright who peers out from behind the mask of the prince"

(376). Greenblatt concludes that the "whiff of criminality is just a fantasy" and does not reflect any reality on the part of either Shakespeare or Prospero (377).

9. Tolkien mentions Shakespeare only a few times in his letters, and twice he does so negatively (*Letters* 88, 143n, 185, 212n, 213).

Works Cited

Auden, W.H. *The Sea and the Mirror.* Ed. Arthur Kirsch. Princeton: Princeton University Press, 2004.

Bakhtin, Mikhail M. "Discourse in the Novel." In *The Dialogic Imagination: Four Essays by M.M. Bakhtin.* Ed. Michael Holquist. Trans. Caryl Emerson and Michael Holquist. Austin: University of Texas Press, 1981. 259–422.

Bates, Jonathan. *Shakespeare Constitutions: Politics, Theatre, Criticism, 1730–1830.* Oxford: Clarendon, 1989.

Berthelot, Anne. "Merlin and the Ladies of the Lake." In *Merlin: A Casebook.* Ed. Peter Goodrich and Raymond Thompson. New York: Routledge, 2003. 162–81.

Bullough, Geoffrey. Ed. *Narrative and Dramatic Sources of Shakespeare.* 8 Vols. New York: Columbia University Press, 1973.

Craig, Hardin, Ed. *The Complete Works of Shakespeare.* New York: Harcourt, 1951.

Geoffrey of Monmouth. *History of the Kings of Britain.* Trans. Lewis Thorpe. New York: Penguin, 1978.

Goodrich, Peter. Introduction. *Merlin: A Casebook.* Ed. Peter Goodrich and Raymond Thompson. New York: Routledge, 2003. 1–90.

Greenblatt, Stephen. *Will in the World: How Shakespeare Became Shakespeare.* New York: Norton, 2004.

Griffiths, Trevor. "'This Island's Mine': Caliban and Colonialism." In *Post-Colonial Theory and English Literature: A Reader.* Ed. Peter Childs. Edinburgh: Edinburgh University Press, 1999. 39–56.

Latham, Jaqueline. "*The Tempest* and King James's *Daemonologie*." *Shakespeare Survey* 28 (1975): 117–23.

Mannoni, Octave. *Prospero and Caliban: The Psychology of Colonization.* Trans. Pamela Powesland. New York: Praeger, 1956.

Montaigne, Michel de. "Of Cannibals." 1580. In *Selected Essays.* Trans. and intro. Donald M. Frame. New York: Black, 1943. 73–92.

Morford, Mark, and Robert Lenardon. *Classical Mythology.* 2nd ed. New York: Longman, 1971.

Orgel, Stephen, ed. Introduction. *The Tempest.* Oxford: Clarendon, 1987. 1–92.

The Post Vulgate Part I: The Merlin Continuation. Trans. Martha Asher. In *Lancelot-Grail. The Old French Arthurian Vulgate and Post-Vulgate in Translation.* Vol. 4. Ed. Norris J. Lacy. New York: Garland, 1993. 167–277.

Robert de Boron. *Merlin and the Grail. Joseph of Arimathea, Merlin, Perceval: The Trilogy of Prose Romances Attributed to Robert de Boron.* Trans. Nigel Bryant. Cambridge: Brewer, 2001.

Shakespeare, William. *The Complete Works of William Shakespeare.* Ed. David Bevington. 5th ed. New York: Pearson, 2004.

Shippey, Thomas A. *J.R.R. Tolkien: Author of the Century.* Boston: Houghton, 2001.

Stewart, R.J., and John Matthews, eds. *Merlin through the Ages: A Chronological Anthology and Source Book.* London: Blandford, 1995.

The Tempest. By William Shakespeare. Dir. Richard Monette. Stratford Festival Theatre, Stratford Canada. 20 July 2005.

The Tempest. Program Notes. Stratford Festival: Stratford, Canada, Summer 2005.

Tolkien, J.R.R. *The Letters of J.R.R. Tolkien.* Ed. Humphrey Carpenter. Boston: Houghton, 1981.

_____. *The Lord of the Rings.* 2nd ed. Boston: Houghton, 1994.

_____. *The Silmarillion.* 2nd ed. Boston: Houghton, 2001.

_____. *Unfinished Tales of Númenor and Middle-earth.* Ed. Christopher Tolkien. Boston: Houghton, 1980.

Vadé, Yvès. "Merlin." In *Companion to Literary Myths, Heroes, and Archetypes.* Ed. Pierre Brunel. Trans. Wendy Allatson et al. London: Routledge, 1988. 796–806.

Vaughn, Alden, and Virginia Vaughn. *Shakespeare's Caliban: A Cultural History.* Cambridge: Cambridge University Press, 1991.

The Vulgate: The Story of Merlin. Trans. Rupert T. Pickens. In *Lancelot-Grail. The Old French Arthurian Vulgate and Post-Vulgate in Translation.* Vol. 1. Ed. Norris J. Lacy. New York: Garland, 1993. 167–424.

"Bid the Tree Unfix His Earthbound Root"

Motifs from Macbeth in J.R.R. Tolkien's The Lord of the Rings

JANET BRENNAN CROFT

While cases may be made for the powerful influence of many of Shakespeare's plays on Tolkien's writing, the one that Tolkien refers to most overtly is arguably *Macbeth*. Some aspects of *The Lord of the Rings* (*LotR*) can almost be read as an answer to the flaws Tolkien perceived in *Macbeth*: "correcting and improving" the play (Shippey, *Author* 193), or both paralleling and reproaching it (Shippey, *Road* 137). There are two very obvious borrowings from *Macbeth* in *LotR*, each solving one of the riddling prophecies the witches revealed to Macbeth, but in an entirely different way from Shakespeare's play and its historical sources. Interestingly, in both cases, an earlier reference in the text of the play, taken in conjunction with the prophecy, could lead logically to the use Tolkien made of the material.

Main Plot Elements

The first example is Tolkien's transformation of the Birnam Wood prophecy and its fulfillment into the Ents. Tolkien uses aspects of this motif in two other places; the hidden path the troops of Rohan take through Stonewain Valley in Druadan Forest is a straightforward interpretation of Malcolm's tactic of concealing his army's numbers and movements by the means of "leavy screens" (*Macbeth* 5.4.4–6, 5.6.1), and the malicious but stationary trees of the Old Forest hint at the even-

215

tual fulfillment of the idea of living, walking trees in the Ents and Huorns.

But of course the main place Tolkien used the Birnam Wood motif was in his inimitable Ents, the wise and ancient Shepherds of the Trees. As Tolkien said in a 1967 interview, he knew that at some point in *LotR* there would be "trouble with treelike creatures" (Norman 6). A long letter to W.H. Auden in 1955 includes a footnote explaining the origin of the Ents:

> Their part in the story is due, I think, to my bitter disappointment and disgust from schoolboy days with the shabby use made in Shakespeare of the coming of "Great Birnam wood to high Dunsinane hill": I longed to devise a setting in which the trees might really march to war [*Letters* 212n].

In *Macbeth,* after the feast disrupted by the ghost of Banquo, Macbeth says "Stones have been known to move, and trees to speak" (3.4.124). It is several scenes later that the witches call up the apparition that tells Macbeth he "shall never vanquished be until / Great Birnam wood to high Dunsinane Hill / Shall come against him" (4.1.91–93). In the original *Holinshed Chronicles,* from which Shakespeare drew many elements of this play, a witch tells Macbeth that "he should neuer be … vanquished till the wood of Bernane came to the castell of Dunsinane" (Boswell-Stone 36). Combining Macbeth's earlier statement with the prophecy, the imaginative audience might expect to see real trees marching on Dunsinane. In contrast to his former fearful reaction to Banquo's ghost, Macbeth's reply to the apparition is arrogant and pragmatic: "That will never be. / Who can impress the forest, bid the tree / Unfix his earthbound root?" (4.1.93–96). It would only be poetic justice to have the trees themselves turn against him.

The freedom of storytelling allows Tolkien to do just that, a feat which would be difficult and unconvincing, if not ludicrous, given the limitations of the stage. As with the stage production of "Puss-in-Boots" Tolkien comments on in "On Fairy-Stories" (OFS), the audience's disbelief would have "not so much to be suspended … as hanged, drawn, and quartered" for a marching forest of sentient trees to come off as believable on stage (OFS 50). Of course in Shakespeare's play the march of the trees turns out to be a trick; Malcolm's men carry branches to conceal their numbers, and from the castle walls it only looks like a forest marching from a distance. It is almost a poke in the ribs of the audience—"see how blinded Macbeth is by his ambition, unable to imagine this interpretation of the prophecy; were you gullible, too?" The audience almost feels cheated. Tolkien certainly did.

But in Tolkien's hands the wonders promised are delivered—twice.

The Huorns march on the orcs at Helm's Deep, and the Ents on the traitor Saruman's stronghold of Orthanc. Like a "howling gale" (3.9. 554), they tear down the walls and turn the Wizard's Vale into a steaming lake. Saruman's arrogance is like Macbeth's; "leaving [the Ents] out of his calculations" (3.9.553) is as foolish as saying "That will never be" to the personifications of Fate. Here Tolkien can preserve the wonder and terror of the prophecy because walking trees *can* happen in Faerie and in the reader's mind. In *Macbeth*, in spite of the presence of Hecate and the witches, we are in the real and historical world where human action matters more than the supernatural, and where a pragmatic and down-to-earth fulfillment of the prophecy is engineered by Macbeth's entirely human enemies. As Harold Bloom pointed out, "[t]he witch-craft in *Macbeth*, though pervasive, cannot alter material events, yet hal-lucination can and does" (Bloom 516). It is always Macbeth's actions in response to the visions he sees that drive the plot, not any direct action by the witches.

The other element taken most directly from *Macbeth* is Tolkien's reworking of the foretelling that "none of woman born / Shall harm Macbeth" (4.1.80–81). In the original *Holinshed Chronicles*, the more specific prophecy was that Macbeth "should neuer be *slaine* with man born of anie woman" (Boswell-Stone 36, emphasis added). In Macbeth's case the fulfillment of this prophecy rests on a technicality; Macduff tells Macbeth he was "from his mother's womb / Untimely ripped" (5.8.15–16); or as he says in *Holinshed*, "was neuer borne of my mother, but ripped out of her wombe" (Boswell-Stone 43). Although in Shake-speare's time, Caesarian sections were being performed on living patients with the expectation that at least some might survive, at the time of the historical Macbeth, a child was only cut out of the womb if the mother was already dead, so that the infant might be baptized. If the mother died, "the newborn was [considered] the child not of a liv-ing woman but of a corpse" (Blumenfeld-Kosinski 1). The audience is cheated yet again—there is no way to tell by looking at Macduff that he was born by Caesarian section, or whether he is even telling the truth about his birth.

However, in *LotR*, Tolkien's completion of the prophecy plays fair—like a mystery writer who abides by the membership oath of the Detec-tion Club, he withholds no vital clues from the reader. There is a popular belief that the Witch-king, leader of the Nazgûl and general of the forces of Mordor, cannot be killed. The wizard Gandalf mentions this prophecy to Denethor, Steward of Gondor, shortly before the charge of the Riders of Rohan: "[I]f words spoken of old be true, not by the hand of man shall he fall, and hidden from the Wise is the doom that awaits him" (5.4.800–801). When confronted by the warrior Dernhelm, the Witch-king thunders, "Thou fool. No living man may hinder me!" (5.6.823). The original prophecy is given in Tolkien's appendixes: after the last king of Gondor defeats the Witch-king, who flees the battlefield, the elf Glorfindel says "Far off yet is his doom, and not by the hand of man will he fall" (App.A.1027). The foretelling is widely known, and not, as in *Macbeth*, known only to the doomed king.

But Dernhelm is actually Éowyn, niece of the King of Rohan, disguised as a man. She fulfils the prophecy simply by being female, as she admits freely and instantly to the Nazgûl: "But no living man am I! You look upon a woman" (5.6.823). Tolkien dropped enough clues that the astute reader will already have guessed that Dernhelm is Éowyn in disguise, and will have a good idea where this sequence is heading, even if unfamiliar with the parallel sequence in *Macbeth*. Macbeth himself has a moment of "sudden doubt" at this instant of confronting his doom, just as the Nazgûl does; he says Macduff's revelation "hath cowed my better part of man" (5.8.18). And technically, it is the overlooked Hobbit, Merry, who strikes the initial blow that hamstrings the Witch-king and breaks "the spell that knit his unseen sinews to his will" (5.6.826).

As with Birnam Wood and the Ents, an earlier phrase in *Macbeth* provides a clue that could lead logically to Tolkien's answer to this riddle. Lady Macbeth's unforgettable tirade, "Come, you spirits / That tend on mortal thoughts, unsex me here" (1.5.40–41), combined with the prophecy "none of woman born," could subtly point to a woman as the solution to this prophecy—although it is not one Shakespeare could use, since *Macbeth* was based on historical events.

Minor Plot Elements

There are two more direct borrowings of scenes and motifs from *Macbeth*, less notable but still interesting. The hobbits and Macbeth both see a vision of a ghostly line of men, the last one significantly different from the others. In Macbeth's case, the witches summon a show of apparitions: eight figures dressed like kings, the last carrying a mirror reflecting yet more kings, and followed by Banquo's ghost (4.1.111–12). These are Banquo's descendants, who will be the kings of England and Scotland for generations to come in spite of Macbeth's usurpation of the throne. Banquo is the maddening conclusion to all of Macbeth's ambitions, and his line stretches on forever—"to th' crack of doom," in Shakespeare's phrase—to torment Macbeth (4.1.117). "For Banquo's issue have I filed [defiled] my mind; / For them the gracious Duncan have I murdered ... To make them kings, the seeds of Banquo kings" (3.1.66–71).

In contrast, the vision seen by Frodo, Sam, Merry, and Pippin, after their rescue from the Barrow-wight by Tom Bombadil, is not sent to torment them but to prepare them to meet Aragorn, heir to the throne of Gondor, that night at the inn in Bree. And what they see also differs in that it is a vision of the past and present only: tall stern men with bright swords, "forgotten kings walking in loneliness," and the last one "with a star on his brow" (1.8.142–43) representing Aragorn, the hopeful conclusion to their years of watchfulness. The source of the vision is not clear, although it seems to come from Tom; the similar visions they see in his house under the influence of his storytelling, and their dreams the first night they stay with him, all reach back into the past.

Comparing how the two authors handle visions and prophecies shows how their concepts of magic and divination differ. Consider the visions Frodo and Sam are shown in the mirror of Galadriel during their stay in Lórien. Galadriel's enchanted basin "shows many things, and not all have yet come to pass. Some never come to be, unless those that behold the visions turn aside from their path to prevent them" (2.7.354). Or unless they turn aside to try to make the visions come true; as Shippey observed, "Someone should have told Macbeth that" before he tried to help destiny along (*Author* 194). Would the prophecies have been fulfilled in the same tragic way if Macbeth had not interfered by murdering Duncan and Macduff's family? Only Banquo questions the motives of the witches: "[O]ftentimes to win us to our harm / The instruments of darkness tell us truths, / Win us with honest trifles, to betray's / In deepest consequence" (1.3.123–26). As with the steward Denethor and the visions shown in the *palantír* by Sauron, Macbeth too saw "only those things which that Power permitted him to see," which "fed the despair of his heart until it overthrew his mind" (*LotR* 5.7.838). The part-truths both believed to be whole led to their downfalls. The witches in *Macbeth* spoke true; one way or another, their prophecies were always fulfilled. Galadriel's prophecies, however, are more nebulous and reveal what might be called "parallel worlds," where history has diverged because of a character's as yet unmade choice; her visions may never come to pass in this world.

The other minor theme repeated in *LotR* is the role of the king as a divine healer. In this case Tolkien does not seem to be answering Shakespeare so much as taking his theme a dramatic step further, by going back to the deepest sources of this belief. Verlyn Flieger traces Tolkien's use of this theme back to early Celtic mythology and shows its kinship with the Maimed King and the Healing King of the Grail stories (Flieger 50). In *Macbeth* there are two mentions of "the most pious Edward ... the holy king" (3.6.27–30), who cures "the king's evil," or scrofula, with his touch and a prayer. This talent is apparently inherited by his successors: "To the succeeding royalty he leaves / The healing benediction" (4.3.156–57). In this depiction Shakespeare flatters his patron, King James I, as he did with the vision of the kings. Macbeth of course does not have this talent; in contrast, his regicide, a crime against the natural, hierarchical order of things, results in owls bringing down falcons and the king's horses attacking each other. The country bleeds under his tyranny; it is the opposite of the true king's healing touch.

Tolkien augments this motif by making the healing touch a sign that reveals the hidden king. The old lore says that "The hands of the king are the hands of a healer," as Ioreth reminds Gandalf, "[a]nd so the rightful king could ever be known" (5.8.842). Aragorn is the only one who can cure Faramir, Éowyn, and Merry in the Houses of Healing. When Faramir calls him King, the healer-woman Ioreth spreads the rumor: "the king was indeed come among them, and after war he brought healing; and the news ran through the City" (5.8.848).

Other Parallels

It is also intriguing to examine a few minor echoes of words and phrases from *Macbeth* in *LotR*. For example, the witches chant "Fair is foul, and foul is fair" in the opening scene of the play (1.1.11). In the chapter introducing Aragorn, Frodo says that spies of the Enemy would "seem fairer and feel fouler" than Aragorn, and he responds "I look foul and feel fair. Is that it?" (1.10.168). The incantations of the witches have the same rhythm and feel as the Barrow-wight's chant over the captured hobbits; compare "Cold be hand and heart and bone, / and cold be sleep under stone" (1.8.138) with "Double, double toil and trouble; / Fire burn, and cauldron bubble" (4.1.10–11). There is also a very faint echo of "To throw away the dearest thing he owed [owned] / As 'twere a careless trifle" (1.4.9–10) in Aragorn's adage, "one who cannot cast away a treasure at need is in fetters" (3.9.550).

Shippey also points out the use of "alliterative assonance" by both authors. *Macbeth* is the only play in which Shakespeare used this Old and Middle English poetic device, in word pairs like life/leaf, fear/fair, and blade/blood, where the vowel changes very slightly to link together alliteration at the beginning and end of words. It is a device Tolkien used frequently in pairs like fail/fall or mock/make (*Road* 183). For example, Tom Bombadil pairs "candle" and "kindle," "song" and "sing"; the swords the Goblins fear most in *The Hobbit* are Biter and Beater; there are paired names among the Dwarves, like Bifur and Bofur; and Treebeard juxtaposes "bear" and "boar" in his list of living creatures.

Stewardship

One of the key underlying themes treated in both these works is the proper role of a Steward. Was it Tolkien's intention to continue his dialogue with *Macbeth*, which began with the borrowing of the two prophecies, by exploring this issue as well? Or is it simply a coincidence, arising from the fact that the plots of both works require reference to the proper relation of a steward to his king? Tom Shippey, for example, does see Tolkien's use of this theme in *The Lord of the Rings* as a rebuke to Shakespeare's *Macbeth* (*Road* 182). Whether it is or not, comparing the attitudes of the two authors provides valuable insights into their contrasting philosophies and historical milieus.

In *LotR*, the honor of a Steward of Gondor resides entirely in how well he keeps the kingdom for his king. There would be no honor in usurping the throne. As Gandalf reminds Denethor, "it is your task to keep some kingdom still against [the return of the king], which few now look to see" (5.1.741). Charles W. Nelson points out that Denethor calls himself "Lord" of Gondor, betraying his possessive pride in his authority; but "as Gandalf reminds him on more than one occasion, he is the *Steward* of Gondor and therefore answerable to a superior.... as Steward, it was [Denethor's] prime responsibility to return the throne to its rightful heir" (Nelson 87). Macbeth's ambition rebels against this natural order; killing his king, his guest, and a man who has honored Macbeth with promotion and has ruled the land well, is a terrible crime; yet it is not unique in history, and is a pragmatic way to gain the power Macbeth and his wife desire.

Boromir, eldest son of the Steward of Gondor, is the closest character to Macbeth in *LotR*, in terms of his political position at the beginning of the work and his ambitious nature. Like Macbeth, Boromir hungers to be more than a mere vassal to a king. He is bitter because his father is still a steward rather than King of Gondor, and earns a sharp rebuke from him, as his brother Faramir reports. "How many hundreds of years needs it to make a steward a king, if the king returns not?" asks Boromir, and Denethor replies, "Few years, maybe, in other places of less royalty.... In Gondor, ten thousand years would not suffice" (4.5.655). At least Boromir was satisfied by Aragorn's claim to the throne, as Frodo reports to Faramir (4.5.649). Denethor's perverse pride might have led him instead to challenge Aragorn; his desire is for Gondor to continue as he has known it all the years of his life—the queen of nations, with an honorable Steward at her head and not some upstart claiming the higher title of King, "last of a ragged house long bereft of lordship and dignity" (5.7.836).

The vision sent to Boromir and his brother, a voice out of the western sky reciting an enigmatic verse about a broken sword (2.2.240), prompts him to make the journey to the hidden valley of Rivendell to puzzle out its meaning. Again his ambition is demonstrated by the fact that he takes this journey on himself, even though Faramir saw the vision first and most often. He learns in Rivendell that Aragorn is the true king, destined to reclaim the throne. He does have sufficient grace and honor, as Macbeth likely would not, to accept the ruin of his hope of kingship, but there remains some sense of tenseness and rivalry between the two. And as the Fellowship travels on its quest, Boromir is more and more maddened by the Ring and the possibilities it presents. He needs no Lady Macbeth to urge him on; the Ring itself serves this purpose for him, undoubtedly preying on his desire for glory the way it played on Sam's dreams of heroism when he briefly held the Ring on the edge of Mordor. Like the witches, the Ring is both "inside and outside" Boromir's mind, "allowing him to interpret things as he wants to see them" (Garber 698).

But it is Galadriel, Lady of Lothlórien, who functions more precisely in the role of the witches for Boromir, tempting him, and in his interpretation, "offering what she pretended to have the power to give"; he claims to have refused to listen, but would not reveal what he thought she had offered him (2.7.349). In the original *Holinshed Chronicles*, the weird sisters were "the goddesses of destinie, or else some nymphs or feiries" (Boswell-Stone 24), perhaps as beautiful and noble as Galadriel, not "secret, black, and midnight hags" (*Macbeth* 4.1.48). What does she reveal to Boromir? When his brother Faramir learns he visited The Lady of the Golden Wood, he wonders "What woke in your heart then?" (4.5.652). Quite likely a vision of himself in command, similar to the one he reveals to Frodo when he tries to take the Ring from him: "How I would drive the hosts of Mordor, and all men would flock to my banner!" Boromir saw himself becoming "a mighty king, benevolent and wise," through the power of the Ring (2.10.389).

As Shippey points out, "[b]oth Tolkien and Shakespeare are aware of prophetic ambiguity, but Tolkien is much more concerned with drawing out its philosophical implications. His point, always, is that his characters have free will but no clear guidance" (*Author* 194). Whatever Galadriel may or may not have revealed to Boromir, she does know his mind and the peril he brought with him to her realm. On the trip down the Anduin after the fellowship's visit to Lórien, Boromir begins to act strangely, culminating with his tragic surrender to the temptation of the Ring at Parth Galen. As with Macbeth, the question is "not ... whether he will do the deed, but ... what the deed will do to him" (Garber, 707). Perhaps because of Tolkien's faith, Boromir is granted a eucatastrophic ending, and turns out not to be past remorse and redemption—unlike Macbeth, defiant to the last and ignominiously beheaded in battle.

Politically, this concern with stewardship and kingship reflects Tolkien's love for ancient Anglo-Saxon England. Shippey points out that the dynasty James I (king of England when *Macbeth* was written) belonged to, the Stewarts, were so named because his ancestors had been High Stewards of Scotland. One had married Robert the Bruce's daughter and their son had initially been named the king's successor. When the king's son David was born, Robert lost this position and was made David's heir apparent instead. Robert served as David's regent while David was in exile, and rebelled against him on his return, then finally succeeded to the throne as Robert II when David died ("Robert II [Scotland]"). According to Shippey, though, the Anglo-Saxon line of kings boasted an unbroken patrilineal descent from the "legendary" past to 1065 (*Road* 182), and Denethor's remark about stewards eventually becoming kings "in other places of less royalty" is a pointed reference to Scotland and Britain. Shakespeare glosses over the irony of James' ancestry in his flatteries to his patron the king, but a recurring theme in his works is that "there is a divine right of kings, and that to usurp the throne is a nefarious crime against all of humanity" (Mabillard).

When Faramir awakens in the Houses of Healing, his first words acknowledge Aragorn as King, before he even knows he has succeeded to the Stewardship. And when Aragorn returns from the last battle to claim the throne, Faramir hands over the symbols of kingship with all proper ceremony, and is rewarded with the added title of Prince of Ithilien. Unlike his father, he accepts Aragorn's claim to the throne without question and hands his trust over gracefully, and unlike his brother, he has no ambitions to rule himself. Macbeth is well aware his actions are not the proper duties of a steward: the king is "here in double trust: / First, as I am his kinsman and his subject, / Strong both against the deed; then, as his host, / Who should against his murderer shut the door, / Not bear the knife myself" (1.7.13–16). Yet he still yields to his ambition.

If Faramir epitomizes the good steward, Aragorn is the image of the perfect king as described by Shakespeare. In a conversation between young Malcolm and Macduff, the son of the murdered king recites a list of "the king-becoming graces / ... justice, verity, temperance, stableness, / Bounty, perseverance, mercy, lowliness, / Devotion, patience, courage, [and] fortitude" (4.3.92–95). Malcolm further describes himself: "I am yet / Unknown to woman, never was forsworn, / Scarcely have coveted what was mine own, / At no time broke my faith, would not betray / The devil to his fellow, and delight / No less in truth than life" (4.3.126–31). While Aragorn may indeed covet what is "his own," desiring the throne of Gondor, the other "king-becoming graces" are quite strong in him. His courage and fortitude are proven in battle; his devotion, perseverance, and patience by his long wait for the hand of Arwen. He dispenses justice tempered with mercy during his first official acts as king. His lowliness or humility was demonstrated while he served as a Ranger, living no better than his men. He is never seen to be less than truthful, generous, or temperate in behavior, and is as stable and dependable a companion on the road as one could desire.

Conclusion

In spite of his stated dislike of the playwright, Tolkien could not totally escape Shakespeare's influence. What English writer could? Tom Shippey comes to the conclusion that Tolkien was "guardedly respectful" of Shakespeare, admiring some aspects of his work but perhaps finding that he had strayed too far from his Warwickshire roots (Shippey, *Author* 194–95). If Tolkien indeed felt that Shakespeare lacked "coherent ideas" (Carpenter, *Inklings* 135) or a consistent underlying philosophy, he tried to remedy this in his own work through "simultaneous immediate relevance, and wider symbolic application" (Shippey, *Author* 196). His themes and motifs reverberate through the levels of his created world in a way difficult to achieve in drama (but not impossible for so brilliant a dramatist as Shakespeare, in spite of Tolkien's misgivings about dramatic plausibility).

The Lord of the Rings is in some ways a response to *Macbeth,* motivated by Tolkien's desire to correct what he saw as Shakespeare's failings, as in the case of the Birnam Wood prophecy. Consciously or not, by referring to and quoting from *Macbeth,* Tolkien keeps the play uppermost in the mind of readers who share his familiarity with it. The rehabilitation of the Birnam Wood motif was deliberate, as shown in his letters. The use of the "no man of woman born" prophecy was also very likely conscious, because it is such an obvious borrowing, although there is nothing in the published letters or in the supplementary material published by Christopher Tolkien to confirm this (*War of the Ring* 326, 34–35, 63–69). It is difficult to tell if the use of other themes, motifs, and quotes was conscious or not, but for a writer as familiar with Shakespeare as Tolkien evidently was, Shakespeare's works form a substratum in the imagination to be drawn on as needed.

Both Tolkien and Shakespeare were also concerned, in part, with two significant themes. First, both define the attributes of a true king and the duties of a faithful steward and explore the possibilities of conflict and harmony between the two roles. Shakespeare dramatizes the tragic example of the false steward Macbeth, and Tolkien writes of the embodiment of kingly virtue in Aragorn, true stewardship in Faramir, and the temptations of Boromir and Denethor. Secondly, both authors examine the ambiguous nature of prophecy and the dangers of acting upon it, as shown in the contrasting prophetic styles of Galadriel and the three witches and the actions of other characters in response. Macbeth succumbs to the temptation to interfere in the workings of prophecy and as a result his life ends in disaster; Sam and Frodo listen to Galadriel's advice about the images in her Mirror and go on to the successful conclusion of their quest in spite of their fears.

Whether or not Tolkien meant his readers to think critically about *Macbeth* while reading *LotR*, his many references to the play encourage us to do so, and in so doing, gain new insights into both works.

Note

Earlier versions of this essay were presented at The Mythopoeic Society's annual conference in Boulder, Colorado, in 2002, and published in *Seven: An Anglo-American Literary Review* 21 (2004): 47–60.

Works Cited

Bloom, Harold. *Shakespeare: The Invention of the Human.* New York: Penguin, 1998.

Blumenfeld-Kosinski, Renate. *Not of Woman Born: Representations of Caesarian Birth in Medieval and Renaissance Culture.* Ithaca, NY: Cornell University Press, 1990.

Boswell-Stone, W.G. *Shakespeare's Holinshed: The Chronicle and the Historical Plays Compared.* 1896. New York: Blom, 1966.

Carpenter, Humphrey. *The Inklings: C.S. Lewis, J.R.R. Tolkien, Charles Williams, and Their Friends.* Boston: Houghton, 1977.

Flieger, Verlyn. "Frodo and Aragorn: The Concept of the Hero." In *Tolkien: New Critical Perspectives.* Ed. Rose A. Zimbardo. Lexington: University Press of Kentucky, 1981. 40–62.

Garber, Marjorie. *Shakespeare After All.* New York: Pantheon, 2004.

Mabillard, Amanda. "Sources for *Macbeth*." 2000. Shakespeare Online. Accessed 22 December 2005 at http://www.shakespeare-online.com/sources/macbethsources.html

Nelson, Charles W. "The Sins of Middle-Earth: Tolkien's Use of Medieval Allegory." In *J.R.R. Tolkien and His Literary Resonances.* Ed. Daniel Timmons. Contributions to the Study of Science Fiction and Fantasy. Westport, CT: Greenwood Press, 2000. 83–94.

Norman, Philip. "The Prevalence of Hobbits." 15 January 1967. Interview. *New York Times.* Accessed 22 December 2005 at http://www.nytimes.com/1967/01/15/books/tolkien-interview.html

"Robert II (Scotland)." *The New Encyclopaedia Britannica.* Vol. 10 (micropaedia). Chicago: Encyclopaedia Britannica, 2002. 104.

Shakespeare, William. *The Complete Works of William Shakespeare.* Ed. David Bevington. New York: Pearson, 2004.

Shippey, Thomas A. *J.R.R. Tolkien: Author of the Century.* Boston: Houghton, 2001.

_____. *The Road to Middle-earth.* Rev. and exp. ed. Boston: Houghton, 2003.

Tolkien, J.R.R. *The Letters of J.R.R. Tolkien.* Ed. Humphrey Carpenter. Boston: Houghton, 2000.

———. *The Lord of the Rings.* 2ndnd ed. Boston: Houghton, 1994.

———. "On Fairy-Stories." In *The Tolkien Reader.* New York: Ballantine, 1966. 3–84.

———. *The War of the Ring.* Ed. Christopher Tolkien. The History of Middle-earth 8. Boston: Houghton, 1990.

The Other

Hidden in Plain View

Strategizing Unconventionality in Shakespeare's and Tolkien's Portraits of Women

Maureen Thum

Both Shakespeare and Tolkien have been charged with confining women to traditional roles that buttress the patriarchal status quo.[1] Recent studies have pointed, however, to subtle strategies used by both authors to resist the dominant patriarchal codes of their respective times.[2] I will make the case that both Shakespeare and Tolkien use similar strategies to disarm reader resistance and to provide a sympathetic view of women in assuming powerful roles. Shakespeare's *Twelfth Night* (*TN*) and Tolkien's *Lord of the Rings* (*LotR*) are cases in point. Both works use carnival strategies to contradict the view that women and power are a toxic combination, or even an abomination resulting in disorder, evil, and chaos, an abomination that must be contained or eradicated. Both *TN* and *LotR* resist traditional stereotypes of women and expand gender roles beyond the limitations imposed by a society in which men were granted power and authority that was not granted to the majority of women.

Like all well-educated Englishmen of his time, Tolkien was closely acquainted with Shakespeare's plays. But there is no indication of a direct connection between his work and Shakespeare's plays, so I therefore wish to refrain from making the case for a one-on-one comparison which would suggest direct influence. Instead, I will propose that both writers drew on a similar tradition of carnivalized literature and that both writers used strategies central to carnivalized literature in order to question and subvert traditional views of women's roles. Both Shake-

speare and Tolkien create alternative fictive worlds that are characteristic of carnivalized literature. In these worlds of fantasy, dream, or
vision, the norms of society can be explored and tested. Gender hierarchies can be shown and analyzed from an unusual, and defamiliarizing, perspective. Within these fictive worlds, both writers use key
strategies of role reversal and masquerade to unsettle normative gender codes. Role reversal demonstrates that social roles are fluid, while
masquerade, understood in its traditional sense as disguise and parody,
confounds the sense of order on which official society is based. Donning a mask signals the adoption of an alternative identity and thereby
blurs normative social and cultural distinctions. In order to demonstrate how Shakespeare and Tolkien use carnival strategies to disrupt
and expand traditional gender boundaries, I will first provide an
overview of Carnival and carnivalized literature and explore the binary
constructions of gender to which the majority of both Shakespeare's
and Tolkien's contemporaries subscribed. I will then focus on how both
writers deploy carnival strategies such as experimental fantasticality,
role reversal, and masquerade to press against restrictive codes confining women to traditionally sanctioned roles.

Carnival and Carnivalized Literature

As M.M. Bakhtin has demonstrated, carnivalized literature derives
from the medieval and early modern pre–Lenten Carnival. In medieval
times, during specific feast days including the Feast of Fools (Twelfth
Night), the strongly enforced social and cultural hierarchies of the
everyday world were suspended (*Rabelais* 15). The custom of carnival
license allowed a permitted or licensed "time-out" from official orthodoxies without the danger of punishment or reprisal. In *TN*, Olivia
refers specifically to carnival license when she states that a licensed
(allowed) fool is not to be reprimanded or censured for criticizing his
social superiors: "There is no slander in an allowed fool, though he do
nothing but rail" (1.5.90–91). Carnival license during specific feast days
permitted role reversals, the wearing of masks, and the assuming of
alternative identities, all of which implicitly put into question the hierarchical structures of the medieval world (Bakhtin, *Problems* 107–9).
Although Carnival was often contained, and served merely as a venting
mechanism,[3] it could lead, as Natalie Zemon Davis (131–50) and Susan
Crane (129–30) have argued, to a permanent state of questioning and
subversion outside the confines of the officially licensed carnival world.
During the Renaissance, especially, the rebellious and unruly spirit of
Carnival often spilled over into the everyday world (Davis 140).

Like Carnival itself, carnivalized literature is infused with the unruly spirit of Carnival and uses recognizable carnival strategies to challenge received ideas, including fixed views of gender and of social class. Fundamental to this challenging of received ideas is the creation of a fictive world which lies outside, yet parallel to, the empirical realities of everyday life. Bakhtin refers to this strategy as "experimental fantasticality" (*Problems* 116). Experimental fantasticality involves the invention of an alternative dream or fantasy world which provides an unusual and defamiliarizing perspective. Both Shakespeare and Tolkien create such imaginary and hypothetical worlds. Within these worlds, the familiar carnival strategies of role reversal and masquerade allow accepted categories, received opinions, and traditional beliefs to be symbolically tested and disrupted. Examining the intersection of gender and Carnival in *TN* and *LotR* allows us to discover how Shakespeare and Tolkien use previously unexplored strategies for questioning and resisting normative codes and for expanding traditional gender boundaries.

Traditional Views of Gender: Shakespeare's and Tolkien's Historical Context

Separated by over three centuries, both Shakespeare and Tolkien wrote in worlds where traditional views of women—while being challenged and tested—still held sway. Numerous studies, especially in the last three decades, have explored the powerful impact of inherited binary views of gender construction on our concepts of both men and women (Ortner 71–72; Rosaldo and Lamphere 1–3). According to a long-standing tradition, men's and women's roles were defined by divine providence, or by natural law, in strictly separated categories. In a tradition dating back to Aristotle, men were viewed as rational, as superior spiritually and intellectually, while women were viewed as inferior. Men were seen as leaders and creators of culture, who played an active, legitimate role in public life. Women, by contrast to men, were viewed as followers, as creators of children rather than culture. Denied an officially sanctioned public role, their activities were seen as properly confined to the household and the domestic sphere where they could exercise power but only within a limited area of activity. While men were deemed by nature to be powerful, active, and independent, women were the reverse: powerless, passive, and dependent (Dunn 15–16). Women in the Renaissance could be powerful and influential, but, with few exceptions, they lacked recognized authority which would legitimize claims to power in the public arena.

During Shakespeare's time, the fixed gender roles were being challenged (Neely 5). The fact that Elizabeth I had remained on the throne successfully for decades and had, through careful negotiation, achieved authority as well as power, disrupted traditional views (Levin and Robertson, Introduction iii). Inherited norms were further unsettled by the fact that, during the sixteenth and seventeenth centuries, numerous upper class women were educated far beyond contemporary expectations for their sex (Dunn 17–28).

However, although the challenging of traditional paradigms led gradually to new views of women's roles, such challenges to normative codes also elicited angry and frightened responses. During Shakespeare's time, sermons, conduct guides, and pamphlets inveighed against unruly women and reaffirmed the patriarchal status quo (Aughterson 68). Thus William Whatley urges, in 1617, that a woman must "[submit] herself with quietness, cheerfully, even as a well-broken horse turns at the least turning, stands at the least check of the rider's bridle, readily going and standing as he wishes that sits upon his back" (Whatley 34). As the title of John Knox's *First Blast of the Trumpet against the Monstrous Regiment of Women* (1558) implies, women who step outside their divinely ordained roles are no less than monsters.

As Knox's diatribe suggests, during this period, women who resisted tradition and who assumed powerful roles were viewed as usurpers in a territory to which they held no claim. Resistance was frequently met by censure, punishment, accusations of heresy and witchcraft, and even execution. It is no accident, surely, that the virulently anti-feminist witch craze was at its height from about 1570 to 1700. During this time between 60,000 and 200,000 witches were executed, over 75% of whom were women. They stood as a powerful warning to those who stepped outside narrowly defined norms (Coudert 61–62). Even Queen Elizabeth, who successfully held a radically unconventional position in Renaissance society, was demonized and accused of being a baby-killer, a murderer, and an unnatural perversion of womanhood (Levin, "Images" 101–5).

Comparing Tolkien's views of women to Shakespeare's might at first seem somewhat astonishing, especially since extreme manifestations of anti-feminism such as the execution of witches had long ceased before Tolkien began writing *LotR*.[1] However, several factors allow for a fruitful comparison. Tolkien's world appears—on the surface—to represent a nostalgic revisiting of an age when patriarchal power structures were still intact, an age similar to that represented by Shakespeare in *TN*. In addition, Tolkien wrote from a relatively traditionalist context. The members of his circle of Inklings, particularly C.S. Lewis, shared strongly conservative views about women. Finally, like Shakespeare's England, Tolkien's mid–twentieth-century Britain was characterized by rapid change and cataclysmic events which brought about a rethinking of accepted orthodoxies, including the place of women in the social order. World War II had thrust numerous women into the workforce to play unconventional roles while men were at war. But, while opportunities opened during the war, a backlash followed after the war ended. The men returned home, and women were encouraged, if not exhorted, to return to the domestic sphere (Friedan 184).

The paradoxes of this period are reflected in Tolkien's writings. During the early decades of the twentieth century, despite vocal and often high profile women's movements for suffrage, equal education, and equal recognition in the workplace, women's roles for the most part remained relatively traditional. Virginia Woolf's *A Room of One's Own* (1929) speaks of the major universities in Great Britain as bastions of male power where women were as yet granted only limited access (6–24). Simone de Beauvoir, writing in the 1950s, argues in *The Second Sex* that women's roles had remained essentially unchanged for centuries. In a thought-provoking article, Patricia Sullivan and Carole Levin compare the attitudes toward women and power during the sixteenth and twentieth centuries, noting that in 1992, Hillary Rodham Clinton was portrayed on the cover of the *American Spectator* as "The Wicked Witch of the West" ("Women" 278). In the same year, Pat Robertson, the self-styled spokesman for the "Moral Majority," spoke out against the passage of an equal rights amendment in Iowa. He censured the amendment as the product of a "feminist agenda" which was part of "a socialist, anti-family political movement that encourages women to leave their husbands, kill their children, practice witchcraft ... and become lesbians" (qtd. in Levin and Sullivan, "Politics" 4). Even now, the question of women and power has remained vexed, and the anxieties concerning female power have not yet been allayed.

During the Renaissance and beyond, mainstream literature reflected, and often reinforced, traditional views of women and power. Powerful, active women in the literature of the Renaissance were frequently demonized and punished, meeting a horrible end. While disobedience was decried, submission was rewarded. In traditional fairy tales deriving from the medieval and the Early Modern periods, passive, silent women, like Sleeping Beauty and Snow White, were allowed happy endings, while active women, such as Snow White's wicked stepmother, were portrayed as evil, and even demonic, and were often killed in the course of the narrative. Such portraits reflected the rejection of powerful, independent women in a patriarchal society. During the twentieth century, witches and witch-like figures continued to appear frequently in literature and film, including the children's books written by Tolkien's friend, C.S. Lewis. In the Walt Disney versions of fairy tales such as *Snow White*

(1937), *Cinderella* (1950), *Sleeping Beauty* (1959), and *The Little Mermaid* (1989), the witch-like figures are even more strongly demonized and more spectacularly punished than in their much earlier fairy-tale counterparts.[5]

Carnival Worlds: Experimental Fantasticality in Shakespeare's and Tolkien's Texts

Both Shakespeare and Tolkien explore, test, and expand the binary constructions of gender by creating alternative worlds in which traditional views can be turned on their head. In the world of Carnival, the very fact that women can dress as men, peasants as kings, laity as monks and bishops, upsets the prescribed social order. Role reversal and masquerade allow Shakespeare and Tolkien to present intelligent, powerful women who are not demonized as witches and punished for their transgressive roles. Instead, their unconventional behavior is validated and even rewarded, indicating that women who step outside traditional roles are neither monstrous nor perverse.

The site for these transgressions is the fictive carnival world where the writers can stage experimental hypotheses concerning the potential for both men and women to think and act outside the boundaries of their traditional roles. In *TN*, the mythical, vaguely medievalized country of Illyria becomes the imaginary site where Shakespeare can subvert fixed concepts of identity associated with gender and social class.[6] Here, male and female roles can be reversed without risk of censure, and a woman can don the mask of a man without fearing the angry responses and reprisals which she would be forced to face in the real world of Shakespeare's time (Levin, *Heart* 126–27; Williams 77). The notion that Shakespeare has created a carnivalized world in *TN* is corroborated by the fact that the title specifically links the play to Carnival and the carnival tradition, referring to the Twelfth Night festival which was also known as The Feast of Fools (Hassel 151).

Like Shakespeare, Tolkien creates a fictional world complete with maps to chart its geography and multiple peoples and languages with their own history and cosmology. Although closer to reality than the half-mythic world of *The Silmarillion*, it is still a world peopled by magical creatures who interact with ordinary and extraordinary mortals. Creating this carnivalized world allows Tolkien, like Shakespeare, to challenge traditional views of power and gender in a setting where the realities of the official, everyday world can be turned upside down. Although the kings, princes, lords, and ladies in Tolkien's writings appear to uphold the ancient hierarchies of the medieval texts from which their images are drawn, a closer look reveals that beneath the veneer of nostalgically re-visioned myth and legend, Tolkien actually invents figures who revise the normative codes even of his own time (Thum 235–38). As with Shakespeare, the alternative perspective of the invented world allows gender hierarchies to be seen from an unusual, defamiliarizing, and critical point of view.

Role Reversal in Twelfth Night *and* The Lord of the Rings

Within the carnivalized worlds of *TN* and *LotR*, expected gender roles are switched. By destabilizing essentialist views of both men's and women's roles as divinely ordained, they suggest that these roles are far more fluid than traditional paradigms would suggest. In *TN*, both men and women exchange expected attributes. Critics and directors alike have frequently viewed the non-traditional male character, Duke Orsino, as a fool because his attributes are not those of the stereotypical male (Hassel 160–61). He is not the epitome of the manly ideal: independent of others, dispassionate, and in charge of his emotions. Instead, he is emotional, overwhelmed by love and by his passions, and dependent on the Countess Olivia, whom he loves from afar and who has consistently refused his offers of marriage. His emotional swings go beyond accepted "courtly" behavior. He even describes himself as "unstaid and skittish" (2.4.18), and claims that he is more emotional and passionate than a woman (2.4.93–103).

Orsino's assumption of a non-traditional role fairly stands for the reversal of gender roles throughout a comedy in which none of the male characters display the expected behavior patterns associated with the traditional ideal of manhood. Sir Toby Belch and Sir Andrew Aguecheek are both dependent on the graces and charity of a woman, Countess Olivia, for room and board. Both men are knights and, therefore, among the higher orders. Nevertheless, both are subject to Olivia's commands as mistress of a large household, over which she holds complete sway. Like Malvolio, the victim of their cruel practical joke, they are prone to folly and cut ridiculous figures throughout the comedy. Viola's brother, Sebastian, weeps openly in grief for his sister and is swayed by an irrational love and admiration for Olivia, whom he met only minutes before. Moreover, he decides to marry her, all the while wondering whether or not he is mad or dreaming.

The female characters, Viola, Olivia, and Maria, all share attributes commonly ascribed to men and, thus, are highly unconventional figures. They are witty, outspoken, and intelligent, and they claim areas of power generally reserved for men. Viola befriends the Duke and gains his confidence dressed as a man, while Olivia runs her estate without the guidance of a male authority figure. Maria, the mastermind of the plot to bring about Malvolio's fall through pride and self-love, has scarcely been mentioned in critical studies, even though she plays the role of "player king," the manipulator of men's destinies. This role of mastermind is generally assigned to a male character, as in *The Tempest*, where it is played by Prospero, or in *Much Ado About Nothing*, where the role is taken by Don Pedro, Prince of Aragon.

In *LotR*, Tolkien has also reversed gender expectations. Critics who view Tolkien as an anti-feminist writer object that he has reproduced female stereotypes. But Tolkien has actually turned traditional paradigms on their head. We see this reversal especially in the expectations attached to the male hero in *LotR*. Jane Chance observes that "Tolkien recast the medieval hero ... in new, unlikely, and multiple forms. These include small Hobbits, suspiciously dark rangers like Strider, sisters and sister-daughters (nieces) like Éowyn ... and second sons like Faramir" (175). Moreover, many of the powerful males in *LotR* prove to be singularly unheroic. They are often weak, subject to temptation, and unable to carry out heroic deeds or exercise their authority. King Théoden is mesmerized by Wormtongue and unable to carry out his kingly duties, while, in a reversal of expectations, Éowyn, a woman, resists Wormtongue's spells. Boromir, the great warrior, cannot resist the temptation to take the Ring from Frodo and thus fails the Fellowship. Ironically, his failure results from his attempt to fulfill the traditional heroic role: to save his people from the enemy. His father, Denethor, Steward of Gondor, fails his sons and abdicates his responsibilities as leader because he has also reached for greater power in order to protect Gondor, but in so doing, he has fallen into the thrall of the Dark Lord. In both cases, traditional heroic qualities—the desire to accomplish great deeds, the desire to shore up and enhance the power of the realms with which they are charged, the desire to challenge the enemy head-on and win the game—all prove to be traps. In a complete reversal of traditional values, among the heroes are Frodo and Sam, "two small dark figures, forlorn, [standing] hand in hand upon a little hill, while the world shook under them" (6.4.930).

By the same token, Tolkien reverses expectations attached to female roles in medieval romance.[7] In Tolkien's anti-epic/romance, women who at first appear to fulfill the stereotype associated with romance genres actually resist the accepted patterns of gender roles associated with the genre. Women—Éowyn, Galadriel, and Arwen—play powerful roles and, contrary to expectations, are not censured or punished for assuming both the power and the authority reserved traditionally for men.

Tolkien, like Shakespeare, turns the gendered roles associated with both
men and women on their heads.

Carnival Masquerade in Twelfth Night

Within these experimental worlds, both Shakespeare and Tolkien
employ traditional carnival maskings and unmaskings in order to
explore the intersection of gender and power in an essentially male-
dominated society. By disguising themselves as men, female characters
escape the confines of the woman's part. By hiding beneath the mask
of conventional femininity, women can even more successfully expand
gender roles, since the conventional masquerade is more subtle and
difficult to detect. Citing Luce Irigaray, Susan Crane has made a strong
case that "resistance to the feminine position is possible through mimicry, that is, through the deliberate acting out of prescribed femininity" (59). Conscious manipulation of gender roles allows women to meet
societal expectations while simultaneously circumventing them. During the Renaissance, as Carol Levin has demonstrated, Queen Elizabeth I participated in this form of disguise by careful manipulation of
the image of the Virgin Queen, who always appears ready to accept a
suitor as her husband, but who puts off matrimony indefinitely by setting up obstacles to the seemingly wished-for union. Elizabeth I thus
provided a model for Shakespeare's heroines who use a similar strategy (Levin, *Heart* 127–28). Tolkien also depicts this form of disguise
when he presents female characters who only appear to fulfill expected
stereotypes, but whose actual role and nature expands gender
definitions in defiance of traditional restrictions.

Viola's Masquerade

With few exceptions, critics and directors have viewed the two main
female characters of *Twelfth Night,* Viola and Olivia, as polar opposites.[8]
Viola has been interpreted as a positive, winsome, endearing young
woman who, despite her unconventional mask, reaffirms traditional
views of gender. Olivia, by contrast, has been viewed negatively, as a
mutilated, narcissistic, frigid, obsessive, and haughty woman who is
unable to love, incapable of connecting with other human beings, and
prone to folly.[9] However, neither of these views fully explores the complexity of Shakespeare's two woman characters. I wish to argue that
Viola and Olivia are far more closely connected than numerous critics
have allowed.[10] Each character uses a different strategy of masquerade
to lay claim to areas of action and to forms of power which would otherwise be closed to them.

To judge from the angry response to cross-dressing in writings by Renaissance moralists, a woman's adoption of male clothing and a male role was seen as undermining the public order (Williams 78). As Levin and Robertson note, "the boy actor challenges biological essentialism and acknowledges, albeit not in our terms, the cultural construction of gender. Femininity becomes simply something played" (Introduction vii). One can extrapolate that masculinity can also be played, putting into question equally fixed ideas about men's roles. Viola's donning of a male mask is hence a subversive and audacious act in itself, an act which is only one of many that demonstrate her intelligence, her ingenuity, and her independence of spirit. Cast upon a foreign shore, uncertain of her reception in a strange land, alone and unprotected, she is at risk in a society which is threatening even to male strangers (3.3.9–11). It is not surprising that she is unwilling to be "delivered to the world"— that is, to allow her identity to be disclosed—"Till that [she] had made [her] own occasion mellow, / What [her] estate is" (1.2.43–44). She wishes to control the outcome of this chance arrival on a foreign shore, but as a woman, she has little leeway for doing so. By taking the initiative and disguising herself, she immediately takes charge of her destiny, allowing herself to claim the freedom of movement otherwise granted only to men.

Viola's mask, while seemingly restricting her love relationship with Duke Orsino, nonetheless allows her an unusual freedom in her relationship with him, thus countering accepted views of the appropriate relationship between men and women who contemplate marriage and even stretching the boundaries of relationships considered appropriate among male friends. Unmarried women were exhorted to avoid the company of men unless escorted by a chaperon (Vives 71). Disguised as a man, Viola has the freedom to become the friend and trusted confidante of the man she comes to love. Thus, they are friends before they become lovers, a completely unconventional approach to traditional views of marriage and the relationships between men and women, especially among the privileged classes. Even among men, the relationship would be unusual, since they are not simply comrades, but have a private, intimate relationship during which Orsino bares his very soul to her.

Significantly, mediated by masquerade, Shakespeare pairs Viola in marriage not only with a partner who has become her friend, but with a man who is himself unconventional and, therefore, more likely to accept a similar unconventionality in a woman. When we first meet him, Orsino is clearly suffering from an even more advanced case of Petrarchanism than Romeo with his imagined love for Rosalind in *Romeo and Juliet*. Shakespeare demonstrates the ludicrous nature of such a stance when, in a sudden and amusing turnabout, Orsino, like Romeo, is instantly cured of his Petrarchan affliction. Reality, as opposed to the conventional projections he had imagined in his amorous fancy, has the power to dispatch the poetic illusion of a distant lover and to readjust Orsino's vision almost without delay. Unlike Romeo who only gets to know Juliet briefly, Orsino has the good fortune to have found a marriage partner to whom he has been able to "unclasp" his bosom and tell his innermost thoughts (1.4.13–14).

Furthermore, Orsino is unconventional in his acceptance of Viola's actions and, especially, her disguise. A stereotypical response would be suspicion and anger, as indicated by the numerous sermons and conduct guides inveighing against female cross-dressing (Levin, *Heart* 127). Unlike the sermons, conduct books, and even the order of James I condemning cross-dressing as an abomination, Orsino does not censure Viola for her disguise, and even though he wishes to see her, finally, in her "woman's weeds," he is not threatened by an intelligent woman who has the independence, the skill, and the sheer bravado to maintain her disguise successfully. Orsino's final words to Viola suggest that their marriage also has the possibility of altering expected male-female power relations in matrimony. His words have at least two possible conflicting meanings, allowing for two opposed readings of their future relationship:

> Your master quits you; and for your service done him,
> So much against the mettle of your sex,
> So far beneath your soft and tender breeding,
> And since you called me master for so long,
> Here is my hand. You shall from this time be
> Your master's mistress [5.1.321–26].

His statement about power relationship between the two remains suffused with irony, since Orsino appears to claim his patriarchal role of master, all the while declaring himself henceforth to be subject to Viola as his mistress. As we have seen in his previous relationship, Orsino is not in charge of women; they hold sway over him.

OLIVIA AND THE MIMICRY OF CONVENTION

Olivia first appears to the audience wearing the mask of conventionality. What we first know of Olivia is only by hearsay. Her identity is concealed by the mask of the cold Petrarchan mistress, distant, unfeeling, rejecting the passionate lover out of cruelty and caprice. Her father and brother have both died, and everyone, including Orsino, expects her to be in want of a protector without whom she can scarcely be expected to run her estate, let alone live a fulfilled life.[11] Olivia has rejected Orsino's advances by claiming that she will not wed until she has grieved for seven years. Critics have interpreted this behavior as evidence of Olivia's morbid introspection, her "self-indulgent posturing as the grief-stricken sister" (Hassel 154), her "ego-reification" and her "refus[al] to interact with others" (Freedman 216), when it is, in reality, a strategy on Olivia's part to avoid an unwanted suitor.

When we actually meet Olivia, the above views of the men who describe her—the Captain, Orsino, and Valentine—are put into question. When Viola, posing as Cesario, a seemingly attractive youth, comes to woo Olivia in the name of Orsino, Olivia after very little prompting removes her veil of mourning. What we discover during their exchange is not the grief-obsessed, folly-ridden woman described by so many critics. Instead, she is witty, ironic, and down to earth. Viola/Cesario begins her petition in the high-flown terms we have come to expect from Orsino, but interrupts herself to state that she does not wish to waste her breath speaking poetry that she has learned by heart if she is not dealing with the "lady of the house." Viola thereby shows her ironic distance from the artificial verses she has "conned" or learned by heart (1.5.170).

Viola's down-to-earth approach strikes a chord in Olivia, who has a similar sense of irony concerning set poems of praise and the poses they represent. Olivia retorts that verses learned by heart are "the more like to be feigned" (I.5.192), revealing with these words that she is not amused by Orsino's posing. Indeed, since she says several times that she does not love Orsino, her apparently exaggerated mourning, like her seeming coldness and inability to respond to Orsino's suits, may actually be seen as her successful fending off of an unwanted suitor (1.5.278). But, since he refuses to accept "no" for an answer, she advances her mourning, at least in part, as a means of keeping Orsino's importunities at bay. The mask of the distant lady who makes somewhat exaggerated claims for mourning is conventionally acceptable, while an outright refusal in order to retain her independence is not. Despite strong pressures to normalize her situation by marrying an appropriate and eligible bachelor, she deflects his advances and maintains her independence without being censured for inappropriate behavior.

Olivia demonstrates that she is ironically and humorously distanced from Orsino's poses. When Viola makes the traditional "carpe diem" argument that Olivia's beauty will go with her to the grave if she does not wed and leave a "copy," that is, a child, Olivia replies ironically by reinterpreting the word "copy" to mean a list of attributes (1.5.239). She then presents a list that parodies the fixed tropes of the conventional love sonnet much as does Shakespeare in his well-known satire, "My Mistress' Eyes Are Nothing Like the Sun":

> Oh, sir, I will not be so hard-hearted. I will give out divers sched-
> ules of my beauty. It shall be inventoried, and every particle and
> utensil labeled to my will: as item, two lips, indifferent red; item,
> two grey eyes, with lids to them; item, one neck, one chin, and so
> forth [1.5.239–44].

Clearly, Olivia is no fool, nor is she the cold, cruel woman Orsino has described. Instead, she is witty, astute, and able to voice her ironic objection to Orsino's taking of the conventional role as the rejected courtly lover. Her itemized list demonstrates that she not only understands the conventions of courtly love, but she also recognizes and rejects the objectification of women which these conventions of male admiration conceal. Significantly, when Orsino does marry, he is able to abandon his former stance with an alacrity that demonstrates the superficiality of his former pose. Olivia clearly understands him better than he understands himself.

Olivia's mask of convention not only hides an intelligent, witty, insightful young woman. It also deflects attention from the fact that she has power and autonomy as an orphan who is subject neither to her father's nor her brother's will. She proves to be quite capable of running an entire estate efficiently and effectively. Sebastian, who arrives just in time to "save" Olivia from an impossible match with a disguised woman, questions her sanity and even his own. And yet, Sebastian recognizes that he cannot be mad, nor can Olivia, for as he observes, "[I]f t'were so, / She could not sway her house, command her followers, / Take and give back affairs and their dispatch / With such a smooth, discreet and stable bearing" (4.3.16–19). Olivia is passionate and independent in her actions. She chooses her lover and marries according to her own wishes, disregarding social class in order to do so.

Indeed, Sebastian's lower social class may be welcome to Olivia, since she may not wish to relinquish her power to an overbearing man, and above all, to a man she does not love. If we are to believe Sir Toby, she has sworn many times never to marry above her station, and thus she refuses to play the subordinate role, either as woman or as a lower ranked spouse who must be grateful for her rise in status (1.3.107–9). Olivia does not put off marriage altogether, as did Queen Elizabeth I. Instead, she makes sure that her partner is willing to play by her rules. Her wish to Sebastian and his response are significant: "Would thou'dst be ruled by me!" Acquiescing to her wish to rule him, Sebastian replies without hesitation, "I will" (4.1.63–64). This is not a partner who will play the expected role of lord and master in the household. Practical and in charge, Olivia follows up immediately by fetching the priest and making the arrangements for the exchange of vows.

Some critics have seen her love for Cesario as a humiliation, and her marriage to Sebastian alternately as a gift of grace, or as a further humiliation. But her comment upon seeing the twins revealed is an undisguised exclamation of pleasure: "Most wonderful!" (5.1.225). These are scarcely words of humiliation and shame.[12] Furthermore, if we accept the fantasy of visually identical twins, male and female, whom the other characters are unable to tell apart, we can also accept the fantasy of a Sebastian who actually is, as Viola tells the audience, similar to her played Cesario in every respect, "For him I imitate" (3.4.385). As Levin notes,

> Olivia, a powerful woman who stays in her female dress but stretches the boundaries of gender expectation, gets what she wants. Olivia is certainly not a direct and complete parallel to Elizabeth, but the queen's presence allowed Shakespeare sympathetically to present— and his audience to accept—a powerful, articulate woman who retains the accoutrements of femininity.... Olivia, like Elizabeth, does not need to cross-dress to be powerful [*Heart* 137].

The humorous ending which rights all wrongs and appears to return the characters from carnival topsy-turvy to the "real world" is, as so often in Shakespeare's comedies, a sprung ending. The harmonious return to convention, which signals closure in many Shakespearean comedies, does not necessarily provide containment for the critical, questioning spirit which has been liberated during the carnival time-out. Like the spirit of Carnival itself, it spills over the accepted boundaries, leaving questions unanswered, issues unresolved, and gender roles destabilized.

Masquerade in The Lord of the Rings

Tolkien, like Shakespeare, uses carnival masquerade in his depiction of two major woman characters, Éowyn and Galadriel. Given the romance/epic genres from which Tolkien drew in his construction of *LotR* (Chance 175), one would expect to find a traditionalist approach to women's roles. Indeed, several critical studies have viewed Tolkien's female characters as traditional women, mere counters who play a symbolic role as objects in male games of power and control. However, Tolkien presents subtle variations similar to the masks described in *TN* which can deflect the attention of his more conservative audience from the unconventional implications of the powerful women in his novel.

ÉOWYN'S MASKS

Éowyn wears two masks: first, the conventional mask of the romance heroine, which is stripped away when she dons a second mask, that of the male warrior, Dernhelm. In both cases, she resists traditional roles to which women have been relegated. Her mask of unconventionality allows Tolkien to depict her independent nature in far stronger terms than if she stated her rebellion against women's traditional roles in overt and clearly discernible forms. When the reader first encounters Éowyn, she is wearing the conventional mask, appearing to fulfill stereotypical expectations of medieval romance. She is simply a "woman clad in white" (3.6.501), an unnamed object, standing in a subordinate position behind King Théoden's chair. But her body language almost immediately resists the implications of the mask she wears. Instead of looking at Théoden as would a subordinate, with unquestioning obedience, "she looked on the king with cool pity in her eyes" (3.6.504). By the same token, she speaks no words and obeys the command to go, seeming to be silent and obedient. Tolkien's description of her also appears to show her as fulfilling the traditional expectations of the beautiful heroine: "Very fair was her face, and her long hair was like a river of gold" (ibid.). But again, the impression is almost immediately contradicted: "Slender and tall she was ... but strong she seemed and stern as steel, a daughter of kings" (ibid.).

Aragorn believes her to be "fair and cold, like a morning of pale spring that is not yet come to womanhood" (3.6.504). But we discover that, contrary to the expectations raised by this male judgment, she is a woman of power, passion, and resolve. Gandalf suggests that she has been viewed as a pawn in Saruman's game—again a typical role for women—since she has been promised as the prize to Wormtongue if he succeeds in undermining Théoden's power. Gandalf's words, spoken once Wormtongue has been banished, seem to suggest that she has been rescued: "Éowyn is safe now" (3.6.509). Nevertheless, reading between the lines, we recognize that this seemingly fragile, beautiful, and typical romance figure, whom we would expect to be relegated to the position of object in a man's world, has demonstrated greater power than Théoden in resisting the spells of Wormtongue, Saruman's emissary. Wormtongue has successfully cast a spell on King Théoden, but he has been unable to overpower Éowyn's will as her pitying glance toward the king suggests. She also appears prominently in all the gatherings of men. This is their sign of respect for her rank and, as the reader discovers, for her qualities which are recognized and applauded by the men of Rohan.

Contrary to traditional expectations, Tolkien presents a society in which the men respect and admire a woman's power, skill, and merit.

Thus, when Théoden plans to go to war, Háma puts Éowyn forward as the leader of the people who remain behind: "She is fearless and high-hearted. All love her. Let her be as a lord to the Eorlingas, while we are gone" (3.6.512). Unlike Viola in *TN*, or the other disguised women in Shakespeare, Éowyn does not simply claim power unofficially, but is officially granted both power and authority. During a special ceremony, she kneels, as would a knight, and receives a sword and "fair corselet" from the king as signs of her office. As the departing Aragorn looks back at her, she appears almost as an emblem of power, standing before the doors of the house in the traditional pose of the knight: "the sword was set upright before her, and her hands were laid upon the hilt. She was clad now in mail and shone like silver in the sun" (3.6.512). The mask of the conventional heroine has been replaced by that of the leader whose power has, astonishingly given the medievalized context of the novel, been officially authorized.

Éowyn uses her authority to empower Merry, a young male Hobbit who, like herself, has been marginalized in the battle preparations. She is marginalized because of her gender and he because of his size as a "Halfling," about the size of a human child of ten. She prepares a tent, weapons, and armor, using her authority to do so. When Merry is to be left behind, she secretly takes him with her, setting him on her horse before her. Tellingly, Tolkien does not reveal her identity to the reader throughout the long trek to Gondor. In *TN*, the audience knows that Viola is disguised, so that the discrepancy between her real and her assumed identity becomes the source of irony and humor. In the case of Tolkien, to avoid the suggestion of a woman warrior, unacceptable to Théoden and his advisors, he conceals Éowyn beneath the male dis-guise of the warrior, Dernhelm.

Unlike Viola, who comments consistently on the burden of her dis-guise, Éowyn is equally at home in the roles of woman and warrior, sub-ject and leader. Unlike Viola, whose inability at swordplay is the source of much horseplay and slapstick humor, Éowyn has a skill equal to that of a man. Unlike Viola, she is fearless, and unlike Viola, she recognizes clearly that traditional women's roles are a trap. Objecting to Aragorn's arguments, she says, "All your words are but to say: you are a woman, and your part is in the house.... But I am of the house of Eorl and not a serving-woman. I can ride and wield blade, and I do not fear either pain or death." When Aragorn asks what she fears, she replies "A cage.... To stay behind bars, until use and old age accept them, and all chance of doing great deeds is gone beyond recall or desire" (5.2.767). It is difficult to imagine a more overtly feminist statement than one ques-tioning the limitations not only of women's accepted roles, but of the heroic desire for doing "great deeds."

When Éowyn with the indispensable help of Merry, a child-like Hobbit, kills the Witch-king and his dragon-like beast, Tolkien's narrator does not express astonishment at the deed. Instead, he validates both her disguise and her role as a warrior. Tolkien makes it clear that only Éowyn was destined to fulfill this role and save the people of Gondor from the devastation of the Witch-king, whom no man could kill. Furthermore, the male characters do not condemn her for donning a disguise in order to go to war. Instead, they recognize and honor her for her qualities as a warrior.

Like Viola, Éowyn marries a man who is her friend. Éowyn abandons her vain admiration for Aragorn, a hero whom she worships from afar, to marry Faramir, a man who not only becomes her friend, but who is her empathetic support in the Houses of Healing while she is recovering from the wound she received in battle. As Leslie Donovan has stated, unlike the Valkyrie whom she resembles, Éowyn is not punished by meeting a dreadful end. Instead, like the other women in the novel, she is allowed "the possibility of human and heroic completion" (109). Tolkien thus validates Éowyn's unconventional role by rewarding her with happiness and fulfillment, not as a man, but as a woman. She is not a male in disguise; she is a powerful woman who retains her womanly characteristics, all the while demonstrating that she can gain public honor in ways normally allowed only to men. In his portrait of this unconventional woman who is both warrior and tender lover, power and femininity do not prove to be a toxic mixture, producing an unnatural being or an abomination. Even at the height of the battle, she remains human and womanly: "slender but as a steel-blade, fair yet terrible" (5.6.823). In Éowyn, the mask does not indicate self-alienation or a sense of a usurped identity. Instead, the mask *is* the woman. Éowyn is a hero.

Galadriel: Masked Power

Critics have frequently overlooked the powerful role played by Galadriel in *The Lord of the Rings*.[13] This is probably not surprising, since, like Olivia, Galadriel wears a conventional mask which deflects the reader's attention and conceals the extent of her power and influence in the novel. At first glance, Galadriel seems to be an expected heroine of romance. She appears to be confined to a garden-like realm, Lothlórien or Blossom of Lórien, where time stands still and where evil is kept at bay. She therefore seems to live in an edenic or fairy-tale world which has little connection with the "real" world of Middle-earth. She does not leave Lothlórien. Like a medieval lady, she presides over a court with Lord Celeborn. She grants gifts to the members of the fellowship, tokens similar to those granted in medieval traditions, and she has admirers who worship her from afar for her beauty. Even Gimli the Dwarf, like the hero of romance, is prepared to fight anyone who disputes his claim that she is the most beautiful of women.

This mask of traditional attributes is not assumed by Galadriel herself. Unlike Viola, Galadriel has no need to dissemble to assert her authority and to exercise power. On the contrary, Tolkien expresses her powers implicitly to make them more acceptable to members of his audience, many of whom still subscribe to more conservative views of women. Behind the mask, however, Galadriel is a woman of unusual power and authority. Unlike women who are confined to the domestic sphere and the garden, Galadriel is not imprisoned in the confines of her garden. On the contrary, she has created this world. As we later discover, she has been entrusted with Nenya, one of the three Elven Rings of Power, which allows her to protect Lothlórien from the spreading evil of the Dark Lord. When members of the fellowship first arrive in Lothlórien, they feel her strong presence. The Elves inform them, "You feel the power of the Lady" (2.6.342). She is no objectified image without identity or subjectivity. Her subjectivity is so powerful as to be felt throughout her realm.

Her garden is not just a limited territory. It extends over many miles and has an Elven city at its center. She runs the defenses of the realm, keeping in direct contact with the guards who meet the Fellowship and destroy the Orcs who have been following them. She protects the realm not just with her powers, but with her wise provisions for secrecy. No one who could betray its secrets may enter the realm unless they are blindfolded. Those who enter may not, under normal circumstances, leave. The realm thus is protected from the growing influence of the Dark Lord.

Her creative powers are reflected as well in the great beauty of her realm. When Frodo first sees the city of Cerin Amroth, which lies at the heart of Lothlórien, he is struck by its unearthly beauty: "It seemed to him that he had stepped through a high window that looked onto a vanished world. A light was upon it for which his language had no name" (2.6.341). Galadriel even has the ability to keep illness and other human imperfections and evils at bay.

In addition to playing the role of creator and protector of the realm—traditionally male roles—she is also shown to possess further powers. She possesses a mirror which can show possible futures; she can read the minds of the members of the fellowship and understand their thoughts without words. They feel, when she looks upon them, as if she had questioned each one of them deeply. Such powers are frequently associated with witchcraft and sorcery. Recognizing the potential prejudice of readers who might deem Galadriel to be a witch and therefore to be evil and perverse, Tolkien preempts such judgments by putting them in the mouths of those who, like Wormtongue, have an evil agenda and whose assessment is not to be trusted. Furthermore, all those in the novel who are good, sympathetic characters see her in a positive light, validating her role as a powerful woman without demonic attributes.

Galadriel's power extends far beyond the realm over which she reigns. As Leslie Donovan (112–18) has indicated, her gifts are similar to those of the Valkyrie, gifts with special powers such as the bow and arrow with which Legolas shoots the Ringwraith in the dark, the phial of light which has the power to keep darkness and evil at bay, the Elven rope which unties itself, the Elven cloaks that conceal members of the Fellowship from their enemies, and the waybread that sustains Frodo and Sam throughout their journey to Mordor. Her presence is so powerful that Gandalf invokes her in song when he exorcises the demonic thralldom of Saruman's minion, Wormtongue, from King Théoden. Galadriel demonstrates political acumen and insight. She calls the first White Council. She advises them to take Gandalf as their leader, advice which proves to be valid in the long term. She even summons the Dúnedain to Aragorn's aid at Helm's Deep. From the time the Fellowship visits her in Lothlórien, her presence and power permeate the novel.

Galadriel's mask of conventionality thus allows Tolkien to validate a powerful and positive woman and to contradict prejudices that would cause women with such powers to be condemned as witches. Indeed, it is significant that while the writings of C.S. Lewis, Tolkien's more conservative friend, feature numerous female witches, Tolkien himself has no female witches whatsoever in his writings. The only witch in Tolkien is male: the Witch-king. In this novel, even the traditional witch figures have been reversed and re-gendered as male.

Conclusion

As Doris Earnshaw notes in her discussion of medieval romance lyric, "the female voice within the overwhelmingly male-dominated literary tradition in written form, can function as a carrier of undercurrents of social values not generally permitted or approved" (13). Shakespeare and Tolkien use similar strategies to disrupt traditional gender paradigms. The fictive carnival worlds in *TN* and *LotR* are not merely used as venting mechanisms which reinforce the status quo after a brief time-out. Instead, these fictional spaces reflect back critically on the normative world of mainstream society. Within these worlds, both Shakespeare and Tolkien reverse expected roles both of men and of women. Both writers depict female characters—Viola and Éowyn—who disguise themselves as men either to escape a position of vulnerability and to enjoy the freedom of movement granted only to men (Viola), or to assume a powerful role otherwise denied to women (Éowyn). At the same time, both writers portray women—Olivia and Galadriel—who appear to be confined to women's traditional spaces, but who, in reality, are not. The fact that their transgressive behavior is concealed allows them greater power and flexibility than overt masquerade. The woman cloaked in conventionality blends in; her mask is invisible, so that she expands gender roles even while her unconventionality remains hidden in plain view.

Notes

1. Those who charge Shakespeare with reinforcing the status quo include Freedman (184) and Greenblatt (86–93). Partridge (179–89), Fredrick and McBride (108), and Stimpson (18) have argued that Tolkien's writings are anti-feminist.

2. Christine Dunn, Irene Dash, and Carole Levin have made a strong case for the power and unconventionality of many of Shakespeare's heroines. Critics arguing for a reassessment of Tolkien's female figures include Leslie Donovan, who compares Arwen and Galadriel to the Valkyrie. See also Melanie Rawls who has interpreted Tolkien's female characters as hybrid mixtures of archetypally masculine and feminine principles.

3. Barber and Hassel view the disruptions of carnival as a reinforcement of the status quo.

4. As Diane Purkiss notes "the popular beatings and lynching of women for witchcraft ... continued into the late nineteenth century" and popular witch stories continued to be circulated as late as 1962 (111).

5. In Perrault's eighteenth-century "Sleeping Beauty," on which the Disney film is based, the wicked fairy plays only a brief, cameo role at the beginning of the tale. In Disney's film, by contrast, the wicked fairy, named Malificent ("evil-doer") appears as a full-fledged witch complete with familiars including a crow and other frightening creatures. The epitome of the monstrous, demonic woman, she is transformed into a dragon which the prince is forced to kill with his sword of virtue and shield of truth.

6. Illyria was "the ancient name of an area of the Adriatic Coast roughly corresponding to what was for long known as Yugoslavia" (Warren and Wells 8). By Shakespeare's time, the name was applied to city states under the governance of the Venetian Republic. But while Illyria has links to an actual area of the Adriatic, it is also a mythic territory and imaginary world.

7. In medieval romance, "the social position occupied by those gendered male becomes conflated with that of humanity at large, exiling those gendered female to the position of difference, otherness, and objectification" (Crane 13).

8. Freedman has viewed both figures negatively: Viola as self-alienated by her mask, and Olivia as self-alienated by her failure to connect with reality (216).

9. For Hassel, Viola and Sebastian are "comic types of the incarnate Christ" and represent "good will and selfless love, forgiveness and humility" (150). Olivia, by contrast, is folly-ridden, obsessive woman engaged in "self-indulgent posturing as a grief-stricken sister" (154).

10. See Irene Dash and Catherine Dunn, who make a strong case that both women are positive, independent, witty, and unconventional characters.

11. In most European countries and Britain, "all widows and unmarried women [were required by law to choose] a male guardian who was to oversee their financial affairs and appear for them in court" (Wiesner 4).

12. Carole Levin notes that her exclamation "sounds like a rapturous triumph" (*Heart* 137).

13. For Frederick and McBride, "Galadriel is a female of great power and importance, yet that power has little relevance to [*LotR*]" (112).

Works Cited

Aughterson, Kate, ed. *Renaissance Woman: A Sourcebook.* New York: Routledge, 1995.

Bakhtin, Mikhail M. *Problems of Dostoevsky's Poetics.* Ed. and trans. Caryl Emerson. Minneapolis, University of Minnesota Press, 1984.

_____. *Rabelais and His World.* Trans. Helene Iswolsky. Bloomington: Indiana University Press, 1984.

Barber, C. L. *Shakespeare's Festive Comedy: A Study of Dramatic Form and Its Relation to Social Custom.* Princeton: Princeton University Press, 1972.

Beauvoir, Simone de. *The Second Sex.* Trans. and ed. H. M. Parshley. New York: Knopf, 1953.

Chance, Jane. "Tolkien's Women (and Men): The Films and the Book." In *Tolkien on Film: Essays on Peter Jackson's* The Lord of the Rings. Ed. Janet Brennan Croft. Altadena, CA: Mythopoeic, 2004. 175–94.

Coudert, Allison. "The Myth of the Improved Status of Protestant Women: The Case of the Witchcraze." In *The Politics of Gender in Early Modern Europe.* Ed. Jean Brink, Allison Coudert and Maryanne Horowitz. Kirksville, MO: Sixteenth Century Journal Publishers, 1989. 61–89.

Crane, Susan. *Gender and Romance in Chaucer's* Canterbury Tales. Princeton: Princeton University Press, 1994.

Dash, Irene G. *Wooing, Wedding, and Power: Women in Shakespeare's Plays.* New York: Columbia University Press, 1981.

Davis, Natalie Zemon. *Society and Culture in Early Modern France: Eight Essays.* Stanford, CA: Stanford University Press, 1975.

Donovan, Leslie. "The Valkyrie Reflex in J.R.R. Tolkien's *The Lord of the Rings*: Galadriel, Shelob, Éowyn, and Arwen." In *Tolkien the Medievalist.* Ed. Jane Chance. New York: Routledge, 2003. 106–32.

Dunn, Catherine. "The Changing Image of Woman in Renaissance Society and Literature." In *What Manner of Woman: Essays on English and American Life and Literature.* Ed. Marlene Springer. New York: New York University Press, 1977. 15–38.

Earnshaw, Doris. *The Female Voice in Medieval Romance Lyric.* New York: Lang, 1988.

Frederick, Candice, and Sam McBride. *Women among the Inklings.* Westpor, CT: Greenwood Press, 2001.

Freedman, Barbara. *Staging the Gaze: Postmodernism, Psychoanalysis, and Shakespearean Comedy.* Ithaca, NY: Cornell University Press, 1991.

Friedan, Betty. *The Feminine Mystique.* 1963. New York: Dell, 1983.

Greenblatt, Stephen. *Shakespearean Negotiations: The Circulation of Social Energy in Renaissance England.* Oxford: Clarendon, 1988.

Hassel, Chris. *Faith and Folly in Shakespeare's Romantic Comedies.* Athens: University of Georgia Press, 1980.

Knox, John. *First Blast of the Trumpet against the Monstrous Regiment of Women.* 1558. In *Renaissance Woman: A Sourcebook.* Ed. Kate Aughterson. New York: Routledge, 1995. 138–39.

Lamphere, Louise. "Strategies, Cooperation, and Conflict among Women in Domestic Groups." In *Woman, Culture, and Society.* Ed. Michelle Rosaldo and Louise Lamphere. Stanford, CA: Stanford University Press, 1974. 9–112.

Levin, Carole. "*The Heart and Stomach of a King*": Elizabeth I and the Politics of Sex and Power. Philadelphia: University of Pennsylvania Press, 1994.

_____. "Power, Politics, and Sexuality: Images of Elizabeth I." In *The Politics of Gender in Early Modern Europe*. Ed. Jean Brink, Allison Coudert and Maryanne Horowitz. Kirksville, MO: Sixteenth Century Journal Publishers, 1989.

Levin, Carole, and Karen Robertson. Introduction. In *Sexuality and Politics in Renaissance Drama*. Lewiston, ME: Mellen, 1991. i–xx.

Levin, Carole, and Patricia Sullivan. "Politics, Women's Voices, and the Renaissance: Questions and Context." In *Political Rhetoric, Power, and Renaissance Women*. Ed. Carole Levin and Patricia Sullivan. New York: SUNY Press, 1995. 1–14.

Lewis, C.S. *The Lion, the Witch, and the Wardrobe*. New York: Collier, 1970.

Neely, Carol. "Constructing Female Sexuality in the Renaissance: Stratford, London, Windsor, Vienna." In *Sexuality and Politics in Renaissance Drama*. Ed. Carole Levin and Karen Robertson. Lewiston, ME: Mellen, 1991. 1–26.

Ortner, Sherry. "Is Female to Male as Nature Is to Culture?" In *Woman, Culture, and Society*. Ed. Michelle Rosaldo and Louise Lamphere. Stanford, CA: Stanford University Press, 1974. 67–88.

Partridge, Brenda. "No Sex Please—We're Hobbits: The Construction of Female Sexuality in *The Lord of the Rings*." In *J.R.R. Tolkien: This Far Land*. Ed. Robert Giddings. London: Barnes, 1983.

Purkiss, Diane. *The Witch in History: Early Modern and Twentieth-Century Representations*. New York: Routledge, 1996.

Rawls, Melanie. "The Feminine Principle in Tolkien." *Mythlore* 38 (1984): 3–13.

Rosaldo, Michelle, and Louise Lamphere, ed. *Woman, Culture, and Society*. Stanford, CA: Stanford University Press, 1974.

Shakespeare, William. *The Complete Works of William Shakespeare*. Ed. David Bevington. New York: Pearson, 2004.

Stimpson, Catharine R. *J.R.R. Tolkien*. New York: Columbia University Press, 1969.

Sullivan, Patricia, and Carole Levin. "Women and Political Communication: From the Margins to the Center." In *Political Rhetoric, Power, and Renaissance Women*. Ed. Carole Levin and Patricia Sullivan. New York: SUNY Press, 1995. 275–82.

Thum, Maureen. "The Sub-Subcreation of Galdriel, Arwen, and Éowyn: Women of Power in Tolkien's and Jackson's *The Lord of the Rings*." In *Tolkien on Film: Essays on Peter Jackson's* The Lord of the Rings. Ed. Janet Brennan Croft. Altadena, CA: Mythopoeic, 2004. 231–58.

Tolkien, J.R.R. *The Lord of the Rings*. 2nd ed. Boston: Houghton, 1994.

Vives, Juan Luis. *The Instruction of a Christian Woman*. 1523. In *Renaissance Woman: A Sourcebook*. Ed. Kate Aughterson. New York: Routledge, 1995. 69–74.

Warren, Roger, and Stanley Wells. Introduction. *The Tempest*. By William Shakespeare. Oxford: Clarendon, 1994.

Whatley, William. *A Bride Bush*. 1617. In *Renaissance Woman: A Sourcebook*. Ed. Kate Aughterson. New York: Routledge, 1995. 31–35.

Wiesner, Merry. "Women's Defense of Their Public Role." In *Women in the Middle Ages and the Renaissance: Literary and Historical Perspectives*. Ed. Mary Beth Rose. Syracuse, NY: Syracuse University Press, 1986. 1–28.

Williams, John. "A Sermon of Apparrell." 1619. In *Renaissance Woman: A Sourcebook*. Ed. Kate Aughterson. New York: Routledge, 1995. 77–79.

Woolf, Virginia. *A Room of One's Own*. 1929. New York: Harcourt, 1957.

Something Is Stirring in the East

Racial Identity, Confronting the "Other," and Miscegenation in Othello and The Lord of the Rings

ROBERT GEHL

"You must speak, my precious, of us that loved it not unwisely but too much." So might Gollum exhort his eulogists before his fatal fall into Mount Doom. Of course, Gollum had no knowledge of Shakespeare's *Othello*, but the confluence of themes in that play and Tolkien's *The Lord of the Rings* (*LotR*) clearly demonstrates that both authors were very concerned with issues surrounding racial and national identity, confronting "others," and miscegenation. By comparing the two works, both written by English authors—one at the dawn of Britain's empire, the other at the close—we see an in-depth exploration of the fear, desire, and problems produced by the system of racism. We see how a nation can confuse racial purity with national identity. We are presented with the very means by which cultures construct race, define its rules and boundaries, and prosecute transgressions against these constructed standards.

Both *Othello* and *LotR* show how power and race are inextricably linked in and to English national identity. In both works, when a dominant culture is confronted and challenged by an outsider, a struggle over racial and sexual identity—that is, a power struggle—ensues, ending with the destruction of the "other." While Tolkien's work does not address gender to the degree that *Othello* does, the lust for the Ring that Frodo, Gollum, and Saruman (among others) exhibit is akin to the sexual lust directed at Desdemona by Cassio, Roderigo, and Othello. Both are fetishistic lusts for dominance. Tolkien's work does, however, deal with race. Gollum's presence is a constant reminder to Frodo and Sam of the possibilities of miscegenation occurring, even in the safe borders of the Shire. Gollum's twisted body is a product of Sauron's will, just as Orcs are produced from Elves and the Uruk-hai from mixing Orcs and Men. For Frodo and his kin to have a place in Middle-earth, nothing short of the defeat of Sauron would suffice; otherwise, the future of the Shire would be at stake, because the future of the race of hobbits would be at stake: they would be made into Gollum-like slaves in Sauron's empire. Likewise, as Brabantio notes in *Othello*, tolerating the Moor's marriage to his daughter would irreversibly alter the face of Venetian society and make "pagans" and "bondslaves" of its statesmen (1.2.101).

This essay proposes to explore these works with a focus on Othello and Gollum. In both works, the characters are trapped between cultures and struggle to find agency. They are caught, to a great degree, within cultural perceptions based on their race. These perceptions are based partly on what is believed to be their essential characteristics and partly on their symbolic representation of the potential of miscegenation and national decay. This is not to say that these characters have no agency; Othello and Gollum also exert, through their subjugation, a sort of power of their own over those that seek to dominate them. As Tolkien stated, "A man who wishes to exert 'power' must have subjects, who are not himself. But he then depends on them" (*Letters* 279). As I argue later, while both Othello and Gollum are subjected and made into "others" in relation to the dominant cultures they encounter, both authors take care to depict their subjugators becoming intimately bound to them. Race is, after all, a symptom of power, a means to a conquering end, but, as Tolkien's statement indicates, power *needs* subjects.

Insular Environments, Insular Audiences

In order to play on their respective audiences' concerns with race, both authors carefully construct environments—Venice and the Shire—which are both familiar to and removed from contemporary England, and then introduce characters—Othello and Gollum—that challenge the hegemony (patriarchy, insularity) of these environments through their very presence. Both of these uprooted characters face an either/or decision to be assimilated or alienated from the dominant culture. As they struggle with this dichotomy, the action is taken farther and farther East (a place whence, as Tolkien put it, "enemies mostly come") (*Letters* 212). There, far removed from the dominant cultures, these characters and those around them finally come to a conflict which resolves the racial anxiety in favor of the dominant culture.

The environments in which these characters attempt to find space, and the environments in which each work was produced, are exceedingly hostile to outsiders. In her study of race and colonialism in Shakespeare's work, Ania Loomba describes Elizabethan London as a place where "questions of difference [were] volatile"; where there were "growing anxieties about being engulfed by outsiders"—among them northern Africans—who were migrating to the city at the rate of 10,000 per annum (15–16). Certainly, London was cosmopolitan, and its inhabitants were interested in the outside world. But, Loomba notes, the vast majority of Londoners got most of their perspective on immigrants and outsiders at The Globe rather than through travel (8). Londoners and the rest of England began to create a sense of national identity in relation to outsiders, rehearsed and observed onstage at the theater. After all, under Elizabeth, England was first blossoming into a world power, one that could defeat the armada of Spain and engage in colonization and commerce the world over. A strong national identity, stemming from a common language, culture, and ethnicity, was necessary if England were to gain power in Europe. The existence of outsiders such as Africans among and around Elizabethans did more to shape English identity than any sort of abstract, internal conception of self (Habib 2).

Furthermore, Shakespeare's decision to stage *Othello* in Venice helped to reinforce English identity. Venice, with its fleets of ships and control of the Mediterranean, was a major rival to the English. It mirrored London in population and surpassed the English capital in prestige. Its architecture and government were equally sophisticated. Venice fascinated the English, who wished to challenge the city in trade and prestige. These views affected popular culture. In writing about Venice, Shakespeare and other Elizabethan authors concentrated "on the idea of Venice as an aristocratic republic and cosmopolitan centre of capitalism, with her exceptional freedom for strangers and her exceptional attraction for travelers in search of sophistication. The image of Venetian society in their ... plays is a refracted projection of London" (Salinger 173).

However, Venice's "freedom for strangers" was a marked contrast to London's. Venice was, in fact, in decline by the time of *Othello*. The English could not only learn from Venice's brand of capitalism and conquest, but also from its cultural mistakes: its heterogeneous culture offered a counterpoint to England's ideology of national solidarity. Shakespeare's plays featuring the Moor of Venice and the Jew of Venice showed the dangers of this freedom for strangers. This could only reinforce the anxiety that many English felt at the influx of Africans into the country.

By Tolkien's lifetime, racial issues in Britain were certainly improved. Alan Rice notes that, especially during World War II and thanks to the 130,000 African-American servicemen who were stationed in the United Kingdom, there was "almost a lost utopian moment of racial harmony" (225). In light of the fight against fascism, African-American and African-British soldiers were treated with respect by the ordinary white British population. The "strange historical nuances of the war" with the broadening influence of African-American troops "dynamically changed sexual and racial mores in Britain" (225).

However, the changes in British culture that resulted from this utopian mix of races proved to be temporary, especially "in comparison to the racist face that the British showed Caribbean migrants over the next fifty years" (225). Love for American troops gave way to fears of dreadlocks and drums. And, even during World War II, the English had a strong fear of miscegenation: however welcome the African-American soldiers were during World War II, they were discouraged from sexual relations with white women, and, when these unions did occur, most of the children born were given up for adoption (224).

These critical descriptions of the pervasive insularity and xenophobia of England, from Shakespeare's London to Tolkien's English countryside, bear remarkable similarity to the insularity of the hobbit homeland, the Shire, and the oldest remaining hobbit settlement, the town of Bree, in Tolkien's work. The Shire, as many critics have noted, is pastoral England idealized.[1] The hobbits are a rural folk of farmers and tradespersons. Crime is low among them; their police force is twelve strong. However, these dozen "shirriffs" are dedicated solely for "Inside Work." The border patrol of the Shire is more involved: "A rather larger body, varying at need, was employed to 'beat the bounds', and to see that *Outsiders* of any kind, great or small, did not make themselves a nuisance" (Prologue 10, my emphasis). At the outset of *LotR*, these bounders

> had been greatly increased. There were many reports and complaints of strange persons and creatures prowling about the borders, or over them: the first sign that all was not quite as it should be, and always had been except in tales and legends of long ago [Prologue 10].

Thus, the environment that produces the heroes of Tolkien's work is insular. Unfortunately, however, the Shire is newly (or again) beset by threats from the outside. The exact nature of this threat is not known; "not even Bilbo yet had any notion of what it portended" (Prologue 10). Yet, as is clear from the high number of Bounders, the Shire is struggling to maintain its homogeneity by denying "Outsiders" any entry.

The other major enclave of hobbits, Bree, is metropolitan to the Shire's pastoral. There, Hobbits live alongside Men. Their relationship, though described as "excellent," is mildly segregated: "[they] were on friendly terms, minding their own affairs in their own ways, but both rightly regarding themselves as necessary parts of the Bree-folk" (1.9. 146). Like Londoners, these rooted Bree-folk avoid travel and get their news of foreign lands in a theatrical manner. Since Bree is situated on an ancient crossroads, travelers at the inn are the chief source of information from outside the town limits. At Barliman Butterbur's Prancing Pony inn, customs and cultures are exchanged through song and dance. When Frodo leaps up onto a table, he speaks a few brief words, but as soon as he pauses, the crowd, eager to observe a hobbit from the Shire, cajoles, "A song! Come on now, master, sing us something we haven't heard before!" (1.9.154).

Beyond these cultural exchanges, news is discussed at the Pony. When Frodo first arrives at the inn, the Bree-folk are trying to manage an influx of immigrants and, like Londoners of Shakespeare's day, are "not pleased at the prospect" (1.9.152). However, as a "squint-eyed ill-favoured" Southerner warns, immigrants from the South would be coming and would take what land they needed. As a major town in the region, Bree is already beset the by the threats of "Outsiders" that the Shire is newly facing.

Beyond this anxiety over assimilating newly arrived peoples, the Bree-folk's reactions to foreigners ranges from tolerance to open hostility. While they "eagerly listened to" tales from the Rangers that visited, they "did not make friends of [the Rangers]" (1.9.146). The innkeeper Butterbur speaks of "Outsiders" from the South and West. But the Bree-lander's hostility and anxiety about others is demonstrated in full when Frodo accidentally disappears while dancing and singing at the Prancing Pony. "We're a bit suspicious round here of anything out of the way," warns Butterbur after the incident (1.9.158).

Thus, the Shire and Bree, like London as described by Loomba, are volatile environments, struggling to cope with an influx of new people. Loomba's discussion of Elizabethan London's (as well as England's) creation of self-identity in relation to their perceptions of the morality and customs of outsiders applies here. The Bree-landers' own mythology is in terms of their relationship to "others"—in this case, the men of Númenor. Furthermore, at the time of Frodo's visit, Bree is entering a paradoxical state where it is becoming "culturally more open, yet in many ways more insular" (Loomba 4).

Enter the Outsiders

The challenges posed by outsiders that Venice and the Shire (as well as England) face are personified in Othello and Gollum. In both cases, the very presence of Othello or Gollum is indicative of the English concurrent fascination with and revulsion by outsiders; it is the underlying cause of both characters' presence. In the case of Othello, the immediate assumption is that his value to Venice is as a general. He is described as "the valiant Moor"; his military skill, we assume, is held in high esteem. However, his status as a general does not bring him fully into Venetian culture; he is charged with fighting the Turks, who are "the *common* enemy"—instead of "*our* enemy." It is a subtle difference, but one that speaks volumes about the outsider status of the Moor. And, since the "common enemy Turk" does not attack in the course of the play, Othello's military value to Venice is never made visible for Shakespeare's audience, and thus his presence in Venice is unexplained. Instead, Othello is a passive character, more a victim than a victor. This passivity is on display from the outset: when the Venetians learn of the imminent Turkish attack on Cyprus, Othello is reluctant to heed the call of the senators. Instead, he "must be found" by a Venetian before he will attend the council (1.2.30). Later, when Cassio discovers him and summons him to see the Duke, Othello notes, "'Tis well I am found by you" (1.6.48). Othello, who is often described by others as a man of action and resolve, instead reveals his passivity, a condition he maintains throughout the play, thus contradicting those descriptions. Rootlessness and a lack of integration into his adopted culture may explain away this contradiction: perhaps on the battlefield Othello is active and resolute, but in the social structure of Venice he is uncertain.

No, Othello's value is not as a general. Shakespeare's play makes it clear that his value in Venice is as an "other." His "Africanness" and background as a redeemed (i.e., now Christian) Muslim seem attractive to the Venetians. His success in Venice stems more from his fascinating history and his ability to tell it than his military feats. His tales are first told in Brabantio's house, where he was asked by the senator to tell "the story of [his] life" (1.3.131). In this Venetian home, African and European cultures come into contact, and these stories fascinate Brabantio and Desdemona because of their descriptions of alien cultures, "cannibals," and "anthropophagi." The immediate result of this encounter is his unexpected and successful wooing of Desdemona. "She loved me for the dangers that I had passed," he reports, "and I loved her that she did pity them" (1.3.169–70). But for the heads of state, such as Brabantio and the Duke, the real value of Othello's stories are as a means by which to measure and confirm the value of their own culture.

These esteemed Venetians, no doubt, are glad that their heads grow *above* their shoulders!

Tolkien's plot is also driven largely by the history and knowledge of a rootless wanderer. Like Othello, Gollum has no home. His family, Gandalf reports, has long disappeared from their dwellings on the banks of the Anduin. Even if they hadn't vanished over time, Gollum was driven from them because of the changes he underwent as a result of his use of the Ring. Gollum "wandered in loneliness" until he found a cave in which to hide from the sun (1.2.52). There he would stay for many years, but he would never feel at home: he was reduced to "nasty furtive eating and resentful remembering.... He hated the dark" (1.2.54). He was finally drawn from this hole when Bilbo accidentally found the Ring. From there he wandered through Mirkwood to Dale, and back toward the west, then south, only to be captured in Mordor.

Gandalf knows this history and tells it to Frodo because of its significance in the history of Middle-earth. Gollum's experience as one under the sway of Sauron tells Gandalf much of the values and motives of the residents of Mordor. No one else, with the possible exception of Bilbo, does more to aid the wizard in his understanding of the effects of Sauron's Ring. He confirms his suspicions of the Ring's ability to work on the will of its user by examining Gollum's history.

"Coursers for Cousins"? What an "Abominable Notion"!

Still, the histories of Othello and Gollum do not solely contribute to the conflicts of either work. Instead, it is when Venetians and Shire-folk realize a potential for miscegenation that fear of these "others" begins to gestate. Desdemona's fascination with Othello's stories leads to their eloping. Othello is thus driven out of his somewhat comfortable space; this is the moment where Othello's accepted role as a general on the "tented field" is brought into direct conflict with his new role as a Venetian husband: a Moorish soldier, yes; a brood of half–Moorish, half–Venetian children, no.

In Gollum's case, his encounter with Frodo in the wilds north of Mordor confirms the hobbit's fears of the effects of Sauron's dominance; while the destruction of Bag End would be horrific enough, the destruction of the hobbit race through the same process that created Orcs (or by mixing with Orcs, for that matter) would be devastating. Before I go into detail, I must digress for a moment. In Shakespeare's play (and time, for that matter), the "godless, bestial, and hideous" Moors and Turks are the race that threatens; those black-skinned peoples were "usually typed as fit only to be saved ... by Christians" (Loomba 91). In Tolkien's work, the race that threatens is the Orcs and their kin. The origin of the Orcs is similar to the "Children of Ham" creation mythology surrounding Africans. Melkor, who is the prime evil in Tolkien's mythology, captured some Elves (who were themselves the products of the supreme deity Eru) and, jealous of Eru's ability to create, twisted the Elves into Orcs. Physically, the conception of an Orc's appearance is in relation to what is seen as beautiful by Europeans: as Tolkien explains, "Orcs are definitely stated to be corruptions of the 'human' form seen in Elves and Men. They are (or were) squat, broad, flat-nosed, sallow-skinned, with wide mouths and slant eyes: in fact degraded and repulsive versions of the (to Europeans) least lovely Mongol-types" (*Letters* 274).

Orcs are not the only genetic perversions. The Nazgûl are derived from men and the Uruk-hai from a mixture of Men and Orcs. In fact, all the races of creatures that Melkor and Sauron (and later Saruman) encountered were twisted into evil creatures. Even Hobbits have their own miscegenated foil in Gollum.

In *LotR*, Gollum represents—especially to the Hobbits—the potential of a mixing between Hobbits and a "dark race" such as Orcs. Sméagol was, as Gandalf states, "of hobbit-kind" once (1.2.51); he was of the Stoor branch of Hobbit-kind. When Frodo first realized that his kind could become blackened by Sauron's power, he was terrified: "I can't believe Gollum was connected to hobbits, however distantly.... What an abominable notion!" (1.2.53). It was a portent of what would no doubt be the fate of the Shire if it were overrun by the Dark Lord. Since Sauron (and his henchman Saruman) had long experimented with the mixing of races, there is little doubt he would do the same with the Shire folk. Thus, although Gollum is not the product of a sexual union between an Orc and a man (such as the Uruk-hai), he is the result of the symbolic union between the hobbit Sméagol and Sauron (via the Ring) and a clear indication of the danger that Frodo and the Shire-folk were facing. This miscegenation would occur as a direct result of Gollum's transmission of his knowledge of "Baggins" and "The Shire" to Sauron; Gandalf wasn't the only one torturing Gollum for information.

Tolkien emphasizes this anxiety in two key scenes. Frodo has two startling encounters with fellow Hobbit Ring-bearers, once with Bilbo in Rivendell and once with Sam in the tower above Cirith Ungol. In the first, the aged Bilbo asks to see the Ring, and when he is presented with it, he becomes "a little wrinkled creature with a hungry face and bony groping hands" (2.1.226). Much later, Frodo recovers the Ring from Sam, who seems to be a "leering and pawing ... foul little creature with greedy eyes and a slobbering mouth" (6.1.891); in short, Orc-like. For Frodo, the despair of watching his uncle and his friend altered into such creatures is all the evidence he needs that the Ring must be destroyed before the Shire is overrun and all the other Hobbits become "sub–Hobbit" creatures like Gollum.

"It Hurts Us, Precious"

For Othello and Gollum, the disconnection from their homes and surroundings that they experience, and the fear that this engenders, causes them to struggle with their identity and agency. In both cases, the characters vividly demonstrate a sort of split identity, and much of their time is spent trying to reconcile this duality. For example, Othello's history as a Moor (as he terms it, a "circumcisèd dog") who lives in Venice is not without its underlying tensions. Despite his "redemption," his past as a Muslim is in direct conflict with his present as a Christian. His current status as a general is in contrast with his past as a slave. After he becomes a husband, Othello tries to become more than a "valiant Moor," but his struggle with identity intensifies. He finds himself criticizing his own speaking ability ("Rude am I in my speech" [1.3.83]), contrasting his lodgings in war with the proper lodgings of a husband ("The tyrant custom ... / Hath made the flinty and steel couch of war / My thrice-driven bed of down" [1.3.232–34]), and explaining his role as a warrior to his new wife ("'Tis the soldier's life / To have their balmy slumbers waked with strife" [2.3.252–53]). His past roles and history haunt his present.

That Gollum is torn between his past and present is just as apparent. His language is based on a duality; he uses "us" and "we" for personal pronouns. "We" includes Sméagol, who existed before the finding of the Ring, and Gollum, the creature who was formed by the influence of the Ring. While his present identity is dominated by Gollum and his lust for the Ring, Sméagol makes his presence known several times, most notably on the stair of Cirith Ungol. More so than Othello, Gollum has neither home nor community: he is afraid of everyone, Dwarves, Elves, Men, Orcs, and Nazgûl. Ironically, however, everyone in Middle-earth is seeking him: he is hunted by Aragorn and enjoys his freedom from the Elves because of a planned Orc attack. However, the only loyalty he has is to his Precious. His most dichotomous moment occurs as Sméagol and Gollum debate over whether or not to take the Ring back from Frodo, a scene that is brilliantly realized in the Jackson production (*Return of the King* scene 6).

Othello's and Gollum's struggles with identity are understandable given their rootlessness and inability to find a space in their respective environments. This conflict, however, is only exacerbated by other characters. Discussing *Othello* and using Todorov's "assimilation/alienation" dichotomy from *The Conquest of America*, Edward Berry states, "Othello's 'Africanness' is crucial to this tragedy not because of what he is, innately or culturally, but because of how he is perceived, by others and by himself" (318). Sujata Iyengar concurs: in *Othello*, "the circumstances of historical existence and of social interactions outweigh the failings of an inherent 'personality' in determining the catastrophe [and the tragedy]" (116). Other characters—specifically Iago, Roderigo, and Brabantio—emphasize the negative stereotypes of Othello's race and culture as a means to drive him from Venetian society. Iago, of course, is the most notorious of these three. His brand of racism is sickeningly witty, playing with the contemporary conception of Africans as bestial: Othello is an "old black ram" who makes "the beast with two backs" with the "white ewe" Desdemona (1.1.90–91, 119–20).

These comments particularly prey on Brabantio, who, as, Joyce MacDonald notes, has a "fund of patriarchal and racial anxieties." His anxiety runs so deep and is so virulent that, "while he grasps desperately at the possibility that his daughter was not in her right mind when she eloped with her new husband, he nowhere questions Iago and Roderigo's ugly racial characterizations of Othello" (188). In fact, he perpetuates Iago's slurs (although certainly not with Iago's wit): how, he asks could "a maid so tender, fair, and happy ... Run from her guardage to the sooty bosom / Of such a thing as [Othello?]" (1.2.67–72). Othello's courtship of Desdemona happened in his home, under his supervision, but seemingly unknown to him. Perhaps it is because their union is unthinkable, even contra-natural; no less than three times he notes its unnatural aspects. Brabantio fears having black grandchildren. However, his fear extends beyond the limits of the "guardage" of his house to encompass this union's consequences on the state; it is, as well, contra-national: "The Duke himself, / Or any of my brothers of the state, cannot but feel this wrong as 'twere their own; / For if such actions may have passage free, / Bondslaves and pagans shall our statesmen be" (1.2.95–99). He may have well used Iago's terminology; instead of "bondslaves," "coursers"; instead of "pagans," "jennets." Thus, his "particular grief" of a Moor "tupping" his daughter is greater than all the military problems of the state; in fact, it "engluts and swallows other sorrows." It threatens the very future of Venice. Indeed, the senators and Duke halt their war plans in order to investigate this transgression; Othello, however, is found to be innocent of "bewitching" Desdemona.

Desdemona, on the other hand, sees "Othello's visage in his mind" (1.3.255) and attempts to ignore race in favor of his full assimilation into her culture. Initially, it appears that she is as uncertain as Othello of her role as a Venetian married to an outsider. Explaining herself to her father and the Duke, Desdemona complains of her "divided duty" between Brabantio and Othello (1.3.183). She senses her duty to her father's house, which is a prominent one in Venetian culture, and Othello's, which is an alien establishment. However, Desdemona's complaint is less above division than about reconciliation. By citing her mother's adherence to the customs of Venice, Desdemona tries to deny the alienness of her marriage; as she sees it, she is doing as her mother did before her, which has nothing to do with Othello's background or customs. She attempts to bring Othello fully into Venetian society by surrendering herself to his lordship as any other Venetian woman was to do for her husband. Here, Desdemona is engaging in "naïve and uncertain assimilationism" (Berry 323).

Of course, neither alienation nor assimilation will work; this polarity only serves to heighten Othello's own identity crisis. "Throughout the play," Berry argues, "Othello sees himself either as an exotic Venetian, a convert in the fullest sense, capable of complete assimilation, or he sees himself as a barbarian, worthy of destruction. His failure to break free of this constricting framework, to achieve a true sense of personal identity, is one of the play's most powerful sources of tragic feeling" (323).

This alienation/assimilation dichotomy is also applicable to *LotR*. The two opposing parties in this dyad are Frodo and Sam, who, after subduing Gollum, debate his nature. For Sam, Gollum is a "hungry villain," "poor wretch," a "nasty," "treacherous," and "dratted creature." Sam sees Gollum as dangerous: since he is willing to eat "worms or beetles or something slimy out of holes" (4.2.610), he certainly would "not [be] too dainty to try what hobbit tastes like" (4.2.607). When Gollum has a moment of doubt about leading Frodo and Sam into Shelob's lair, Sam sees him lightly and almost affectionately caress Frodo and accuses Gollum of "pawing at master" (4.8.699). At that point at least, it is Sam's perception of Gollum, not Gollum's nature or lust for the Ring, which drives the creature on with his murderous scheme. Sam even contemplates murdering Gollum in his sleep (4.2.609). Certainly Sam is afraid of Gollum because of the lack of food and Gollum's reputation as a treacherous murderer, but Sam's fear runs deeper than this. As the travelers pick their way through the Dead Marshes, Sam quips, "Three precious little Gollums we shall be, if this goes on much longer" (4.2.614). Sam sees Gollum as a threat to his master Frodo; Gollum will lead them astray, and time is precious, because Frodo feels the weight of the Ring growing heavier. Frodo will soon join Gollum in his existence as a little Ringwraith, and faithful Sam would follow Frodo there.

Sam's reaction to Gollum (after he perceives Gollum's dual identity, he refers to Gollum as "Slinker and Stinker") allows Gollum no space to negotiate his struggles with his cultural identity. Frodo, on the other hand, recognizes Gollum's struggles as his own and emphasizes Gollum's hobbit heritage, thus attempting to redeem Gollum from his time with the Ring. This begins with Frodo's pity: "I will not touch the creature. For now that I see him, I do pity him" (4.1.601). Frodo tries to assimilate Gollum in order to recover him from the grip of the Ring. This attitude was influenced by Gandalf, who also hoped Gollum could be saved (4.6.671). When Sam names Gollum a "sneak," Frodo tells him, "Don't take names to yourself, Sméagol.... It's unwise" (4.8.700). Frodo's desire to reform Gollum is based on combating perceptions of the creature as much as it is on kind treatment. Like Desdemona, Frodo "sees the visage in Gollum's mind," and, to use Berry's terms, engages in "naïve assimilationism."

Alien and Akin: Fetishes and the Union between Subjugator and Subjugated

However, while Frodo does admirably work to cure Gollum, he has been appointed to destroy the Ring. This responsibility trumps any personal needs he has, including a belief in a life after the destruction of the Ring. In this capacity, Frodo is an agent of the state, serving its interests. For his own homeland as well as for the rest of the West, his goal is to prevent Sauron from overwhelming the world and enslaving and blackening its inhabitants. If Gollum is brought back from his Ring-sickness, so much the better. But Frodo is always mindful of Gandalf's constant assertion that Gollum would have a role to play in the quest, and, of course, it is Gollum who inadvertently hurls the Ring into the fire and destroys it.

Thus, Frodo needs to subjugate Gollum to prevent the creature from trying to recover the Ring. To do this, he uses his personal experience with the Ring to enter into a promissory and dominant relationship with Gollum. Frodo's knowledge of the Ring's power over its bearers allows him to subjugate Gollum. Gollum, on bended knee, swears to "be good" "on the Precious." Sam witnesses the power of this bond:

> [H]is master had grown, and Gollum had shrunk: a tall stern shadow, a mighty lord who hid his brightness in grey cloud, and at his feet a little whining dog. Yet the two were in some way akin and not alien: they could reach one another's minds (4.1.604).

Like Frodo, Iago sees the benefit of binding himself to Othello in order to better control the Moor. Unlike Frodo, Iago is never mindful of the interests of the state; "In following [Othello]," he declares to Roderigo, "I follow but myself—/ Heaven is my judge, not I for love and duty / But seeming so for my peculiar end" (1.1.60–62). However, there is no doubt that, given his racism, Iago is keen to drive the Moor out of Venice because of sexual jealousy and the threat of miscegenation. "For that I do suspect the lusty Moor / hath leaped into my seat, the thought whereof / Doth like a poisonous mineral gnaw my inwards; / And nothing can or shall content my soul / Till I am evened with him, wife for wife" (2.1.296–300). For Iago, advancement of rank would be an agreeable consequence of his plots, and the senators would certainly reward him for exposing Othello for what they all believe him to be.

To accomplish this, he also enters into a pledged bond. In a moment meant to mock the ceremonies of marriage, Othello and Iago both drop to their knees and pledge their service to each other, although Othello's pledge centers on violence and revenge against Cassio more than his love of Iago. Functioning in place of a ring in this mock-nuptial is another fetish—an Egyptian handkerchief. This handkerchief has magical properties not unlike the Ring:

> That handkerchief
> Did an Egyptian to [Othello's] mother give.
> She was a charmer, and could almost read
> The thoughts of people. She told her, while she kept it
> 'Twould make her amiable and subdue my father
> Entirely to her love, but if she lost it
> Or made a gift of it, my father's eye
> Should hold her loathèd and his spirits should hunt
> After new fancies (3.4.57–65).

This fetish, this trifle, which has the power to subdue, and if lost incites an eye to loathe, changes hands throughout the play. It is highly symbolic of Othello's mystical, pagan past, of Desdemona's virtue, and of Iago's malice. Just as Gollum's screams of "Baggins" and "Shire" incite Sauron to start the war to seek out his Ring, Shakespeare's plot turns on this piece of cloth. When Iago reveals that Cassio has it, Othello has all the proof he needs, and his pledge to Iago to seek revenge marks the beginning of the final conflict.

The bonds between Iago and Othello and Frodo and Gollum are wholly dependant on the ability of these characters to understand the desires and impulses of one another. Frodo's understanding of Gollum is analogous to Iago's understanding of Othello: each understands their respective subject's jealousies and lusts. Frodo knows how devastating Gollum would find it if he had to see the Ring on Sauron's finger, or on his own. This desire drives Gollum to battle Frodo at Mt. Doom and ultimately fall, Precious in hand, into the fire, thus saving Middle-earth from Sauron's domination. Lustful and covetous Iago knows full well that Othello, like any patriarch, would enter into a blind rage at the thought of his wife committing adultery, the "ocular proof" of which is her handkerchief in another man's hand. This rage ends in Desdemona and Othello's death in their bed; the site of their sexual union becomes the grave of miscegenation in Venice.

Conclusion

As I hope is clear from this essay, the issue of race problematizes both of these texts. In the case of *Othello*, this is very clear; much of the criticism I have cited considers race (as well as gender and sexuality) to be central facets of the text. What I argue here is that Tolkien's trilogy is just as concerned with race as Shakespeare's play. This is not to suggest that Tolkien was virulently racist; I disagree with the critics who argue that *LotR* is about whites rising against a tide of black-skinned foes. However, I also disagree with critics such as Sandra Straubhaar and Patrick Curry who look to intercultural marriages (such as Faramir and Éowyn's) as evidence of Tolkien's carefree multiculturalism. Clearly, as English writers who are associated with mythologies of England and empire, race is at the heart of both Tolkien's and Shakespeare's works.

In the end, the result of these authors' works is a heightened awareness in the reader of the process and means by which racial identity is created through "othering." In Shakespeare's time, Elizabethans gained a conception of themselves in relation to those from the East, as well as in relation to Venetians. To use the language of performance studies, they learned the scripts by which to play their roles by examining onstage the sexual and cultural values of an "other" such as Othello. The pernicious byproduct of this conception, of course, is the pseudo-scientific, Darwinian categorization of people by skin tone in order to justify the colonial practices of the Empire. For readers of Tolkien in his day and today, the result is certainly more subtle. Within the text, the fallout of Gollum's plunge into Mt. Doom is the end of the Third Age, which sees the "rise of the race of Men." The rise of Men means the fall of Orcs, who are not redeemed by Aragorn the king. However, the Uruk-hai and their forebears are problematic: they are part–Man, part–Orc. Upon Aragorn's ascension to the throne, the Dunlendings and Haradrim, both groups of Men, were cleared of past transgressions. By contrast, Orcs and other races (Trolls, for instance) are left to hide in the hills. Little is said of them.

Thus, the miscegenated peoples of Middle-Earth, the Uruk-hai and half–Orcs, are extremely problematic. Is their human heritage enough to redeem them in the Fourth Age? Or will their Orc and Troll blood mean that they will suffer the same fate as their full-blooded Orc brethren? Is there a measurement or scale, similar to the South's complicated system of racial heritage and categories (such as mulatto and quadroon), on which to judge the degree of their sins? As for Gollum, had he survived, would he have joined Bilbo, Frodo, and Sam over the sea as a fellow Ring-bearer? Or would he have joined the Orcs and Trolls?

External from the text, readers have used the tome to symbolize the struggle between environmentalists and corporations, the struggle between pacifists and hawks, and, disturbingly (especially to the reader that loves these books), Tolkien's work has been categorized as "must reading" by white supremacist groups such as the British National Party and Aryan Nations (Potts). Images of "beautiful Nordic heroes"—that is, stills from the Jackson production depicting blonde-haired Elves and Rohirrim—have circulated the Internet.[2]

Because Tolkien's work can certainly inspire this simplistic reading, the specter of race must be dealt with. Like the vision of Africans, Turks, and Venetians presented to audiences in the Globe who saw *Othello*, *LotR* presents to its audience a complex vision of how race is constructed as two cultures collide. Ultimately, we must temper our love for the Bard and the father of Fantasy with acknowledgment of the problematic role of race in their works.

Notes

1. The Shire, to be fair, is also pastoral England criticized; Tolkien's description is also at times sarcastic. "They were, in fact, sheltered, but they had ceased to remember it" (Prologue.5). For an exploration of the pastoral mode of *LotR*, see Patrick Curry's *Defending Middle Earth*.

2. In particular, see http://www.stormfront.org/archive/t-3273Beautfiul_White_Nordic_images.html.

Works Cited

Berry, Edward. "Othello's Alienation." *Studies in English Literature* 30.2 (Spring 1990): 315–33.

Curry, Patrick. *Defending Middle-earth: Tolkien, Myth and Modernity.* Boston: Houghton, 2004.

Habib, Imtiaz. *Shakespeare and Race: Postcolonial Praxis in the Early Modern Period.* New York: University Press of America, 2000.

Iyengar, Sujata. "White Faces, Blackface: The Production of 'Race' in *Othello*." In *Othello: New Critical Essays*. Ed. Phillip Kolin. New York: Routledge, 2002. 103–32.

The Lord of the Rings: The Return of the King. Special extended DVD. Screenplay by Peter Jackson et al. Dir. Peter Jackson. 2002. New Line, 2003.

Loomba, Ania. *Shakespeare, Race, and Colonialism.* Oxford: Oxford University Press, 2002.

MacDonald, Joyce G. "Black Ram, White Ewe: Shakespeare, Race, and Women." In *A Feminist Companion to Shakespeare.* Ed. Dympna Callaghan. Oxford: Blackwell, 2001. 188–207.

Potts, Leanne. " '*Lord of the Rings*' Unleashes Debate on Racism." *Albuquerque Journal,* 26 Jan. 2003. Accessed 1 March 2003 at http://www.abqjournal.com/shock/827891fun 01-26-03.htm

Rice, Alan. "'Heroes across the Sea'": Black and White British Fascination with African Americans in the Contemporary Black British Fiction of Caryl Phillips and Jackie Kay." In *Blackening Europe: The African American Presence.* Ed. Heike Raphael-Hernandez. New York: Routledge, 2003. 217–31.

Salinger, Leo. "The Idea of Venice in Shakespeare and Ben Jonson." In *Shakespeare's Italy: Functions of Italian Locations in Renaissance Drama.* Ed. Michele Marrapodi. New York: Manchester University Press, 1993. 171–84.

Shakespeare, William. *The Complete Works of William Shakespeare.* Ed. David Bevington. 5th ed. New York: Pearson, 2004.

Tolkien, J. R. R. *The Letters of J.R.R. Tolkien.* Ed. Humphrey Carpenter. Boston: Houghton, 2000.

_____. *The Lord of the Rings.* 2nd ed. Boston: Houghton, 1994.

Self-Cursed, Night-fearers, and Usurpers

Tolkien's Atani and Shakespeare's Men

ANNA FÅHRAEUS

To say that Tolkien shared with Shakespeare a fascination with the effects of the fact of mortality on the shaping of human life is perhaps to state the obvious, and to make a claim that can be said of any number of other writers. However, two things make a comparison with Shakespeare immediately attractive. First, like Shakespeare, Tolkien separated the issue of death from that of decay. In the work of both authors, there is a strong recognition that decay (as the experience of ever-increasing loss) is as much a part of life as it is of death. This would make a study of their respective treatments of loss and the parallels between Shakespeare's Romances and Tolkien's Elves profitable, but unfortunately that lies outside the scope of this essay. Instead, in this essay I will focus on the human relationship to death and how it influences the characterization of Tolkien's Atani and Shakespeare's Men.

A second point that makes a comparison between the two authors profitable is their shared interest in history and the pivotal role of wars and disputes, and how the nature of Men impacts on those struggles. They both explore the effects of confronting mortality in moments of crisis. They seem to have been equally fascinated by how the fact of death shapes human lives. Both writers also implicitly accepted the fact that history as they wrote it was a construct, yet also that as a construct— or perhaps even particularly as a construct and in narrated form—history has power over the human mind. As early as 1592, Thomas Nashe saw in Shakespeare's *Henry VI Part 1* an attempt to make the past live again for his audiences. Considering that ten of his thirty-seven plays were histories, it is apparent that Shakespeare recognized that his audiences liked seeing the past enacted and wrote works to accommodate their taste. Tolkien deliberately set out to construct Middle-earth and its history as a mythic English past to rival other European mythologies.

Both authors were fascinated by the history of England in particular and conceived of it as fertile soil for the creative imagination. It does not seem too far-fetched to imagine that along with the obvious *Macbeth*, Tolkien would have paid particular attention to Shakespeare's history plays, especially the depiction of the medieval War of the Roses. The aim of this essay is to illustrate possible ways in which Tolkien taps into Shakespeare as part of the "soup" of material available on England and its history. The intent is not to prove that Tolkien used Shakespeare's plays as a direct source for his work. Tolkien's objective was manifestly to create a mythic epic, a faery tale of a history of an age long past, while Shakespeare's was to recreate—with creative license— a more recent and much more limited past. However, I will argue that in creating the conditions of mortality for Men in *The Silmarillion* and *The Lord of the Rings* (*LotR*), Tolkien echoes and alludes to images (and motifs) in Shakespeare, and that he does so in a way that is indirectly both poetic praise and reproach of images that occur in the two history plays *Richard II* (*R2*) and *Richard III* (*R3*).

Shakespeare's Men and Tolkien's Atani

There have been innumerable studies on Shakespeare's Men, from the early character studies that emphasized an empathetic response to a proliferation of psychoanalytic studies of Shakespeare's characters that probe the make-up of their minds and personalities. Since Samuel Johnson's *Preface* to Shakespeare (1765), Shakespeare has been thought to embody the general in the particular in his characters. A strong consensus has been that he provides plausibility and credibility, which is to say coherence for his characters.

King Richard in *R2* is obsessed with names and words more than concrete action and his obsession gives his ineffectuality, his despair and his suicide believability. His obsession is contrasted with Bolingbroke's pragmatic attitude, which allows him to usurp the throne and King Richard's title. The issue of names and the power they signify is socially divisive and decisive in the play and engenders crises of identity (Maus 946). Tolkien would recognize this connection between names and identity and exploit it creatively in introducing Aragorn, Elendil's heir to the throne of Gondor and the wielder of Andúril, as a Ranger when he firsts enters the story. Gandalf's names likewise encompass his history and his power: Olórin, Incánus, Tharkûn, Grey Pilgrim, Grey Wanderer. He is also known as Mithrandir by the Elves, Gandalf Stormcrow and Láthspell by Men, and has the titles Gandalf the Grey and later Gandalf the White.

It has been noted that in *R3*, Shakespeare begins to psychologize inner motives and that Richard's deformity is presented as "less the cause of his evil nature than its sign" (Greenblatt 509). This process vividly comes to life in Tolkien but in reverse, when Théoden son of Thengel, King of the Mark of Rohan, is released from the evil bondage of Saruman. He regains both his strength and his vigor. He goes from being bent to standing straight. The evil that has deformed him has been purged. Greenblatt further argues that the dead in *R3* are more than psychological projections; they are metaphysical realities. Yet what Richard is haunted by is curses, words. Tolkien, of course, gives his sinister dead a much more tangible reality as the Ringwraiths but also as the more neutral but equally malicious barrow-wights.

There are varying opinions about how Shakespeare's plays, including *R2* and *R3*, present human nature and what is central to the human experience, but both these plays focus on a nostalgia for an idealized English past and issues of self-shaping. Both also include vivid portrayals of the fear of death. All three aspects tie them to Tolkien's work and his conceptualization of Men as a race with specifically English affiliations.

For his part, Tolkien's separation of different aspects of the human into different races makes a comparison between his Men and Shakespeare's conceptualization of the conditions of mortality somewhat easier than it might otherwise be, because it compelled him to delineate more concretely specific characteristics for each race. It can be assumed that he left something he thought was rudimentary but fundamentally important in the race of Men. The perspective of the early days of mortal Men is given in Tolkien's letters and in *The Silmarillion*. The latter is an account given by the Elves, but it gives insight into how Men were perceived from the beginning of their emergence in Arda:

> The Atani they were named by the Eldar, the Second People; but they called them also Hildor, the Followers, and many other names: Apanónar, the After-born, Engwar, the Sickly, and Fírimar, the Mortals; and they named them the Usurpers, the Strangers, and the Inscrutable, the Self-cursed, the Heavy-handed, the Night-fearers, the Children of the Sun [*Silmarillion* 103].

What is immediately evident is that the image of Men and their identity is multiple, and that most of the later epithets are negative. This draws attention to the fact that the names are not self-designations nor can they be taken as objectively neutral terms. It can instead be assumed—and this is intimated—that the Elven use of them is based on hearsay and, to a lesser extent, on interactions with Men. Similarly, because these are the terms that have been passed on, and not others, it can be assumed that they are regarded as prominent features of Men—at least to the Elves, and perhaps to the other races of Arda. This essay will focus particular attention on three of the epithets: Men as Night-fearers, as Self-cursed, and as Usurpers. I will argue that that each of these has a context as they mirror how the fascination and the dread of Men is intimately tied to their unique status and history on Arda. The status of Men is given by Ilúvatar, who differentiates Men from Elves in that the Elves are immortal and Men are not, and that what happens to Men after death is known only to him, their creator. The second differentiation of Men in Tolkien is interestingly one that in the context of Shakespeare has been defined as belonging not to medieval depictions of humanity but as emerging in the early modern era: Ilúvatar makes inherent in their nature a restless desire. First, let us take a look at the depiction of the role of death in shaping men in Tolkien, and in Shakespeare.

The Fear of Death

Men's mortality is both a source of grief and of envy to the Elves (*Silmarillion* xv), but few things are more human than the fear of death, and it is thus not surprising that it is central to the characterization of Tolkien's Men. The way the connection between Men and their preoccupation with death is introduced in *LotR* is through contrast with the idyllic world of the Shire. Several of the images Tolkien uses as a basis for his story can be seen as expansions of images that Shakespeare used in a very famous dream sequence in *R3* that is likewise concerned with the fear of death.

The Duke of Clarence has a nightmare while he is being held prisoner in the Tower of London. He dreams that he has escaped the Tower and is in a boat with his brother Gloucester. They are crossing a river. Gloucester stumbles and causes Clarence to fall into the water. He feels himself dying and surrounded by death, and then dreams that he is actually dead. It is hard to imagine Tolkien not having read this particular scene and being struck by it. There are arresting echoes of Clarence's dream in the beginning sequences of *LotR*. What makes a connection plausible, aside from the images themselves, is the fact that Tolkien's use of them has obvious parallels with his reaction to the fulfillment of the prophecy that Macbeth would not die until the Great Birnam wood moved against him. What in Shakespeare is prophetic metaphor becomes literal in Tolkien. The trees become sentient beings that move. The same is the case with Clarence's dream. Its images become literal events or characters in Tolkien.

> Methought I saw a thousand fearful wracks;
> Ten thousand men that fishes gnawed upon;
> Wedges of gold,
> ...
>   unvalued jewels,
> All scattered in the bottom of the sea.
> Some lay in dead men's skulls, and in the holes
> Where eyes did once inhabit there were crept,
> As 'twere in scorn of eyes, reflecting gems,
> That wooed the slimy bottom of the deep
> And mocked the dead bones that lay scattered by [1.4.23–33].

There are four images thus far that Tolkien chose either from this source, or from somewhere else, and embroidered upon until he had full-fledged narrative elements: the image of two brothers fighting in a boat until one falls into the water (Smégol and Déagol); being surrounded by masses of dead men floating and rotting but not yet decomposed (the Dead Marshes); a ring that is "unvalued" that has been seemingly carelessly lost and that now rests on the bottom of the sea; and glowing skull eyes that mock the dead but that are also dangerously seductive (Frodo's fall into the Dead Marshes). Tolkien's adaptation of these images makes the dream itself literal in various ways, thus implicitly commenting on and criticizing what seems to him to have been Shakespeare's—and realism's—generally shabby way of treating things with fantastic details. He transforms and concentrates the image of, for example, the "wedges of gold" that are "scattered" at the bottom of the sea by focusing on one ring and giving it a dark, sinister history. It is an "unvalued" jewel, but with a twist: its own power is what is underestimated.

Clarence's dream continues after he is dead when he is brought across the river by "that sour ferryman which poets write of, / Unto the kingdom of perpetual night" (1.4.46–47). In *LotR*, the three parts of this classic image of death are reinterpreted and again expanded. Frodo and Sam cross the Brandywine into a land dominated by the shadow in the East as night is falling. Their boat lacks a ferryman but after they have crossed the river and entered the inn at Bree their fate becomes intertwined with that of a Man, Aragorn, who at first seems grim and has an air of ominous mystery. He will become their companion on this darker side of Middle-earth.

Tolkien reinforces the traditional image of crossing a river with the added image of crossing an actual threshold to stress that the hobbits have entered a drastically different world. Both events, the crossing of the river and their entrance into the inn are portrayed as occurring at night and with great drama. They are literal and mundane yet they are filled with the suspense and the foreboding of the unknown. The world they have entered is much less safe and secure than the Shire. It is also where the hobbits encounter Men en masse for the first time. The Men of Middle-earth live on this other side; a side where death reigns.

Though Aragorn fulfills part of the role of ferryman he quickly loses his menacing quality, but Tolkien includes a different type of "ferryman" which is much more menacing and which spans the border between life and death literally. The hobbits are pursued to the river and prevented from backtracking to the Shire by the Ringwraiths. The hobbits are "accompanied" unwillingly by these wraiths of Men, who are not quite dead. On the Bree side they will eventually have an encounter with them on Weathertop in which Frodo will be stabbed. Shakespeare includes a vivid description of Clarence's experience of being pursued in the realm of death that runs parallel to Frodo's:

> With that methought a legion of foul fiends
> Environed me, and howlèd in mine ears
> Such hideous cries that with the very noise
> I trembling waked, and for a season after
> Could not believe but that I was in hell [1.4.58–62].

As Clarence's dream encounter leaves him shaken and for "a season after" feeling as if he was in "hell," Frodo's actual encounter with the Morgul blade of the Witch-king leaves him on the brink of hell, with a strong unwillingness to even relive the experience in memory. Tolkien echoes Shakespeare's imagery and conceives of the Ringwraiths in much the same terms as Clarence's "legion of foul fiends." The image is, not surprisingly, expanded as the fiends, that is, Ringwraiths, are given a terrifying history and even a mission (to retrieve the Ring at all costs). The "hideous cries" of Shakespeare's "foul fiends" become the shrill shrieks of the Nazgûl that freeze the blood and stop breath. Fear is the weapon of these beasts that bear the Ringwraiths and the power of their cry is to pierce the heart with "poisonous despair" (5.4.791).

Self-Cursing and Unfulfillable Desire

Reading this it is possible to object that Frodo and Sam are Hobbits, not Men, but what is important in this section of *LotR*, for this study, is that the hobbits are passing into the part of Middle-earth dominated by Men and by the fear of Sauron. The effect of the Nazgûl on

Men is no different from their effect on hobbits. Beregond admits to Pippin that "the very warmth of my blood seems stolen away" when he hears their cries (5.1.749), and he equates the Nazgûl with the Shadow of the Dark Lord and his coming with a malignant night, which brings death and worse than death. Other Men, too, "stand stricken with a passing dread" (5.4.798), and even the "stout-hearted" quail and "their weapons fall from nerveless hands while into their minds a blackness came, and they thought no more of war; but only of hiding and of crawling, and of death" (5.4.805).

What is surprising is that in *The Silmarillion* death is said to have been originally given to Men as a gift and only Men's reaction to it has made it a source of trouble; Tolkien refers to death as simultaneously "the Gift" and "the Doom" of Men (*Silmarillion* xiv). Men's fear of death and of dark shadows thus has a history that has led the Elves to refer to Men as "Self-Cursed" by what was meant to be a blessing. Two of these events or reasons can be found in *The Silmarillion*. On the one hand the basic tenet of the argument seems to lie in the effect it has on the Númenorean Men when they are rewarded with longer life after helping defeat Sauron for the first time. They become increasingly possessive towards their own achievements and they want more time to enjoy them, which is to say that they want to forestall death (*Silmarillion* xxii). Ultimately their preoccupation with their possessions and with not dying leads to their corruption and the destruction of Númenor. A second reason is given that applies to all Men and not just the aristocratic Númenorians: fear. Death begins to bother Men because they associate it with "the shadow of Morgoth" and his malignant darkness. As a result they grow "wilful and proud and would not yield, until life was reft from them" (*Silmarillion* 265).

Of course the desire to not die is ultimately unfulfillable. And it is in this intersection between death and the drive or ambition created by the unfulfillable desire to not die that Tolkien echoes a motif in *R2*, restless desire. This motif is not confined to Shakespeare's play—in fact, it permeates much of the literature of the early modern period—but the words Shakespeare's King Richard uses are worth looking at and considering in connection with Tolkien. In the next to last scene of the play, King Richard ruminates on his own status after he has been unseated from the throne:

> Then am I kinged again, and by and by
> Think that I am unkinged by Bolingbroke,
> And straight am nothing. But whate'er I be,
> Nor I, nor any man that but man is,
> With nothing shall be pleased till he be eased
> With being nothing [5.5.36–41].

His own identity is in crisis. He was king but is king no longer and he cannot accept that. His comment on the nature of man can be read in two ways. Either no man can be pleased with having nothing and so must fight to gain some sort of foothold in life until he dies, or no man is ever pleased regardless of what he has and will always want more. Read as the latter, Richard's statement would be in harmony with what Robert Watson identifies as the modern notion of desire that emerged in the early modern era: desire as perpetually unsatisfied, restless and unfulfillable. It is seen as characterized by "an infinite regress"; there is always something more to be done before one's desire is fulfilled (Watson 161).

The motif of restless desire is bound up in the English early modern mind with an obsession with identity or self-fashioning. Much of the best scholarship on Shakespeare in the last twenty years has revolved around the threat and fascination of self-shaping: the ability of man to modulate his exterior (and thus his reception) and change his destiny, and the vulnerability that this malleability entails. Stephen Greenblatt states that during the early modern period the idea of self-fashioning was fraught with fear, a very literal fear that the self was so intrinsically tied to one's identity that one could be literally annihilated if the foundation of that (social) identity was eroded (257). This is King Richard's position. He cannot accept that he is no longer king and reshape himself to fit his new circumstances; he feels annihilated. He concludes quite literally that he is nothing. Most of the play deals with Richard's gradual confrontation of the fear of death but also the realization that there is something worse: to be nothing.

It is this complexly drawn connection between mortality and desire as infinitely forestalled that finds its way into Tolkien, complete with the early modern tension between self-shaping and a divine or supremely ordained order. Men are unique in Tolkien's world because in creating Men, Ilúvatar gives them two gifts. The first is the gift of death. The second is a "new gift" that is linked to the conditions of mortality for Men:

> [H]e willed that the hearts of Men should seek beyond the world and should find no rest therein; but they should have a virtue to shape their life, amid the powers and chances of the world, beyond the Music of the Ainur, which is as fate to all things else (*Silmarillion* 41).

Read carefully, this gift has two parts, or is itself two gifts that are bounded by mortality or death and that are paradoxical in nature. One part of the gift is a restless desire for something other than what Men already have; to continually "seek beyond the world." The second is the ability to choose for themselves what they will be and do and how they will contribute to the Music of the Ainur. Men are given what the evil Vala Melkor wrongfully desired: the right to add things to the creation music of Ilúvatar. It is this dual gift, of restless desire and the power to shape life—bounded by "the powers and chances of the world"—that is the crux of what it means to be a man or woman, to be among the Atani of Arda. It is a fantastic gift, but it is contrary to the order by which all the other races are governed, and not surprisingly this sets Men apart from them and makes the other races, including the Elves, suspicious of them.

As in Shakespeare, the insatiable desire for more becomes tied to ambition and to the fear of annihilation. Nowhere is this more apparent in Tolkien for Men as a race than in the downfall of Númenor, but it is most plainly seen in an individual character in Denethor's reaction to Sauron and the return of the heir of Elendil. His desire to fight for Gondor is overshadowed by his fear of being made redundant as a Steward by the return of the King. In his blackest moment of insanity, a core of Denethor's desire for something beyond what life has given him, beyond his identity and limitation as a Steward of Gondor, is revealed in his orchestration of an ancient pagan burial rite: "No tomb for Denethor and Faramir. We will burn like heathen kings" (5.4.807). It is in this clinging to his image of himself as a ruler of importance that Denethor's fear of invalidation most echoes Shakespeare's King Richard. Like Denethor, who discharges Pippin, Richard discharges those who would dissuade him from despair and seeks to evade nullification as ruler by embracing death.

> By heaven, I'll hate him everlastingly
> That bids me be of comfort any more.
> Go to Flint Castle. There I'll pine away;
> A king, woe's slave, shall kingly woe obey [3.2.207–10].

Richard has, in fact, already been given counsel on how to conquer death by the Bishop of Carlisle:

> My lord, wise men ne'er sit and wail their present woes,
> But presently prevent the ways to wail.
> ...
> Fear, and be slain. No worse can come to fight;
> And fight and die is death destroying death,
> Where *fearing dying pays death servile breath*
> [3.2.178–85, emphasis added].

Denethor equates the return of the King and the loss of his early power and status with death on earth, and like King Richard, embraces literal death to avoid being figuratively annihilated as a ruler. He refuses to serve under a King.

For Men in general on Middle-earth, Tolkien literalizes the foe and the servitude. Death and Men's fear of it become embodied in Sauron and his instruments, the Ringwraiths, Men who have literally faded almost into the most horrible of nothings through their desire to not die and retain their earthly power. The Elves, who envy the gift of mortality, write that the Valar (powers for good with a stewardship over Middle-earth) entreated Men to trust in the purposes of Ilúvatar so that death does not become "a bond" that constrains them (*Silmarillion* 265). The Men of Middle-earth are unable to; they fear the Valar rather than love them. They are instead like the Macbeths who refuse to accept the limitations of Macbeth's position as Thane of Glamis. The over-reaching of Lady Macbeth for the crown leads to contact with a supernatural evil that brings its own destruction in the form of madness. It puts Macbeth on a collision course with the rest of the world until the earth— in the shape of Great Birnham wood—seems to literally move against him. Like the Macbeths, Tolkien's Men are cursed but they bring the curse upon themselves.

Images of Usurpation

The name and history of Men on Arda are complicated. In *The Silmarillion*, the history of Men is intertwined with that of the Elves. We are told that the Valar use the designation of Atani for the race of Men. Though Atani and the Sindarin Elvish form, Edain, are most often straightforwardly equated, the Grey Elves clearly distinguish the Edain from the general race of Men. In the "Akallabêth," or the account of the downfall of Númenor, not all Men belonged to the Edain, only those who turned from evil and wandered westward and came at last to Beleriand (*Silmarillion* 259).[1] Though Men are peripheral to most of the accounts in *The Silmarillion*, their appearance in Beleriand is in the end decisive.[2] They arrive with the first sunrise and are, thereafter, connected to each decisive turn of events on Middle-earth, and the fate of the Edain becomes intertwined with that of the Elves (103). Their coming signals the beginning of the fulfillment of the prophecy that the Elves will wane and Men increase. It is, therefore, unsurprising that the Elves reconstruct their own history and reduction in importance as a consequence of the "triumph of Morgoth" (the name given to Melkor after he escapes to Middle-earth) and the fact that "Men *usurped* the sunlight" (105; emphasis added). The epithet "usurper" in relation to Men has a broader application and history as the prophecy is increasingly actualized in the lives of both races.

Though we are not told how the First Fall of Men in Tolkien's Arda came about, we are told that it resulted in "an inner weakness" in Men, whereby rewards are more dangerous for Men than punishment (*Silmarillion* xxi). It is therefore ironic that after helping defeat Morgoth (the Edain and the Elves enter into an alliance), the Edain are given "rich rewards" and a land to dwell in near Valinor. This eventually leads to a "Second Fall" of Men in Middle-earth and to the alteration of Arda that prevents all but the Elves from finding the straight road to the Undying Lands. Though the island of Númenor is drowned by the sea, it remains an ideal that haunts the Men of Middle-earth, especially Aragorn, who traces his heritage to the Númenorean kings.

It is at this point that echoes of a particular image from Shakespeare's historical drama *R2* comes into play. Phyllis Rackin has commented that this play in particular (and *R3* as well), is marked by nostalgia for a more idealized England that has been lost. As a reader of Tolkien and Shakespeare, it is hard not to think of Númenor when reading the dying Gaunt's description of England:

> This royal throne of kings, this sceptred isle,
> This earth of majesty, this seat of Mars,
> This other Eden, demi-paradise,
> This fortress built by nature for herself
> Against infection and the hand of war,
> This happy breed of men, this little world,
> This precious stone set in the silver sea,
> Which serves it in the office of a wall—
> Or as a moat defensive to a house,
> Against the envy of less happier lands,
> This blessèd plot, this earth, this realm, this England [2.1.40–50].

Line by line there are parallels in the island given to the Edain. It is separated from all other lands by the sea, but is within sight of both Valinor and the island given to the Elves, Tol Eressëa. As the seat of the Edain it becomes the "royal throne of king" and is adorned with flowers and fountains brought by the Elves. It shimmers in "a golden haze" as Men approach it and is a country "fair and fruitful" (*Silmarillion* 261). On it Men live longer than the normal span granted to Men on Middle-earth, and they grow prosperous and strong under the protection of the Valar and wise through the friendship of the Eldar. To use Shakespeare's words, it is the "envy of less happier lands" in Middle-earth and it eventually becomes a terrifying "seat of Mars."

The image of Shakespeare's "sceptred isle" seems to superimpose itself on Númenor and vice versa—the more so because Gaunt's description is ironic. The picture of England that he gives is of a time past. In his own time, the position of the English ruling class is ambiguous; they are "Feared by their breed and famous by their birth" (2.1.52). Shakespeare's King Richard governs legitimately and by divine right, but he is presented as simultaneously weak and ineffectual and tyrannical. Shakespeare leaned on several historical accounts for this interpretation. Among them Raphael Holinshed's *Chronicles of England, Scotlande, and Irelande* (1577), in which King Richard is painted as "prodigal, ambitious and lustful" (Healy 55). In the play, he has put the country in debt with his blank charters (2.1.64). Gaunt's tone is thus one of deep sadness and regret as well as nostalgia: "this dear, dear land ... Is now leased out" (2.1.57, 59).

Tolkien had, of course, no actual historical source to draw on for his imaginary king, but his portrayal of Ar-Pharazôn echoes Shakespeare's text. By Ar-Pharazôn's time, the Edain and especially their Kings are corrupted. Instead of aiding and protecting the other Men on Middle-earth, they lay them under tribute. They grow prideful and become estranged from both the Eldar and the Valar. The tributes become increasingly taxing on Middle-earth as the Edain start seeking to be "lords and masters" rather than "helpers and teachers" (*Silmarillion* 266–67).

The Edain grow increasingly troubled by the inevitability of death. Concern turns to fear. Fear turns to ambition. They become so powerful that Sauron, who had grown in power on Middle-earth, feared them "lest they should invade his lands and wrest from him the dominion of the East" (267). His fear is realized, and Ar-Pharazôn brings Sauron back to Númenor as his prisoner. Once in Númenor, Sauron acts the Machiavellian deceiver. He uses their fear and ambition to persuade Ar-Pharazôn to make war on the Valar.

Shakespeare's drama of King Richard, like Tolkien's story of Númenor and Ar-Pharazôn, raises two issues: what should determine who rules? And what should be done when a ruler is unjust?

The verdict is out on whether Shakespeare's plays should be read as a support of inherited office or rule by merit. Yet, even though *R2* illustrates "inconsistencies in Renaissance theories of kingship," it can definitely be seen as implicitly arguing that history supports the hereditary rule of the monarchy (Maus 944). After King Richard has been deposed and murdered, civil war ensues, fulfilling prophecies in the play of destruction and the shedding of blood in the wake of Bolingbroke's usurpation of the throne. Tolkien's epic supports inherited office but complicates it by the lead role the hobbits play in the Fellowship and in securing the possibility for Aragorn, as the last Númenorean King, to ascend to the throne of Gondor.

The answers Shakespeare and Tolkien give to the second are more strikingly similar. Tolkien, in fact, echoes Shakespeare's *R2*. Unable, as a supporter of the divine right of Kings, to act on behalf of his brother the Duke of Gloucester, who has been unjustly killed on the order of King Richard, Gaunt says:

> God's is the quarrel; for God's substitute,
> His deputy appointed in His sight,
> Hath caused his death; the which if wrongfully,
> Let heaven revenge, for I may never lift
> An angry arm against His minister [1.2.37–41].

He later refuses to support Bolingbroke's rebellion but allows him into his home to rest. The Men on Númenor that are faithful to the Valar face the same questions and the results are the same. Amandil's advice to his son Elendil is "To meddle not in the war, and to watch" (*Silmarillion* 276). Elendil does not move with Ar-Pharazôn, but neither does he move against him.

The similarities between the stories of King Richard and Ar-Pharazôn are mostly superficial, but the connections between the deeper issues are not. Among these shared and connected issues are kingship, usurpation, self-shaping, and a fear of death, issues central to an understanding of human nature in the works of both authors. In portraying the overthrow of Ar-Pharazôn and the downfall of Númenor as a "Second Fall" of Men, Tolkien is echoing the words of Richard's Queen, who calls the news of Richard's deposition "a second fall of cursèd man" (3.4.76). With his characteristic twist, Tolkien makes Shakespeare's words literal. What is metaphorical in Shakespeare once again becomes amazingly concrete, as well as amazing new literature, in Tolkien.

Notes

1. Despite their rejection of Morgoth, Men were not uniformly welcomed by the Elves even though the latter knew that eventually Men would come and live among them (140–49).

2. The Edain are also distinguished from the remaining races of Men on Middle-earth through the three intermarriages between Elves and members of the Edain: Beren and Lúthien (grandparents of Elwing), Eärendil and Elwing (the parents of Elrond and Elros), and much later, Aragorn and Arwen.

Works Cited

Greenblatt, Stephen. *Renaissance Self-Fashioning: From More to Shakespeare.* Chicago: University of Chicago Press, 1980.

Healy, Margaret. "*Richard II.*" In *Shakespeare: Texts and Contexts.* Ed. Kiernan Ryan. London: Macmillan, 2000. 49–80.

Johnson, Samuel. "The Preface to Shakespeare." 1765. In *The Norton Anthology of English Literature.* Ed. M. H. Abrams. 6th ed. Vol. 1. New York: Norton, 1993. 2393–2401.

Maus, Katherine Eisaman. Introduction to *Richard II*. In *The Norton Shakespeare*. New York: Norton, 1997. 952–1014.

Nashe, Thomas. "*1 Henry VI*." 1592. In *The Norton Shakespeare*. Ed. Stephen Greenblatt et al. New York: Norton, 1997. 3322.

Rackin, Phyllis. *Stages of History: Shakespeare's English Chronicles*. Ithaca, NY: Cornell University Press, 1990.

Shakespeare, William. *The Complete Works of William Shakespeare*. Ed. David Bevington. 5th ed. New York: Pearson, 2004.

Tolkien, J.R.R. *The Lord of the Rings*. 2nd ed. Boston: Houghton, 1994.

_____. *The Silmarillion*. 2nd ed. Boston: Houghton, 2001.

Watson, Robert. "Tragedies of Revenge and Ambition." In *The Cambridge Companion to Shakespearean Tragedy*. Ed. Claire McEacharen. Cambridge: Cambridge University Press, 2002. 160–81.

Gollum and Caliban
Evolution and Design

LISA HOPKINS

In this chapter I want to explore the parallels between Gollum and Caliban and to suggest that these have two principal effects. The first relates to the idea of the *translatio imperii*, which postulated that the cultural authority of Troy and Rome had been ultimately transferred to England. Tolkien was acutely aware of attempting to create an epic for England, and therefore of working within the tradition established by Homer and Virgil; *The Tempest*, with its Virgilian echoes, is a play deeply rooted in the idea of the *translatio imperii*. The second reason I want to propose for Tolkien's interest in Caliban is that by the time Tolkien turned to him, Caliban had developed from his Shakespearean beginnings to become intimately associated with the theory of evolution. The figure of Gollum thus allows Tolkien to pit ideas of evolution and chance against those of design and order as a complex part of the book's overall sense of historical pattern and of human perception of it.

Parallels and Echoes

Although Tolkien claimed to dislike Shakespeare, whom he considered, amongst other things, implicated in the "debasement" of the word "Elves" (*Letters* 185), he did record enjoying a performance of *Hamlet* in 1944 (88), and there are many references to Shakespeare in his works. In *The Hobbit*, the dwarves want cakes and ale when they come to tea in Bag End (1.19), as Sir Toby Belch does in *Twelfth Night*; the Master of Laketown changes the people's minds as Antony does in *Julius Caesar* (14.264); and there are numerous echoes of *A Midsummer Night's*

Dream (see Hopkins, "*Hobbit*"), not least in the way in the way the uncanny doubling between Saruman and Gandalf parallels that between Theseus and Oberon. In *The Lord of the Rings* (*LotR*), another comedy is echoed when Aragorn tames Gollum by denying him drink and food (2.2.247) as Petruchio does to Katherine. History plays are also remembered. *Henry IV* is recalled when Pippin, Falstaff-like, questions the good of honor (5.4.790), while *Richard II* is echoed in Sam's recognition that he is fitted to be a gardener, not a ruler (6.1.881), and *Richard III* is remembered in the way Aragorn resembles Richmond when the day of battle is black (5.3.277–80) like the darkness which comes from Mordor (5.3.783). Moreover, both are aided by an army of the dead, and both come to claim a long-lost kingship which each of them seals by marriage (in fact the end of Gollum in Peter Jackson's film of *The Return of the King* is strikingly reminiscent of that of Ian McKellen's Richard III in Richard Loncraine's film of the play).

Nor is tragedy forgotten: one of the Tooks of the past was named Fortinbras (*Letters* 291), and the wheel of fire imagined by Frodo (6.3.910) recalls *King Lear*. That play is also echoed when Frodo, after his fall on the Emyn Muil, thinks he has gone blind (4.1.593) (a motif also found in the blindfolding in Lórien and Ithilien); when Prince Imrahil holds his vambrace to Éowyn's lips (5.6.827) as Lear watches Cordelia's; when the deposed Saruman is found wandering with Wormtongue (6.6.960–62) as Lear and the Fool do on the heath; and above all in the persistent play on the closeness between wisdom and folly (Gandalf at the Council of Elrond proposes "Let folly be our cloak!" [2.2.262]; Boromir views the plan to destroy the Ring as folly [2.10.389]; Denethor calls Gandalf "the Grey Fool" [5.7.835]; and when Frodo puts on the ring at the Crack of Doom Sauron understands his own folly [6.3.924]). The trees that walk and the Ringwraith who cannot be killed by any man of woman born evoke *Macbeth*, a play also alluded to when Tolkien writes in a letter speaks of how "being tied to the stake [I] stayed the course as best I could" (*Letters* 390) and when Sam says of Frodo: "If he screws himself up to go" (2.10.394).

It is, I think, significant that Shakespearean plays of a variety of genres are recalled in Tolkien, because his own work spectacularly defies traditional generic classifications. It is, therefore, unsurprising that the work of Shakespeare's to which *LotR* most insistently recurs is itself one which transcends genre, *The Tempest*, generally described only by the nonce-term "last play." Haldir refers to the Elves of Lórien as being on an island (2.6.339), something which has no basis in the actual situation but which both echoes the location of *The Tempest* and has obvious psychological resonance, especially given the wartime context of both the conception and the composition of *LotR*, and the importance of

Britain's island status both in its wartime defense and in Shakespeare's imagination. Gollum runs with bent back (2.6.340), recalling Sycorax, "who with age and envy / Was grown into a hoop" (1.2.259–60). Frodo is lost in wonder in Lórien and finds, like so many characters in *The Tempest*, that his language is inadequate for the description of what he sees: "A light was upon it for which his language had no name" (2.6.341). The falling towers towards the end of *The Return of the King* (6.3.925), too, closely recall Prospero's vision of dissolution in *The Tempest*:

> The cloud-capped towers, the gorgeous palaces,
> The solemn temples, the great globe itself,
> Yea, all which it inherit, shall dissolve [4.1.152–4].

Most notable are the parallels between Gollum and Caliban—a comparison which Tolkien himself made when he wrote to his son Christopher that Sam "treats Gollum rather like Ariel to Caliban" (*Letters* 77), and which others have since drawn: "The shadow is on the other side of our psyche, the dark brother of the conscious mind. It is Cain, Caliban, Frankenstein's monster, Mr. Hyde. It is Vergil who guided Dante through hell, Gilgamesh's friend Enkidu, Frodo's enemy Gollum" (Le Guin 53–54). Both Caliban and Gollum like glitter, as is seen when Gollum steals Frodo's cast-off mail shirt (6.2.904); both are isolates, with a suggestion of deformity or degeneration attached; both are linguistic outsiders who do not speak as those around them do— Gollum calls the moon the White Face (4.1.602) while Caliban refers to the sun and moon as "the bigger light and ... the less" (1.2.338)— and both plan treachery whilst their masters are asleep. Both are associated with fish, something all the more striking in Gollum's case because he has never actually seen the sea, though he dreams of fish from it (4.2.619); both function in their respective narratives as knowledgeable but unreliable guides to a strange environment. Both, too, have a claim to ownership with is acknowledged to varying degrees in their respective texts. Caliban says "This island's mine, by Sycorax my mother" (1.2.334), and though modern Shakespeare criticism has been much more willing to see the justice of this than the majority of Shakespeare scholars were in Tolkien's day, Tolkien himself was no unthinking supporter of Empire—he remarked that "the treatment of colour nearly always horrifies anyone going out from Britain ... Unfort. [*sic*] not many retain that generous sentiment for long" (*Letters* 73)—and he does fully register that Gollum had as much right to the ring as Bilbo. Even if Gollum's ultimate regaining of it will finally bring him nothing but death, it does save the world from Sauron—and perhaps we should notice here that what Sauron plans to do is in fact very close to the colonization of other lands.

The most striking point of comparison between Gollum and Caliban is, of course, that the relationship of Gollum and Frodo so clearly mirrors that of Prospero and Caliban. This thing of darkness Frodo does, indeed, acknowledge his, as he explains to both Sam and Faramir. Here, again, it might be possible to see a critique of *The Tempest*, or at least *The Tempest* as it was understood in the 1940s, for though Prospero does acknowledge Caliban, he does so in less than gracious terms, which the majority of Shakespeare scholars in Tolkien's day would have regarded the play as a whole as endorsing. In the case of Frodo and Gollum, however, there is not only a literal relationship—Gollum is of Hobbit descent—but a strongly established pattern in which, as Gandalf predicts, their two destinies prove to be inextricably interwoven, and in which the similarities between them ultimately matter more than the differences.

Translatio Imperii

I want to suggest that there are two principal effects of these parallels between Gollum and Caliban. The first relates to the idea of the *translatio imperii*. This is the idea that the cultural authority of Troy and Rome had been ultimately transferred to England via Brutus, great-grandson of the Trojan refugee Aeneas, who had allegedly traveled to Britain and named it after himself. Tolkien was well aware of this story, because *Sir Gawain and the Green Knight*, which he edited, opens with a retelling of how "fer ouer [th]e French flod Felix Brutus / On mony bonkes ful brode Bretayn he settez wyth wynne" (Tolkien and Gordon 1), an episode which Heide Estes argues is of considerable importance for the poem as a whole (Estes 65). Along with the idea of the *translatio imperii* traditionally went the analogous idea of the *translatio studii*, the transfer of knowledge and letters. Tolkien was acutely aware of attempting to create an epic for England: he told one correspondent that "I was from early days grieved by the poverty of my own beloved country: it had no stories of its own" (*Letters* 144), a second that his aim was "to restore to the English an epic tradition and present them with a mythology of their own" (231), and a third that the Eagles were a "machine," which he clearly meant in the sense of epic machinery (271). He knew, therefore, that he was working within the tradition established by Homer (who sang of the fall of Troy) and of Virgil (who hymned Aeneas), and above all Milton, who before turning to *Paradise Lost* had thought of an epic either on Macbeth or on King Arthur, another figure who is echoed in *LotR* in Aragorn the sword-claimer. Indeed Tolkien referred directly to both the relationship of his legendarium to North

Sea traditions, one of which he identifies as centering on an ancestor of the queen's (*Letters* 347), and to the fact that "The Mouths of Anduin and the ancient city of Pelargir are at about the latitude of ancient Troy" (376). *The Tempest*, with its Virgilian overtones and echoes and its motif of arrival in a new land, is a play deeply rooted in the idea of the *translatio imperii*: indeed Ferdinand's opening words to Miranda, "Most sure the goddess" (1.2.425) directly echo the first words spoken by Virgil's Aeneas on landing in Africa, "O dea certe" (see also Tudeau-Clayton). As such Tolkien's echoes of it may help us to see the extent to which *LotR* is a condition of England novel which is interested above all in the idea of the present's relation to the past, in the shape of the lost language of Númenor, with its obvious parallels to Latin (Tolkien told a correspondent that "The archaic language of lore is meant to be a kind of 'Elven-latin'" [176]), its ruins, its history of decadence, and the importance of the eagles who recall those which flew over Roman legions.

Evolution

The second reason I want to propose for Tolkien's interest in Caliban is evolution. In this respect, what matters is not just what Caliban might have meant to Shakespeare, but also the additional meanings which had accrued to him by the time Tolkien wrote. The first of these is the weight of subsequent literary reuses of the figure of Caliban, perhaps the most notable of which for my purposes was Mary Shelley's *Frankenstein* (Small 122–23,125), where the Monster, like Gollum, cannot correctly name the moon and becomes an outcast from society. Concomitantly, Mary Shelley's text was linked to the proto-evolutionary ideas being disseminated by Charles Darwin's grandfather Erasmus Darwin, whom Mary Shelley mentions. Caliban and evolution come together again in Aldous Huxley's *Brave New World* (first published in 1932), where genetic engineering triumphs in a world in which Shakespeare is outlawed, and in which John's Savage plays an ironic Caliban to Lenina's lustful Miranda. Evolution is also an important idea in *The Lord of the Rings* and indeed in Tolkien's work in general, and one to which the figure of Gollum and his relationship to Shakespeare functions as a key. "Three precious little Gollums in a row we shall be, if this goes on much longer," muses Sam (4.2.614); there is no such concern in Shakespeare, where Prospero acknowledges a relationship but is nevertheless a securely separate entity. This idea is, as we shall see, entirely characteristic of the cultural uses made of Shakespeare from the late nineteenth century, as too is the eugenic concern found in the remark that Prince Imrahil "was of high blood, and his folk also, tall men and proud with sea-grey eyes" (5.1.734).

The Lord of the Rings, and indeed all Tolkien's work, has deep roots in texts directly influenced by the idea of evolution. In George MacDonald's *The Princess and Curdie*, the sequel to *The Princess and the Goblin* and a text in which Tolkien was interested (*Letters* 178), the old princess with her light and water prefigures Galadriel, while her fire of renewal in turn recalls Ayesha. The monstrosity of MacDonald's goblins consists primarily in the fact that they have no toes; neither does Tolkien's troll (2.5.316), while the Ents have variable numbers of toes and fingers (3.4.469). Sources for Tolkien can also be traced in another children's writer, Rudyard Kipling, whose poem on the camel's hump and whose mode of describing the accompanying illustrations both anticipate *The Father Christmas Letters* (Kipling 24, 26).

Tolkien's most marked debt, however, is to Kipling's close friend Rider Haggard, who is also a strong influence on Lewis, and who wrote of the Africa where Tolkien was born and which he never ceased to remember (in letters, he noted that he had read several books on African exploration and referred several times to his early memories of Africa [*Letters* 30]). In *She and Allan* (1921), for instance, Allan and his party follow the Amahagger through a marsh in which there is foul gas and strange lights like will-o'-the-wisps, as in the Dead Marshes; later, smoking pipes, they look at the mountain which is their goal (Haggard 112–113, 126). Tolkien was also influenced by Bram Stoker, another writer keenly interested in evolution (see Hopkins, *Giants*). This is most strongly marked in *The Two Towers*, where Gollum's descent down the Emyn Muil so insistently recalls Harker's view of Dracula crawling down the walls of his castle:

> Down the face of a precipice, sheer and almost smooth it seemed in the pale moonlight, a small black shape was moving with its thin limbs splayed out. Maybe its soft clinging hands and toes were finding crevices and holds that no hobbit could ever have seen or used, but it looked as if it was just creeping down on sticky pads, like some large prowling thing of insect-kind. And it was coming down head first, as if it was smelling its way. Now and again it lifted its head slowly, turning it right back on its long skinny neck, and the hobbits caught a glimpse of two small pale gleaming lights, its eyes that blinked at the moon for a moment and then were quickly lidded again (4.1.598).

Compare this with Jonathan Harker's account of Dracula emerging from Castle Dracula:

> I saw the whole man slowly emerge from the window and begin to crawl down the castle wall over that dreadful abyss, *face down*, with

his cloak spreading out around him like great wings ... I saw the fingers and toes grasp the corners of the stones, worn clear of the mortar by the stress of years, and by thus using every projection and inequality move downwards with a considerable speed, just as a lizard moves along a wall (Stoker, *Dracula* 34).

Finally, there are also echoes of that other writer influenced by Stoker and Haggard, Buchan. Aragorn summons the dead by the Black Stone (5.9.856), the name of the conspiracy in *The Thirty-Nine Steps*, and in Buchan's *The Long Traverse* there is mention of a great forest called Mirkwood (36). In Buchan's short story "The Frying-pan and the Fire" we find the "glen of the Hollin" (202), and in *Huntingtower*, Mrs. Morran's cottage "had a green door and a polished brass knocker" (27), like Bilbo's, while Dickson the grocer buckling on his pack and taking his pipe on a journey (6), and later contemplating burglary (49), also recall Bilbo, and again it is jewels which are at stake and which Dickson must conceal on his person.

Haggard, Stoker and Buchan all draw strongly on Shakespeare (and in Haggard's case also on the story of the *translatio imperii*, since his African queen first lures a young man away from his duty and then dies by fire, just as Virgil's had done). In Buchan's *Prester John*, for instance, the obvious Shakespearean echo of "Unarm, Eros.... The long day's task is done" (181), from *Antony and Cleopatra*, is supplemented by the quieter invocation of *Richard III* in Laputa's accusation that "[y]ou stole my horse. That is why I am dying" (179), and Laputa himself from the outset obviously suggests Othello. As for Stoker, he was influenced in this as in so many other things by his close friendship and professional connection with the great Shakespearean actor Henry Irving, of whose Lyceum Theatre he was the stage manager, and consequently his works are full of allusions to Shakespearean plays, particularly but by no means exclusively those in which Irving appeared. Finally, Haggard's most famous novel, *She*, contains a sustained strand of reference to *Hamlet*. At the Amahaggers' party, we are told that "Caesar's dust—or is it Alexander's—may stop a bunghole, but the functions of these dead Caesars of the past was to light up a savage fetish dance" (211); this clearly alludes to Hamlet's speculations with Horatio on the fate of Caesar's dust, and when Ustane's body is dragged away through the curtains of Ayesha's boudoir (222) we may also recall Polonius, who seems again to be remembered at a significant moment when Holly notes that on the approach to the Place of Life "we went up like a crab, sideways" (258).

The Lord of the Rings, like its predecessors and indeed like all Tolkien's texts, is also configured by this confluence of Shakespearean allusion and evolutionary ideas. In his *Letters*, Tolkien wrote of his plan for a story in which "plants and animals change from one fantastic shape to another but men ... don't change at all" (81) and referred to the world as divided into Morlocks and Eloi (121); he also worried over whether "Elves and Men are evidently in biological terms one race, or they could not breed and produce fertile offspring" (189), and referred in overtly Darwinian terms to the "struggle for life" in his garden (402–3). In *The Hobbit*, the fish in Gollum's lake have clearly evolved: "their eyes grew bigger and bigger and bigger from trying to see in the blackness" (5.82). There are also strange flowers in Beorn's garden (7.131) and "Black emperor" butterflies in Mirkwood (8.159–60).

As for *LotR* itself, Tolkien concurred with a correspondent's idea that the Fell Beast ridden by the Witch-king was pterodactylic (*Letters* 282), and there are also many other signs of an interest in evolution. Hobbits, for instance, have changed noticeably over time: "they have dwindled, they say, and in ancient days they were taller" (Prologue 1–2)—a process which is reversed after Pippin and Merry drink of the Ent-draughts and subsequently grow. Gandalf tracks the kinship of Gollum and Bilbo rather as Darwin postulates common ancestry for finches, dogs, and horses (1.2.51), and we hear of the Men of Bree that "According to their own tales they were the original inhabitants and were the descendants of the first Men that ever wandered into the West of the middle-world" (1.8.146). As in evolutionary theory, change is a key word, and a key concept: the landscape in front of the entrance to Moria has changed (2.4.293); Gollum is changed when he appears at the Crack of Doom (6.3.922); and the steed of the Nazgûl also shows clear signs of evolutionary change:

> if bird, then greater than all other birds, and it was naked, and neither quill nor feather did it bear, and its vast pinions were as webs of hide between horned fingers; and it stank. A creature of an older world maybe it was, whose kind, lingering in forgotten mountains cold beneath the Moon, outstayed their day, and in hideous eyrie bred this last untimely brood, apt to evil (5.6.822).

At the close of the epic cycle, the entire Third Age will pass away, taking with it for ever many forms of life once familiar in Middle-earth, who will effectively have become extinct. Here again, though, the evolutionary perspective proves compatible with the religious one, for we are never in any doubt of the existence of a benevolent creator.[1]

In this context, it is worth noting that as well as the parallels between Frodo and Prospero, there are also parallels between Gandalf and Prospero, in that both are powerful and essentially benevolent controllers of magic. This introduces another aspect of the books, their interest in parallels, as when in *The Hobbit* "A pang of fear and loss, like an echo of Gollum's misery, smote Bilbo" (5.99), or as when Bilbo's transformation when he sees the Ring again (*LotR* 2.1.226) recapitulates and "fast-forwards" the change it has wrought in Gollum. This interest in parallels is something strongly marked in the films, where not only does Gollum's ongoing psychomachia clearly indicate that he is himself bifurcated into the two antithetical figures of Gollum and Sméagol, but he is also echoed by a number of other characters. The most obvious, and perhaps the most troubling, of these is Frodo, who looks at Gollum and says "I have to believe he can come back" and to whom Sam cries out "Can't you hear yourself? Don't you know who you sound like?" (*Two Towers* scene 28). To add to the complexity of the patterning here, when Frodo plunges into the Dead Marshes (which are themselves a mirroring surface) he recalls Déagol. In the theatrical cut of *The Two Towers* it is, significantly, immediately after this that Frodo identifies Gollum as Sméagol (scene 14), and as he does so he starts off another chain of echoing and resonance, because Gollum's response of "My name" anticipates Gandalf's similar reply when Aragorn addresses him by name: "That was what they used to call me" (scene 15). Moreover, the way Faramir watches Gollum's psychomachia clearly hints that he is experiencing one himself (*Two Towers* scene 42), while Jackson's film of *The Return of the King* is framed by images of Gollum and of Bilbo looking unnervingly similar (scenes 1, 76). In this context, the necessity of acknowledging one's own relationship to the thing of darkness seems urgent indeed. However, the predominance of doubling effects also emphasizes the importance of pattern and narrative order in the books, and serves as an emblem of overarching construction and control. In many nineteenth-century novels, written in the immediate aftermath of Darwinian theory, uncanny doublings work to echo the disturbing effect of Darwin's insidious suggestion that things which appear different—such as man and monkey—might be at base the same; to counteract this nightmare scenario, a sense of providential force often accrues to overt examples of narrative patterning in these novels, in a crude but comforting formula of author-is-like-God, and both are ultimately in control.

Pattern and Change

It is in this context, too, that the idea of the *translatio imperii* becomes important. For several nineteenth-century writers, the tradition of Trojan ancestry had provided a very comforting alternative to the Darwinian idea of descent from animals. Haggard is particularly prominent in this respect because the long recital of the Vinceys' unbroken descent from classical times at the start of *She* so obviously echoes the tradition of descent from Troy, just as Haggard's Africans echo the Greeks and Trojans of his friend Andrew Lang's reworking of the *Iliad*. Again, pattern and development are pitted against the idea of change as mere mutation or random adaptation. Tolkien was too good a scholar not to acknowledge the force of the evidence for evolution; it would indeed have been virtually impossible for him to ignore during the course of his long residence in Oxford, where the Natural History Museum contained the remains of the dodo which inspired Lewis Carroll while its next-door neighbor the Pitt-Rivers Museum encoded in its very structure an idea of gradual change as part of General Pitt-Rivers' philosophy of evolution rather than revolution (Van Keuren 1989).

Indeed the idea of pattern, particularly as it is emerges from chance or change, is crucial to the story of Middle-earth. In Tolkien's theory of "eucatastrophe" (*Letters* 100), the concept of hope is crucial: the books' mantra might well be Aragorn's words to Sam when Frodo is wounded, "Do not give up hope, Sam!" (1.12.198). In *The Hobbit* the dwarves in Mirkwood "would soon have come, if they could have kept up their courage and their hope, to thinner trees and places where the sunlight came again" (8.157), and *LotR* repeatedly stages moments when loss of hope causes an unnecessarily gloomy apprehension of the situation: Gandalf says of himself at Crickhollow, "Then for a while hope left me, and I did not wait to gather news, or I might have been comforted" (2.2.256); Legolas says of Boromir and Aragorn in the snow on Caradhras, "They despaired, until I returned and told them that the drift was little wider than a wall" (2.3.285); and most strikingly of all, as Tolkien himself noted to a correspondent, "Frodo's face goes livid and convinces Sam that he's dead, just when Sam gives up *hope*" (*Letters* 101). As Gandalf says, "No counsel have I to give to those that despair" (3.6.503), while Gandalf calls the Lord of the Ringwraiths "the Captain of Despair" (5.4.801) and, for all Tolkien's professed dislike of allegory, the encounter of Gandalf and Denethor over the bier of Faramir reads like an allegory of Hope meeting Despair (5.7.835).

This emphasis on hope matters particularly because ultimately, as Tolkien makes clear in a letter, he, like his nineteenth-century predecessors, sees God as the Writer of the Story (*Letters* 253), so this is a providential narrative. As Pippin so presciently says, "Whatever may be in store for old Gandalf, I'll wager it isn't a wolf's belly" (2.4.290); this is indeed a narrative with a *telos*, in which destiny plays a part, as when Faramir says to Sam, "If you seem to have stumbled, think that it was fated to be so" (4.5.666). Most notably, the Lord of the Nazgûl falls on the fifteenth of March (App. B. 1068), the day, as Shakespeare's *Julius Caesar* reminds us, on which Caesar died, while Sauron is defeated ten days, later on the 25th, which was, as the devoutly Catholic Tolkien would be well aware, the Feast of the Annunciation, being nine months before Christmas. The symbolism is sufficiently obvious.

In terms of construction of a providential narrative, allusion to Shakespeare, as so often in nineteenth-century counter-evolutionary texts, is an obvious card to play. Allusion to Shakespeare often provided a potent counter-discourse to oppose to the ideas of change and instability in human nature which had been suggested by Darwinian theory. This was particularly true of *Hamlet*, with its investigation of the human condition which, however bleak in other respects, at least never doubts the 'human' element of the equation. Indeed Shakespeare in general becomes, paradoxically, a crucial reference point for both evolutionary and counter-evolutionary discourses. The dichotomy so beloved of the Victorians between apes and angels can be traced back to *Measure for Measure*, where Isabella complains that man like "an angry ape / Plays such fantastic tricks before high heaven / As makes the angels weep" (2.2.125–27), and though the now clichéd phrase "*Hamlet* without the prince" may sound like one of those truisms which have no particular origin, "to leave the Prince out of *Hamlet*" appears in fact to have been first said by the dinosaur hunter Edward Drinker Cope as a critique of "Darwin's failure to recognize the progressive element in evolution" (Desmond 148); Cope used the metaphor to express his objection to *The Origin of Species*' implication that humanity did not represent the *telos* of species development. "On this new hypothesis of evolution 'what a piece of work is man!'" exclaims Daniel Wilson in *Caliban: The Missing Link* in 1873, before proceeding to argue of Shakespeare that "To him of all men the distinction between man and his lower fellow-creatures seemed clear and ineffaceable" (93, 188) (the equation between Caliban and the Missing Link was still being made nearly a century later by John Wain, the pupil of Tolkien's friend C. S. Lewis [Bratman 49]). In this context, the play's image of a man holding an obviously *human* skull plays resonantly against Victorian paleontologists' obsession with change and development in skulls.

The Tempest is a particularly suitable text in this respect, not only because the figure of Caliban had proved such a powerful recuperative tool for allowing nineteenth-century writers to assimilate the threatening new idea of evolution within the contours of the known, but also because it is a text which pits Art against Nature, staging its highly artificial masque of Juno, Iris and Ceres in provocative proximity to the much more crudely motivated rebellion of Caliban, Stephano, and Trinculo. It thus serves to highlight both the essential decadence of Elvish culture—something to which Tolkien drew repeated attention in his letters—and the extent to which this is ultimately bound to be dispossessed by the inexorable forces of change. As in Middle-earth at the close of the Third Age, the necessity of development is delicately weighted against what is beautiful, but doomed. Tolkien knew that the Elves were backward-looking, and that they would inevitably fade. He also, however, knew that without them there could be no narrative, any more than there can be much to say about Valinor in the years before Melkor blighted it. To hark back so insistently to a dramatist 400 years dead offers a powerful emblem of this, while also allowing Tolkien to recognize the power of change as embodied in evolution but simultaneously to assert the ultimate dominance of providential order and design, as a story which goes back to the Fall of Troy is seen to be still steadily unfolding.

Notes

1. On the acceptance of evolution by the Catholic Church, see, for instance, Gould.

Works Cited

Bratman, David. "Caliban between the Worlds." *Mythlore* 12.4 (1986): 48–53.
Buchan, John. "The Frying-pan and the Fire." In *The Best Short Stories of John Buchan*. Vol. 1. Ed. David Daniell. London: Panther, 1984. 197–232.
_____. *Huntingtower*. 1922. Far Thrupp, U.K.: Alan Sutton, 1993.
_____. *The Long Traverse*. 1941. Thirsk, U.K.: Stratus, 2001.
_____. *Prester John* .1910. Harmondsworth, U. .K.: Penguin, 1956.
_____. *She*. 1887. Harmondsworth, U.K.: Penguin, 1994
Desmond, Adrian. *Archetypes and Ancestors: Paleontology in Victorian London, 1850–1875*. London: Blond & Briggs, 1982.
Estes, Heide. "Bertilak Reads *Brut*: History and the Complications of Sexuality in *Sir Gawain and the Green Knight*." *Essays in Medieval Studies* 17 (2001): 65–79.
Gould, Stephen Jay. "Nonoverlapping Magisteria." *Natural History* 106 (1997): 16–22. Accessed 22 December 2005 at http://www.stephenjaygould. org/library/gould_noma.html
Haggard, H. Rider. *She and Allan*. 1921. London: Macdonald, 1960.
Hood, Gwenyth. "Sauron and Dracula." In *Dracula: The Vampire and the Critics*. Ed. Margaret L. Carter. Ann Arbor, MI: UMI Research Press, 1988. 215–30.
Hopkins, Lisa. *Giants of the Past: Popular Fictions and the Idea of Evolution*. Lewisburg, PA: Bucknell University Press, 2004.
_____. "*The Hobbit* and *A Midsummer Night's Dream*." *Mallorn* 28 (1991): 19–21.
Huxley, Aldous. 1946. *Brave New World*. London: Granada, 1977.
Kipling, Rudyard. 1902. *Just So Stories*. London: Macmillan, 1996.
Le Guin, Ursula K. "The Child and the Shadow." In *The Language of the Night*. New York: Berkley, 1979. 49–62.
The Lord of the Rings: The Return of the King. Special Extended DVD. Screenplay by Peter Jackson et al. Dir. Peter Jackson. 2002. DVD. New Line, 2003.
The Lord of the Rings: The Two Towers. Special Extended DVD. Screenplay by Peter Jackson et al. Dir. Peter Jackson. 2001. DVD. New Line, 2002.
Shakespeare, William. *The Complete Works of William Shakespeare*. Ed. David Bevington. 5th ed. New York: Pearson, 2004.

Small, Christopher. *Ariel Like a Harpy: Shelley, Mary and* Frankenstein. London: Gollancz, 1972.

Stoker, Bram. *Dracula.* 1897. Ed. A.N. Wilson. Oxford: Oxford University Press, 1983.

_____. *Personal Reminiscences of Henry Irving.* Vol. 1. London: William Heinemann, 1906.

Tolkien, J. R. R. *The Hobbit.* 2nd ed. Boston: Houghton, 1966.

_____. *The Letters of J.R.R. Tolkien.* Ed. Humphrey Carpenter. Boston: Houghton, 2000.

_____. *The Lord of the Rings.* 2nd ed. Boston: Houghton, 1994.

Tolkien, J.R.R., and E. V. Gordon, eds. *Sir Gawain and the Green Knight.* Oxford: Oxford University Press, 1967.

Tudeau-Clayton, Margaret. *Jonson, Shakespeare and Early Modern Virgil.* Cambridge: Cambridge University Press, 1998.

Van Keuren, David K. "Museums and Ideology: Augustus Pitt-Rivers, Anthropological Museums, and Social Change in Later Victorian Britain." In *Energy and Entropy: Science and Culture in Victorian Britain.* Ed. Patrick Brantlinger. Bloomington: Indiana University Press, 1989. 270–88.

Wilson, Daniel. *Caliban: The Missing Link.* London: Macmillan, 1873.

Of Two Minds

Gollum and Othello

CHARLES KEIM

If you turn to a handbook or companion guide to *The Lord of the Rings* for information on *Gollum*, you might be directed to look under the entry entitled *Sméagol*. On the other hand, if you look under *Sméagol*, you might be sent back to *Gollum*. Such duplicity is not due to the capriciousness of editors, but to an underlying and unresolved tension in the character himself. In this essay, I will argue that the psychology of Gollum is more complicated than we may initially believe; and to properly define the extraordinary psychology of Gollum, I will first examine the nature of his character as it develops from the time of his murder of Déagol to his final moments clutching his precious in the heart of Mordor. Rather than attempting to apply modern psychoanalytic terms or criteria to Gollum, I wish to demonstrate the literary connection existing between J.R.R. Tolkien and Shakespeare. In order to help us appreciate the psychological complexity of this fallen character, I believe that we need to reconsider the character of Othello. While Shakespeare's *Othello: The Moor of Venice* may seem more appropriate for a study that likens Gollum to the devilish Iago, it is in Shakespeare's depiction of Othello's tortured and divided consciousness that Tolkien may have found the crucial example of a character who has become alienated from himself. Even though Tolkien was not an enthusiastic supporter of Shakespeare's works, it is this very source that could have provided him with a convincing portrait of "one who loved not wisely but too well."

In his cinematic adaptation of *The Lord of the Rings*, Peter Jackson depicts Gollum as a single person housing two separate drives. We are all of us aware of the old cartoon image where the protagonist is depicted with a good angel on one shoulder and a fallen angel on the other. Typically, both sides plead the merits of their case before the central consciousness of the character (often while taking shots at the opposing side). In such a scenario, the character is shown to be much like a judge who must decide in favor of one voice; and while the results are often humorous, the opposing voices are but secondary figures, actors in a pseudo-courtroom drama, to the judiciary authority of the person on whose shoulders they are seated. For Marjorie Garber, Othello exemplifies *psychomachia*, the literary term defining the struggle between two forces for a man's soul; but the "tug-of-war with Othello at its center" is internal and external, occurring within Othello's mind and reflected in the depravity and purity of Iago and Desdemona (593). "Iago is the 'bad angel,' and Desdemona the 'good,'" Garber writes (613), even though they are both "real dramatic characters, not hallucinations" (593).

The bifurcated nature of Gollum is similar to this situation, since there are two voices vying for his authority within the larger battle between good and evil; but what is unique and disturbing is the seeming erosion of a consciousness to arbitrate between the voices. Sam labels what he sees to be the two sides of Gollum's character "Slinker" and "Stinker," and Jackson draws attention to this duplicity when he has Gollum speak to his reflection in the standing waters of Mordor (*Return of the King* scene 6). The effect Jackson achieves in this scene is a high point in the movie, and it visibly represents the loss of a central and unified consciousness while presenting the psychic turmoil of such a condition. Though looking upon the glassy water, Gollum is unable to reflect upon the consequences of his actions on future events from a central, stable perspective: he is both the face peering into the water and the watery image returning the gaze, and he is neither. Gollum is not schizophrenic, since both parts of his consciousness are completely aware of the other's presence, yet he cannot arbitrate between these two positions.

The chasm within Othello's divided self is less precipitous and is not given as much time to develop, which is to be expected given the demands of a stage drama that is viewed in one sitting. But after having been duped into arranging the death of his faithful Lieutenant and strangling his sweet Desdemona in her bed, Othello recognizes his terrible error and distances himself from what has been done by his hands. When Lodovico enters the scene with his officers, he asks, "Where is this rash and most unfortunate man?" Othello responds, "That's he that was Othello. Here I am" (5.2.291–2324). The reply points to a crucial Shakespearean invention, which is the depiction of a character who has disassociated his acts from himself. Othello's response implies a distance between the person talking and the person formerly known as Othello, who was a great and noble warrior. But unlike Gollum, Othello's consciousness is less evenly balanced, for when he takes himself by the throat and plunges his knife into his body, the fallen Othello offers no resistance. Gollum and Sméagol achieve an uneasy alliance, but while Shakespeare depicts Othello becoming distanced from what he has become, he does not present him locked in a psychic wrestling match with himself. His judgment on himself is as swift as a falling sword.

Gollum's psychology is divided more clearly than Othello's, and the epic allows Tolkien greater time and liberty to develop his character. In terms of the cartoon imagery I mentioned earlier, it is as though Gollum is the two voices pleading their cases; he is not a character who cannot make up his mind, but rather, one who has two minds. Further complicating this demarcation is the fact that neither side is wholly good. Gollum's "minds" do not embody the classic struggle of good and evil (*psychomachia*), a fact witnessed by their decision to join forces and regain the Ring from Frodo; nor have their sallies fully destroyed Gollum's central consciousness, which even late in the narrative comes to the surface when he declares, "I did escape" (4.3.629). The psychology of Gollum is complex and more difficult to define than his conversations with his watery reflection would imply. In particular, I wish to investigate the nature of his mental dilemma and explore how he has become disassociated from himself, for it is in this crucial aspect that Gollum comes to most closely resemble Othello, who in his fall conceives of himself as someone other than "he who was Othello."

Who Is Gollum?

In terms of the narrative, Gollum began as Sméagol, of the Stoor branch of hobbit-kind. This variety was the last to cross the Misty Mountains, and, at the time of Tolkien's epic, they had come to inhabit the Marish and Buckland regions, their preference being flat lands and riversides; of all the hobbits, this group alone enjoyed aquatic pursuits like swimming, fishing, and boating. And so it is while fishing that Déagol "happens" to catch the Ring, for which he is murdered by his cousin Sméagol, who then takes his "precious" into hiding by a lake beneath the Misty Mountains. The title "Gollum" refers to Sméagol's repugnant habit of noisily clearing his throat, and from the outset he is of questionable integrity.

We first encounter Gollum in *The Hobbit* when Bilbo Baggins comes upon a cold, gloomy lake while trying to find his way out of the labyrinthine passageways beneath the Misty Mountains. There lives Gollum, who makes his wretched home on a slimy island of rock in the middle. Though his possessions are meager, he unwittingly counts among them that on which the entire destiny of Middle-earth rests—his most treasured "precious." It is surprising that his use of the Ring is occasional, since his existence revolves around its intoxicating possession. At first, he wore it continually, but soon discovered that it was the Ring that was wearing him out; then he kept it in a pouch next to his skin, until the potency of its evil "galled him" (5.91). We find that he now keeps it hidden in a small hole in the rock on his island, to which he feverishly and compulsively returns to look upon its circular beauty and singular perfection. If a goblin should happen to wander down to this watery region, however, Gollum slips on the Ring and strangles it from behind; should the demands of his appetite warrant it and his courage support it, he may also use the Ring to sneak undetected into the goblins' territory and hunt them there.

In the original version of Bilbo's meeting with Gollum (1937), Tolkien had presented a tamer, less malevolent picture of this creature; but in the second edition (1951), Gollum is a much darker and more complex figure. More importantly, for the concerns of this essay, Tolkien originally used the phrase "my precious" as Gollum's reference to himself, while the second edition makes the phrase appear to refer to the Ring (*Annotated Hobbit* 120n8). This revision is crucial for the integrity of the trilogy, since it shows that even at this early stage Gollum's psychological state is divided. He cannot refer to himself as "my precious" because he has lost a sense of himself as a unified and coherent consciousness—he is comprised of two "I's," two unmediated and uncontrolled drives that seek to impose their own will upon him.

The "blessing" of the Ring is its curse. After Gollum overtakes him in the tunnel and races past, less than a yard away, Bilbo comes to realize that wearing the Ring makes one invisible. Only in the dazzling light of the midday sun, the narrator tells us, can the wearer's shadow be seen, and then only faintly by keen eyes. But I want to suggest that the invisibility offered by the Ring intimates its metaphorical consequences, since wearing it similarly occludes the individual's consciousness. The voices that the characters hear within themselves are positions or stances that the character must decide to follow or abandon; but the Ring seriously impairs an individual's ability to mediate between their various internal drives, as though rendering the individual both physically and psychically invisible.

In this way, Gollum is unique among the villains presented in *The Hobbit* and *The Lord of the Rings* (*LotR*). Unlike the other dark characters, Gollum is neither wholly evil, nor does he pursue his "precious"

with a determination that is single-minded; and Gollum expresses little interest in using the Ring to rule Middle-earth. Tolkien depicts him
carrying on an inner dialogue as he weighs the options between selfishness and selflessness; as the narrative progresses, however, his inward
state becomes increasingly divided and antagonistic, essentially cleav-
ing his consciousness into two separate halves. This separation is not
unlike the internal conversation of Sam when he convinces himself to
embark on the final ascent of Mount Doom: "'I'll get there, if I leave
everything but my bones behind,' said Sam. 'And I'll carry Mr. Frodo
up myself, if it breaks my back and heart. So stop arguing!'" (6.3.918).
The crucial difference between Sam Gamgee and Gollum is that Sam
is able to negotiate between these two positions; that is, he weighs his
options and then decides what he will do. He enjoys the possession of
a stable consciousness that can evaluate, discern, and choose between
the voices in his head, all of which are evidence of a healthy mental
state; and it is this stable ego, this ability to arbitrate, that we would say
is Sam, who chooses not to turn back but to press on. It is a tribute to
his iron will that Sam not only pledges to give his all for Frodo, but also
terminates the interior discussion to pursue physical action. Gollum
enjoys no such happy state: he is suspended between his own contrary
impulses.

When Bilbo first meets him, all he sees of Gollum are two "pale
eyes sticking out at him" (*Hobbit* 2.83). Just before this meeting, the
narrator describes him as "dark as darkness, except for two big round
pale eyes in his thin face" (5.82). Bilbo likens these eyes to "green
lamps," as though he can see through these windows of the soul to the
jealousy and envy that consume this slimy creature; and yet I think that
we can also see Tolkien preparing us for an interpretation of Gollum
as two "I's." In *LotR*, Gollum refers to himself in the plural, not the singular. And, like his two big eyes, he is defined by the two individual
minds, Gollum and Sméagol, that both desire autonomy.

Who Is Othello?

Bilbo sees in Gollum's eyes "green lamps" (5.94) and Iago cautions
Othello about the perils of jealousy; it is, he says, "the green-eyed monster, which doth mock / The meat it feeds on" (3.3.178–79). Othello,
like Gollum, abandons precaution and becomes wholly consumed by
jealousy; while Gollum jealously pursues the Ring, it is Othello's jealousy and sense of injured merit that brings him to destroy his most precious Desdemona. Who is this valiant Moor and how is it possible that
he should commit such a grim crime? In truth, we know surprisingly

little of this famous character. He is a Moor, which means that he is presumably of North African descent (where Mauritania, the place of origin of the "Moors," was located); but criticism has yet to resolve the question of how dark his complexion is. Iago refers to him as an "old black ram," a "Barbary horse," and as having "thick lips"; however, we should be on our guard when listening to the vengeful Ancient, for the Duke is correct in reminding Brabantio that his "son-in-law is far more fair than black" (1.3.293). More importantly, Othello is the character least at home in the tragedy—he is the Moor *of* Venice. Since he is not a native of Venice, he is in the peculiar position of protecting a country to which he does not belong. Even his marriage to the daughter of a Venetian senator cannot place him in the inner circle of Venetian society—he is an outsider.

In arguing that we can locate Gollum's precursor in the figure of Othello, let me first note some of the differences between their characters. Othello is less responsible for his own downfall. Unbeknownst to him, Iago is working his devilish magic, contaminating the perspective of Othello so that he will believe the virtuous Desdemona to be stealing moments of affection with Cassio. Iago is, as Harold Goddard says, a "moral pyromaniac" (77). He is completely at home in the play, and there is no other character that is able to counteract his venomous plans. If only we had a Hamlet or a Falstaff to expose his malicious ploys, then we would not have to wait for Emilia, his wife, to bring his duplicitous acts to light. But this is false hope, for there is no Gandalf, Aragorn, or other medicinal person to immunize Othello from Iago's charms, and we are left to watch Iago perform his devilish magic unchallenged.

Othello is a type of war god, a tremendous warrior who has but to utter eleven menacing monosyllabic words to immediately quell a possible street riot: "Keep up your bright swords, for the dew will rust them" (1.2.59). Othello himself presents the scant historical details we discover. If we are to trust him, we find that his career began at the tender age of seven (1.3.85), he was sold into slavery (1.3.140), and his battles have taken him into exotic regions of the globe (1.3.141–47). Presumably, Othello has converted to Christianity, since he refers to himself as "circumcisèd" (5.2.365). Regardless of this ritual, however, Othello's dark skin marks him forever as someone other than the "curled darlings" of Venice. Psychologically, the consequences of Othello's fall are every bit as unnerving as Gollum's, since by the midpoint of the play we begin to hear Othello refer to himself in the third person, as though he inhabits some point outside of himself or is an actor watching the drama of his character "strut and fret his hour" upon the stage. Despite his valor, he will always be an outsider, someone who is of Venice but not a Venetian; ironically his marriage to Desdemona further alienates him from the society that he guards and has married into. Emotionally, Othello's fall exacts a tremendous toll on the audience. Dr. Samuel Johnson famously remarked that because the play was so painful he could bring himself to read it only once. By contrast, we encounter Gollum only as the fallen pursuer of the Ring, and we learn of his earlier life as Sméagol from someone else. In this way, we do not come to invest in him as an unambiguously sympathetic character; only in his moral ruins do we come to know him, even though the tremendous loss offers glimpses of a creature once potentially good.

It is Othello's presence as an alien, a dark, unknown person that most galls Brabantio, who manifests his racism by happily listening to Othello's stories and embracing his protection, while considering the prospect of him as a son in law opprobrious. So it is that Brabantio disrupts the Venetian war council to have them interrogate the nature of Othello's marriage to his daughter. In responding to these imprecations, Othello provides a moving, beautifully articulated speech chronicling his past while giving fair grounds for his courting of the lovely Venetian:

> the battle, sieges, fortunes...
> Of moving accidents by flood and field,
> Of hairbreadth scapes i'th'imminent deadly breach,
> Of being taken by the insolent foe
> And sold to slavery, of my redemption thence
> And portance in my travels' history [1.3.132–41].

In addition to his personal adventures, Othello speaks of the strange places and people that he has encountered, of cannibals and the men "whose heads / Do grow beneath their shoulders" (1.3.146–47). Small wonder, then, that Desdemona should "seriously incline" and devour his discourse with a "greedy ear"; in fact, Othello's powerful rhetoric has a similar effect on his audience, for the Duke immediately responds by conjecturing that this tale would "win my daughter too." Othello's grand speech endears him to his audience, and it is important to recognize the nobility and power of his speech so that we can appreciate more fully the magnitude of his fall.

To turn from this eloquent speech to Othello's later conversations with Iago and Desdemona is to witness a monumental transformation in his language. Gone are the subtle phrases and delicate constructions, gone are the references to exotic and mysterious places, gone is the warm love that he had for his delicate bride. In abandoning his noble rhetoric, Othello embraces the cold, warlike, and bestial language of Iago. Earlier, we heard of Iago's distasteful reference to Othello and

Desdemona's act of nuptial intimacy as "making the beast with two backs" (1.1.119–20); but once he suspects his wife, Othello declares that he "had been happy if the general camp, / Pioneers and all, had tasted her sweet body, / So had I nothing known" (3.3.361–63). He accompanies this repulsive analogy by asking Iago to be sure to "prove my love a whore" (3.3.375); and yet before any proof has been found, he exclaims, "Damn her, lewd minx" (3.3.491). Not only is there a general contracting of Othello's speech, but he adopts Iago's fondness for animal imagery, too. Desdemona notices this change that has come over him, asking him why he speaks "so startingly and rash" (3.4.81). As readers, the degenerative effects of Othello's transformation are fully realized when we hear him reply to Iago's specious remembrance of Cassio's lusty dream of Desdemona: "—Pish! Noses, ears, and lips?—Is't possible?—Confess—handkerchief!—O devil!" (4.1.42–43). The audience is forgiven if they find Othello's speech impenetrable, for the images are brusquely joined without the mediation of a mind contextualizing them, as though he were speaking in a type of shorthand or synecdoche. Garber notes how the "[l]oss of language here, as elsewhere in Shakespeare, is emblematic of loss of humanity" (612). The crumbling of consciousness is visibly portrayed by the stage directions, which call for the actor playing Othello to fall into a trance after delivering these lines.

If Othello's language, like Gollum's, reflects his psychological deterioration, his actions, too, visibly signal his internal decline. Though he may not strangle goblins, Othello commits a far more gruesome act than Gollum by strangling his innocent Desdemona in her bed. The entire play has been building toward this terrible act, and with its completion and the revelation of Iago's treachery, Othello recoils and judges himself, a judgment that cries out for his own blood. The execution is immediate: "I took by th' throat the circumcisèd dog / And smote him, thus" (5.2.365–66). The animal imagery invoked earlier by Othello and earliest by Iago reaches its grim end in the Moor's definition of himself as a "circumcisèd dog."

Gollum or Sméagol?

The ritual of circumcision recalls the original covenant established between Abraham and God (Genesis 17:9–14), where the physical act was intended to consciously declare the new external and immutable covenant between God and Abraham. It marked the individuality of each Jew and the beginning of his spiritual life. From early times, the practice took on a symbolic importance, representing new life; it was

invested with a spiritual import that silently declared dedication and
fidelity to the Hebrew God. Othello is circumcised; but, like his marriage, the act has not initiated him into the larger cultural context.
Though Tolkien's narrative is situated as occurring long before the time
of the Hebrew scriptures, Gollum finds himself in a similar situation,
since he began as a hobbit but is now someone who is neither fish nor
fowl, so to speak. Later in the narrative, when Frodo fights off Gollum's
attempt for the Ring, the narrator sees this creature as a "lean, starved,
haggard thing" (6.3.922). "Thing" may also apply to the noble Othello,
for while his circumcision visibly identifies him as no longer a Moor,
his skin proclaims that he is not and never can be a Venetian.

Gollum has come to a similar point but in opposite fashion, for he
is a hobbit that can no longer be identified as such—he incarnates a
type of physiological no man's land. Like his physical person, Gollum's
core identity is uncertain, and it is witnessed not only by the question
of what name he should be indexed under, but also in the hobbits'
response to him. In Garber's discussion of Othello, she repeatedly draws
attention to the binary poles embedded in the play. Not only do Desdemona and Iago stand at two ends of the spectrum, but there is also
"Venice and Cyprus. Light and darkness. Black and white" (592). These
categories are complicated by Shakespeare, however, for while "Othello
looks black ... it is Iago who becomes the pole of moral negativity" (592).
The difficulty in understanding Gollum is that *psychomachia* cannot be
applied as easily to him as to Othello. Gollum/Sméagol does not constitute two forces battling for supremacy, and our understanding is further
problematized by the responses of the hobbits, who themselves seem
unsure of him. In addition, while Iago and Desdemona function as a
type of objective correlative to Othello, crystallizing the moral poles he
vacillates between, there are no characters serving this role for Gollum.

Neither is there evidence that Gollum has internalized the moral
positions held by Iago and Desdemona, because it is never clear whether
Gollum operates only out of selfishness, a concern for a higher moral
principle, or necessity. Sam and Frodo cannot be sure that he can be
trusted, since he may very well follow them, as Iago follows Othello, to
"serve his own ends." It is precisely this uncertainty and the danger it
holds that compels Sam to warn Frodo of trusting Gollum. In naming
the two aspects of Gollum "Slinker" and "Stinker," Sam signals his own
distrust and disgust, Slinker being an only slightly less reprehensible
character than Stinker. Sam conjectures that Gollum is the "dark side"
or alter ego of "the long submerged Sméagol"; and it is Stinker who
plots the capture of "precious," who casts the stones at Sam, bites the
ring-bearing finger off of Frodo, and who "overbalances" and falls into
the river of lava. But Slinker is inextricably bound up in this drama as

well, for Slinker seems a willing accomplice in the machinations of Stinker. Furthermore, Sam sees in Slinker's eyes an abiding desire for the ring, a desire that will gleefully employ the treachery of Stinker. Sméagol may well be submerged, but he was never someone who could be trusted in the first place. His murder of Déagol, for instance, was made all the more alarming by the alacrity of his decision and his lack of remorse.

Even though Sam is not sympathetic to Gollum, he does use two names to refer to him. In this way, even the skeptical Sam recognizes in this character two "people." And so does Frodo. But he possesses a special knowledge of the torment that Gollum endures, since he too knows the tremendous burden and perilous attraction of the Ring. Despite Sam's continual suspicion, he retains an abiding empathy for Gollum, an empathy that informs his final decision to spare him on the gloomy heights of Mount Doom. "At last I can deal with you," Sam threatens with "drawn blade ready for battle" (6.3.923). But Sam does not take Gollum's life into his own hands; instead he defers the decision to the hand of fate.

That Sam's decision is informed by an abiding belief in the power of Sméagol to overcome Gollum is unlikely; but Frodo does express trust in some old vestiges of good still present in this character. When Sam and Frodo finally meet this tricky fellow at the broken feet of the Emyn Muil, Frodo refers to him by both his names, and not the ones used by Sam, either. Replying to Gollum's plea for life, Frodo answers that they will not kill him. "'But we won't let you go, either. You're full of wickedness and mischief, Gollum. You will have to come with us, that's all, while we keep an eye on you'" (4.1.601). There is a subtle irony in Frodo's words, since while they will try to "keep an eye" on Gollum, it is only through his cunning that they will navigate a path to the Fire of Mount Doom while avoiding the evil "eye" of Sauron.

But after stating their intention to keep a close eye on Gollum, Frodo replies to his question of where they are planning to go with the Ring by saying, "You know that, or you guess well enough, Sméagol.... We are going to Mordor, of course. And you know the way there, I believe" (4.1.601). Frodo's address is extraordinary. Nothing has changed in the intervening lines, and, throughout this section, the narrator refers to Gollum as Gollum, not Sméagol. Does Sméagol know Mordor in a way that Gollum does not? Both beings have passed through those dark lands; and it would seem more likely that Gollum would have discovered the hidden path than Sméagol. Yet, since Frodo refers to Sméagol, not Gollum, as knowing the way to Mordor, and since Gollum does not protest and claim glory, we can surmise that both sides are equally knowledgeable of the dangerous path.

Frodo's response to Gollum further complicates our reading of this psychologically dynamic character. "You're full of wickedness and mischief, Gollum," Frodo asserts; are we to assume that he is here referring to the creature before him, or to that part of the creature that is known as Gollum? If Frodo really believes that Gollum is wholly wicked and mischievous, then he could not be trusted to guide them to Mordor; furthermore, if Gollum were fully wicked, there would be no psychological divergence within him. But either Gollum is not wholly bent on evil or else his power is limited, which Frodo acknowledges when he says, "twice now we have been in your power, and you have done no harm to us" (4.3.626). At this point, we verge on committing the error of interpreting Gollum and Sméagol as two sides of a single character rather than separate personalities within a single body; but we still cannot be certain that it is Gollum who is full of wickedness and Sméagol who can be trusted. Sméagol is not the unfallen Gollum, nor does he represent an innate sense of goodness. He is as desperate as Gollum to retrieve the Ring. It was Sméagol, after all, who first murdered Déagol for it.

Frodo is a resourceful hobbit, one whose intelligence compensates for his size and relative physical weakness. And it would seem more than serendipity that he invokes the name of Sméagol when trying to get him to act in a manner worthy of his trust. Gollum may well be "full of wickedness and mischief," but Sméagol is another matter, and in crediting him with the knowledge of Mordor's secret entrance, Frodo appeals to the embers of morality that may still smolder in him. In reprimanding the baseness of Gollum, Frodo exposes the baseness of his motives to the eyes of Sméagol. Twice the hobbits have been spared; twice Gollum's malice has been subverted: might they now trust him for a third time?

Sam's cautionary names find their counterpart in Frodo, who recognizes the treachery of Gollum and the knowledge of Sméagol, for which they have great need. Both Sméagol and Gollum know the hidden pathway into Mordor, since both of them have clearly made the journey, psychology not being something that one abandons at the boundaries of a country. What is fascinating to consider, however, is how Sméagol refers to himself when describing his explorations. An anonymous and detached voice relates his exploits: "There is another way.... Another way, darker, more difficult to find, more secret. But Sméagol knows it. Let Sméagol show you!" (4.3.624). It could be argued that this is Sméagol talking, but whoever is talking is not claiming responsibility. The speaker does not use "I" as Sméagol normally does when referring to his own actions. Instead, we are told that Sméagol knows of another way into Mordor and he is willing to guide our hobbits along it. We have, however, not come any closer to discovering who this speaker is that knows Sméagol's secrets but is not Sméagol.

Gollum implies that it is Sméagol who knows of another way into the land of Mordor: "Yess! Yess indeed! There *was* another way. Sméagol found it. Let's go and see if it's still there!" (4.3.624). That Gollum refers specifically to Sméagol, rather than saying "I" or "we," tacitly acknowledges a time when he was not submerged but dominant. If indeed it was Sméagol who discovered the alternate path, then would not Gollum be as aware of it as him? "Let's go," the voice counsels; and yet the plural can refer to Gollum, Sam, and Frodo, as well as to Gollum/Sméagol. The difficulty that we face in attempting to separate Gollum from Sméagol is that we cannot know if there was a time when they were separate. Was it the murder of Déagol that gave birth to Gollum, or was it the Ring and its power to pervert that slowly formed him?

We cannot be sure if Gollum could still resist his evil motives and embrace right action, but we can assuredly say that he is still capable of referring to himself as an "I." When Frodo questions him about the possibility of a third passage (Cirith Ungol), Gollum replies that though fraught with peril it will allow passage into the dark land. But first Sam and Frodo wish to know whether Gollum escaped or was set free by the enemy; in short, can they trust him to lead them into Mordor without delivering them over to Sauron? "I did escape," Gollum protests, "The Precious was ours, it was mine I tell you. I did escape" (4.3.629). Immediately, Frodo is struck by this response: "he noted that Gollum used *I* [which seemed to indicate] that some remnants of old truth and sincerity were for the moment on top" (4.3.629). It is a tribute to Tolkien's optimism that even at this stage in the narrative, after Gollum has carried his precious for hundreds of years (he carried the Ring from 2463 to 2941), a vestige of hope remains.

It is a dimming hope, however, and one that flickers in the shadow of his increasing desire. Later in the narrative, Frodo himself recognizes the difficulty of knowing how to address such a divided character: "Come now, Gollum or Sméagol if you wish, tell me of this other way" (4.3.626). Frodo's twofold reference is sympathetic and diplomatic, recognizing the rift within Gollum while placing the burden of identification on him: which name does he use? Despite his depravity, the character Frodo calls Gollum never wholly loses the latent promise incarnated in the person of Sméagol. When Sam brandishes his blade on the gloomy heights of Mount Doom, Sméagol responds not with Gollum-like ferocity but rather falls prostrate and begs for his life: "Don't kill us.... Let us live, yes, live just a little longer. Lost lost! We're lost" (6.3.923). Frodo had placed the burden of identity on Gollum, but

Gollum himself resists this identification, choosing instead to refer to himself in the plural.

This is a significant turn of phrase. Gollum says that they are lost, and since he has been carefully guiding Sam and Frodo to this physical location and is familiar with the geography of Mordor, then he must be referring to his mental (spiritual?) state. Yet are we to understand that both Gollum and Sméagol are lost? That Gollum should be lost strikes us as sound doctrine and just, given the terrible deeds he has committed; but should Sméagol be lost, too? If they are both lost, then it upsets an easy understanding of their relationship that would see the loss of Gollum as the salvation of Sméagol. Or are we to see that they are both lost because they have become locked in a kind of psychic stalemate that will not allow either side to gain the upper hand? But such an impasse would condemn this character to a continual wringing of the hands; that is, he would only agonize over a decision without ever being able to make one. Gollum suffers from no such paralysis of the will, however, and even with his divided consciousness there is a considerable amount of plotting and persuasion exerted by each side to further its own interests. Perhaps Gollum says that they are "lost" because the continual internal skirmishes have eroded the authority of a central consciousness that could mediate between the competing interests. We cannot be sure. Nonetheless, it is abundantly clear by this point in the narrative that Gollum is not an "I" but rather a collection of "I's," like the two big pale eyes that define his physical person in *The Hobbit.* And this brings a profound irony to light; namely, that in pursuing self-interest within the dominion of the evil "eye" of Sauron, Gollum has lost his sense of selfhood—he has become "I-less."

This is not to say, however, that Sméagol does not desire the Ring as voraciously as Gollum, since both sides of his character are united in their yearning for its possession, though unwilling to share it with the other. As Sam carries Frodo up the final ascent of Mount Doom, he is knocked to the ground by a rock hurled by Gollum, who hisses, "Wicked masster cheats us; cheats Sméagol, *gollum.* He mussntn't go that way. He musstn't hurt Preciouss. Give it to Sméagol, yess, give it to us! Give it to uss!" (6.3.922). The alliteration of "s" sounds produces an effect similar to that of a serpent, and Gollum's physical posture reflects the magnitude of his moral depravity, since he is now bent forward on all fours, more closely resembling an animal than a hobbit. And, as his desire for the Ring increases, so is he drawn ever more closely to the earth, until his final fall into the river of lava in Mount Doom.

But now I wish to draw attention to Gollum's words to Sam. Since we have been following the fortunes of Gollum and tend to place the burden of depravity on him, it is surprising to then hear Sméagol, not

Gollum asking for the Ring: "give it to Sméagol, yess, give it to us! Give it to uss!" Given what we know of him should it not be Gollum who is asking for the ring? It may be objected that Gollum is in fact in charge and is using the name Sméagol to aid his case, but such a conjecture diminishes what we know to be true—both Gollum and Sméagol are fallen; both want the Ring. It is wildly ironic that the Ring should momentarily unite them, since it was a desire for and possession of the Ring that marked the genesis of Gollum and drove the psychic wedge between him and Sméagol.

His years spent with the Ring have exacted a tremendous price. His deteriorated mental condition is reflected in his physical body; he is now but a whisper of his former self, crawling on all fours like a beast. Not only has his visage suffered the ravages of evil, but his speech has been coarsened, too. When Bilbo first meets him, it is Gollum's hiss combined with his wretched swallowing sound that cause him to jump "nearly out of his skin" (5.83). The degradation he has suffered is symptomatic of the Ring's power, since Frodo, too, feels its terrible weight around his neck drawing him closer to the ground.

In this manner, we can see many similarities between the degeneration of Gollum and John Milton's depiction of Satan in *Paradise Lost*. Satan begins first as Lucifer, the unfallen Seraph; but with his lust for power and rebellion against God and subsequent exile to hell, Satan loses his beauty and brightness. Throughout Milton's epic, Satan declines. Seeking to turn Adam and Eve from God, he sneaks into their bower at night so that he might, "forge / Illusions as he list, Phantasms and Dreams" (4.803–4), and there Gabriel and his band of angels find Satan, "Squat like a Toad, close at the ear of Eve" (4.800). In contrast to his former upright state, Satan is now, like Gollum, down on all fours, resembling a beast; and even though he resumes his former shape when confronted by Gabriel, he remains unrecognizable. "Know ye not mee?" Satan asks incredulously. That his former "colleagues" do not recognize him demonstrates the magnitude of Satan's disfigurement, since he fell less than three weeks previous.

Satan's disfigurement continues when he enters the mouth of the serpent and assumes his body to tempt Eve (9.186), and he experiences his ultimate humiliation later, in hell, when,

> His visage drawn he felt to sharp and spare,
> His arms clung to his Ribs, his Legs entwining
> Each other, till supplanted down he fell
> A monstrous Serpent on his belly prone
> Reluctant, but in vain: a greater power
> Now rul'd him, punisht in the shape he sinn'd [10.511–16].

Satan would speak and tell his angels of his achievement, but in the place of words, "hiss for hiss return'd" (10.518). Gollum is not a serpent, nor is he supernaturally transformed into one. Yet like his physical posture, he has become more like a serpent than a hobbit, though he is neither. Like Satan after his fall from the bright morning star known as Lucifer, Gollum no longer reflects the original unspoiled potential of Sméagol. And, like Satan, should he have seen what he was to become and the magnitude of his suffering, he would have recoiled in disgust and fear.

The Fall of Othello

There is a certain grim irony in comparing Othello and Gollum, since both characters die clutching their precious; for both of them, death has come at their own hands, and only in their death is a moral balance restored to the world they inhabit. The concept of balance is crucial, I think, not only because Gollum loses his balance and falls into the river of lava, but because both of them lose their psychic balance. The distinction between Gollum and Sméagol is more apparent than that found in the unwinding of Othello's consciousness. While Othello originally responded to Brabantio's allegations with poise, panache, and an unflagging conviction of himself as incorporating the varied roles of warrior/protector/groom, Iago's poison later infects his mind and subverts this uneasy alliance, compelling him to question and renounce his former identity:

> Farewell the tranquil mind! Farewell content!
> Farewell the plumèd troops and the big wars
> That make ambition virtue!
> ...
> Farewell! Othello's occupation gone (3.3.364–73).

It is curious that Othello should so rashly disavow himself from his station, because Iago has only suggested Desdemona's infidelity—no ocular proof has been sought or found. Yet Othello already declares his farewell to arms, implying that all has been lost and, like Brabantio, that his worst fears have been realized. Othello's identity is inextricably bound up in the pomp and circumstance of war, the "plumèd troops and the big wars." And so his moving farewell to his former occupation must by necessity involve a farewell to the Othello of that realm; such an adieu nonetheless carries with it the ache of memory and the sobering realization of how much has been lost.

But how does one disassociate from that which has driven and defined one's life? Slowly, it would seem, for Othello is not immediately transformed into a person who views himself from a point outside of himself. It is not until after the final, terrifying bedroom scene and Othello's discovery of the magnitude of Iago's deception that he retreats from the horror that he has become. Even after Desdemona is strangled, Othello continues to refer to himself in the first person as he contends with Emilia over Desdemona's fidelity and Iago's honesty. But when the truth is revealed and Othello finds himself at his "journey's end," he asks, "Where should Othello go?" (5.2.280). His reference to himself in the third person does not mark a definitive turn, since in his penultimate speech he petitions his audience to "speak of me as I am"; but his psychological condition is not so stable as it was in the beginning, for he then immediately speaks of himself as "one that loved not wisely but too well" (5.2.354).

The impersonal pronoun "one" prepares us for his final act of disassociation when he asks them to set down this:

> And say besides that in Aleppo once,
> Where a malignant and a turbaned Turk
> Beat a Venetian and traduced the state,
> I took by th' throat the circumcisèd dog
> And smote him, thus (5.2.362–66).

In stabbing himself, Othello carries out his final act of justice, restoring the balance of the play, though not mitigating the force of the tragedy. Interestingly, unlike Tolkien, Shakespeare allows his supreme villain to live on; true, Iago is wounded and he is promised future torture, but he is alive. What is most central to our treatment of Shakespeare's influence, however, is the way in which he has Othello refer to himself. It is surprising to witness Othello's suicide, because on first hearing him speak he seems to be referring to someone else. What is especially troubling is Othello's use of the word "I." Who or what is this I of which he speaks? And since he is "the circumcisèd dog" that he has taken by the throat, how is it that he can interpret himself as the executor of justice and not as the executed? Recoiling from the horror of his misjudgment and monstrous act, Othello psychologically removes himself. He refers to himself in the third person, and by doing so he establishes a critical distance between him and his self.

As with Gollum, we cannot interpret Othello as schizophrenic, but we do recognize that he is of two minds. The Othello who has committed the heinous act of strangling his innocent wife does not visibly protest his fate. For Othello to die is an act of mercy, since who could live with the knowledge of such dark deeds? Only Iago, who has fully committed himself to carrying out his sinister designs while reveling in their insidious fruition, seems capable of living in the shadow of his art. Throughout the entire play, no evidence can be found of Iago questioning his own motives: he does not hesitate or waver in his plan to reduce the world of Othello to ashes. Though Iago enjoys eight soliloquies (Othello only three), never once do we encounter him engaged in a soul-baring internal dialogue. Unlike the Satan of *Paradise Lost* or even Othello himself, Iago wholly embraces his own dark genius, and in so doing, he enjoys the possession the stable and unified consciousness—he is at war with everything *outside* of himself.

Unlike Iago, Othello's war is almost entirely an inward war; and it is a war that he is ill equipped to fight. A war against the Turkish fleet may well have provided Othello with the necessary salve for Iago's insinuations; but with the destruction of the fleet by natural causes, the warrior is stripped of his context. Earlier, Othello had protested to the Venetian senate that he would not "scant" the business of the state, though taking his new bride along with him to Cyprus might seem a conflict of interest. In truth, he declares, the moment that Cupid "taints" and dulls his judgment, "Let huswives make a skillet of my helm" (3.3.275). Othello is unmatched in waging war against an external foe; but he is ill matched to defend himself from Iago's ironic suggestions, which once planted cannot be rooted from his mind.

The inward movement of Othello is terrible in that it feeds upon itself even as it drives him to believe the absolute worst of Desdemona and Cassio. Once Iago has infected Othello's mind, the valiant Moor is left to interpret all external reality through the green lens of his inner eye. A similar phenomenon is at work in Gollum, since his entire existence is bent on recovering the Ring. All manner of people are evaluated solely on their relation to the Ring or on their usefulness for obtaining it, not on the basis of good or evil. Significantly, we witness in both their characters the manifest reality of inner actions producing an outer (public) consequence. Othello is a prominent social figure, and his actions are projected onto the larger screen of public focus; but even though Gollum lives out his existence in the margins of Middle-earth, his actions affect the entire world. In both characters, the momentum of their inner desire is balanced by an awareness of that inwardness, rendering their psychological states cloven.

Conclusion

Unlike Othello, Gollum is never able to see himself for what he has become. Or, if he does recognize the ruins of he who was once Sméagol, he is not able to detach himself from that reality to execute justice. Othello refers to himself as "the circumcisèd dog"; but such an insight is available only to one who has come to see the magnitude of his error and the bestiality of his actions. And by taking the "dog" and smiting him "thus," Othello purges himself of that negative element responsible for the atrocity. Othello's character is divided, and his slaying of the part that has become consumed by jealousy and plotted revenge is a type of inward cleansing or circumcision. "O bloody period!" exclaims Lodovico at the sight of Othello's suicide (5.2.367); but it is Othello's blood alone that can repair the damage that is a result of his hand. And while the period is "bloody" it nonetheless marks the final grim conclusion of the tragedy: no more blood is spilled after this death. There is a strange parallel between Othello's last moments and Gollum's, since they both die clutching their "precious" after having put it to their lips; but for Othello it is the final sign of his contrition and stands as a visible monument to "One that loved not wisely but too well" (5.2.354). Gollum, too, dies as a result of having "loved not wisely," and yet his death is not sacrifice but the price of selfishness. In spite of whether their final actions are selfless or selfish, both characters die a death that does not hold the promise of a regenerative afterlife. Othello's chilling remark that this look of Desdemona "will hurl [his] soul from heaven, / And fiends will snatch at it" (5.2.283–84) applies equally well to Gollum.

Only by death is peace restored to the worlds of Othello and Gollum. But it is a peace that has been dearly purchased. The genius of Shakespeare and the critical example Tolkien may have found there is how to represent a psychologically divided character. Ambivalence, in the Freudian sense, is the presence of at least two strong contrary desires, but in Gollum the mediating presence of an Ego is largely absent. The divided self surfaces only briefly in Othello, and yet it is this appearance that may have lit the way for Tolkien's highly developed depiction of a character permanently at war with himself. Unlike Othello, Gollum/Sméagol plummets to his death without having resolved the central inner tension. He does not deliver justice but is delivered to justice. A ring is a powerful symbol; in a wedding ceremony, it incorporates within itself the image of eternity and the mysterious arc of two people metaphorically joining to become one flesh. Gollum and Sméagol's pursuit of the Ring, however, symbolically places them on either side of the ring's band, so that they never join and are forever alienated from each other. While the journey of the Ring brings it full circle, reconciling its beginning with its end and restoring peace, Gollum and Sméagol are left to plummet to their death separated forever by the distance of a ring.

Works Cited

Garber, Marjorie. *Shakespeare After All*. New York: Pantheon, 2004.

Goddard, Harold. *The Meaning of Shakespeare*. Vol. 2. Chicago: University of Chicago Press, 1951.

The Lord of the Rings: The Return of the King. Special Extended DVD. Screenplay by Peter Jackson et al. Dir. Peter Jackson. 2002. DVD. New Line, 2003.

Milton, John. *Paradise Lost*. Ed. Merritt Y. Hughes. New York: Odyssey, 1962.

Shakespeare, William. *The Complete Works of William Shakespeare*. Ed. David Bevington. 5th ed. New York: Pearson, 2004.

Tolkien, J.R.R. *The Annotated Hobbit*. Annotated by Douglas A. Anderson. Rev. and exp. ed. Boston: Houghton, 2002.

_____. *The Hobbit*. 2nd ed. Boston: Houghton, 1966.

_____. *The Lord of the Rings*. 2nd ed. Boston: Houghton, 1994.

About the Contributors

Jessica Burke, a native New Yorker, is working on her MA in English. Her first experience with Tolkien came after an excursion to the New York Public Library at age five; she borrowed a recording of Professor Tolkien reading "Riddles in the Dark" from *The Hobbit*. Ms. Burke is co-chair of the New York Tolkien Society and co-author of "Humiliated Heroes: Peter Jackson's Interpretation of *The Lord of the Rings*," which appeared in *Translating Tolkien* (Walking Tree Publishers, 2004).

Annalisa Castaldo is currently assistant professor of English at Widener University in Chester, Pennsylvania. She received her BA in English and Medieval/Renaissance studies from Wellesley College, and her PhD in English with a concentration in Shakespeare and cultural studies from Temple University. She has published on a variety of subjects, including Shakespeare in Neil Gaiman's *Sandman* comics. Most recently she was the fiction editor of a forthcoming encyclopedia on Shakespeare and pop culture.

Janet Brennan Croft is head of Access Services for the University of Oklahoma Libraries. She is the author of *War and the Works of J.R.R. Tolkien* (Praeger, 2004), which won the Mythopoeic Society Award for Scholarship in Inklings Studies in 2005, and editor of *Tolkien on Film* (Mythopoeic Press, 2004). She is also the author of *Legal Solutions in Electronic Reserves and the Electronic Delivery of Interlibrary Loan* (Haworth Press, 2004). She is currently the editor of *Mythlore*, the scholarly journal of the Mythopoeic Society.

Rebecca-Anne C. Do Rozario received her doctorate at Monash University, Melbourne, where she now teaches fantasy and children's literature. She has published various articles on the fairy tale, musical theatre and children's film and fiction in journals including *Women's Studies in Communication*, *TDR* and *The Journal of Dramatic Theory and Criticism*.

Anna Fåhraeus is a PhD candidate in the English Department at Gothenburg University in Sweden. She is the editor of the international volume *Textual Ethos Studies: Or Locating Ethics* (with AnnKatrin Jonsson). She has written on Thomas Rawlins's *The Rebellion*, a little-known play that has been overlooked in the major studies of race during the Renaissance but that is important in its fictional treatment of the expulsion of the Moors from Spain. She is the editorial secretary for the *Nordic Journal of English Studies*, and is currently working on a thesis titled "Horror, Race, Sex: Miscegenation and Social Signification in Four Renaissance Plays."

Robert Gehl is working on his PhD in cultural studies at George Mason University. He has published work in *The Atlantic Online, Nebula, MindFire Renew,* and *The Glass Eye.* He lives in Alexandria, Virginia, with his wife and his dog, Violet.

Lisa Hopkins is professor of English at Sheffield Hallam University. She is primarily a Renaissance specialist, and her publications include *The Shakespearean Marriage* (Palgrave, 1998) and *Beginning Shakespeare* (Manchester University Press, 2005). She is also interested in the impact of evolutionary theory on literature and teaches a course called "Making Monsters: Literature and Evolution," which has resulted in a book called *Giants of the Past: Popular Fictions and the Idea of Evolution* (Bucknell University Press, 2004).

Allegra Johnston teaches English at the University of Colorado, Colorado Springs. She is a former U.S. Air Force officer and has also taught at the U.S. Air Force Academy. While she has taught everything from technical writing to medieval legends, her real interest and research is in British literature and lore. Her presentations on Tolkien's work and on Arthurian legend have been well-received at the International Medieval Congress and the Southeastern Medieval Association Conferences, and she has several publications forthcoming on those topics. When not writing academically, Allegra writes fiction; her story "The Blue Woman Concerto" was recently selected for inclusion in the "Best of the Year" 2006 issue for the online publication *Apollo's Lyre.*

Charles Keim is currently an assistant professor of literature at Nazarene University College in Calgary, Alberta. He received his PhD with a concentration on early modern studies, especially John Milton, from the University of British Columbia. His current research interests are the Garden of Eden in *Paradise Lost* and the ancient Hebrew Temple.

Judith J. Kollmann is professor of English at the University of Michigan–Flint, where she has taught English literature since 1968. Her field is medieval literature, which has given her a strong interest in medieval-ism and fantasy. As a consequence she has published a number of arti-cles on the Inklings member Charles Williams, as well as articles on Brother Cadfael, on centaurs, on Sheridan Le Fanu, and on other assorted interesting writers and themes. She contributed an essay to *Tolkien on Film* (Mythopoeic Press, 2004).

Romuald I. Lakowski teaches Shakespeare, children's literature and introductory literature (including Tolkien) at Grant MacEwan Col-lege in Edmonton, Canada. He has published several articles and reviews in *Early Modern Literary Studies, Renaissance Forum, Disputatio, Ben Jonson Review, The Sixteenth Century Journal* and *Mythlore*. His current research interests include the geographical background of Thomas More's *Utopia* and the drafting of *The Lord of the Rings*.

Nicholas Ozment received his BA (and will soon receive his MA) in English from Winona State University in Minnesota, where as an instructor he taught a topics in literature course on *The Lord of the Rings*. His master's thesis, *The Inklings: Modern Mythmakers*, examined the mythopoeic theories of Tolkien and C.S. Lewis. His poetry has appeared in such publications as *Mythic Circle, Mythic Delirium*, and *Weird Tales*, and he received honorable mention in the *18th Annual Year's Best Fantasy and Horror.*

Anne C. Petty has a PhD in English from Florida State University with emphasis in comparative mythology and creative writing. Her dis-sertation topic was the mythopoeic structure of J.R.R. Tolkien's *The Hob-bit* and *The Lord of the Rings*. She has taught composition and literature at the university and secondary level, presented numerous convention seminars on writing and fantasy literature, and written articles for both literary journals and popular magazines. She is the author of *Dragons of Fantasy* (2004), *Tolkien in the Land of Heroes* (2003), and *One Ring to Bind Them All: Tolkien's Mythology* (University of Alabama Press, 2nd ed., 2002). Her dark-fantasy novel *Thin Line Between* (Book 1 of The Wand-jina Quartet) was published in May 2005 by Cold Spring Press/Simon & Schuster. Book 2, *The Dangerous Place*, followed in 2006. She lives with her husband and two opinionated cats on the Florida Gulf Coast.

Frank P. Riga teaches in the English Department of Canisius Col-lege in Buffalo, New York, where he also directs the Graduate Schol-arship Office. He has taught courses in English and European Romanticism, Byron and Byronism, Keats and his circle, children's lit-erature, and C.S. Lewis and the Oxford Christians. His book *The Index to the London Magazine* appeared in 1977, and he has published articles on St. Augustine, C.S. Lewis, Byron, George MacDonald, Maria Louisa

Molesworth, and Jean Rhys. He has also published a series of articles on Christmas traditions, including Santa Claus, La Befana, the Magi, and the crèche.

Leigh Smith is an assistant professor of English, specializing in medieval literature as well as teaching a Tolkien class, at East Strouds-burg University. She received her PhD from the University of Houston. Her publications include *Middle English Hagiography and Romance in Fifteenth-Century England: From Competition to Critique* and several entries in the *Encyclopedia of Medieval Folklore*. Her current research interest is medieval prison literature as a subgenre of contemplative literature.

Maureen Thum has published articles on the Grimm Brothers, Chaucer, Milton, and the German literary fairy-tale writer Wilhelm Hauff, in *The Germanic Review, The Philological Quarterly, Milton Studies,* and the *MLA Children's Literature Annual Journal.* She has presented numerous papers on topics ranging from Shakespeare to children's lit-erature and the Victorian novel, and contributed an essay to *Tolkien on Film* (Mythopoeic Press, 2004). She is the director of the Honors Pro-gram at the University of Michigan–Flint.

Daniel Timmons received his PhD from the University of Toronto and has published several articles and reviews on the work of J.R.R. Tolkien. With George Clark, he co-edited the essay collection *J.R.R. Tolkien and His Literary Resonances: Views of Middle-earth* (Greenwood Press, 2000) and contributed an essay to *Tolkien on Film* (Mythopoeic Press, 2004). Timmons was also the writer, director, and producer of a literary documentary, *The Legacy of* The Lord of the Rings. Dr. Timmons died in December 2005, as this volume was nearing completion.

Kayla McKinney Wiggins is the chair of the English Department at Martin Methodist College in Pulaski, Tennessee. In addition to numer-ous articles on film, drama, and folklore, she is the author of *Modern Verse Drama in English* (Greenwood Press, 1993); she also contributed an essay to *Tolkien on Film* (Mythopoeic Press, 2004).